ABOUT THE AUTHOR

Dr Sharon Beder is associate professor in the Science, Technology and Society programme of the University of Wollongong. After several years as a professional engineer, she returned to academic life. The positions she has held include Director of the Earth Foundation Australia and President of the Society for Social Responsibility in Engineering.

HER BOOKS INCLUDE:

Toxic Fish and Sewer Surfing (1989)

The Nature of Sustainable Development (1993 and 1996)

Global Spin: the Corporate Assault on Environmentalism (1997 and 2000)

The New Engineer: Management and Professional Responsibility in a Changing World (1998)

✧ ✧ ✧

CRITICAL PRAISE FOR SHARON BEDER'S PREVIOUS BOOKS

Global Spin

'Examines the systematic stifling of independent critical thought by multinational corporations – in alliance with the media and government. Beder's analysis is comprehensive, steely and clinical.' – Harold Pinter, naming it as one of his favourite books of the year, *Guardian*, 24 December 1997

'If you beg, steal, borrow or buy only one book this year, make it this one – it is the most important contribution to the environmental debate I have read.' – David Edwards, *Ecologist*

'It is hard to find words sufficiently enthusiastic to describe Sharon Beder's new book.... This is a must read, not just for environmentalists, but for everyone who doesn't have a vested interest in the continued destruction of our planet.' – Allen Myers, *Green Left Weekly*

'If you care a fig for either democracy or the environment, then *Global Spin* is a book for you. It is a thorough – and thoroughly shocking – account of the sophisticated techniques being used around the world to undermine environmentalism and reset the agenda to status quo.' – *New Internationalist*

'I would urge anyone who is concerned about the current environmental crisis to read *Global Spin*. Allow Dr Beder to heighten your awareness about what's really going on in the corporate world.' – *Social Alternatives*

'*Global Spin* is an ambitious, important analysis of corporate propaganda in all its gory splendour, which ought to be read carefully by anyone who wants to understand how public opinion and policy are moulded and twisted in modern society.' – Sheldon Rampton, *Texas Observer*

'Highly thought-provoking and most definitely worth reading.' – *Environmental and Planning Law Journal*

'This is the most frightening book I have ever read, except for Theo Colborn's *Our Stolen Future*, which is equally frightening. But read it we must.' – *Pacific World*

'Rarely does a book live up to the songs of praise printed on its back cover. This one does. Sharon Beder has written a very important and disturbing book. I urge everyone to read it....' – *Australian Rationalist*

❖

The Nature of Sustainable Development

'This book is in the vanguard of contemporary statements on sustainability.' – *Australian Journal of Environmental Management*

'This is an excellent book which is an ideal text to use with students on any course in environmental politics.' – *Environmental Politics*

❖

The New Engineer

'After reading it I think every engineer should be nailed to a chair and made to read it regardless.' – *New Zealand Engineering*

'It should be required reading for all engineers.' – *Canberra Times*

Selling the Work Ethic
From Puritan Pulpit to Corporate PR

Sharon Beder

Scribe Publications
AUSTRALIA

Zed Books
LONDON and NEW YORK

Selling the Work Ethic: From Puritan Pulpit to Corporate PR was first published in 2000 by
Zed Books Ltd., 7 Cynthia Street, London N1 9JF, UK and
Room 400, 175 Fifth Avenue, New York, NY 10010, USA

Distributed in the USA exclusively by St Martin's Press, Inc.,
175 Fifth Avenue, New York, NY 10010, USA.

Published in Australia by Scribe Publications Pty Ltd,
PO Box 287, Carlton North,
Victoria 3054

Copyright © Sharon Beder, 2000

Cover design by Andrew Corbett
Set in 10½/13 pt Monotype Garamond
by Long House, Cumbria, UK
Printed and bound in Australia
by Australian Print Group, Maryborough

The rights of the author of this work has been asserted by her
in accordance with the Copyright, Designs and Patents Act, 1988

A catalogue record for this book
is available from the British Library

US CIP has been applied for

ISBN   1 85649 884 0 hb (Zed Books)
        1 85649 885 9 pb (Zed Books)
        0 908011 48 2 pb (Scribe Publications)

❖ Contents ❖

———

✧ PART II ✧
Motivating Work –
Coercion and Persuasion   93

✧ PART III ✧
Motivating Work – Conditioning   193

✧ Abbreviations ✧

All dollars are US dollars unless otherwise indicated

ACOSS   Australian Council for Social Services
ACS   Australian Contracting Solutions
ACTU   Australian Council of Trade Unions
AFDC   Assistance to Families with Dependent Children
AMA   American Management Association
APESMA   Association of Professional Engineers, Scientists and
             Managers of Australia
CBPP   Center on Budget and Policy Priorities
CEO   Chief Executive Officer
CES   Commonwealth Employment Service
FAIR   Fairness and Accuracy in Reporting
GDP   Gross Domestic Product
IMF   International Monetary Fund
NAM   National Association of Manufacturers
OECD   Organisation for Economic Cooperation and Development
PEPI   Personal Effectiveness Programme Initiative
PR   Public relations
SBA   Small Business Association
TANF   Temporary Assistance for Needy Families
TCFU   Textile Clothing and Footware Union
TVEI   Technical and Vocational Education Initiative
UNDP   United Nations Development Programme
UPS   United Parcel Service of America
WEP   Work Experience Program
WHO   World Health Organisation
WIN   Work Incentive Program

To Richard Gosden, who inspired this book
and who has cultivated personal qualities
far more valuable than a work ethic.

◇ 1 ◇

Introduction

In *Global Spin: the Corporate Assault on Environmentalism*[1] I described how corporations have used their financial resources and power to counter the gains made by environmentalists, to reshape public opinion and to persuade politicians against increased environmental regulation. Yet this is only part of the explanation for the failure of nations to deal with environmental problems adequately. In this book I examine the way capitalist culture gives power and influence to these corporations and at the same time promotes and reinforces lifestyles and behaviours that are damaging to people and to the environment, particularly in English-speaking countries. Of central importance are the underlying cultural imperatives for production and consumption.

As we begin the twenty-first century, work and production have become ends in themselves. Employment has become such a priority that much environmental degradation is justified merely on the ground that it provides jobs. And people are so concerned to keep their jobs that they are willing to do what their employers require of them even if they believe it is wrong or environmentally destructive. The social benefit of having the majority of able-bodied people in a society working hard all week goes unquestioned, particularly by those who work hardest. Few people today can imagine a society that does not revolve around work. They never stop to consider why they work and whether they want to work. How did paid work come to be so central to our lives? Why is it that so many people wouldn't know what to do with themselves or who they were if they did not have their jobs?

As Dominique Méda observed in *International Labour Review*, work 'has come to be regarded as an inherent feature of the human condition, as the only means of fulfilling all individual and social aspirations'. It 'has come to dominate the entirety of individual and social time and space' and to be the 'main vehicle for the formation of social relationships and for self-fulfilment'.[2]

1

Employers have gone to a great deal of trouble to ensure this is so and they have been aided in their endeavours by governments, preachers, teachers, social scientists and others. To make sure there is no social identity outside of employment, the unemployed are stigmatised. They tend to be portrayed in the media as either frauds, hopeless cases or layabouts who are living it up at taxpayers' expense. Work is seen as an essential characteristic of being human. No matter how tedious it is, any work is generally considered to be better than no work.

An ideology of work has been promoted in Western societies since the early days of modern capitalism. Those who don't have to do manual labour have extolled its dignity and nobility.[3] A. R. Gini and T. J. Sullivan observe in their book on work and the person that the work ethic 'has often been used as a means of masking the drudgery and necessity of work.... [T]he tradition of the work ethic glorified and legitimized work and gave it a teleological orientation – a sense of purpose or design – which helped to both sustain individual effort and ameliorate its temporal brutishness.'[4]

The work ethic, which has been at the heart of capitalist culture, has evolved from a religious principle originating in the sixteenth century to a success ethic advanced by writers, businessmen and teachers in the nineteenth century. Today the work ethic is promoted primarily in terms of work being a responsibility, both to family and to the nation. The hard work of citizens is advocated as being necessary to national prosperity. For half a millennium hard work has been seen as an indicator of good character.

The work ethic, however, is based on assumptions and premises that are fast becoming outdated. Those pushing the work ethic today claim that every person needs to work, and work hard, if productivity is to increase. All progress, it is argued, depends on increasing productivity. The fallacy of this assumption is becoming clear as fewer and fewer people are required in the workforce and more and more products are being forced on consumers.

But the call to ever-increasing productivity is seductive. Even when dissidents challenge capitalism they are usually loath to advocate the dismantling of the ethical foundations and institutions that underpin national productivity, particularly the work ethic. Robert Heilbroner noted decades ago:

> The striking characteristic of our contemporary ideological climate is that the 'dissident' groups, labour, government, or academics, all seek to accommodate their proposals for social change to the limits of adaptability of the prevailing business order....[5]

This is particularly true of modern environmentalists in their search for solutions to the environmental crisis. It is for this reason that sustainable development has become so popular as a solution. Sustainable development embraces the idea that economic growth and environmental protection are compatible. Sustainable development seeks reforms that do not challenge the political, institutional or cultural status quo: this is why the doctrine has been unsuccessful at achieving the sorts of significant changes that are necessary to protect the environment.[6] National and international sustainable development policies leave power in the hands of the corporations that are responsible for some of the worst instances of environmental degradation and avoid any measures that might reduce rates of production and consumption that are clearly unsustainable.

The compulsion to work has clearly become pathological in modern industrial societies. Together with the obsession with creating wealth and consuming, it provides the impetus to go on producing goods at the expense of everyone's quality of life. Millions of people are being encouraged and coerced to work long hours, devoting their lives to making or doing things that will not enrich their lives or make them happier but will add to the garbage and pollution that the earth is finding difficult to accommodate. They are so busy doing this that they have little time to spend with their family and friends, to develop other aspects of themselves, or to participate in their communities as full citizens. And the best brains of a generation are engaged in persuading them to go on doing this without question.

Escalating production and consumption are degrading the environment at rates that undermine any improvements that can be achieved through technological and legislative change. Lester Brown notes in his introduction to the Worldwatch Institute's well-respected *State of the World 1998*:

> While economic indicators such as investment, production, and trade are consistently positive, the key environmental indicators are increasingly negative. Forests are shrinking, water tables are falling, soils are eroding, wetlands are disappearing, fisheries are collapsing, rangelands are deteriorating, rivers are running dry, temperatures are rising, coral reefs are dying, and plant and animal species are disappearing.[7]

Similarly, the *Human Development Report 1998* states that: 'Runaway growth in consumption is placing unprecedented pressures on the environment through pollution, waste and the growing deterioration of renewables: water, soils, forests, fish and biodiversity.'[8]

But despite the international efforts to do something about this degradation, development and economic growth have such priority that changes are minor and no real reform can be effected. The European Environment Agency found in 1998 that in the 44 countries it surveyed there had been little progress on environmental improvements since its previous assessment in 1995. The loss of species had not been halted and waste from

3

manufacturing, mining and urban centres had increased by 10 per cent since 1990.[9]

Both the international conferences that have taken place in the last decade and the agreements signed in the same period have failed to address the key cause of the problem, the burgeoning production and consumption of the world's most affluent nations. Surveys show that the majority of people in most countries are not only concerned about the environment but also think that the well-being of the environment should be given priority over economic growth, and that governments should regulate to protect it.[10] Yet this public concern is not translating into either cultural change or government action.

Unless the work/consume treadmill is overcome there is little hope for the planet. History has shown that both the values underlying such compulsions as the work ethic and the respect accorded to those who accumulate wealth are socially constructed and temporal (see chapters 2 and 3). They are not inevitable; they are not an essential part of human nature; they are historical and they are shaped and reinforced by corporate interests and by all of the major institutions in modern societies.

It is time to reconsider our unquestioned submission to employers and the value we accord to work and wealth creation. We need to recognise the historical roots and modern underpinnings behind industrial culture, and to consider alternatives. This book sets out to clear the way for that task, by exposing some of the key cultural foundations and myths supporting the capitalist value system and the way those foundations and myths are constantly reinforced in the face of a different reality. The chapters that follow will uncover the part played by ideas, values and beliefs in the rise and dominance of capitalism in modern societies and the conditioning of the community to the authority of employers, and corporations in particular. They will examine how certain ideas and beliefs served business interests and were adopted and promoted by those interests so successfully that they became widely held beliefs and values in the wider community.

It is time to question the priority we give to paid work, wealth generation and consumption of material goods and the influence that those who provide these things have over our decision making. Cultures can change, and we need to recognise that industrial culture has become dysfunctional and is in need of a major overhaul.

NOTES

1 Sharon Beder, *Global Spin: the Corporate Assault on Environmentalism* (Devon: Green Books and Melbourne: Scribe Publications, 1997).

2 Dominique Méda, 'New Perspectives on Work as Value', *International Labour Review*, Vol. 135, No. 6 (1996), p. 633.

3 David Bleakley, *Work: the Shadow and the Substance* (London: SCM Press, 1983), p. 36.

4 A. R. Gini and T. J. Sullivan, 'A Critical Overview', in A. R. Gini and T. J. Sullivan (eds), *It Comes with the Territory: an Inquiry Concerning Work and the Person* (New York: Random House, 1989), p. 9.

5 Quoted in Ralph Miliband, *The State in Capitalist Society* (London: Quartet Books, 1969), p. 193.

6 Sharon Beder, *The Nature of Sustainable Development*, 2nd edn (Melbourne: Scribe Publications, 1996).

7 Lester Brown, 'The Future of Growth', in Lester Brown *et al.* (eds), *State of the World 1998* (Worldwatch Institute, 1998).

8 'UNDP: Runaway Consumption Widens Gap Between Rich, Poor', *Go Between* (October/November 1998), p. 16.

9 'Bearing the Brunt of Pollution', *News Direct* (9 June 1998).

10 Riley E. Dunlap, George H. Gallup Jr and Alec M. Gallup, 'Of Global Concern: Results of the Health of the Planet Survey', *Environment*, Vol. 35, No. 9 (1993).

PART I

Work, Wealth and Inequity

◆2◆

The Virtue of
Work and Wealth

All paid jobs absorb and degrade the mind.
Aristotle[1]

A rich man will exploit you if you can be of use to
him, but if you are in need he will forsake you.
Ben Sira, 180 BC[2]

He, that hath a trade, hath an estate; and he, that
hath a calling, hath an office of profit and honour.
Benjamin Franklin[3]

The man who builds a factory builds a temple. The
man who works there, worships there.
Calvin Coolidge[4]

The concept of work as a determinant of personal value and identity and as
an indicator of good character and good morals would have been alien in
many past societies. It was following the Reformation in the sixteenth and
seventeenth centuries that work acquired this moral dimension and became a
central defining characteristic of human existence. People worked hard to
serve God and to prove their worthiness to others. This helped create a diligent and reliable workforce.

Similarly, the idea of money making being the primary goal of the most
admired people in society, the goal of nations, and the major determinant of
social success would have been strange indeed to previous societies. Prior to the
Reformation those whose primary goal had been money making had been
looked at with suspicion and even contempt. The acquisition of wealth
became an approved and worthy goal with the emergence of modern capitalism and the support of Protestant teachings.

Once the capitalist spirit took hold it no longer needed the support of a religious ethos although the Churches continued to promote the work ethic. Yet if we are to understand the foundations of the modern work ethic we need to understand its religious origins. Similarly, if we are to recognise the work ethic as historically based and socially constructed we need to recognise that it is a relatively recent phenomenon in human societies that resulted from the conjunction of ideas and interests in Europe some three hundred years or more ago.

The rise of modern capitalism represented a complete turnaround in commonly held beliefs and attitudes from those held in previous times: 'It required the almost total dismantling of the mediaeval and classical system of thinking, their concepts, understandings and perceptions. In order to change the world it was necessary to change men's understanding of it.'[5] This chapter will consider the social changes that occurred in Europe in the sixteenth and seventeenth centuries which have 'converted a natural frailty into a resounding virtue'.[6] It will examine the way that work was imbued with moral qualities, and how wealth seeking acquired social legitimacy, through religious sanction.

CHANGING CONCEPTIONS OF WORK

At the heart of the work ethic is the idea that work is worthwhile for reasons other than the rewards it brings in terms of pay, products and profit. The work ethic gives work an intrinsic value:

> Dedicated work is considered a mark of good character.... For people who accept this belief, dedicated work is a positive virtue, much like honesty or loyalty. Implicit in this belief is an ethical demand that a person ought to be diligent and industrious.[7]

The idea of hard work and diligence as a virtue, although it is not unique to Western culture, is not universal. The way people view work is shaped by their culture and their social setting. Modern capitalist societies tend to imbue work with a moral value that other societies would find strange. Past civilisations have treated work as a degrading pursuit to be carried out by those at the bottom of their cultural hierarchy. For example, for 'the society of New Spain (i.e. Mexico and South America) work did not redeem and had no value in itself. Manual work was servile. The superior man neither worked nor traded.'[8]

In earlier, non-market societies the separation between work and other activities was not so apparent. People were not paid to work; they just did what was required to provide their needs and much of this was done collectively. Their labours were natural and inevitable. With the rise of more complex societies, however, a division of labour developed and work became not only a separate activity but also a different activity for different people.

Work in ancient Greece had no moral value and the Greek philosophers often disparaged it. Homer claimed that humans had to work because the gods despised them.[9] Greek writers generally expressed disdain for hard manual work. Indeed Greek society had no need for an ideology that exalted work as slaves didn't have to be self-motivating.

In reality, many Greek citizens did work, but it was something they had to do, an unwelcome necessity that had neither status nor morality attached to it. Often they worked alongside slaves, doing the same work for the same pay, but this only served to denigrate the value of that work. Even artisans and craftsmen were considered little better than slaves, at least by the aristocracy, although there is some evidence that individual artisans took pride in their work.[10]

Whilst it is difficult to know how Greek workers thought of themselves, as they were illiterate and left no historical record, there is no doubt that the philosophers, poets and aristocracy held work in low regard. Poets made fun of politicians who had manual occupations and it was also a means of insulting an opponent in the law courts. Attitudes to work also varied somewhat from city to city.[11] In general, however, working for someone else was thought to be especially degrading as it meant you were dependent on others and therefore not free.[12] Greeks valued their freedom above any economic attainment and 'preferred the insecurity of a daily-changing labour market to regular assured work' that limited their freedom to work as needed and when civic duties permitted.[13]

Aristotle, like many of the Greek thinkers, viewed work as interfering with the duties of citizens and distracting them from more virtuous pursuits such as politics, art and philosophy.[14] These could only be mastered through a long education which took time and leisure. Those who spent their time mastering the techniques of the mechanic or the artisan were spoilt in mind and body for contemplation and philosophy.[15] The only good purpose of work was to earn enough money for a person to have leisure to contemplate philosophical issues, the most noble of activities.[16] He wrote:

> A state with an ideal constitution – a state which has for its members men who are absolutely just, and not men who are merely just in relation to some particular standard – cannot have its citizens living the life of mechanics or shopkeepers, which is ignoble and inimical to goodness. Nor can it have them engaged in farming; leisure is a necessity, both for growth in goodness and for the pursuit of political activity.[17]

Plato also argued that work interfered with leisure which was necessary for the 'practice of the art of government' and therefore those engaged in it should not be part of the governing class. Plato cited Socrates as claiming that not having to work is necessary to leading a virtuous life and to being a good leader or governor.[18] P. D. Anthony points out:

> We have become used to paying a certain respect to workers upon whose efforts our economic structure rests, but in a society in which economic values were subordinated to cultural and political ends, to be at the bottom of the economic structure was to be at the bottom of the dung heap.[19]

As Greek culture spread to other parts of the world during the Hellenistic period, particularly to the Mediterranean region, so did this attitude to work. The Romans of the Roman Republic adopted a similar attitude to the ancient Greeks when it came to work. The Latin for work, *labor*, means 'extreme effort associated with pain' and apparently comes from the same root as *labare* which means 'to stumble under a burden'.[20] Cicero reflected common Roman thought in his belief that manual work and craft work or 'the hiring out of a person's arms' was 'vulgar, dishonoring and beneath the dignity of a Roman citizen'.[21] He wrote:

> we have been taught, in general, as follows. First, those means of livelihood are rejected as undesirable which incur people's ill-will, as those of tax-gatherers and usurers. Unbecoming to a gentleman, too, and vulgar are the means of livelihood of hired workmen whom we pay for mere manual labour, for in their case the very wage they receive is a pledge of their slavery. Vulgar we must consider those who buy from wholesale merchants to retail immediately, for they would not get profits without a great deal of downright lying; ... And all mechanics are engaged in vulgar trades.... [22]

For Romans the most honourable pursuits were war and politics. Even professional work requiring intelligence and education, such as that done by doctors, architects and teachers, was considered to be unfit for the nobility. As in Greece, freemen worked alongside slaves in many occupations including crafts. This association helped to degrade the value of these occupations. Craftsmen were unable to take part in government and there is some evidence that the low esteem accorded to manual workers, merchants and craftsmen was not limited to the aristocracy.[23] A former apprentice to a sculptor stated:

> If you become a stone-cutter you will be nothing more than a workman, doing hard physical labour.... You will be obscure, earning a small wage, a man of low esteem, classed as worthless by public opinion, neither courted by friends, feared by enemies, nor envied by your fellow-citizens, but just a common workman, a craftsman, a face in a crowd, one who makes his living with his hands.[24]

The ancient Jews, too, thought of work as a painful necessity, although in their society everyone was expected to work and there was nothing to be ashamed of in being a worker.[25] After all, according to the Old Testament, God worked at creating the world and on the seventh day he rested. Many Jewish leaders cited in the Old Testament also worked, particularly in agriculture, and so too some of the great rabbis earned a living with their hands.[26]

In the Book of Genesis Adam and Eve did not have to work in the Garden of Eden but when they disobeyed God he imposed work on them as part of their punishment: 'cursed is the ground because of you; in toil you shall eat of it all the days of your life.... In the sweat of your face you shall eat bread till you return to the ground....'[27] The Jews accepted work as 'expiation through which man might atone for the sin of his ancestors and cooperate with God in the world's salvation'.[28] Work in Jewish society therefore had a religious value that it lacked in Greek and Roman culture, but it was still considered unpleasant and had no intrinsic moral value apart from atonement.[29]

Early Christians adopted a similar attitude to the Jews in considering work as God's punishment for original sin. Jesus came, by all accounts, from a working family, his father a carpenter and his disciples fishermen, one of the lowliest occupations in the Roman world according to Cicero. Whilst he did not judge people by their occupations, Jesus did not seem to put much value on work and labour either:

> Consider the lilies how they grow: they toil not, they spin not; And yet I say unto you, that even Solomon in all his glory was not arrayed like one of these.[30]

One of Jesus's more influential followers, Paul, was far more positive about the value of work. A tentmaker by trade, he valued work for the independence and self-respect it gave a person and the means it offered to be charitable to others. Working to be able to give charity was also a theme of the early Church, and the early monasteries incorporated all types of work in order to be self-sufficient.[31] Work was valued in the monasteries as a way of serving the monastery and as a means of fostering brotherly love. Work had no intrinsic value, nor was it to be done to gain wealth: it was a means to a religious end, 'an instrument of purification, of charity, of expiation'.[32]

Over time work took on more value but was always secondary to the more important task of contemplating God. Religious work was better than work to obtain material needs, but higher still was 'pure contemplation, passive meditation on divine matters'. Those who didn't need to work for a living were best off spending their time praying and contemplating God.[33]

In later years it was often the lay people who did the manual work necessary to provide the material needs of the community while the monks did the intellectual and religious work.[34] The Church, which had once had an ideal of egalitarianism, embraced the idea of a stratified society as part of God's plan.

This hierarchy had those who devoted themselves to the religious life at the top.[35] Saint Thomas Aquinas actually drew up a scale of occupations according to their value to society, with agriculture at the top (but still below religious work) and commerce at the bottom.[36]

The traditional workers in the Middle Ages also had no great love of work, nor did they imbue it with special qualities or virtue. The traditional worker in the Middle Ages 'commonly lived to a good round age, worked when necessity demanded, ceased his labour when his wants were supplied'.[37] They would take days off when they felt like it, spend many hours socialising, work short days and 'move freely in and out of work and from one task to another according to personal inclination'.[38]

Food was the major expense of an ordinary worker and when food was cheap and plentiful labour was in short supply. As late as 1694 Josiah Child complained: 'In a cheap year they will not work above two days in a week.'[39] In contrast to the modern worker's experience, higher wages resulted in less work, not more. Weber noted: 'The opportunity of earning more was less attractive than that of working less.' Workers did not, 'by nature', want to earn more money but rather to earn enough to provide for their needs. Work was not done for self-development or improvement, nor was it done as a duty.[40]

WORK AS A VIRTUE

It was within Protestantism that work was imbued with a moral quality and became a central defining characteristic of human existence. Max Weber in *The Protestant Ethic and the Spirit of Capitalism* (1904–5) described how work became a religious calling, a way of worshipping God.[41]

The idea of a 'calling' is a religious idea and refers to a task set by God. It does not have its roots in either the Old or the New Testament but within the Catholic Church. A 'vocation' or 'calling' originally referred to the work of monks, nuns and priests who served God by removing themselves from daily life and serving the Church. In this way they could achieve salvation and attain God's grace.

To some extent the teachings of the early Protestant leaders were aimed at undermining the power of the Catholic Church which they believed had become corrupt. The Catholic Church advocated the idea that personal salvation could be achieved through good works set out by the Church. The Church even raised money by selling 'indulgences' which enabled people to buy forgiveness for sins.

Martin Luther, originally a Catholic friar himself, argued that the religious work of the monks and priests deserved no special status or influence. Luther accused the monks of being parasitic – living off the work of others.[42] He claimed God's grace was not restricted to the religious orders of the Church; that whatever one's work was, it was a way of serving God. He argued that a divine calling could be followed no matter what one's occupation.[43] Thus elevated, non-religious work was no longer a punishment but was, in Luther's thinking, a blessing, something sacred to be enjoyed.[44]

John Calvin, a French theologian and Protestant, was also influential in shaping the Protestant ethic. He argued that God had already decided who would be blessed after death, even before they were born. Most people were born in a state of sin and were unable, through their own actions, to save themselves from damnation and hell. A few people, however, through God's grace, were predestined to everlasting life and would be called out of the state of sin and blessed.[45]

Calvinism eliminated the priests and the Church hierarchy from the relationship between an individual and God. The individual stood alone before God. No intermediaries could interfere with what had already been predestined. It was because of this that 'there arises at the very heart of the Calvinistic system a tremendous emphasis upon individualism'.[46]

For Catholics, doing good works could lead to salvation. But for Calvinists, since God's blessing was decided in advance, doing good works would not change one's fate. People who were blessed did good works, however, so doing good works was a 'sign' that one had been blessed. People who wanted to convince themselves or others of their state of grace had to do good works and devote themselves to their calling.[47] Good works were not the means to salvation but the 'means of assurance' of salvation.[48]

Unlike the Catholics, Calvinists could not be forgiven for occasional lapses; rather, such lapses were a sign that a person was not one of the elect. In particular, dislike of work was a sign that one was not one of the elect. So self-discipline was all the more important if Calvinists wanted to feel sure that they would be saved. Their work could at no time be sloppy or inconsistent. It had to be 'methodical, disciplined, rational, uniform'.[49]

For believers work was not done for the purpose of earning a living but to glorify God and demonstrate one's state of grace. No matter how much money one had, one still had to work for more. Hard work served God, and wasting time was therefore the deadliest of sins.[50] Work had not only a moral value but a status value. Even if they lacked a work ethic and didn't believe in the virtue of work, it was necessary for Protestants to work hard so as to be respected in the community, to persuade others that they were amongst God's elect.

The idea of the moral value of work spread through Europe and to English Protestants. The English Puritans, in particular, embraced the gospel of work.[51] The work ethic helped to supply the new entrepreneurs with 'sober, conscientious, and unusually industrious workmen, who clung to their work as to a life purpose willed by God'.[52] Those Protestant sects which adopted Calvinism, including the Puritans in England and others in Germany, became known for their industry and their frugal lifestyles.[53] Puritan writers embraced the moral value of work, the need to work long and hard and continuously: 'Idleness also and negligence of our Callings, is sinful....'[54] Only by hard work could one serve God and at the same time avoid the temptations of fleshly indulgence.

From England the Puritans took this idea of work as a calling to America where, as in England, preachers made it a topic of sermons. 'In terms of work values, it remained the keystone of Christian thinking about work until well into the eighteenth century.'[55] Work had become a good in itself and 'the core of the moral life'.[56] (This was less so in the South, where slave labour was employed and wealthy landowners emulated an aristocratic way of life.)

Prominent sociologist C. Wright Mills noted that 'the gospel of work has been central to the historical tradition of America, to its image of itself, and to the images the rest of the world have of America'.[57] And Robert Eisenberger in his book on the loss of the work ethic in America noted that

By the middle of the nineteenth century, the personal work ethic had three strong intertwined components: a perceived moral duty as a worthwhile person to work hard; a willingness to exert high effort to achieve material well-being; and a pride in one's work skills and in the quality of the product or service that resulted.[58]

UNEMPLOYMENT AS A VICE

The most obvious manifestation of the work ethic as a moral value has been in the way unemployed people have been treated since the Protestant Reformation. Whereas beggars had been tolerated in medieval society as natural and part of the normal God-given order, even glorified because of the opportunity they gave Catholics to do good deeds, they were despicable to Protestant society: 'begging, on the part of one able to work, is not only the sin of slothfulness, but a violation of the duty of brotherly love'.[59]

The early Christian emphasis on brotherly love meant riches had value only in so much as they were used to express that love by giving to the poor. Early Christian communities are believed to have lived communally at first but even after that they were known for their charity, both to members of their own community and to outsiders who needed help. But in Protestant societies idleness was seen as a sin and the destitute were seen as being responsible for their state through their own wickedness. They argued that charity should not extend to those who were able to work for themselves.[60]

Both Luther and Calvin condemned laziness and living off others' work. Luther despised vagrants for their idleness and believed they should either be made to work or banished.[61] Calvin proclaimed there was 'nothing more disgraceful than a lazy good-for-nothing who is of no use either to himself or to others but seems to have been born only to eat and drink'.[62] Whilst Catholics believed in an imperfect human race in which individuals who had been diverted from a virtuous life into sin could be saved, Protestants, following Calvin, believed that sinners could not be saved and were quite different types of people from those granted grace. They deserved no compassion or charity but should be avoided at best.[63]

There was little recognition from those who condemned beggars that many people were unemployed because of circumstances beyond their control. From the second half of the fifteenth century through to the seventeenth century economic and social changes displaced many rural workers, causing a flood of people seeking work that was in scarce supply. In England the enclosing of the commons was one such factor forcing peasants from the land. Work provided by merchants was irregular and depended on insecure markets, and there wasn't enough work to provide for all those who wanted it.

Unemployment was also exacerbated by an increasing population throughout Europe in the sixteenth century, which resulted from an increasing life expectancy. The growth of economic activity did not keep up with population growth. As a result thousands of people were without means to support themselves.[64] 'This European-wide problem of increased population, food scarcity, and price increases combined to create a class of seemingly worthless idlers who, in reality, were people without prospects and hope.'[65]

These people were mercilessly criticised by Luther and later Protestant leaders who labelled them as idlers who wouldn't work. They had no calling and clearly were not amongst God's chosen. 'Neither the ministers nor their secular counterparts distinguished between the poor and the unemployed, and in many instances identified both with beggary.'[66] There was no concept of bad luck or lack of opportunity in the Protestant conception of the world. These people were poor because they were immoral and didn't work hard enough.

In England, from the sixteenth century, people who were caught begging in a town, or who couldn't account for themselves as residents or having legitimate business there, could be whipped, forced into compulsory service or put in prison.[67] Thomas More (1478–1535) noted that in England those who had been displaced by the enclosures became 'tramps and beggars' and were 'put into prison for being idle – when nobody would give them a job, however much they want one'.[68]

In 1531 an English statute attempted to differentiate in favour of the deserving poor, who were granted licences to beg; the others, under a 1536 statute, were required to work or be whipped (and even have part of an ear severed) and sent back to where they came from. It was single, able-bodied men in particular who were considered undeserving and most frequently whipped.[69]

Workhouses were set up for the destitute in various parts of Europe in the seventeenth century (the first in Amsterdam in 1596) to teach work skills and the value of hard work.[70] The English Poor Laws of 1597 and 1601 made provision for children of the poor to be apprenticed out and adults to be institutionalised in workhouses and poorhouses for the disabled. During the seventeenth century workhouses became a standard way of dealing with the poor: they were cheaper than paying relief, imposed work and unpleasant living conditions on the poor and ensured that welfare was not an attractive alternative to low-paid work outside the workhouse. Some entrepreneurs even set up their own workhouses in order to take advantage of the cheap forced labour.[71]

In Europe and America in the seventeenth and eighteenth centuries the unemployed poor were seen as defying God in their unwillingness to work. They were subject to humiliation and punishment. In Europe city gates were locked against vagrants at night. They were treated like criminals, put on chain gangs, publicly whipped and put in stocks, and branded. And if they stole food they could be executed.[72] Such attitudes were perpetuated in colonial America where whipping was also used to punish idleness, and preachers such as Cotton Mather said of the unemployed, 'let them starve'.[73]

> Through all of this ran a common thread. To be without work was to be an idler, a person of poor character, an ingrate of the first order. Unemployment (a term not used at this time), poverty, and vagrancy were of the same cloth. Not to work was a willful misuse of time, a denial of effort that would damage both the individual and the community. In short, a tinge of evil equated with the absence of paid labor.[74]

Throughout the seventeenth and eighteenth centuries the number of work-houses increased (to some 2,000 in Europe by 1776). Despite the presence of structural unemployment it was assumed by English opinion makers that 'those who *really* wanted work could find it'. They did not deserve sympathy, com-passion or charity, and the workhouse conditions were purposefully harsh.[75]

Workhouses, almshouses and 'bettering' houses were also established in every seaport in colonial America to cope with the flood of new immigrants. They proliferated during the eighteenth century. These institutions, like the English workhouses, were 'designed to be harsh' and less desirable than having a job. Some strove to 'instil improved behaviour and work habits'.[76] Puritan thought and leadership were important in shaping attitudes to the poor and unemployed in the American colonies.[77]

PROFIT MAKING AS A VIRTUE

Just as poverty came to be a sign of wickedness and sin, so wealth came to be a sign of God's blessing. Following the Protestant Reformation the acquisition of wealth became an approved and worthy goal perhaps for the first time in history and this was a major factor in the rise of capitalism in Western society. The new capitalists no longer felt the guilt that encumbered medieval businessmen. Rather, they came to be considered 'the very pinnacle of morality itself since they testified to the bourgeois virtues of thrift, diligence, hard work, dedication, and persistence. Profits were the result, not of personal greed, but of application in a profession or vocation.'[78] R. H. Tawney states in his *Religion and the Rise of Capitalism* that the significance of Calvinism consisted

> in its admission to a new position of respectability of a powerful and growing body of social interests, which, however irrepressible in practice, had hitherto been regarded by religious theory as, at best, of dubious propriety, and at worst, as frankly immoral.[79]

In the society of the Middle Ages, capitalistic activities involving trade and profit were tolerated as necessary but were neither praised nor 'ethically justified and encouraged'.[80] The Church looked upon those who devoted themselves to making money through trade or manufacture with suspicion, even though their activities might be honest and their work useful to the community. Moneylending in particular was despised by both the Church and the wider society. Charging interest on money lent was called usury, and anyone who engaged in it was likely to be denied the privileges of the sacraments. Those who made fortunes were likely to renounce them in old age or donate their money to the Church in order to atone, before their death, for a lifetime of profit seeking. Others sought respectability by buying land and becoming part of the landed gentry.[81]

Such attitudes to commercial activities have long antecedents in human history. In ancient Greece the acquisition of wealth was distrusted and the only good purpose of wealth was thought to be to free a person from work and to become self-sufficient. Aristotle condemned 'the piling up of superfluous fortunes'[82] and in the *Laws* Plato assigned industry, trade and business activities to migrants.[83] None of this was fit for the ideal Greek citizen to undertake: 'The idea that trade and marketing was incompatible with wholehearted participation in social and political life was deeply rooted.'[84]

In his history of Roman civilisation, Will Durant argues that the Romans were somewhat hypocritical in their attitude to money: 'Nearly everybody in Rome worshipped money with mad pursuit, and all but the bankers denounced it.'[85] Whilst having money was desirable, trade and moneylending were considered the lowest of occupations and money made in this way was the least prestigious. Land was the most respected form of wealth, and without ownership of land citizens were held to be inferior. No matter how much money a person made, if they were not born into the aristocracy then they were not granted high status by the elite of Roman society.[86] Cicero argued that the wise man would only seek a fortune in order to exercise virtues such as generosity.[87]

Members of the senatorial class were forbidden to invest in commerce or industry and none of the aristocratic families were directly involved in either manufacturing or trade. Some families, however, used freedmen to invest on their behalf. Nevertheless, these men who made money for them were looked down upon. Members of the senatorial class required money to fulfil their obligations as officials in unpaid public posts. For them money was very much a means to an end and they 'upheld rule by birth' over rule by money.[88]

In the third century the Roman emperor Gratian proclaimed that a man who bought merchandise 'in order that he may gain by selling it again unchanged and as he bought it, that man is of the buyers and sellers who are cast forth from God's Temple'. Six centuries later Charlemagne issued a capitulary which stated: 'Those who by various manoeuvres dishonestly plan to amass goods of all kinds with the express aim of making money are acquiring ill-gotten gains.'[89]

Early Christian, Hebrew, Roman and Greek philosophy all contain the idea that humans once lived in a golden age, communally and in harmony, sharing all that they had, and that the struggle for individual possessions spoiled that harmony and created conflict between humans.[90] For example, Roman philosopher Seneca stated:

> This fellowship remained unspoiled for a long time, until avarice tore the community asunder and became the cause of poverty.... But avarice broke in upon a condition so happily ordained, and, by its eagerness to lay something away and to turn it to its own private use, made all things the property of others, and reduced itself from boundless wealth to straitened need.[91]

Martin Hengel in his *Property and Riches in the Early Church* says that the 'thesis that private property came into being as a result of the Fall had great influence on the history of the church'. For example, fourth-century preacher John Chrysostom, whom Hengel names as the 'greatest Christian preacher of antiquity', said 'that concerning things that are common [sun, air, earth, and water] there is no contention but all is peaceable. But when one attempts to

20

possess himself of anything, to make it his own, then contention is introduced.'[92]

The Old Testament story of Cain is in part a story of how greed turned a man into a liar and a murderer. The name Cain is thought to mean 'be envious of possessions' as it derives from two Hebrew words: *qana,* which means 'acquire', and *qana'* which means 'to be envious'.[93] Both Old and New Testaments tend to attack the rich, particularly those who exploit others to gain their wealth, rather than blame the poor.[94] The Hebrew prophets 'identified the rich and powerful with the wicked' and the poor as 'holy and righteous'.[95] Many were highly critical of the rich landlords who dispossessed the poor and exploited them. For example, Isaiah states: 'Woe to those who join house to house, who add field to field, until there is no more room.'[96]

In Exodus the Jews were told, 'If you lend money to any of my people with you who is poor, you shall not be as a creditor, and you shall not exact interest from him.'[97] In Deuteronomy, it was stated that every seven years all debts were to be forgiven. There was also provision for a percentage of every person's income (at least 2 or 3 per cent and up to 20 per cent) to be tithed for the poor.[98]

Jesus saw wealth as a danger to the soul and a hindrance to righteousness: 'No man can serve two masters: for either he will hate one and love the other; or else he will hold to the one, and despise the other. Ye cannot serve God and Mammon.' Better-known, perhaps, is his statement: 'It is easier for a camel to go through the eye of a needle than for a rich man to enter into the Kingdom of God.'[99] Jesus also showed his contempt for commercialism in a well-known episode when he threw the money changers and vendors from the outer court of the Temple, knocking over their tables.

> And Jesus entered the temple of God and drove out all who sold and bought in the temple, and he overturned the tables of the money changers and the seats of those who sold pigeons. He said to them, 'It is written, "My house shall be called a house of prayer"; but you make it a den of robbers.'[100]

From all accounts Jesus himself had no possessions and required his followers to give up their possessions and he promised that this renunciation of worldly goods would be recognised by God.[101] He told his disciples: 'Blessed be ye poor: for yours is the kingdom of God…. But woe unto you that are rich! for ye have received your consolation'[102] and 'Sell that ye have, and give alms…. For where your treasure is, there will your heart be also.'[103]

The Christian disciples followed this line. Paul, for example, advised Christians to be content with food and clothing and to avoid the love of money.[104] He warned that those who sought riches 'fall into temptation … and into many foolish and hurtful lusts…. For the love of money is the root of all evil.'[105] This last saying had precedents in popular Greek as well as Jewish philosophy.[106]

The establishment of monasteries in earlier centuries resulted from Christian advice to live a communal life of voluntary poverty. Charging interest on loans of money was forbidden and consumption for pleasure was seen as sinful. Augustine stated that 'Business is in itself an evil' and Jerome claimed that 'A man who is a merchant can seldom if ever please God.'[107]

The early Protestants did not wholeheartedly embrace the pursuit of wealth as a virtue either. Luther, reflecting the values of the community he lived in, didn't consider commerce as real work and disapproved of the hoarding of wealth.[108] He praised manual labour that produced a tangible product but 'denigrated the efforts of merchants who produced neither goods nor food'. The idea of buying goods and selling them at a profit without adding to their value in any material way did not fit with Luther's idea of work and he considered it to be sinful. He felt business people exploited the labour of peasants and artisans.[109] He thought Christians should keep away from 'the world of trade, banking, credit, and capitalist industry'.[110] In this Luther held traditional views.

Calvin was more accepting of business activity than Luther but was still concerned about the dangers that wealth could lead to, such as greed, degeneracy and idleness. Calvin differed from his predecessors in his acceptance of moneylending or usury as a necessity for commerce and the moneylender as a useful member of society.[111] He allowed that wealth was a sign of God's blessing for one's labours.

THE RISE OF MODERN CAPITALISM

Both Luther and Calvin condemned as evil the selfish use of wealth to satisfy personal desires and both disapproved of work aimed at maximising profits. It was some years before business activity was actively supported by Protestants.[112] Even early Protestants could build up their wealth in good conscience, however, provided it did not lead to 'idleness and the temptations of the flesh' nor 'distraction from the pursuit of a righteous life'.[113]

The Puritans took this further, 'teaching that it is one's duty to extract the greatest possible gain from work'.[114] Profits showed that God had blessed a person and approved of their work. In this way seeking wealth became a religiously endorsed activity, which one could pursue in good conscience. The labour and the profit were supposed to be for God, however, not for one's own pleasure. So hand in hand with the pursuit of wealth went an ethic of austerity and abstinence, of asceticism. Weber explained:

22

asceticism looked upon the pursuit of wealth as an end in itself as highly reprehensible; but the attainment of it as a fruit of labour in a calling was a sign of God's blessing. And even more important: the religious valuation of restless, continuous, systematic work in a worldly calling, as the highest means to asceticism, and at the same time the surest and most evident proof of rebirth and genuine faith, must have been the most powerful conceivable lever for the expansion of that attitude toward life which we have here called the spirit of capitalism.[115]

Richard Baxter, one of the better-known English Puritan writers, stated in his *Christian Directory*, a compendium of Puritan ethics:

> It is a sin to desire riches as worldlings and sensualists do, for the provision and maintenance of fleshly lusts, and pride. But it is no sin, but a duty to labour not only for labour's sake, formally resting in the act done, but for that honest increase and provision, which is the end of our labour; and therefore to choose a gainful calling rather than another, that we may be able to do good, and relieve the poor.[116]

The asceticism of Protestantism ensured that the money made by capitalists was not wastefully spent but was reinvested to make more capital. Traditionally, economic activity had been aimed at satisfying needs. Capitalism involved 'a struggle for profit free from the limits set by needs'. Profits were not spent or lent but reinvested in the business to make it even more profitable. Capitalism was not merely synonymous with a desire to acquire money and goods, nor with trading for profit. Commercial activity undertaken by the new breed of entrepreneurs and traders was methodical, calculated, rationalised. The capitalist ethic involved the pursuit of profit for an end other than the goods, pleasure and position it could buy.[117]

In this way capitalists were not working for personal happiness but for business success and the sense of achievement that brought. Such an approach would seem irrational and strange in other cultures. Even in Rome, which was one of the most materially rich civilisations of the ancient world, citizens who became rich used their wealth to buy position or to live in outrageous luxury.[118]

Traders and merchants in the Middle Ages did not seek to continually increase and expand their business, nor to invest most of their profits back into the business.

> The majority of merchants, traders and small craft manufacturers were content to make only a comfortable profit and, similarly, to enjoy the benefits of a comfortable standard of living.... Chance opportunities for personal gain were quick to be exploited, but the systematic creation of wealth through ceaseless efforts in the marketplace [was] seen to be the prerogative only of ambitious and greedy persons who were personally inclined to such pursuits....[119]

Those that became rich spent their money on luxury: magnificent homes and furnishings, jewellery, clothing, servants and land.[120] The new breed of capitalist traders and merchants, however, had a very different approach. They were methodical and tireless in their relentless drive to continually expand their businesses, making more and more money which they did not spend on themselves but reinvested. Despite their wealth they lived modestly and were highly self-disciplined.[121]

Although trade for profit has existed throughout history, modern capitalism involves a society-wide system of trade, and a common, shared way of life, as opposed to individuals trading here and there. It requires a system of values that revolve around economic meanings and goals. Capitalism had existed in earlier societies but without the spirit or ethos that guides modern capitalism.[122]

The capitalist ethos exemplified in the 1750s by the preaching of Benjamin Franklin, a founding pilgrim father of the USA, was a complete reversal of more traditional ways of understanding the purpose of life and virtuous living. For example, Franklin preached:

> Remember, that *time* is money. He that can earn ten shillings a day by his labour, and goes abroad, or sits idle, one half of that day, though he spends but sixpence during his diversion or idleness, ought not to reckon that the only expense; he has really spent, or rather thrown away, five shillings besides.[123]

Weber pointed out that Franklin was not merely giving rules or providing wisdom to guide the unwary, but rather was delivering a moral code, an ethos.[124] Not surprisingly, Franklin, although not religious himself, was brought up in a Calvinist family, his father strictly religious.[125] In earlier times the sentiments expressed by Franklin would have been considered 'as the lowest sort of avarice'. Now they became the ethos of a nation.

ROLE OF THE CHURCH

The teachings of the early Protestant reformers were by no means obvious interpretations of the Bible, which is ambiguous and contradictory enough to support various views of work and capitalism. But coinciding as they did with the rise of a middle class in Europe and an increase in commercial and business activity, their teachings were attractive to a sector of the population which was itself becoming more powerful. Calvin preached to people who valued virtues such as diligence, thrift and entrepreneurial endeavour: 'It is no accident that these urban merchants, bankers, and artisans were among the earliest and most fervent supporters of Calvinism. They found in this faith a reinforcing rationale for their belief in hard work and enterprise.'[126]

During the transition to capitalism, the Church was a powerful force in people's lives, and the clergy and their preaching were 'decisive influences in the formation of national character'.[127] Those who worked hard were respected and those who made money were honoured. The clergy promoted the work ethic throughout the sixteenth and seventeenth centuries in Europe.[128]

Once the capitalist spirit took hold it was hard to resist or turn back. When businesspeople became capitalists, those in the same business either had to follow suit and give up their leisurely and relaxed way of doing business, or go out of business because they couldn't compete with the ever-expanding capitalist entrepreneurs.[129]

The religious roots of the spirit of capitalism 'died out slowly, giving way to a utilitarian worldliness'.[130] By the time the American colonies were being settled by the Puritans, the Protestant ethic had become a secular ethic, part of the culture of the new immigrants.[131] Nevertheless, their ministers continued to preach about the importance of industriousness and hard work as part of a righteous life: 'Protestant ministers found that sermons stressing diligence and the divine justification of material wealth were well received by those reaping the benefits of hard work.'[132] They gave weekly sermons promoting the 'gospel of work'.[133]

Modern churches continue to reinforce the message of the value of work. For example, at its second assembly the World Council of Churches called upon society to provide all its members with the opportunity to work and stated that 'all work honestly done, whether undertaken for the sake of earning a livelihood, or for the sake of the community, or out of spontaneous joy in creative effort, has genuine value and meaning in the purpose of God'.[134]

The Catholic Church also belatedly attempted to create a work ethic from biblical material through papal statements. In this way the Catholic Church is one of many social institutions supporting capitalist values in the modern world. Papal encyclicals throughout the twentieth century emphasised the value of work. In his 1981 encyclical 'Laborem Exercens (On Human Work)', Pope John Paul II counselled: 'Work is one of the characteristics that distinguish man from the rest of the creatures, whose activity for sustaining their lives cannot be called work.'[135]

Pope John Paul II referred to the biblical text 'In the sweat of your face you shall eat bread' when he said:

> And yet in spite of this toil – perhaps, in a sense, because of it – work is a good thing for man…. It is not only good in the sense that it is useful or something to enjoy; it is also good as being something worthy, that is to say, something that corresponds to man's dignity, that expresses his dignity and increases it. If one wishes to define more clearly the ethical meaning of work, it is this truth that one must particularly keep in mind.[136]

These statements were reconfirmed in following encyclicals in 1987 and 1991.[137]

The National Center for the Laity today promotes 'the spirituality of work' amongst Catholics: 'Catholics must understand that all baptized Christians – not only priests and religious – can respond to the call to holiness through their careers and their daily responsibilities.'[138] Writing in the *Journal of Business Ethics*, Michael Naughton and Gene Laczniak claim that the Catholic social tradition provides 'an orientation that perceives work as an act of virtue as well as a means to a financial end'.[139] In fact one commentator, writing in *The Christian Century*, noted that the Protestant work ethic is 'now more honored, ironically enough, in Catholic social teaching than it is among mainline Protestants'.[140]

CONCLUSION

There is some debate about which came first, the Protestant ethic or the beginnings of modern capitalism. But one doesn't need to prove a causal relationship between one and the other to argue that the Reformation provided moral support and legitimacy to a class of people who had an interest in raising the status and influence of commerce and industry. In fact Weber acknowledged that for ideas to become influential they need to be taken up by people who have an interest in their acceptance.[141] Ideas and interests are mutually reinforcing.

Protestantism provided a conducive environment for capitalism to flourish in and the moral high ground from which to pursue profit freely and with good conscience. Similarly the new businessmen supported a church and faith that told them that what they wanted to do was in keeping with what God wanted them to do. Tawney stated:

> The shrewd, calculating commercialism which tries all human relations by pecuniary standards, the acquisitiveness which cannot rest while there are competitors to be conquered or profits to be won, the love of social power and hunger for economic gain – these irrepressible appetites have evoked from time immemorial the warnings and denunciations of saints and sages. Plunged in the cleansing waters of later Puritanism, the qualities which less enlightened ages had denounced as social vices emerged as economic virtues.[142]

In England, Holland, Scotland, Geneva and America the combination of Protestantism and capitalism wrought social change of huge dimensions. In England it overturned the power of a feudal aristocracy 'contemptuous of the economic virtues … more interested in maintaining customary standards of consumption than in accumulating capital for future production'. It transformed a farming system based on subsistence farming by serfs indebted to landlords. It provided those who were discontented with the old order of things with 'the dignity and momentum of a religious and a social philosophy' to carry forward the changes they sought.[143]

Whilst few people today consider their work to be a calling or service to God, hard work is still viewed as a sign of good character. As will be seen in the following chapters, secular institutions have taken over from the churches in preaching the virtues of work:

> The identification of labour and enterprise with some sort of higher service remains with us – less God-centred, but still associated with notions of 'good behaviour'. Our major political, industrial and cultural institutions are permeated with the work ethic – party leaderships preach the message; unions and management display solidarity on the issue.[144]

This identification is not just a remnant of earlier times, but something that was reinforced in the centuries following the Protestant Reformation by those who had most to gain from such attitudes, in particular employers and businesspeople who profited from a hard-working workforce.

Capitalism no longer requires Protestantism to support it and give it a moral base. In fact, the fear of the Church that money making and wealth seeking would become ends in themselves rather than means of glorifying God, and that people would be distracted from God by their attachment to their money, was well founded. Over time, wealth became a measure of worldly success and status, as we shall see in the next chapter. For Benjamin Franklin, although he grew up in a Calvinist family, money making was an end in itself rather than a sign of God's blessing.[145] And in the twentieth century even the asceticism of Protestantism was lost, as consumerism became a driving force in human affairs – a theme we revisit in Chapter 12.

NOTES

1 Quoted in Ernie J. Zelinski, *The Joy of Not Working: a Book for the Retired, Unemployed, and Overworked* (Berkeley, California: Ten Speed Press, 1997), p. 57.

2 Quoted in Martin Hengel, *Property and Riches in the Early Church: Aspects of a Social History of Early Christianity*, translated by John Bowden (London: SNM Press, 1974), p. 16.

3 Extract in Alfred D. Chandler and Richard S. Tedlow, *The Coming of Managerial Capitalism: a Casebook History of American Economic Institutions* (Homewood, Illinois: Richard D. Irwin, 1985), p. 10.

4 Quoted in 'The Modern Temper: America in the 1920s', *Publishers Weekly*, Vol. 242, No. 17 (1995), pp. 67–8.

5 P. D. Anthony, *The Ideology of Work* (London: Tavistock Publications, 1977), p. 39.

6 R. H. Tawney, 'Religion and the Rise of Capitalism', in Robert W. Green (ed.),

Protestantism, Capitalism and Social Science: the Weber Thesis Controversy (Lexington, Mass.: D. C. Heath and Co., 1973), p. 104.

7 David J. Cherrington, *The Work Ethic: Working Values and Values That Work* (New York: AMACON, 1980), p. 26.

8 Barry Jones, *Sleepers, Wake! Technology and the Future of Work*: Oxford University Press, 1983), p. 192.

9 Adriano Tilgher, *Work: What It Has Meant to Men Through the Ages*, translated by Dorothy Canfield Fisher (London: George G. Harrap, 1931), p. 3.

10 Herbert Applebaum, *The Concept of Work: Ancient, Medieval, and Modern* (Albany, NY: State University of New York Press, 1992), p. 36.

11 *Ibid.*, pp. 35–7.

12 Anthony, note 5, p. 4; Applebaum, note 10, p. 31.

13 Hannah Arendt, quoted in Anthony, note 5, p. 18.

14 *Ibid.*, p. 17.

15 Applebaum, note 10, pp. 64–6.

16 A. R. Gini and T. J. Sullivan, 'A Critical Overview', in A. R. Gini and T. J. Sullivan (eds), *It Comes with the Territory: an Inquiry Concerning Work and the Person* (New York: Random House, 1989), p. 6.

17 Aristotle, quoted in Applebaum, note 10, p. 34.

18 *Ibid.*, pp. 35, 61.

19 Anthony, note 5, p. 20.

20 Gini and Sullivan, note 16, p. 5.

21 Roger B. Hill, 'Historical Context of the Work Ethic'. http://www.coe.uga.edu/~rhill/workethic/hist.htm (1992); Tilgher, note 9, p. 8.

22 Cicero, quoted in Applebaum, note 10, p. 95.

23 *Ibid.*, pp. 96–7, 101, 120.

24 Quoted in *ibid.*, p. 117.

25 Lukas Vischer, 'The Work of Human Beings as Creatures of God', *The Ecumenical Review*, Vol. 48, No. 3 (1996).

26 Applebaum, note 10, p. 181.

27 Quoted in Gini and Sullivan, note 16, p. 5.

28 Stanley Parker, *The Future of Work and Leisure* (London: MacGibbon and Kee, 1977), p. 34.

29 Tilgher, note 9, p. 12.

30 *The Holy Bible*, King James edn (Oxford: Oxford University Press, n.d.), Luke 12.22–12.27.

31 Applebaum, note 10, pp. 184–8.

32 Tilgher, note 9, p. 35.

33 *Ibid.*, p. 41.

34 Hill, note 21.

35 Applebaum, note 10, p. 209.

36 Tilgher, note 9, p. 39.

37 P. Gaskell, quoted in Anthony, note 5, p. 40.

38 Gordon Marshall, *In Search of the Spirit of Capitalism: an Essay on Max Weber's Protestant Ethic Thesis* (London: Hutchinson, 1982), p. 124.

39 Quoted in John Hatcher, 'Labour, Leisure and Economic Thought before the Nineteenth Century', *Past and Present* (August 1998).

40 Max Weber, *The Protestant Ethic and the Spirit of Capitalism*, translated by Talcott Parsons,

2nd edn (London: George Allen & Unwin, 1967), pp. 59–60.

41 *Ibid.*

42 Kemper Fullerton, 'Calvinism and Capitalism: an Explanation of the Weber Thesis', in Robert W. Green (ed.), *Protestantism, Capitalism and Social Science: the Weber Thesis Controversy* (Lexington, Mass.: D. C. Heath and Co., 1973), p. 15.

43 Marc Kolden, 'Work and Meaning: Some Theological Reflections', *Interpretation*, Vol. 48, No. 3 (1994).

44 Applebaum, note 10, p. 323.

45 Weber, note 40, pp. 99–100.

46 Fullerton, note 42, p. 17.

47 Weber, note 40, pp. 100–14.

48 Anthony Giddens, Introduction to Weber, note 40, p. 5.

49 Tilgher, note 9, pp. 59–60.

50 Weber, note 40, p. 157.

51 Paul Bernstein, *American Work Values: Their Origin and Development* (Albany, NY: State University of New York Press, 1997), pp. 38, 69–71.

52 Weber, note 40, p. 177.

53 Applebaum, note 10, p. 329.

54 Richard Baxter quoted in *ibid.*, pp. 330–1.

55 Bernstein, note 51, p. 39.

56 Gini and Sullivan, note 16, p. 8.

57 Quoted in *ibid.*, p. 8.

58 Robert Eisenberger, *Blue Monday: the Loss of the Work Ethic in America* (New York: Paragon House, 1989), p. 7.

59 Weber, note 40, p. 163.

60 Tilgher, note 9, p. 29; Hengel, note 2, pp. 31–2, 42–4.

61 Applebaum, note 10, p. 324.

62 Bernstein, note 51, p. 56.

63 Tilgher, note 9, p. 56.

64 Bernstein, note 51, p. 2.

65 *Ibid.*, p. 46.

66 *Ibid.*, p. 50.

67 Joe R. Feagin, *Subordinating the Poor* (Englewood Cliffs, NJ: Prentice-Hall, 1975), p. 18.

68 Quoted in Bernstein, note 51, p. 42.

69 *Ibid.*, pp. 101–4.

70 *Ibid.*, p. 51.

71 Feagin, note 67, pp. 19–21.

72 Bernstein, note 51, pp. 3, 41.

73 Quoted in *ibid.*, p. 137.

74 *Ibid.*, p. 51.

75 *Ibid.*, pp. 97, 105–7.

76 Lydia Morris, *Dangerous Classes: the Underclass and Social Citizenship* (London: Routledge, 1994), p. 59.

77 Feagin, note 67, p. 27.

78 Marshall, note 38, p. 107.

79 Tawney, note 6, pp. 90–1.

80 Weber, note 40, p. 58.

81 Marshall, note 38, pp. 106–7; Fullerton, note 42, pp. 8–9.

82 Tilgher, note 9, pp. 9–10.
83 Cited in Anthony, note 5, p. 16.
84 Applebaum, note 10, p. 70.
85 Will Durant, *Caesar and Christ: a History of Roman Civilization and of Christianity from Their Beginnings to AD 325* (New York: Simon and Schuster, 1944), p. 332.
86 Applebaum, note 10, pp. 93, 120, 166.
87 Tilgher, note 9, pp. 9–10.
88 Durant, note 85, p. 96.
89 Quoted in Earl Shorris, *A Nation of Salesmen: the Tyranny of the Market and the Subversion of Culture* (New York: W. W. Norton, 1994), p. 61.
90 Hengel, note 2, pp. 1–5.
91 Quoted in *ibid.*, p. 6.
92 Quoted in *ibid.*, p. 2.
93 *Ibid.*, p. 1.
94 Thomas H. Naylor, William H. Willimon and Rolf Osterberg, *The Search for Meaning in the Workplace* (Nashville: Abingdon Press, 1996), p. 45.
95 Tilgher, note 9, pp. 16–17.
96 Quoted in Hengel, note 2, p. 13.
97 Quoted in Shorris, note 89, p. 58.
98 Hengel, note 2, pp. 14, 20.
99 Quoted in Tilgher, note 9, pp. 24–5.
100 Matthew 21:12 quoted in Shorris, note 89, p. 60.
101 Hengel, note 2, p. 26.
102 Luke, note 30, 6.20 and 6.24.
103 *Ibid.*, 12.33–12.34.
104 Tilgher, note 9, p. 31.
105 Quoted in Jeffery L. Sheler, 'Is God Lost as Sales Rise?', *US News and World Report*, Vol. 118 (13 March 1995), p. 63.
106 Hengel, note 2, pp. 10–11.
107 Quoted in Rodney Clapp, 'Why the Devil Takes Visa', *Christianity Today*, Vol. 40, No. 11 (1996).
108 Hill, note 21.
109 Bernstein, note 51, pp. 1, 33, 83.
110 Applebaum, note 10, p. 324.
111 Tawney, note 6, p. 92.
112 Bernstein, note 51, pp. 33, 55.
113 Weber, note 40, p. 157.
114 Applebaum, note 10, p. 325.
115 Weber, note 40, p. 157.
116 Quoted in Applebaum, note 10, pp. 330–1.
117 Weber, note 40, pp. 53, 64, 68.
118 Durant, note 85, pp. 130–3, 337.
119 Marshall, note 38, pp. 105–6.
120 *Ibid.*, p. 105.
121 Fullerton, note 42, pp. 11–12.
122 Weber, note 40, pp. 19, 52, 55.
123 Quoted in *ibid.*, p. 48.
124 *Ibid.*, p. 51.

125 Applebaum, note 10, p. 334.

126 Bernstein, note 51, p. 60

127 Weber, note 40, pp. 155.

128 Cherrington, note 7, p. 34.

129 Weber, note 40, p. 68.

130 *Ibid.*, p. 176.

131 Hill, note 21.

132 Eisenberger, note 58, p. 2.

133 Cherrington, note 7, p. 35.

134 Quoted in Vischer, note 25.

135 Pope John Paul II, 'Laborem Exercens (On Human Work): Encyclical Letter 1981', in Gini and Sullivan, note 16, p. 59.

136 *Ibid.*, p. 63.

137 Vischer, note 25.

138 William Droel, 'The Spirituality of Work', *Momentum*, Vol. 28 (August/September 1997).

139 Michael Naughton and Gene R. Laczniak, 'A Theological Context of Work from the Catholic Social Encyclical Tradition', *Journal of Business Ethics*, Vol. 12, No. 1 (1993).

140 Dennis P. McCann, 'Apology of the Hireling: a Work Ethic of the Global Marketplace', *The Christian Century*, Vol. 112 (17 May 1995).

141 Tony Watson, *Sociology, Work and Industry*, 2nd edn (London: Routledge and Kegan Paul, 1987), p. 48.

142 Tawney, note 6, p. 105.

143 *Ibid.*, pp. 99, 101.

144 David Bleakley, *Work: the Shadow and the Substance* (London: SCM Press, 1983), p. 81.

145 Fullerton, note 42, p. 31.

◇ 3 ◇

Work, Status and Success

Life depends, not upon birth and status, not upon breeding or beauty, but upon effort, effort that will be rewarded in riches, in material goods, which are a sign that the effort was made, that one has in the language of childhood been 'good'.
Margaret Mead[1]

In some large factories, from one-fourth to one-fifth of the children were either cripples or otherwise deformed, or permanently injured by excessive toil, sometimes by brutal abuse.
Robert Dale Owen[2]

Every penny bestowed, that tends to render the condition of the pauper more eligible than that of the independent labourer, is a bounty on indolence and vice.
Sir Edwin Chadwick[3]

With the rise of capitalism work came to be valued according to its productivity and wealth-creating potential. Success in business was measured solely in terms of profits. Wealth, as the supposed fruits of hard work, became an indicator of a person's worth and determined their social standing. The emphasis on work as a religious calling was gradually superseded by a materialistic quest for social mobility and material success.

This success-oriented work ethic encouraged ambition, hard work, self-reliance, and self-discipline and held out the promise that such effort would be materially rewarded. Rather than emphasising religious virtues, the revised work ethic focused on character: 'Desirable character traits included perseverance, industry, frugality, sobriety, punctuality, reliability, thoroughness, and initiative.'[4] If one had these character traits then one would be successful.

Today the ambition for material success is so ingrained in all industrialised countries that people assume it is so natural and unavoidable 'that material wealth is an ultimate human motive'.[5] In his book *The Illusion of Choice: How the Market Economy Shapes Our Destiny*, Andrew Bard Schmookler argues that people have come to accept the market as the adjudicator of value, even their own value. The way they 'evaluate their lives' now conforms with 'the way the market system keeps score'.[6]

A person's value is assessed by others according to what they do for a living and how much money they have or earn. In this context it is little wonder that so many people work, not just to provide their needs, but to improve their status and increase their wealth. Yet we have seen that such values had to overcome a previous set of human values that regarded the naked pursuit of personal wealth as greed and avarice that should be avoided.

In capitalist societies there has been no shortage of wealthy people and those who depended on them to preach 'the new gospel of the morality of wealth'.[7] It was in their interests to present the capitalist system of inequalities as based on merit, with social advancement open to anyone of good character who was willing to work hard.

SOCIAL MOBILITY

Throughout the medieval period a fixed social hierarchy was considered essential to social order.[8] People were born to a particular station in life, be it peasant or nobleman, and generally they accepted this as part of the natural order of things. The idea of a fixed order was reinforced by the Church, which presented it as God-given. Thomas Aquinas's model of society had a place for everyone, each contributing to a higher order in a preordained way: 'one played one's allotted role in a drama scripted elsewhere'. Those who ruled did so for the benefit of the whole society, or at least this was the story given by the Church to the peasants on behalf of the feudal aristocracy of the times.[9]

The desire to raise one's social status through changing jobs was considered by early Christians to be mere vanity.[10] Work was not supposed to be a means of social mobility but a way to earn one's living and atone for one's sins. The fourteenth-century schoolman Henry of Langenstein argued:

> He who has enough to satisfy his wants and nevertheless ceaselessly labors to acquire riches, either in order to obtain a higher social position, or that subsequently he have enough to live without labor ... all such are incited by a damnable avarice, sensuality, or pride.[11]

33

Luther, too, believed that one's place in the world and one's calling were assigned by God and were not means of social mobility. Predestination for Luther meant accepting one's position in life as having been ordained by God. Everyone's work had equal spiritual dignity as long as they served God. In this he reflected the ideas of the times.[12]

Calvin, however, opened the way for work to become a means of social mobility. Unlike Luther and those who had gone before, Calvin did not claim that one's occupation was assigned by God and was therefore immutable. Although he did not advocate changing jobs for material gain or personal betterment, he argued that people should find the occupation that was of greatest value to society and in which one could best serve God.[13]

The idea that hard work was a 'sign' of being one of God's chosen was an essential first step in the association between work and status. Because a person's fate was predetermined, work was a way of demonstrating to others that s/he was one of the chosen. Wealth was supposed to be the fruit of hard work and the sign of God's blessing. The social status gained by the wealthy as a result of these beliefs turned out to be a more powerful incentive to work than the need to prove oneself to a distant God.

Subsequent Puritan preachers held not only that one could change one's calling but that there was even a duty to do so. The English Puritan leader, Richard Baxter, said: 'When God shows you a way in which you can lawfully make more [money] without danger to your soul or to others than you can in some other way, and when you reject this way and follow the way that brings in less, then you cross one of the purposes of your calling. You refuse to be God's steward and to accept his gifts….'[14]

Work was 'thus freed from the hampering ideas of caste and … endowed with the greatest possible initiative'.[15] But although Luther and Calvin saw the value of work in serving God and the community, and warned about doing work for the purpose of making money, and although early Puritan preachers warned against ambition as a sin, work gradually came to be glorified as a means of personal fulfilment.[16] By the late seventeenth century the Puritan divines were declaring worldly success evidence of God's grace.[17]

The idea of work as a religious calling was soon replaced by the idea of working for self-interest and personal betterment: 'The spirit of self-improvement and belief in an opportunity ethic was subtly pushing God into the background.'[18] Businesspeople no longer needed to see their work as a religious calling to be motivated to work hard; they could see the value of their industry in terms of profits and advancement. Hard work and diligence were good ways of gaining wealth, and for the middle classes vocation came to be seen as a way of becoming wealthy rather than a way of serving God.[19]

In England, through the seventeenth and eighteenth centuries, social

34

position was increasingly based on market relations rather than tradition. Wealth had traditionally been associated with property, particularly land owner-ship, but 'Wealth became identified with money, or with property which could be transformed into money by sale on the market.'[20] Merchants and professionals worked hard for financial success and 'nobles and yeomen vied for wealth and upward mobility rather than spiritual merit'.[21]

Unlike the French aristocracy, the English aristocracy more readily embraced the new men of wealth, grudgingly accepting them into their society, sending their sons into business or (often the same thing) to marry into a merchant family. In turn the successful merchants sought to become gentlemen by acquiring land and titles.[22]

In parts of Europe and in America wealth, rather than being a manifesta-tion of virtue and the 'favourable spiritual state of the inward man', became an end in itself 'leaving but the dry husk of material success to define the purpose of human existence'. And when material success became the end goal, religious virtues such as piety were gradually superseded by 'virtues' that led to that success: 'initiative, aggressiveness, competitiveness, and forceful-ness',[23] qualities that might have been frowned on in earlier times. 'Protes-tantism had begun to elevate the concept of wealth, and the pragmatism that developed in America raised it still higher.'[24]

For white people, eighteenth-century America offered the opportunity for social advancement through hard work: 'Advancing within your occupation not only meant greater wealth and personal success; it was also a mark of good character.'[25] Middle-class Americans, particularly farmers, merchants, teachers and artisans, embraced the work ethic and it gradually spread to other strata of American society.[26]

In the slave-owning southern states of America the social order was far more fixed and the work ethic less central. It was the Northerners who sought to propagate the culture of work and money. Their middle classes 'controlled the major institutions of social influence' – the schools, churches, factories, political offices and publishing companies – and used them to propagate their values:[27]

Like a brightly lighted beacon, the moral preeminence of work beamed unwa-veringly from all the early moralists. Influential statesmen, clergymen, and authors all taught that success came through hard work, diligence, persever-ance, honesty and thrift. Young people were confronted on all sides with advice about dedicated work, the wise use of time, and the importance of character.[28]

Benjamin Franklin was one of the best-known propagators of such values and has ever since been held up as the paragon of American virtues and to exemplify the national character in that period. He wrote:

The way to wealth, if you desire it, is as plain as the way to market. It depends chiefly on two words, industry and frugality; that is, waste neither time nor money, but make the best use of both. Without industry and frugality nothing will do, and with them everything. He that gets all he can honestly and saves all he gets will certainly become rich....[29]

Poor Richard and Franklin's autobiography sold millions of copies at the time and were translated into many languages for sale abroad. He epitomised the spirit of self-improvement.[30] In his 'Advice to a Young Tradesman' he urged thrift, industry, pursuit of money and hard work.[31]

Foreigners observed the industriousness of Americans as somewhat alien. They were 'amazed at the intensity with which Americans approached work and business. They were both fascinated and appalled by the American dedication to get ahead, and were aghast over what appeared to be a crass effort at social mobility and money making.'[32]

> There is, probably, no people on earth with whom business constitutes pleasure, and industry amusement, in equal degree with the inhabitants of the United States of America. Active occupation is not only the principal source of their happiness, and the foundation of their national greatness, but they are absolutely wretched without it.... Business is the very soul of an American: he pursues it, not as a means of procuring for himself and his family the necessary comforts of life, but as the fountain of all human felicity....[33]

This singular devotion to business was also noted in England after the industrial revolution. Foreigners were sometimes disturbed by the English businessmen's determination to make money whilst ignoring the poverty in their midst. Ralph Waldo Emerson noted in 1856 that 'the Englishman has pure pride in his wealth, and esteems it a final certificate'.[34]

INDUSTRIAL REVOLUTION

The industrial revolution in England in the late eighteenth and early nineteenth centuries was marked by rapid increases in production, trade and population. Manufacturing rose to prominence over agriculture as the engine of development.[35] Established landowners benefited from the industrial revolution and some became capitalists in their own right, for example by developing mines on their land.[36] But alongside the landowners who were able to take advantage of the new business opportunities, a new class of people found their place at the top of society, particularly manufacturers.

This new class of wealthy manufacturers generally did not emerge from the more established wealthy classes of landowners, bankers and merchants but from farmers, shopkeepers and tradesmen:[37] 'anyone who could borrow a little money and was prepared to work like a slave and to live like a slave master. Many of them came of yeoman stock....'[38]

And just as a new elite emerged, a new industrial working class was also formed. E. P. Thompson, in his classic study *The Making of the English Working Class*, describes how it forged a class-consciousness, giving rise to working-class political expressions such as trade unions. This new class was subject to various forms of political, educational and religious indoctrination aimed at keeping it docile and submissive and hard-working.[39]

Manufacturers established factories and employed large numbers of workers. Much of the manufacturing centred around textile production. Prior to the factories, spinning and weaving had been done by hand in people's own homes. Men did the weaving, whilst women and children did the spinning. Home workers had worked long hours to make a living, and worked their children too, but the factories took away the measure of control they had over their work and replaced it with the factory discipline dictated by machines, clocks and constant supervision. People were forced to work for 12–14 hours a day in hot airless rooms, often locked in, without water, where they could be fined for opening a window, fined for being dirty, fined for washing themselves during working hours, and even fined for being sick.[40]

David Dickson identifies four reasons why factories were set up in England:

> The merchants wanted to control and market the total production of the weavers so as to minimize embezzlement, to maximize the input of work by forcing weavers to work longer hours at greater speeds, to take control of all technical innovation so that it could be applied solely for capital accumulation, and generally to organize production so that the role of the capitalist became indispensable.[41]

It was a time of rapidly growing population and the population was on the move. People were being forced off the land by enclosures and changes in agriculture, they were migrating to England because of starvation in Ireland, and large numbers of men were being released from the army after a long war.[42] People flocked to the towns and provided the workforces for the new factories.

These people were not trained as factory workers, however, and had difficulty adapting to the factory discipline. As described in the previous chapter, traditional workers had not been in the habit of working long and regular hours. They would only work when they needed the money. Workers were criticised for being 'of loose and wandering habits'.[43]

Discipline was therefore a problem for employers. Andrew Ure described the problem in his 1835 book *Philosophy of Manufactures*:

> To devise and administer a successful code of factory discipline, suited to the necessities of factory diligence, was the Herculean enterprise.... [I]t is found nearly impossible to convert persons past the age of puberty, whether drawn from rural or from handicraft occupations, into useful factory hands. After struggling for a while to conquer their listless or restive habits, they either renounce the employment spontaneously, or are dismissed by the overlookers on account of inattention.[44]

Getting skilled workmen to submit to factory discipline was particularly difficult, and manufacturers looked for mechanical ways of replacing their labour so that most factory tasks could be reduced 'to the exercise of vigilance and dexterity – faculties ... speedily brought to perfection in the young'.[45]

> Women and children could be employed in such work. They were naturally more timid and easier to rule; their slender and more pliant fingers were better adapted to the tasks required of them; their shorter stature made it possible to place them in corners, and underneath machines where a man neither could nor would consent to be placed.[46]

Children as young as four or five years old were employed for 12 hours a day and up to 18 hours a day. Children from the workhouses were locked up during the night to prevent them running away. In 1802 legislation was passed that limited the working hours of children from workhouses to 12 hours per day in the cotton mills. In 1815 another law prohibited the employment of children under ten years of age and limiting those under eighteen to ten and a half hours a day.[47]

Disciplining adults to work hard all day was a more difficult matter. 'Industrialization, then, was more than a question of producing goods in a new way. It also entailed a process of socialization which aimed at stabilizing and inculcating fidelity among those whose labor was being conscripted.'[48] The ideal solution was a workforce that was motivated to work for work's sake. Many factory owners, despairing of the traditional lackadaisical attitudes of their workers, 'launched "moral crusades" and attempted to convert whole sections of their labour force' to Protestantism in the hope of creating 'an efficient, diligent, and reliable' workforce.[49]

For many such factory owners, the new evangelical branches of Protestantism such as Methodism seemed to serve the purpose well. Methodists tended to have 'methodical' habits, to pay careful attention to instructions, to fulfil contracts on time, and not be inclined to embezzle materials.[50] They were imbued with a work ethic and were generally sober, hard-working, obedient employees. The following directive was issued at the Methodist Conference in 1766:

We must never forget the first rule, 'Be diligent. Never be unemployed for a moment. Never be triflingly employed. Never while away time; neither spend any more time at any place than is strictly necessary.'[51]

METHODISM

For the workers at the beginning of the industrial revolution, the established church represented little more than the established authorities.[52] Whilst the Protestant ethic had suited the growing middle classes of the sixteenth and seventeenth centuries, and provided a rhetoric to encourage workers, a significant proportion of the new industrial workers could not identify as being one of God's chosen, nor did they see work as a means of social mobility.

Methodism was one of the first branches of Christianity to welcome the industrial workers and offer them salvation.[53] It prompted a religious revival in England. Methodist preaching style was fervent and passionate and attracted thousands of people:

> Rather than imitate the fashionable sermonizers by reciting well-prepared addresses of a polished and pedantic character, they improvised their sermons and aimed at generating violent emotions in their listeners, at filling them with the terror of hell, or, more precisely, with dread of sin, which is the true hell.[54]

The aim of this type of sermon was to produce a 'crisis of despair' followed by a cathartic release leading to 'a mood of blissful peace'. Indeed, people listening to them would faint and have convulsions. Thousands were converted, and the preachers' popularity led to them being disbarred from preaching in churches so that they preached outside the churches, in the streets, in the market place, in the fields.[55]

The rise in the popularity of Methodism amongst both workers and their employers served also to reinforce the work ethic. Rather than teaching predestination, whereby only a few were saved and nothing could change that, Methodist preachers believed in 'free will and justification by works'.[56] They taught wretched, poorly paid workers that they could look forward to happiness in a future world after death. God's grace could be attained by everyone, even the lowliest worker. Those who laboured hard, not for money but as an act of virtue, were blessed.[57]

Methodist preachers taught their followers to submit to authority and be obedient: 'Even if those in authority are evil or without faith, nevertheless the authority and its power is good and from God....'[58] Elie Halévy notes that Methodist leaders had declared their intention of 'promoting loyalty in the middle ranks as well as subordination and industry in the lower orders of society'.[59]

Thompson argues that workers accepted Methodism in part because they were indoctrinated. The Methodist Sunday schools were very active and often the only source of 'education' for poor children. These schools were more concerned with teaching good behaviour and submission than teaching reading and writing. In fact, Methodist Sunday schools, like Anglican Sunday schools, discouraged the teaching of writing. Methodists believed children were naturally sinful, and education tended to be aimed at their moral rescue. They were not allowed to play freely; their play had to be channelled into useful activities such as chopping wood and digging:[60]

> Break their will betimes. Begin this work before they can run alone, before they can speak plain, perhaps before they can speak at all. Whatever pain it costs, break the will if you would not damn the child. Let a child from a year old be taught to fear the rod and to cry softly; from that age make him do as he is bid, if you whip him ten times running to effect it.... Break his will now, and his soul shall live, and he will probably bless you to all eternity.[61]

Not all Methodist preachers and Sunday school teachers were as tough and uncompromising as Methodist doctrine expected, however, and there was enough humanity and sense of community to attract workers and keep them. The chapels ran various activities such as sewing groups, meetings and fund-raising activities, which provided important opportunities to socialise for people who had been uprooted from their traditional communities and extended families. The chapels helped people feel they were accepted and belonged and were of some worth.[62] There were opportunities for workers to participate in the running of the chapel and the chapel community provided recognition and status for religious, sober, and pious members.[63] Sinning meant not only a fall from grace but also being expelled from the community.

The repression and discipline expected of everyday life was given an outlet at chapel where people were encouraged to become emotional and expressive and pour out their feelings. Thompson describes the process:

> These Sabbath orgasms of feeling made more possible the single-minded weekday direction of these energies to the consummation of productive labour. Moreover, since salvation was never assured, and temptations lurked on every side, there was a constant inner goading to 'sober and industrious' behaviour – the visible sign of grace – every hour of the day and every day of the year. Not only 'the sack' but also the flames of hell might be the consequence of indiscipline at work. God was the most vigilant overlooker of them all.[64]

Methodism was a religion that suited employers not only because it furnished an obedient and disciplined workforce but also because it emphasised the qualities that they prided themselves on, including thrift, hard work and personal responsibility for success.[65] But although it was taken up by the proprietors of the factories, Methodism was particularly popular amongst the poorest and most wretched of workers. 'For the miner or weaver, the Chapel with its summons to the emotions, its music and singing, took the place that theatres, picture galleries, operas, occupied in the lives of others.'[66] This limited sense of social well-being, together with the promise of a better life afterwards, enabled the poor downtrodden worker to carry on. And Methodism was more attractive to workers than the Puritan faiths that provided salvation for the limited few who could demonstrate their virtue by counting their money.

Methodism taught patience, resignation and acceptance of the established social order: 'poor men were persuaded to practise virtues which enriched their masters rather than brought worldly success to themselves and to seek individual salvation when many of their leaders were urging the need for collective action'.[67] For the workers it taught that the riches and power that were beyond their reach were not everything, that the poor could also be blessed.

Not all workers were Methodists, however, and by 1851 the census showed that only a minority remained religious.[68] Other means were necessary to invoke hard work amongst the working classes. The undesirability of work for most industrial workers made it necessary 'for the industrial state to glorify work in order to maximise productivity and profit; so, the work ethic has been preached powerfully'.[69]

MYTH OF THE SELF-MADE MAN

The social mobility of the early part of the industrial revolution in England was lauded in books, newspapers and official reports as evidence of the fairness of a social system which rewarded hard work. In the 1855 novel *North and South,* the mill owner stated that it is 'one of the great beauties of our system that a working man may raise himself into the power and position of a master by his own exertions and behaviour'.[70]

Organisations such as the Bettering Society promoted thrift and self-improvement and criticised measures to aid the poor.[71] Samuel Smiles was one of the foremost advocates of 'the spirit of self-help'. His 1859 book *Self-Help* argued:

> In many walks of life drudgery and toil must be cheerfully endured as the necessary discipline of life.... He who allows his application to falter, or shirks his work on frivolous pretexts, is on the sure road to ultimate failure ... even men with the commonest brains and the most slender powers will accomplish much, if they will but apply themselves wholly and indefatigably to one thing at a time.... Nothing that is of real worth can be achieved without courageous working.[72]

Workers were urged to work hard towards success, to be independent and to raise themselves above their lowly stations in life through saving, striving and industry.[73] Whilst many of the early English manufacturers started off as workers themselves, they tended to come from the middle classes; and as time went by the opportunity for working people to become capitalists declined as the gap between them widened.[74] The rapid increase in economic growth did not benefit all. Whilst the wealthy reaped the gains, the poor seemed to get even poorer. One report showed that between 1796 and 1815 the wages of weavers in Glasgow had been reduced by 75 per cent whilst the cost of provisions had increased 100 per cent. Richard Pilling wrote in 1843: 'I was twenty years among the hand-loom weavers, and ten years in the factory ... and the longer and harder I have worked the poorer and poorer I have become every year, until at last, I am nearly exhausted.'[75]

Once steam engines and power machines and large-scale factories employing hundreds of workers became the norm, a great deal of money was needed to become a manufacturer and the small entrepreneur was squeezed out. An important pathway from worker to capitalist was closed and classes became more rigid.[76]

> In fact the much publicised gospel of improvement and self-help served only to obscure the very limited prospects and achievements of the self-made men within early and later Victorian society, and investigations of the steel and hosiery industries, for instance, have shown how little recruitment occurred from the ranks of the workers to those of the entrepreneurs.[77]

Yet there remained enough oft-repeated stories of individuals moving from poverty to wealth to keep alive, at least in the minds of the well-to-do, the idea that hard work could lead from rags to riches – even if this was not the case for the vast majority of people, who were born in poverty and died in poverty after a lifetime of hard work.[78] In this way the affluent were able to feel comfortable about poverty in their midst, blaming it on individual weakness rather than societal failings.

As opportunities became more limited in England and other parts of Europe, many of those wanting to make their fortunes migrated to America. America had a reputation as a land of opportunity, a place where people could advance socially through hard work. A large portion of the early migrants had been indentured servants who were given land with their freedom at the end of a set period of time. Hard work on frontier farms had been rewarded, and the migrants prospered and gained respect in their communities. The children learned the value of hard work from their parents and this was reinforced by schoolteachers and school-books, and by ministers who continued to preach the work ethic and the wickedness of idleness.[79]

The idea of social position depending on hard work and initiative helped perpetuate the myth that America did not have a class system. It was claimed that no matter what the social position of their parents, a person's own social position would be determined by the effort they put into their occupation. This was in contrast to the class structure of Britain and Europe, which limited the social mobility of those born to the working classes. In Britain, for example, the class a person was born into would influence the type of education their children would get, the neighbourhood they lived in, the types of services they had access to, the way other people treated them, and their opportunities and expectations for social advancement. It was this hereditary limiting of opportunities for social advancement of working-class children that was supposed not to exist in America.

During the nineteenth century people came to worship economic success and to 'enshrine wealth as the essence of value'.[80] Hard work was promoted as the route to this success and 'received the endorsement of a continuing stream of writers, workers, businessmen, and politicians'. Books and stories illustrating the work ethic flourished. They emphasised 'hard work, punctuality, and reliability'.[81] A key part of the propaganda was the promotion of the idea of the 'self-made man' which reinforced the idea that any man could make a fortune, no matter what his origins, provided he worked hard and was reasonably intelligent. Through example and reiteration, the myth that anyone could become rich in America if they tried hard enough became firmly established.

In the US 'newspapers, books, interviews, speeches, and literature abounded with praise of the successful who had made it on their own'. Success was defined in terms of doing well in business and making lots of money. '[E]ntrepreneurship was idolized in every precinct from the pulpit to the political podium.'[82] Owning one's own business was supposed to be a route to success that was open to all, as Abraham Lincoln explained in an 1861 speech to Congress:

> there is not of necessity any such thing as the free hired laborer being fixed to that condition for life…. The prudent, penniless beginner in the world labors for wages awhile, saves a surplus with which to buy tools or land for himself, then labors on his own account for awhile, and at length hires another new beginner to help him. This is a just, and generous, and prosperous system; which opens the way to all – gives hope to all, and consequent energy and progress, and improvement of conditions to all.[83]

Children's literature promoted work values as part of good character and the formula to success.[84] McGuffey's Eclectic Readers were perhaps the most widely read children's books in the nineteenth century, with 122 million copies of the six readers sold to an estimated four-fifths of US school children.[85] These books taught middle-class values, including the work ethic and success through hard work: 'Work, work, my boy, be not afraid; Look labor boldly in the face.'[86]

Other children's books such as the Peter Parley books and the stories of Horatio Alger also taught work values. Alger's books, some 20 million copies of which were sold – *Strive and Succeed, Ragged Dick, Mark the Matchboy, Risen from the Ranks, Bound to Rise* – told of poor boys who became self-made men through their own efforts and perseverance. Such boys were also honest and faithful to their employers and displayed initiative and self-reliance.[87]

In Alger's story *Bound to Rise or Up the Ladder*, Harry Walton, a boy from a very poor family, is inspired by reading about Benjamin Franklin and tells his mother, 'I don't expect to be a great man like him. But if I try hard I think I can rise in the world, and be worth a little money … I read in the country paper the other day that many of the richest men in Boston and New York were once poor boys.' He sets out on the road at 14 years of age to earn enough money to pay off a family debt and finds work as a shoemaker's assistant. He has his money stolen from him twice but good luck outweighs the bad, and the reader is encouraged to believe that this is because of his good character, which will always win out in the end. He comes home triumphant six months later, pays off the debt and more, and then sets off to start his apprenticeship to a printer, ready to work his way up from the bottom, confident that he will make it.[88]

Maria Edgeworth was an English author whose stories, such as *Idleness and Industry,* were also published in America for over a century. They taught that hard work could lead to success and wealth, and reinforced the model of the self-made man. William T. Adams wrote books such as *Work and Win,* with heroes who were 'industrious, useful, and reliable'.[89]

Many writers were in fact Protestant clergymen, including Horatio Alger, who was forced to leave his ministry after allegations of sexual activities with boys. Protestants sought to reconcile their 'teachings with popular materialism' and to ensure that the church remained relevant. Such literature stressed the triumph of good character over obstacles such as poverty, lack of innate talent and skills, and lack of education.[90]

In Britain the myth of the self-made man was evident in the popular music-hall songs of the nineteenth century, such as *Work, Boys, Work* by Harry Clifton:

… labour leads to wealth
and will keep you in good health,
so it's best to be contented with your lot.

Work, boys, work and be contented,
As long as you've enough to buy a meal,
The man, you may rely, will be wealthy by and by,
If he'll only put his shoulder to the wheel.[91]

Self-help books supplemented fiction in showing the way to success. Andrew Carnegie, himself a self-made man who started out as a poor immigrant and became one of the wealthiest men in America, published essays advising young men how to succeed in business. At the turn of the twentieth century he wrote that success was a 'simple matter of honest work, ability, and concentration' and so was available to 'the sober, frugal, energetic and able mechanic' as well as to the office boy and clerk of similar character.[92]

Yet Carnegie's own career was the exception rather than the rule. The wealthy and the top industry people, even in the nineteenth century, were not men who had worked their way up from poor beginnings; mainly they came from privileged backgrounds.[93] Nonetheless the myth was perpetuated in an effort to promote hard work and industry amongst workers, and the occasional story of the boy who did make it, like Carnegie, was told over and over to give veracity to the myth. Such stories were popular in the community because they offered hope. A favourite of the early twentieth century was that of Henry Ford, who became one of the most famous and wealthiest businessmen of his time after starting life as a farm boy and a mechanic. Self-improvement books at the turn of the twentieth century, with names such as *The Conquest of Poverty, Pushing to the Front* or *Success under Difficulty*, all preached the message of how any motivated, hard-working individual could overcome life's obstacles and reach the pinnacle of success: wealth and power.[94]

The American Dream is a twentieth-century embodiment of the success-based work ethic with its emphasis on social mobility. The American Dream was founded on the presumption of equal opportunity: that America offered all its citizens the opportunity to improve their material standard of living if they were willing to take opportunities and work hard. Success was deserved, as was failure, and each person was responsible for his or her own fate.

> America's reputation as a land of opportunity rested on its claim that the destruction of hereditary obstacles to advancement had created conditions in which social mobility depended on individual initiative alone. The self-made man, archetypical embodiment of the American dream, owed his advancement to habits of industry, sobriety, moderation, self-discipline, and avoidance of debt.[95]

The promise of the American Dream was promoted in the twentieth century by politicians and businessmen, despite increasing evidence to the contrary. In the 1920s Calvin Coolidge, then President of the US, argued that success was directly related to 'the amount of hard work put into it'.[96]

During the Depression years the National Association of Manufacturers (NAM) and other organisations published advertisements extolling the leaders of industry as self-made men: 'A typical advertisement featured a construction worker high on a steel girder looking down and waving at a man in a chauf-feured limousine. The headline reads: "I knew him when he pushed a wheel-barrow", and the text purports to show that, in America, every man and his offspring have an equal chance of success.'[97] A 1940s NAM pamphlet stated: 'Your future is strictly up to you.... Your opportunities will be limited only by your vision of what your future may become, your abilities and how you use them, your character and your determination.' Poverty and lack of education were obstacles that could be overcome by those who had 'what it takes'.[98]

Children continued to learn at school about how various successful Americans had started from humble origins. In the 1940s the American Schools and Colleges Association presented an annual Horatio Alger Award to businessmen whose 'rise to success symbolizes the tradition of starting from scratch under our system of free competitive enterprise'.[99]

In Britain, too, the myth of the self-made man persisted in children's liter-ature into the twentieth century. Philip Cohen notes:

> When I was growing up in the early 1950s it was still possible to get given 'improving books' for one's birthday, consisting of biographies of self-made men, engineers, inventors, industrialists, entrepreneurs, philanthropists and the like. These men, and they were all men, had usually lived in the 'heroic' age of nineteenth-century capitalism and the books themselves were clearly prepared for the edification of the young.[100]

BLAMING THE POOR

Not all immigrants to America prospered. Many immigrants found destitution in the new lands and as time went by workhouses were established in the larger towns. By the eighteenth century many of these workhouses had become combined prisons, almshouses and workhouses.[101] The mixing of the unemployed, the poor and the criminal in workhouses reflected common attitudes to poverty and unemployment as being the result of the same immoral character most clearly displayed by criminals.

By this time Puritans happily embraced wealth seeking as compatible with a God-fearing life, and poverty as a sign of godlessness, moral weakness and idleness: 'presumptive evidence of wickedness'.[102] The myth of the self-made man also had the corollary that those who were poor were that way because of personal inadequacies, particularly laziness.

Workhouses expanded and by the nineteenth century sometimes lodged thousands of inmates. The workhouse was part punishment, part deterrent. In towns where there was no workhouse, cash relief was miserably low. The idea was to ensure that there was little choice for those offered extremely low wages for regular work outside of the workhouses.[103] At the same time prominent members of the public questioned whether these people should be aided with public taxes: 'if the poor had pauperized themselves through drunkenness, impiety, idleness, extravagance, and immorality, public relief would only reinforce such habits'.[104] Efforts were made to reform the poor through conversion to a Christian life of hard work and sober living and through teaching middle-class values.[105]

In England, similarly, reformers such as J. T. Becher described early nineteenth-century English workhouses as 'a system of secluded restraint and salutary discipline, which, together with our simple yet sufficient Dietary, prove so repugnant to their dissolute habits that they very soon apply for a discharge, and devise means of self-support, which nothing short of compulsion could urge them to explore'.[106] A Royal Commission into England's Poor Laws in 1832 recommended that 'people supported by the parishes should not enjoy the same lifestyles as workers' and that cash relief payments should be abolished. Anyone who wanted help would have to come and live in a workhouse. Similar measures to deny relief to the able-bodied were established in Scotland.[107]

Both Christians and businessmen feared the contamination of the working class with morally inferior people. Women were separated from men, and children were separated from their parents, in part as punishment, and in part to protect the children from the bad habits and immorality of their parents.[108] Thomas Malthus claimed that the Poor Laws encouraged vice by providing assistance to the unworthy.[109] An eminent opponent of poor relief, he argued:

> the increasing proportion of the dependent poor, appears to me to be a subject so truly alarming, as in degree to threaten the extinction of all honourable feeling and spirit among the lower ranks of society, and to degrade and depress the condition of a very large and most important part of the community.[110]

Such attitudes to the poor in the UK and the US continued into the twentieth century. Writing in 1911, Norman Pearson demonstrated a common view of the poor and unemployed:

> It is to be feared that the confirmed loafer and the habitual vagrant are seldom capable of being reformed. It is a mistake to suppose that the typical pauper is merely an ordinary person who has fallen into distress through adverse circumstances. As a rule he is not an ordinary person, but one who is constitutionally a pauper, a pauper in his blood and bones. He is made of inferior material, and therefore cannot be improved up to the level of the ordinary person.[111]

The Great Depression of the 1930s provided a huge challenge to such views. So many people lost their jobs that it became clear that the unemployment resulted from business and market failure rather than individual failure. In the face of this reality, businesspeople stepped up their propaganda in the US.

The President of NAM told members that people were homeless and unemployed because of their lack of thrift and, as we have seen, they stepped up advertisements extolling the self-made man.[112]

Despite mounting evidence to the contrary, the attitude that the unemployed had only themselves to blame led to government policies in which work relief was much preferred to cash relief, that is direct monetary payments: 'In city after city, investigations were staged to weed out welfare "chiselers" and newspapers railed against "boondogglers" and "shirkers".'[113] Henry Ford labelled unemployment 'little more than leisure on a mass scale'.[114]

There were numerous calls toward the end of the 1930s for reductions in welfare spending and in 1941 much of the work relief and other programmes were cut back even before jobs were available for many unemployed. The programmes that remained, including old age and unemployment insurance and some public assistance for families with dependent children, were opposed by business groups as threatening to undermine individual initiative.[115] It was no accident that many unemployed people had no access to these schemes and were left to their own devices to manage as best they could.

CONCLUSION

Although the work ethic shifted from the concept of a vocation serving God, the idea of wealth and success as being God-ordained continued. Hard work remained a virtue and wealth a sign of that virtue. The newly formulated work ethic gave the social system of inequality a moral legitimation, ensuring most people saw it as fair, and protecting it from those who might question or challenge it.

America's reputation as a land of opportunity rested on its claim that the destruction of hereditary obstacles to advancement had created conditions in which social mobility depended on individual initiative alone. The self-made man, archetypical embodiment of the American Dream, owed his advancement to habits of industry, sobriety, moderation, self-discipline, and avoidance of debt.[116]

The myth of the self-made man was based more on folklore than fact.[117] By exaggerating the opportunities available to ordinary working people, businesspeople and their supporters reinforced materialistic values and material success as the goal to aspire to, and promoted business enterprise as the pinnacle of human achievement. Those who prospered deserved to, those who suffered also deserved their fate, and the social hierarchy was therefore just.[118]

The promotion of wealth as a just reward for hard work, good character and initiative, as well as the idea that unemployment and poverty are the consequence of individual character defects and laziness, generated hard-working employees and dissuaded people from 'dropping out' or becoming unemployed. This ensured employers a competitive labour market from which they could choose a hard-working workforce. It also ensured that the wealthy gained not only profits but also social rewards and influence. These are discussed further in the next chapter.

***

NOTES

1 Quoted in Robert E. Lane, *Political Ideology: Why the American Common Man Believes What He Does* (New York: The Free Press, 1962), p. 57.
2 Quoted in J. T. Ward, *The Age of Change 1770–1870* (London: A. and C. Black, 1975), p. 127.
3 Quoted in *ibid.*, p. 127.
4 Joseph L. DeVitis and John Martin Rich, *The Success Ethic, Education, and the American Dream* (Albany, NY: State University of New York Press, 1996), p. 11.
5 Andrew Bard Schmookler, *The Illusion of Choice: How the Market Economy Shapes Our Destiny* (Albany: State University of New York Press, 1993), p. 148.
6 *Ibid.*, p. 144.
7 *Ibid.*, p. 148.
8 Adriano Tilgher, *Work: What It Has Meant to Men Through the Ages*, translated by Dorothy Canfield Fisher (London: George G. Harrap, 1931), p. 40.
9 Tony Watson, *Sociology, Work and Industry*, 2nd edn (London: Routledge and Kegan Paul, 1987), pp. 72, 75.
10 Tilgher, note 8, p. 31.
11 Quoted in Paul Bernstein, *American Work Values: Their Origin and Development* (Albany, NY: State University of New York Press, 1997), p. 36.
12 Tilgher, note 8, pp. 47–9.
13 Bernstein, note 11, pp. 15, 38.
14 Baxter, quoted in Kemper Fullerton, 'Calvinism and Capitalism: an Explanation of the Weber Thesis', in Robert W. Green (ed.), *Protestantism, Capitalism and Social Science: the Weber Thesis Controversy* (Lexington, Mass.: D. C. Heath and Co., 1973), p. 27.
15 Tilgher, note 8, p. 61.
16 Lukas Vischer, 'The Work of Human Beings as Creatures of God', *The Ecumenical Review*, Vol. 48, No. 3 (1996); M. J. Kitch, *Capitalism and the Reformation* (London: Longman, 1967), p. 148.
17 M. J. Kitch, *Capitalism and the Reformation* (London: Longman, 1967), p. 147.
18 Bernstein, note 11, p. 5.
19 *Ibid.*, p. 93.
20 T. Kemp, *Industrialisation in Nineteenth Century Europe* (London: Longmans, 1969), p. 12.
21 Bernstein, note 11, p. 95.
22 Ward, note 2, pp. 4–5.
23 Schmookler, note 5, pp. 145–6.
24 Perry Pascarella, *The New Achievers: Creating a Modern Work Ethic* (New York: The Free Press, 1984), p. 34.
25 David J. Cherrington, *The Work Ethic: Working Values and Values That Work* (New York: AMACON, 1980), p. 32.

26 Robert Eisenberger, *Blue Monday: the Loss of the Work Ethic in America* (New York: Paragon House, 1989), p. 2.

27 Cherrington, note 25, pp. 32–3.

28 *Ibid.*, p. 31.

29 Quoted in Matthew Josephson, *The Robber Barons: the Great American Capitalists 1861–1901* (London: Eyre and Spottiswoode, 1962), p. 10.

30 *Ibid.*, p. 9; Daniel Bell, *The Cultural Contradictions of Capitalism* (London: Heinemann, 1976), p. 57.

31 DeVitis and Rich, note 4, pp. 12–13.

32 Bernstein, note 11, p. 160.

33 Quoted in Eisenberger, note 26, p. 5.

34 Quoted in Ward, note 2, p. 11.

35 D. P. O'Brien, *The Classical Economists* (Oxford: Clarendon Press, 1975), p. 17.

36 Ward, note 2, p. 15; J. L. Hammond and Barbara Hammond, *The Town Labourer 1760–1832*, Left Book Club edn (London: Victor Gollancz, 1937), p. 21.

37 Elie Halévy, *England in 1815*, translated by E. I. Watkin and D. A. Barber, first paperback edn, 6 vols, Vol. I, *A History of the English People in the Nineteenth Century* (London: Ernest Benn, 1960), p. 277.

38 Hammond and Hammond, note 36, p. 20.

39 E. P. Thompson, *The Making of the English Working Class* (London: Penguin, 1980), pp. 212–13.

40 Hammond and Hammond, note 36, pp. 23, 32.

41 David Dickson, *Alternative Technology and the Politics of Technical Change* (Great Britain: Fontana/Collins, 1974), p. 73

42 Hammond and Hammond, note 36, pp. 25–6.

43 Thompson, note 39, p. 394.

44 Ure, quoted in *ibid.*, pp. 395–6.

45 Ure, quoted in *ibid.*, p. 396.

46 Halévy, note 37, p. 279.

47 *Ibid.*, pp. 279–87.

48 Stuart Ewen, *Captains of Consciousness: Advertising and the Social Roots of the Consumer Culture* (New York: McGraw-Hill, 1976), p. 6.

49 Gordon Marshall, *In Search of the Spirit of Capitalism: an Essay on Max Weber's Protestant Ethic Thesis* (London: Hutchinson, 1982), p. 125.

50 Thompson, note 39, p. 395.

51 Quoted in Harold B. Jones, 'The Protestant Ethic: Weber's Model and the Empirical Literature', *Human Relations*, Vol. 50, No. 7 (1997), p. 762.

52 Hammond and Hammond, note 36, p. 289.

53 Malcolm I. Thomis, *The Town Labourer and the Industrial Revolution* (London: B. T. Batsford, 1974), p. 171.

54 Halévy, note 37, pp. 36–7.

55 *Ibid.*, pp. 36–7, 389.

56 *Ibid.*, p. 392.

57 Thompson, note 39, pp. 399–401.

58 *Ibid.*, p. 399.

59 Quoted in Thomis, note 53, p. 166.

60 Thompson, note 39, pp. 412–15; Thomis, note 53, pp. 173–5.

61 Robert Southey, quoted in Thompson, note 39, p. 412.

62 *Ibid.*, pp. 416–17; Thomis, note 53, p. 171.
63 Hammond and Hammond, note 36, p. 292; Thompson, note 39, p. 417.
64 Thompson, note 39, p. 406.
65 *Ibid.*, p. 393; Thomis, note 53, p. 168.
66 Hammond and Hammond, note 36, p. 294.
67 Thomis, note 53, p. 170.
68 Thomis, note 53, p. 74.
69 David Bleakley, *Work: the Shadow and the Substance* (London: SCM Press, 1983), p. 35.
70 Quoted in Thomis, note 53, p. 86.
71 John Roach, *Social Reform in England 1780–1880* (London: B. T. Batsford, 1978), p. 69.
72 Quoted in Ward, note 2, pp. 22–3.
73 Thomis, note 53, pp. 106–7.
74 Hammond and Hammond, note 36, p. 21.
75 Quoted in Ward, note 2, pp. 99–100.
76 Thompson, note 39, pp. 220–1.
77 Thomis, note 53, p. 86.
78 Adrian Furnham, *The Protestant Work Ethic: the Psychology of Work-related Beliefs and Behaviours* (London: Routledge, 1990), p. 198.
79 Eisenberger, note 26, pp. 4–5; Roger B. Hill, 'Historical Context of the Work Ethic', www.coe.uga.edu/~rhill/workethic/hist.htm (1992)
80 Schmookler, note 5, p. 145.
81 Bernstein, note 11, pp. 7, 153.
82 *Ibid.*, pp. 141, 173.
83 Quoted in Ely Chinoy, *Automobile Workers and the American Dream*, 2nd edn (Urbana and Chicago: University of Illinios Press, 1992), p. 4.
84 Bernstein, note 11, p. 141.
85 Cherrington, note 25, p. 36.
86 Quoted in Bernstein, note 11, p. 161.
87 Bernstein, note 11, pp. 7, 161; Chinoy, note 83, p. 1; Wellford W. Wilms, 'Captured by the American Dream: Vocational Education in the United States', in Jon Lauglo and Kevin Lillis (eds), *Vocationalizing Education: an International Perspective* (Oxford: Pergamon Press, 1988), p. 82.
88 Horatio Alger, *Bound to Rise or Up the Ladder* (Chicago: Saalfield Publishing, 1900).
89 Bernstein, note 11, pp. 160–1.
90 DeVitis and Rich, note 4, pp. 3, 15.
91 Transcribed from Harry Clifton. *Work Boys Work. On. The Birth of the Music Hall.* Wellington: World Record International, n.d. record.
92 Quoted in Bernstein, note 11, p. 172 and in DeVitis and Rich, note 4, p. 17.
93 *Ibid.*, p. 18.
94 William H. Whyte, *The Organization Man*, 2nd edn (Harmondsworth, Middlesex: Penguin, 1960), p. 235.
95 Heather Richardson, 'The Politics of Virtue: a Strategy for Transforming the Culture', *Policy Review* (Fall 1991).
96 Bernstein, note 11, p. 156.
97 Richard S. Tedlow, *Keeping the Corporate Image: Public Relations and Business, 1900–1950* (Greenwich, Connecticut: Jai Press, 1979), p. 66.
98 Quoted in Chinoy, note 83, p. 6.
99 Quoted in *ibid.*, p. 1.

100 Philip Cohen, 'Teaching Enterprise Culture: Individualism, Vocationalism and the New Right', in Ian Taylor (ed.), *The Social Effects of Free Market Policies: an International Text* (New York: Harvester Wheatsheaf, 1990), p. 61.

101 Joe R. Feagin, *Subordinating the Poor* (Englewood Cliffs, NJ: Prentice-Hall, 1975), pp. 24–8.

102 Bernstein, note 11, pp. 75–6.

103 Feagin, note 101, pp. 28–9.

104 Quoted in *ibid.*, p. 30.

105 *Ibid.*, p. 30.

106 Quoted in Roach, note 71, p. 73.

107 Ward, note 2, pp. 134, 138.

108 Matthew Colton, Ferran Casas, Mark Drakeford, Susan Roberts, Evert Scholte and Margaret Williams, *Stigma and Social Welfare: an International Comparative Study* (Aldershot, UK: Avebury, 1997), p. 16.

109 Daniel Bell, 'Work and Its Discontents (1956)', in A. R. Gini and T. J. Sullivan (eds), *It Comes with the Territory: an Inquiry Concerning Work and the Person* (New York: Random House, 1989), p. 122.

110 Quoted in Ward, note 2, p. 130.

111 Quoted in J. R. Hay, *The Development of the British Welfare State, 1880–1975* (London: Edward Arnold, 1978), p. 62.

112 Stuart Ewen, *PR! A Social History of Spin* (New York: Basic Books, 1996), p. 235.

113 Charles Trout, quoted in Feagin, note 101, p. 41.

114 Quoted in Bernstein, note 11, pp. 157, 187.

115 Feagin, note 101, p. 43.

116 Richardson, note 95.

117 Chinoy, note 83, p. 3.

118 P. D. Anthony, *The Ideology of Work* (London: Tavistock Publications, 1977), p. 71.

◆4◆

Justifying Wealth

———

Men do not desire to be rich, but to be richer than
other men.
J. S. Mill [1]

Nobody talks more of free enterprise and competition and of the best man winning than the man
who inherited his father's store or farm.
C. Wright Mills [2]

As wealth came to symbolise the fruits of hard work, those who were wealthy
gained status. They wielded power over others through being able to hire
them or otherwise pay for their services and favours. And as wealth became a
measure of worthiness and success, money became an even more effective
means of inducement to manipulate and sway others.

In the late nineteenth century business leaders used this high public esteem
and plenty of money to make their influence felt in all realms of society.
Matthew Josephon in *The Robber Barons* described the wealthy businessmen as
'invading hosts … they overran all the existing institutions which buttress
society... they took possession of the political government (with its policy,
army, navy), of the School, the Press, the Church....' [3]

In short order the railroad presidents, the copper barons, the big dry-goods
merchants and the steel masters became Senators, ruling in the highest councils
of the national government, and sometimes scattered twenty-dollar gold pieces
to newsboys of Washington. But they also became in even greater number lay
leaders of churches, trustees of universities, partners or owners of newspapers
or press services and figures of fashionable, cultured society. [4]

These 'robber barons' attributed their success to their hard work and

53

ability. They felt righteous in their faith that their rewards were God-given. When criticised for giving the Church tainted money, John D. Rockefeller, founder of the giant Standard Oil Trust, exclaimed, 'God gave me my money.'[5] Wealthy businessmen bought the support of the Church through large donations, recognising that it still had significant power over the masses of people:

> Filled with gratitude, the soldiers of the Church needed no direct marching orders from their chief benefactors, the captains of industry. In their thousand-fold activities throughout the world, as missionaries, as therapeutic agents, as healers of the sick and the poor, they contributed to the defense of the established order ... in the slums of the cities they sought to 'save the souls' of the strayed, and return them to sober and diligent toil.[6]

Through a similar strategy – large donations of money – businessmen made their presence felt in the universities. They set up technical institutes and effected a shift from classical humanities to more practical areas of science and technology that could serve business ends. Their donations resulted in the silencing or dismissal of many critics of business within the universities.[7]

Businessmen also used their money to influence the press, either by bribing reporters with gifts, using their advertising payments as leverage to get favourable stories and 'puff' pieces, or buying newspapers directly: 'Papers on the financial rocks, indeed, had a way of drifting into portfolios of big-time investors, who recognized the utility of having press spokesmen on their side.'[8]

The entry of men with business backgrounds into politics went largely unchallenged in the US. As one newspaper editor wrote, they were 'types of that American pluck and enterprise and those traits of industry that have built up the greatness of the nation. As such he would indeed be bold who would challenge their right to sit in the highest assembly of the country as representatives of the American people.' So many business people entered the Senate that it became known as the 'Millionaires' Club'. Once there, they blatantly pursued their own interests in the name of national prosperity.[9]

Business leaders did not hesitate to buy and bribe politicians. One of the railroad magnates wrote in 1877 that if a decision maker would not made the 'right' decision without being bribed, 'I think the time spent will be gained when it is a man's duty to go up and bribe the judge.'[10] Another railroad chief said 'it was the custom that when men received nominations to come to me for contributions and I made them and considered them good paying investments for the company; in a Republican district, I was a strong Republican, in a Democratic district I was Democratic....'[11] The costs of political influence were factored into the price of the products.

At first the wealthy businessmen were quite blatant about buying poli-ticians, taking bags full of cash to Washington or 'giving out stock to other Congressmen that they might be prompted to look after their own property.' As the price for political favours escalated, however, and bribery became too hard to conceal, more subtle methods for inducing political bias were conceived. Politicians would be loaned money at no interest or given the opportunity to buy land or make other investments at far below market price so they could then sell up at large profits to themselves. Junkets would be organised. Lobbyists were used – people who were paid a retainer because of their ability to persuade a group of politicians, through their contacts and friendships.[12]

By 1912 Woodrow Wilson could say in a campaign speech:

> The masters of the government in the United States are the combined capital-ists and manufacturers of the United States. It is written over every intimate page of the records of Congress ... the men really consulted are the big men who have the biggest stake – the big bankers, the big manufacturers, the big masters of commerce, the heads of railroad corporations, and of steamship corporations.... Every time it has come to a critical question, these gentlemen have been yielded to and the demands treated as the demands that should be followed as a matter of course.[13]

One of these capitalists, Frederick Townsend Martin, wrote:

> We are not politicians or public thinkers; we are the rich; we own America; we got it, God knows how; but we intend to keep it if we can by throwing all the tremendous weight of our support, our influence, our money, our political con-nection, our purchased senators, our hungry congressmen, our public-speaking demagogues into the scale against any legislation, any political platform, any Presidential campaign, that threatens the integrity of our estate....[14]

The wealthy men of the late nineteenth century and early twentieth century had power and influence through their ability to buy others and because of the prestige and status they gained from being wealthy and successful. As the supposed epitome of humanity, those who best displayed the virtues and character of self-made men, they were admired and accorded leadership and authority in their own right. People listened to them, and the views of the John D. Rockefellers and J. P. Morgans determined much government and social policy.[15]

LAISSEZ-FAIRE ECONOMICS

The concentration of wealth and power in industrialising countries was not accompanied by new obligations and responsibilities for the rich towards their employees. The obligations and responsibilities that the wealthy in the earlier feudal society had owed to their tenants and employees disappeared with the industrial revolution, and such relationships became merely a matter of business.

Sir Walter Scott noted that 'A man may assemble five hundred workmen one week and dismiss them the next ... without having any further connection with them than to receive a week's work for a week's wages, nor any further solicitude about their future fate than if they were so many old shuttles.'[16] Shelley called it the 'unmitigated exercise of the calculating faculty' and Thomas Carlyle noted that everything was ruled by calculations with 'cash payment as the sole nexus'.[17]

Those who prospered were those most willing to embrace the capitalist spirit of commercialism and rational calculation where 'everyone endeavours to purchase at the lowest price and sell at the highest, regardless of equity in either case'.[18] This seemed to fly in the face of traditional Christian precepts such as 'do unto others as you would have them do unto you'. It required some element of deceit and a willingness to pay workers less than they needed to live on whilst selling the goods they made for large profits. To such a worker the employer 'would simply insist that he had paid him to the last sixpence of the agreed terms and conditions and that he had nothing further to do with the man's condition'.[19]

Attempts by reformers to improve the conditions of the working classes by regulating wages and legislating maximum working hours for children were opposed by employers. Their opposition was given enormous support by proponents of the new economic philosophies of the time who argued against government intervention in economic matters. It was contended that regulating wages would reduce the competitiveness of manufacturing industries and therefore hurt both employers and employees, who would lose their jobs. Wages had to be decided by supply and demand; it was unfortunate if as a result workers and their families went hungry, but it couldn't be helped. Even attempts to restrict child labour were opposed on the grounds that government should not interfere with the labour market and economic freedom.[20]

The prevailing economic philosophies enabled employers to clothe their selfish interest in increasing profits as being beneficial to the wider community. Of prime and early importance was Adam Smith, who in 1776 published *An Inquiry into the Nature and Causes of the Wealth of Nations* – the foundation of classical economics. Smith argued that the pursuit of economic self-interest by businessmen served the public good. Even though a businessman 'intends only his own gain ... he is in this, as in many other cases, led by an invisible hand to promote an end which was no part of his intention'.[21] The reason for this was that competition enabled production to match

consumer demand without the need for centralised planning. Thus the self-
ishness of the businessman in trying to get rich was beneficial to society,
including workers and consumers. Smith wrote:

> It is not from the benevolence of the butcher, the brewer or the baker that we
> expect our dinner, but from their regard to their own self-interest. We address
> ourselves, not to their humanity but to their self-love, and never talk to them
> of our own necessities but of their advantages.
>
> Every individual is continually exerting himself to find out the most advan-
> tageous employment for whatever capital he can command. It is his own
> advantage, indeed, and not that of society, which he has in view. But the study
> of his own advantage naturally, or rather necessarily leads him to prefer that
> employment which is most advantageous to the society.[22]

Competition was supposed to guarantee that those who raised prices to
take unreasonable profits would be priced out of the market by others who
charged less. Those who paid workers low wages lost workers to those who
were willing to pay higher wages (assuming there was not an oversupply of
workers and employers did not collude in wage setting). These market trans-
actions were carried out freely and voluntarily because people were free to
pursue their own interests without interference or coercion. They could
choose their jobs and they could choose the products they would buy; as
both workers and consumers they were free to choose.[23]

Smith was no lackey of the capitalists. He was in fact challenging a system
of government power and interference that favoured the traditional ruling
classes.[24] His theory, however, was taken up and popularised by the emerging
ruling classes. Smith 'captured the spirit of the new industrial and commercial
system and presented its theoretical defense in a form which dominated the
thought of the most influential writers of economics for the greater part of
the [nineteenth] century'.[25]

To economists the beauty of an economic system based on competition
was that it was efficient – the producer who could produce goods at the least
cost won. But for businesspeople the theory had its merit on a political
level.[26] It disguised the power that they wielded, it relabelled their greed as
public service and it provided an argument against government regulation of
business activities.

Adam Smith and his followers freed the businessman from guilt over his
pursuit of self-interest in a way that religion could not. Protestantism, whilst
providing solace to the wealthy man that his profits were God's blessing for
his hard work, did not approve of the selfish and single-minded pursuit of
profits. For Protestant teachers and preachers, work should be service to God
and the wealth that resulted incidental.[27]

Following Smith, a number of British economists and philosophers refined and added to his theories, reinforcing the capitalist system as they did so. They attempted to separate morals and ethics from economics,[28] leaving a bare, cold rationality that was without compassion. David Ricardo and Thomas Malthus attributed low wages and poverty to the fact that workers had so many children. In a free market the oversupply of labour through population growth lowered wages.[29]

Malthus argued that poverty was inevitable if population growth was unfettered because it tends to outstrip the means of subsistence. Although his argument was complex, 'The doctrine that poverty was inevitable and incurable put a soft pillow under the conscience of the ruling class.' The ruling class inferred from his writings that charity and government poor relief could do more harm than good because 'if the conditions of the poor were improved, population would quicken its pace still further', which would only exacerbate the problems of the poor.[30]

Similarly, Ricardo's theories about the workings of the market and the forces of supply and demand were interpreted by the ruling classes as implying that there tended to be a 'natural' price for labour, at subsistence level, and therefore the existing distribution of wealth in the society was inevitable.[31] Poverty couldn't be helped. Jeremy Bentham argued that industrialists should be able to follow their own interests in order that the majority would benefit. Some people might lose out from such a system but the goal should be the 'greatest good for the greatest number'. The Italian economist Vilfredo Pareto added that 'constancy of inequality in the distribution of income reflects inequality of human ability, which is natural and universal'.[32]

Economic ideology was selectively taken up by politicians to obstruct legislation in favour of workers. William Pitt rejected the idea of wage regulation by arguing that 'trade, industry, and barter would always find their own level, and be impeded by regulations which violated their natural operation and deranged their proper effect'.[33] Similarly public relief provided to the poor interfered with the natural supply and demand balance between workers and employers and was opposed by businesspeople. For this reason paupers could not receive aid that was any higher than the lowest of wages. 'Political economy often seemed like a charter of manufacturer's rights to pursue business without restriction in whatever way he thought best.'[34]

Businesspeople argued that a legislated ten-hour day would destroy the competitiveness of British industry and in this they were supported by economists. Nassau Senior, Professor of Political Economy at Oxford, put forward the case for 12-hour working days for workers, including children, in terms of 'the great proportion of fixed to circulating capital, which makes long hours of work desirable; and secondly, the extraordinary lightness of the labour, if labour it can be called, which renders them practicable'. He argued that the proposed ten-hour day would either destroy profits, reduce wages or raise prices and so 'would be utterly ruinous'.[35] Other economists argued that wage regulation was in fact unnecessary because it was in the employer's self-interest to take care of his workers and pay them a living wage, just as he took care of his equipment, because otherwise workers would not be well maintained, fit for service and productive.[36]

The economic ideology promoted by these economists dominated the first half of the nineteenth century and came to be known as *laissez-faire* because it opposed government interference in the market and business affairs. The role of government, it was believed, should be limited to protecting property rights and keeping social order amongst the populace. 'The control of the economy should be in terms of a natural aristocracy to be determined by the competitive struggle of the market, which eliminates the weak and incompetent and chooses those with initiative, vision, judgement, and organizing ability.'[37]

SOCIAL DARWINISM

Economists have played a major role in providing a legitimising philosophy that justifies not only the unbridled accumulation of wealth and power in the hands of businesspeople but also the poverty of working people. In the late nineteenth century this justification was reinforced by developments in the natural sciences. The continued presence of large numbers of poor people, the growth of unions for unskilled and semi-skilled workers, riots amongst the unemployed and the increased radicalism amongst the working classes raised concerns about whether poverty threatened the social order.

Darwin's theories of evolution were used most effectively by those who sought to defend *laissez-faire* capitalism against the infringement of the state.[38] In 1859 Darwin argued in *The Origin of Species* that in the struggle for life only the fittest – those with a genetic advantage – survive. In this way species evolve to be better adapted to the conditions of life.[39] Social Darwinists suggested the same natural selection process was occurring in human societies. They concluded that English Victorian society was at the top of the evolutionary tree and the English people were, therefore, biologically superior to other peoples. Within English society, they claimed, the lower classes were poorer because they were genetically inferior.

Social Darwinism reinforced the idea, already promoted by the work ethic and economic theory, that those who were successful deserved their wealth and position because they were better people. The theory was used to justify the competition between men for financial advantage over each other as being natural and selecting for the 'best'-quality person. The claimed 'naturalness' of the process meant that the social hierarchy could not be challenged as a manifestation of greed or the operation of vested interests. Rather inequality was a natural consequence of varying abilities and qualities of individuals and the question of fairness did not arise. The existence of poverty was inevitable.

In its extreme form Social Darwinism was used as a weapon against welfare spending and charity as well as to support imperialism and racism. It was argued that to give aid to the poor would be to interfere with the evolutionary struggle for existence that promoted a genetically superior race. For example Herbert Spencer, a leading Social Darwinist, argued that government action to reduce poverty impeded social progress as failures in economic competition were 'unfit' and should not be given assistance to survive and consume resources that were better used by others.[40]

Darwin himself was not averse to extrapolating the results of his findings to human societies:

We civilized men, on the other hand, do our utmost to check the process of elimination; we build asylums for the imbecile, the maimed, and the sick; we institute poor-laws.... Thus the weak members of civilized societies propagate their kind. No one who has attended to the breeding of domestic animals will doubt that this must be highly injurious to the race of man.[41]

Social Darwinists condemned the poor as being genetically inferior, just as those before them had condemned them for not working hard enough (see previous chapter) and having some sort of character defect or moral deficiency. Social Darwinism was used as a scientific base from which to 'legitimise political and social divisions' in society.[42] For example, Thomas Huxley supported the social structure of English society by suggesting: 'In so far as the struggle for the means of enjoyment tends to place such men in possession of wealth and influence, it is a process which tends to the good of society.'[43]

Social Darwinism spread to the US, where it was taken up by clergymen, businessmen, politicians, academics and others: 'In the late nineteenth century, Conservative Darwinism was standard doctrine in thousands of American pulpits, universities and newspaper offices.'[44] The ideas of Herbert Spencer were particularly popular in America and his articles were published in magazines such as *Atlantic Monthly* and *Popular Science Monthly*.[45]

Some very influential Americans were influenced by Social Darwinism. James G. Kennedy, in his book on Herbert Spencer, tells how at the end of the nineteenth century 'three justices of the Supreme Court were avowed Spencerians and participated in decisions recognizing corporations as individuals, and disallowing government regulation of contracts with regard to hours of work, a minimum wage, or child labor'.[46]

Social Darwinism fitted well with the myth of the self-made man. Wealthy businesspeople in particular found Social Darwinism a useful doctrine to justify their own success and also the huge differences in wealth between themselves and ordinary people. For example, one railroad entrepreneur used it to justify railroad monopolies by arguing that 'the fortunes of railroad companies are determined by the law of the survival of the fittest'.[47] Similarly Rockefeller told Sunday school children:

The growth of a large business is merely a survival of the fittest.... The American Beauty rose can be produced in the splendor and fragrance which bring cheer to the beholder only by sacrificing the early buds which grow up around it. This is not an evil tendency in business. It is merely the working-out of a law of nature and a law of God.[48]

William Graham Sumner, an American follower of Spencer, argued that 'The millionaires are a product of natural selection.... They may fairly be regarded as the naturally selected agents of society for certain work. They get high wages and live in luxury, but the bargain is a good one for society.'[49] In 1908 banker Henry Clews told students at Yale:

You may start in business, or the professions with your feet on the bottom rung of the ladder; it rests with you to acquire the strength to climb to the top. You can do so if you have the will and the force to back you. There is always plenty of room at the top.... By dint of greater effort or superior skill, or by intelligence, if he can make better wages, he is free to live better.... Birth is nothing. The fittest survive. Merit is the supreme and only qualification essential to success.[50]

Darwinism was used not only to justify the success of large corporations in suppressing competition but also to legitimise the growth of high levels of personal wealth in a nation still having significant poverty. The wealthy calmed their consciences by assuring themselves and others that this was only natural and that those who could not drag themselves out of poverty were morally or biologically inferior. They were assisted in this by influential intellectuals, such as Sumner, who claimed that wealthy businesspeople had been selected for their wealth and were therefore paragons of virtue, leading the evolution of civilization. He argued that the 'strong' and the 'weak' were 'equivalent to the industrious and the idle, the frugal and the extravagant'.[51]

AN ELITE CLASS

The myth of the self-made man, which had been reinforced by the Social Darwinists, faded during the twentieth century as increasing numbers of people were employed in dead-end jobs. Unlike the self-employed farmer, merchant or artisan of earlier times, factory workers had little hope of working their way to prosperity. The proportion of self-employed workers fell dramatically through the nineteenth and early twentieth centuries in the US – from 80 per cent in 1800 (compared with less than 50 per cent in Britain) to 20 per cent in 1920.[52]

Towards the end of the nineteenth century and early in the twentieth century a wave of mergers of businesses in the US created huge corporations. Between 1898 and 1902 over 2,600 firms went out of existence as the result of mergers.[53] Naomi Lamoreaux notes in *The Great Merger Movement in American Business, 1895–1904* that in a few short years the US was 'transformed overnight from a nation of freely competing, individually owned enterprises into a nation dominated by a small number of giant corporations'.[54] Further mergers took place during the First World War and during the late 1920s, so that by the end of that decade the giant corporation, run by professional managers, had come to dominate not only most industries but also economic life in the US.[55]

Nevertheless newspapers, movies and magazines continued to promote the entrepreneurial route to success, publishing story after story of those who had started small and built up a fledgling business into a multimillion-dollar success.[56] The automobile industry of the early twentieth century provided plenty of case studies, beginning with that of Henry Ford. The automobile industry followed the course of other industries, however, in becoming monopolised by a few large corporations. Between 1902 and 1908 there were some 77 companies successfully producing and selling cars; by 1923, ten companies were turning out 90 per cent of the cars; and by the Great Depression this had been reduced to three: General Motors, Ford and Chrysler. The opportunities for those starting out in the automobile business were therefore limited to peripheral services such as selling second-hand cars, operating gas stations and car repair.[57]

Automobile workers, although they got relatively high wages, often did not have work for the whole year because of seasonal lay-offs and found it difficult to save to start a business. When they did, the risks associated with a small business were high. Ely Chinoy notes in his book *Automobile Workers and the American Dream* that in the 1950s about 30 per cent of new businesses did not even last a year, and almost half did not last more than two. The more profitable business opportunities had been concentrated in the hands of large corporations and everyone else competed for the scraps, the marginal and risky businesses.[58]

Over time the opportunities to advance in many industries became scarcer and it became obvious that most of those at the top had not started at the bottom at all. Despite the supposed lack of classes in American society, there was clearly an elite class. Upton Sinclair described it in various novels in the early part of the century[59] and C. Wright Mills in his classic 1956 text, *The Power Elite*, described an elite structure in the US which included a network of very rich families, closely connected with multimillion-dollar corporations, top politicians, military generals and company executives: 'The people of the higher circles may also be conceived as members of a top social stratum, as a set of groups whose members know one another, see one another socially and at business, and so, in making decisions, take one another into account.'[60]

Despite the lack of a landed gentry or aristocracy in the US, there were gradations of wealth and power and the people who were wealthiest and most powerful saw themselves as a class, whose membership was exclusive – they were class-conscious. They believed that they deserved their privileges and were ready to defend them, whilst publicly denying their power.[61] Mills wrote:

> Members of the several higher circles know one another as personal friends and even as neighbors; they mingle with one another on the golf course, in the gentlemen's clubs, at resorts, on transcontinental airplanes, and on ocean liners. They meet at the estates of mutual friends, face each other in front of the TV camera, or serve on the same philanthropic committee, and many are sure to cross one another's path in the columns of newspapers, if not in the exact cafes from which many of these columns originate.[62]

The boards of directors of corporations had interlocking and overlapping memberships drawn from this class[63] and when government intervention threatened to weaken the power of these corporations with the New Deal they infiltrated the government and its executive, ensuring that politicians and top civil servants were also increasingly drawn from the same pool of people.

Mills studied the richest Americans between the Civil War and the decade that followed the Second World War. He found that most of them came from the middle or upper classes and this trend increased over time. The 1900 generation of richest men included 39 per cent who were sons of lower-class parents, whereas the 1950 generation only had 9 per cent (less than one in ten). Only 2 per cent of the 1950 generation of very rich were foreign-born, a proportion far lower than in the general population. Most of the wealthy were Protestants, most had attended Ivy League schools.[64]

> The reality and the trend are clearly the upper-class recruitment of the truly upper class of propertied wealth. Wealth not only tends to perpetuate itself, but as we shall see, tends also to monopolize new opportunities for getting 'great wealth'.[65]

Similarly, in Britain, the ruling class was made up of the business leaders, leading politicians, top civil servants, judges, those at the top of the various institutions – including the Church, the military and the government – and leading professionals. In Britain as in the US, Ralph Miliband notes in his book *Capitalist Democracy in Britain*:

> there is a high degree of homogeneity among the members of the dominant class, much of it based on a marked similarity of social background, education, and 'life-styles'. A majority are of middle- and upper-class origin, and have had a public-school and Oxford or Cambridge education. Many of them are linked by ties of kinship.... They constantly cross each other's paths in an incessant round of meetings, lunches, dinners, functions, and ceremonies, and as members of boards, commissions, councils, committees, and institutions of the most varied kind.[66]

Miliband notes that these people shared similar ideologies and political views and that those who joined the power elite from outside soon learned to take on elite values and behaviour as an essential requirement of success.[67]

The alternative route to wealth – by rising up the corporate hierarchy – was just as restricted for poor people. The hierarchical structure of business organisations mirrors the class structure of the society they are in. In Britain, those at the top of the organisational hierarchy have tended to be those of higher class. Because of their education and upbringing they fitted in with the company power brokers better: for a man to be promoted to the top ranks of a company 'he must be like those who are already in, and upon whose judgements his own success rests.... To be compatible with the top men is to act like them, to look like them, to think like them', or at least to give that impression. Upper-class men possess a 'cultural capital', including a manner and style and way of speaking, that enables them to fit in with ease and tends to give them authority with subordinates, a quality expected of senior executives.[68]

Similarly, in the US, when Mills studied the top chief executives of the largest companies in each generation from 1900 to the 1950s, he found that they too were 'a quite uniform social type which has had exceptional advantages of origin and training'. They were mainly American-born of American-born fathers, college-educated, Protestant, white, and from upper- or upper-middle-class families. Seven out of ten had fathers who were businessmen or professionals. And the proportion coming from working-class families was falling over time, with only 2.5 per cent of chief executives under 50 in 1952 coming from such families.[69]

ACCEPTING THE AMERICAN DREAM

This lack of opportunities for working people did not stop businesspeople from continuing to promote the idea of success through hard work. Businesspeople self-servingly stressed the value of hard work throughout the twentieth century. Standard Oil executive A. C. Bedford told employees that 'work was more important than love, learning, religion, and patriotism' because these things could not exist without work. And Chinoy noted in 1955 that there was 'an unceasing flow of newspaper material and public speeches' affirming the 'reality of opportunity and the possibility of success' and advising how this could be achieved.[70]

When asked how they had 'made it', 'America's Fifty Foremost Business Leaders' told B. C Forbes in 1947 that it was their character traits such as enthusiasm, confidence, energy, courage, foresight, judgement, determination and self-control.[71] Alfred Sloan, Chairman of General Motors, wrote: 'Think of the corporation as a pyramid of opportunities from the bottom toward the top with thousands of chances for advancement. Only capacity limited any worker's chances to grow, to develop his ability to make a greater contribution to the whole and to improve his own position as well.' Yet a government committee noted a year earlier 'that substantial opportunity does not exist for a large proportion of workers in either small or large corporations.... Most of them, therefore, must look forward to remaining more or less at the same levels, despite the havoc this might visit upon the tradition of "getting ahead".'[72]

Nevertheless, younger factory workers often held on to the dreams fed to them by self-interested employers. Many in Chinoy's study saw their work at the factory as temporary until they went on to something better, whilst others dreamt of starting their own business or buying a farm as a way of getting out of the mindless, alienating boredom of factory work. For most this was little more than a dream because they were unable to save the capital necessary to make it come true. This situation was exacerbated by the fact that spending their money in their free time was their only compensation for enduring their working hours. After they married, family responsibilities meant that the wages went on children, mortgages, doctors' bills and the like. As they grew older and became resigned to their lack of mobility, factory workers shifted their hopes of upward mobility to their children.[73]

When Robert Lane interviewed fifteen working- and lower-middle-class men in the American town of Eastport in the late 1950s, he found that they generally 'accepted the view that America opens up opportunity to all people, if not in equal proportions, then at least enough so that a person must assume responsibility for his own status'.[74]

Whilst recognising that not everyone is born equal – some are born into wealth and others into poverty – Lane's interviewees believed the opportunity was available to improve one's social status and position through effort, education and ability. Therefore, in the end, people deserve their status. What is more, they believed that inequality and differences in status are necessary to provide an incentive for everyone to work hard and display initiative. Lane explained this in terms of the life experience of those he interviewed. They themselves had worked hard to achieve what they had, forsaking leisure and pleasure in pursuit of middle-class respectability. The idea of making the world equal would deprive them of the benefits they had worked so hard to obtain as well as their purpose in life. Their life goals were 'structured around achievement and success in monetary terms'.[75]

Although the increasing living standards of those interviewed were not generally due to promotions but rather reflected improving economic circumstances in the US at the time — rising wages, shorter hours, increasing productivity — their better circumstances, especially when compared with their fathers, were nevertheless credited to their own effort and affirmed their belief in the American Dream.[76]

> The experience of the workingman in America leads him to believe that, generally speaking, business is the source of legitimate earned money.... The processes by which business earns its money are familiar and ... they seem sound and fair. They are fair because they represent an exchange of one thing for another; they are sound because businesses, like people, and like children on allowances, must have earned their money in order to have it.[77]

When David Cherrington and his colleagues conducted a survey of the attitudes and values of some 3,000 American workers in 1975, they found that 'the work ethic continues to be a significant force in the lives of many American workers'. Most agreed that workers should do their best even if they disliked their work and that they should do a good job whether or not the supervisor was around. They also believed that occupational success depended on the amount of effort a person put into their work rather than luck or knowledge.[78] A 1980 *Wall Street Journal*/Gallup poll found that most executives said they still believed in the ideal of self-made people. Another 1980 survey found that chief executives tended to agree that 'inner' character, hard work and self-reliance were the means to success.[79]

In Australia, the myth of an egalitarian, classless society has parallels with the American Dream. Its origins are similar, stemming from the pioneer spirit of a newly colonised country with many opportunities for the new settlers. As in the US, however, the myth is not based in reality and 'bears little relation to the actual distribution of wealth, privilege, and power in the affluent and highly urbanised society' of twenty-first-century Australia.[80]

R. W. Connell found in his 1970s study of Australian children that they had been socialised as they got older to accept inequalities as the result of differing effort. When they were asked about social inequalities, younger children mostly felt they were unfair but older children – teenagers – generally thought they were fair. The younger children thought that the poor should have more. The teenage children thought inequalities in the society were justified as reward for degree of effort. Connell notes that his findings 'make it very clear that the gospel of work is more widespread among the children, and more fundamental in their outlook, than any doctrine of equalitarianism or social hierarchy'.[81]

In Britain, which is clearly a more class-conscious society, the success-oriented work ethic is nevertheless strong. Researcher Adrian Furnham concluded in 1993 that 'the work ethic is alive and well in Britain'. He found that most people agreed that 'a good indicator of a person's worth is how well they do their job' and that two-thirds of 15- and 16-year-olds agreed that 'hard work makes someone a better person'.[82]

CONCLUSION

Through much of the nineteenth and twentieth centuries inequality was portrayed by businessmen, politicians and writers as the result of individual variability in terms of character, virtue and endeavour, rather than a structural feature of a social system that rewarded some activities over others and favoured those who already had advantages in terms of wealth and position.[83]

This individualist view was bolstered by Social Darwinism and also by the economic ideology of *laissez-faire*. *Laissez-faire* philosophy reinforced the prior Protestant moral endorsement of profit seeking as a virtuous activity but went further by equating self-interest with moral duty.[84]

The individualism incorporated in the work ethic, the American Dream and the myth of the self-made man, and the supporting philosophies of the classical economists and the Social Darwinists, secured the acceptance of a social system that promoted inequality and disparities of wealth and power whilst ensuring that the poor continued to work hard and accept their lot. Social Darwinism added a scientific rationale for the naturalness of inequality. As Stephen Asma notes in his article on 'The New Social Darwinism': 'It is truly remarkable that the power elite of [the US] has been able to convince the middle class that its enemy is the poor.'[85]

For all that, the reality that most hard-working people cannot possibly succeed was one that became increasingly evident in the late twentieth century. The next chapter will consider the declining opportunities for social mobility through hard work in recent times, and how faith in the fairness of the capitalist system has been maintained despite this.

———

NOTES

1 Quoted in Adrian Furnham, *The Protestant Work Ethic: the Psychology of Work-related Beliefs and Behaviours* (London: Routledge, 1990), p. 33.

2 Quoted in *ibid.*, p. 126.

3 Matthew Josephson, *The Robber Barons: the Great American Capitalists 1861–1901* (London: Eyre and Spottiswoode, 1962), p. 316.

4 *Ibid.*, p. 317.

5 Quoted in *ibid.*, p. 318.

6 *Ibid.*, p 323.

7 *Ibid.*, pp. 324–5; Upton Sinclair, *The Goslings: a Study of American Schools* (Pasadena, California: Upton Sinclair, 1924); Upton Sinclair, *The Goose-Step: a Study of American Education*, revised edn (Pasadena, California: Upton Sinclair, 1923).

8 Quoted in Richard S. Tedlow, *Keeping the Corporate Image: Public Relations and Business, 1900–1950* (Greenwich, Connecticut: Jai Press, 1979), p. 8.

9 Josephson, note 3, pp. 316, 347.

10 Quoted in *ibid.*, p. 355.

11 Quoted in Alfred D. Chandler and Richard S. Tedlow, *The Coming of Managerial Capitalism: a Casebook History of American Economic Institutions* (Homewood, Illinois: Richard D. Irwin, 1985), p. 553.

12 Josephson, note 3, pp. 355–8.

13 Quoted in Karl Schriftgiesser, *The Lobbyists: the Art and Business of Influencing Lawmakers* (Boston: Little, Brown and Co., 1951), p. 35.

14 Quoted in Josephson, note 3, p. 352.

15 John Kenneth Galbraith, *The Anatomy of Power* (London: Hamish Hamilton, 1984), p. 49.

16 Quoted in J. T. Ward, *The Age of Change 1770–1870* (London: A. and C. Black, 1975), p. 7.

17 Quoted in Malcolm I. Thomis, *Responses to Industrialisation: the British Experience 1780–1850* (Newton Abbot: David and Charles, 1976), p. 83.

18 Southey, quoted in *ibid.*, p. 104.

19 Carlyle, quoted in *ibid.*, p. 106.

20 *Ibid.*, pp. 96–7.

21 Quoted in Galbraith, note 15, p. 112.

22 Quoted in D. P. O'Brien, *The Classical Economists* (Oxford: Clarendon Press, 1975), p. 30.

23 Andrew Bard Schmookler, *The Illusion of Choice: How the Market Economy Shapes Our Destiny* (Albany: State University of New York Press, 1993), pp. 38–43.

24 Ward, note 16, p. 2.

25 Ellen Frankel Paul, *Moral Revolution and Economic Science: the Demise of Laissez–Faire in Nineteenth-Century British Political Economy* (Westport, Connecticut: Greenwood Press, 1979), p. 9.

26 John Kenneth Galbraith, *American Capitalism: the Concept of Countervailing Power*, Sentry edn (Boston: Houghton Mifflin, 1956), p. 24.

27 M. J. Kitch, *Capitalism and the Reformation* (London: Longman, 1967), p. 11.

28 *Ibid.*, p. 183.

29 Cited in Galbraith, note 15, p. 116.

30 J. L. Hammond and Barbara Hammond, *The Town Labourer 1760–1832*, Left Book Club edn (London: Victor Gollancz, 1937), p. 221.

31 *Ibid.*, pp. 222–3.

32 Quoted in Galbraith, note 15, pp. 117–18.

33 Hammond and Hammond, note 30, p. 217.

34 Thomis, note 17, pp. 95, 99.

35 Quoted in Ward, note 16, pp. 151–2.

36 Hammond and Hammond, note 30, pp. 218–19.

37 Joseph L. DeVitis and John Martin Rich, *The Success Ethic, Education, and the American Dream* (Albany, NY: State University of New York Press, 1996), p. 4.

38 Greta Jones, *Social Darwinism and English Thought: the Interaction between Biological and Social Theory* (Sussex: The Harvester Press, 1980), p. 55.

39 Charles Darwin, *The Origin of Species* (New York: Collier Books, 1962).

40 Jones, note 38, p. 56.

41 Quoted in Joe R. Feagin, *Subordinating the Poor* (Englewood Cliffs, NJ: Prentice-Hall, 1975), pp. 34–5.

42 Jones, note 38, p. 143.

43 Thomas H. Huxley, *Evolution and Ethics and Other Essays* (New York: D. Appleton and Co., 1897), p. 42.

44 Eric F. Goldman, quoted in Feagin, note 41, p. 35.

45 Stephen T. Asma, 'The New Social Darwinism: Deserving Your Destitution', *The Humanist*, Vol. 53, No. 5 (1993).

46 Quoted in *ibid.*

47 Quoted in Feagin, note 41, p. 35.

48 Quoted in *ibid.*, p. 35.

49 Quoted in John Kenneth Galbraith, *The Culture of Contentment* (London: Penguin, 1992), pp. 80–1.

50 Quoted in William H. Whyte, *The Organization Man* (Harmondsworth, Middlesex: Penguin, 1960), pp. 18–19.

51 Quoted in Feagin, note 41, p. 36.

52 Robert Eisenberger, *Blue Monday: the Loss of the Work Ethic in America* (New York: Paragon House, 1989), p. 15; Paul Bernstein, *American Work Values: Their Origin and Development* (Albany, NY: State University of New York Press, 1997), pp. 116, 143.

53 Chandler and Tedlow, note 11, p. 554.

54 Quoted in Roland Marchand, *Creating the Corporate Soul: the Rise of Public Relations and Corporate Imagery in American Big Business* (Berkeley: University of California Press, 1998), p. 10.

55 Louis Galambos, *The Public Image of Big Business in America, 1880–1940* (Baltimore: The John Hopkins University Press, 1975), p. 9.

56 Ely Chinoy, *Automobile Workers and the American Dream* (Urbana and Chicago: University of Illinois Press, 1992), p. 4.

57 *Ibid.*, pp. 13, 16–17

58 *Ibid.*, pp. 6, 17.

59 For example, Upton Sinclair, *The Metropolis* (New York: Moffat, Yard & Co, 1908); Upton Sinclair, *The Money Changers* (New York: B. W. Dodge, 1908).

60 C. Wright Mills, *The Power Elite* (Oxford: Oxford University Press, 1956), p. 11.

61 *Ibid.*, pp. 11–17.

62 *Ibid.*, p. 281.

63 *Ibid.*, p. 283.

64 *Ibid.*, pp. 105–7.

65 *Ibid.*, p. 105.

66 Ralph Miliband, *Capitalist Democracy in Britain* (Oxford: Oxford University Press, 1982), p. 7.

67 *Ibid.*, p. 7.

68 Tony Watson, *Sociology, Work and Industry* (London: Routledge and Kegan Paul, 1987), p. 189; Mills, note 60, p. 141.

69 Mills, note 60, pp. 127–8.

70 Chinoy, note 56, p. 2.

71 *Ibid.*, p. 7.

72 Quoted in *ibid.*, pp. 3–5.

73 *Ibid.*, pp. 82–3, 90, 114–17, 126.

74 Robert E. Lane, *Political Ideology: Why the American Common Man Believes What He Does* (New York: The Free Press, 1962), p. 61.

75 *Ibid.*, pp. 62, 76, 78.

76 *Ibid.*, pp. 262–3.

77 *Ibid.*, p. 265.

78 David J. Cherrington, *The Work Ethic: Working Values and Values That Work* (New York: AMACON, 1980), pp. 45–8.

79 Bernstein, note 52, pp. 175, 181.

80 A. F. Davies and S. Encel, *Australian Society: a Sociological Introduction* (Melbourne: Cheshire, 1970).

81 R. W. Connell, *Ruling Class Ruling Culture: Studies of Conflict, Power and Hegemony in Australian Life* (Cambridge: Cambridge University Press, 1977), pp. 143–6.

82 Adrian Furnham, 'Curse of the Drinking Classes', *New Scientist* (3 April 1993), pp. 49–50.

83 Feagin, note 41, p. 22.

84 P. D. Anthony, *The Ideology of Work* (London: Tavistock Publications, 1977), p. 67.

85 Asma, note 45.

❖ 5 ❖

Legitimising Inequality

If I had gone to college, I would be higher up in
this world.
Anonymous[1]

Until you know the income bracket of a stranger,
and he knows yours, your mutual relationship is
unsatisfactory and incomplete.
Geoffrey Gorer[2]

In many countries today, including the wealthiest, it is not only becoming
more and more difficult for the poor to become rich through talent, effort
and opportunities, but the differences in income between the wealthy and the
ordinary worker have increased. The rich have been getting richer whilst the
average worker has been getting poorer. Social mobility between generations
can no longer be taken for granted.

Social mobility can be achieved as an employee or as a businessperson. As
the opportunity to start a small business diminished, so the link between hard
work and prosperity became more tenuous. By 1984 less than 8 per cent of
workers in the US were self-employed.[3] The path to success and advancement
within a corporation is largely limited to white-collar workers, and more particularly to well-educated men. Despite the rhetoric of business leaders that
the lowliest employee can rise through the ranks through sheer determination,
ability and hard work, factory workers with little skill or education have little
hope of being promoted up the ranks of the corporation.

In large plants employing over a thousand employees (by 1947 this accounted for 84 per cent of factories, with 64 per cent employing more than 2,500
employees), personal recognition for merit or hard work is difficult to gain.
This is particularly so because the work is so regimented and controlled that

71

there is little room for initiative and the timing of work tasks is decided by others. The career ladder for factory workers has few rungs and is unlikely to go beyond foreman.[4]

Although it is increasingly obvious that hard work often does not lead to success, businesspeople, politicians and writers have continued to promote the myth of the self-made man. And although there is a growing proportion of working poor in modern societies, increasing levels of poverty have continued to be attributed to deficiencies in the poor rather than structural aspects of the society. This chapter examines the way that inequalities have been justified in the twentieth century in terms of individual hard work, character and education, despite evidence to the contrary.

THE DISAPPEARING DREAM

Throughout American history, according to economic measures, the standard of living has doubled about every 30 years.[5] To the extent that the American Dream meant better material living conditions through the generations, experience seemed to bear it out. This is no longer the case, despite increasing wealth overall. People are realising, as Edward Kennedy pointed out in *USA Today*,

> that economic growth and prosperity no longer benefit all Americans fairly.... Superficial signs of prosperity abound – the stock market hitting record highs, inflation consistently low, unemployment down – but the prosperity is less than it seems. Americans are working harder and earning less. Their standard of living is stagnant or sinking.... For the vast majority of families, the American Dream today has a sign over it that says, 'Only the Wealthy Need Apply'.[6]

Similarly, John Schwarz notes in *Illusions of Opportunity* that 'the number of Americans closed out of minimally adequate opportunity surpasses the total populations of the one hundred largest American cities combined'.[7] Schwarz argues that whilst unemployment in the US is low, the number of jobs paying an adequate wage to support a family at a 'minimally dignified' standard of living falls far short of the number who need them. And if the jobs are not there, neither is the opportunity that is supposed to be at the heart of the American Dream.

One factor contributing to the increasing shortage of adequate jobs (and diminishing opportunity to live the Dream) has been the decline in wages for most workers. The purchasing power of average hourly wages in the US in 1995 was less than the average worker received in 1965, 30 years earlier.[8] In the 1950s the federal minimum wage was about the same as the minimum wage necessary to live a respectable lifestyle. By 1989 the minimum wage was only 55 per cent of the amount necessary for such a lifestyle. In the 1990s, a family can have two workers earning the minimum wage and still not achieve a respectable lifestyle with private bathroom, running water, telephone and hotwater heater.[9]

Eighty per cent of the workforce have experienced a decline in real wages since 1979.[10] In order 'to reach their 1973 standard of living, they must work 245 more hours, or 6-plus extra weeks a year.'[11] Between 1973 and 1988 'families headed by high school dropouts increased their work effort by nearly 12 percent, yet ended up with 8 percent less annual income'.[12] Hard work pays off less than it used to.

In the US, the world's richest nation which prides itself on being a land of opportunity, wealth is far more concentrated in the hands of a minority than in any other industrialised nation, and this concentration has increased in recent decades. The richest 1 per cent of families own 45 per cent of the country's wealth. This 45 per cent compares with 20 per cent owned by the richest 1 per cent in 1970. Even in the UK, supposedly the bastion of class privilege, the wealthiest 1 per cent own only 18 per cent of the country's wealth.[13] The United Nations Development Programme's *Human Development Report 1998* notes that despite its wealth, booming economy and low unemployment, 16.5 per cent of people live in poverty in the US (the highest proportion in the developed world).[14]

The reason for the growing inequity has little to do with hard work. Increasingly wealth comes from capital gains from investments, particularly real estate, and corporate stock. And the wealthiest 10 per cent of families in the US already own 'about 90 percent of stock shares, bonds, trusts, and business equity, and 80 of non-home real estate'.[15] Similarly in Australia the wealthiest 10 per cent of households own 90 per cent of privately owned shares.[16]

The average worker is unable to invest because s/he is unable to save enough. The poorest third of the population in the US has never been able to save anything from their meagre incomes. The middle third used to be able to save but since the 1980s that is no longer the case. It is only those who have wealth to start with who are able to realise the capital gains on that wealth to become even wealthier.[17]

During the 1980s the trend for the rich to get richer and the poor to get poorer became most evident (see Table 5.1). The poorest 40 per cent of families (accounting for 60 per cent of the workforce) have had falling incomes since the mid-1970s, the middle 40 per cent have had fairly stagnant incomes, and the wealthiest 20 per cent have had spectacular increases in wealth (100 per cent increases for the top 1 per cent and 30 per cent increases for the top 5 per cent).[18]

TABLE 5.1 PERCENTAGE CHANGE IN FAMILY INCOME (1967–89)

	Low income Poorest 10%		Middle income	High income	Wealthiest 10%
1967–73	21.9	12.4	17.3	20.6	21.8
1973–76	–1.2	0.2	3.5	5.0	6.2
1979–87*	–8.7	–1.4	2.4	7.7	10.1

* Median family income in the mid-1990s was down another 7 per cent from 1989.[19]
Source: Clinton E. Boutwell, *Shell Game: Corporate America's Agenda for Schools* (Bloomington, Indiana: Phi Delta Kappa Educational Foundation, 1997), p. 57.

Whilst the poor are getting poorer and the middle classes are making little headway, the wealthy are booming. Reuters news agency reported at the end of 1999 that 'Not since the early twentieth century has the United States experienced such mansion-building.'[20] Meanwhile, home ownership rates have declined.[21] In 1991 a study of the children of middle managers found that they were not as well off as their parents at the same age and were perhaps 'the first generation in American history that will not do better economically than its parents'.[22]

Social mobility between generations has become a thing of the past, not just in the US but in Australia, Canada and the UK also. In Canada, inequality in weekly earnings increased during the 1980s.[23] In Australia, whilst companies are making record profits and aggregate personal wealth has increased by more than 40 per cent in the last decade, average wages have hardly changed and wages have fallen for the bottom third of male Australian workers.[24] An Australian National University report found that boys between 15 and 19 earn the equivalent of $96 less per week (30–50 per cent less) than boys did 20 years ago, and are more likely to remain poor as they grow older. They are less likely to find full-time work and less able to support a family than their parents were.[25]

In Australia, as in the US, the rich have been getting richer whilst the poor have been getting poorer. The wealthiest 200 people in Australia have increased their wealth by $21 billion in just three years. The richest 10 per cent of households own 48.7 per cent of the total household wealth (compared with 44.9 per cent five years ago).[26] At the same time the number of people living in poverty has almost doubled since 1973 to 11.5 per cent of the population.[27]

In Britain, too, a recent government report reveals that 'the proportion of people living in households with relatively low incomes has more than doubled between the end of the 1970s and the beginning of the 1990s'.[28]

According to the Secretary of State for Social Security, Alistair Darling, one in three children live in poverty and this is 'three times the number in 1979'.[29] Since 1980 the wages of the lowest 20 per cent of workers have not changed whilst the income of the top 10 per cent have grown by 50 per cent in real terms.[30]

In no earlier period in the twenteith century did average wages decline (in terms of purchasing power) whilst per capita GDP was rising.[31] There has been no trickledown of wealth in English-speaking countries over the last two decades. US workers have benefited in neither time nor income from productivity gains estimated to be over 25 per cent between 1973 and 1994. During this time manufacturing costs fell and prices rose, ensuring huge profits in which workers did not share.[32] Between 1982 and 1996 the value of the New York Stock Exchange increased 400 per cent whilst the real wages of the average worker went down by 15 per cent.[33]

In contrast, corporate executives have seen their incomes go up 21 per cent on average.[34] The difference is even more pronounced when one considers the top executives. The average chief executive officer (CEO) of the 500 largest firms in the US received $US4.06 million in remuneration in 1995 (including base salary, bonuses, perks and stock options), up 16 per cent from the previous year. In 1996 the average compensation for the CEOs of the largest companies went up another 52 per cent, and in 1997 it went up a further 35 per cent.[35]

CEOs now get over 400 times the wages of the average US worker, compared with 41 times in the mid-1970s. CEO salaries have increased by 1,000 per cent in the last 20 years, while the average hourly wages for workers have diminished in real terms during the same time period.[36] All the benefits of economic growth have gone to those at the top. Even when they are 'downsized' the CEOs do much better than ordinary workers. In Britain recently, a CEO who had retrenched 750 workers got a £17 million redundancy package for himself.[37]

These CEOs also preside over empires that employ Third World workers who are paid a pittance. For example, Disney CEO Michael Eisner earns $750,000 per year in salary, plus bonuses up to $15 million. He received over $575 million compensation for his work in 1997 (including money made from stock options). Florida employees at Walt Disney World earn $5.95 per hour and after three years can earn $13,541 per year. Contractors in Haiti producing Disney-branded clothes are paid 28 cents per hour. *New Internationalist* magazine estimated that it would take these workers 156 years to earn what Eisner earns in one hour.[38]

The huge salaries that CEOs get no longer seem to be tied to performance, either. When General Dynamics lost $500 million and laid off 27,000 workers, it paid its CEO an $800,000 salary and $4 million worth of stock options. In the year that United Airlines profits went down by 71 per cent, the CEO received $18.3 million in compensation.[39]

Whilst US CEOs earn more than CEOs in other countries, the disparities exist elsewhere. In Britain company directors earned an average of £800,000 in 1998 after giving themselves an average raise of 18 per cent in 1997, compared with a 3 per cent inflation rate. This income compared with the average of £16,100 for their employees; that is, company directors earned as much each week as the average person earned in a year.[40]

In *A Class Act: the Myth of Britain's Classless Society* Andrew Adonis and Stephen Pollard describe the 'rise of the Super Class' over the last 30 years in Britain. The Super Class consists of 'a new elite of top professionals and managers', including chief executives, corporate solicitors, accountants and stockbrokers. Some make their money from huge executive salaries. Others have made the most of opportunities arising from financial deregulation or privatisation. This Super Class is 'very highly paid yet powerfully convinced of the justice of its rewards, and increasingly divorced from the rest of society by wealth, education, values, residence and lifestyle'.[41]

In Australia the average annual income for company executive officers was $A797,420 ($US476,700) in 1997.[42] The average income for the lowest-paid 20 per cent of the Australian population was $6,300. The income for the highest-paid 20 per cent of the population accounted for 47.5 per cent of all income earned in the financial year 1996/7.[43]

In the US, social mobility between generations is today incremental with small steps up the occupational ladder being the norm.[44] Joseph DeVitis and John Martin Rich observe in their book *The Success Ethic, Education and the American Dream* that 'The idealistic notion … that with the right traits one can rise in one's lifetime from poverty to the top of the occupational ladder is not borne out by research … only rarely does a son obtain a job much higher or lower than his father's in occupational prestige.' Family background is still an important factor in occupational status.[45]

The idea that the US offers more opportunity to those who are willing to work is no longer true, if it once was. A 1996 OECD study which compared income mobility in eight developed countries found that fewer workers in the bottom 20 per cent income bracket in the US were able to move into the top 60 per cent than in any of the other countries.[46] In fact, the proportion of children growing up in poverty in the US is now double that of other affluent countries and the situation is getting worse.[47]

In the US as elsewhere, poverty tends to be concentrated geographically and amongst those of particular racial backgrounds, such as blacks and Latinos. Whilst 13 per cent of the population was officially defined as poor in

1997, 26.7 of blacks and 27 per cent of Hispanics were defined as poor.[48] The percentage of people able to work their way out of poverty in the US is far lower than in other industrialised countries, as can be seen in Table 5.2.

TABLE 5.2 PERCENTAGE OF POOR PEOPLE WHOSE INCOMES INCREASED ABOVE THE POVERTY LINE WITHIN A YEAR

Country	Per cent
The Netherlands	44
Sweden	37
France	28
Germany	26
Ireland	25
USA	13

Source: Clinton E. Boutwell, *Shell Game: Corporate America's Agenda for Schools* (Bloomington, Indiana: Phi Delta Kappa Educational Foundation, 1997), p. 54.

CONTINUING PROPAGANDA

In the face of the growing inequities in modern industrialised nations, particularly English-speaking nations, it is hard to maintain a success-based work ethic. In a US survey, 57 per cent of people said that the American Dream was out of reach for most families, and more than two-thirds were concerned that their children would not live as well as they had. One-third were concerned about losing their jobs soon.[49] In another study 59 per cent of blacks said that they thought the American Dream was impossible to achieve.[50]

To counter such perceptions, modern US politicians still frantically promote the American Dream. Bill Clinton, like other presidents before him, gave speeches on it. He claimed that if a person works hard and respects the law the only limit to advancement is ability. The House Republicans put out a book in 1995 entitled *Restoring the American Dream* which claimed that anyone in America could succeed, whatever their skin colour or current income level.[51] In his book *To Renew America*, US House Speaker Newt Gingrich argued that 'Part of the American genius has been that, at every level of society, people can improve their own lot. We have no caste system, no class requirements, no regulated professions, no barriers to entry.'[52]

In 1995 and 1996 a whole spate of books were published on how to promote and rejuvenate the American Dream, including *Reviving the American Dream* by Alice Rivlin, *The Success Ethic, Education and the American Dream* by De Vitis and Rich, *Facing up to the American Dream* by Jennifer L. Hochschild, *The American Dream* by Edmund Morris, *Recovering the American Dream Through the*

Moral Dimension of Work, Business and Money by Robert Wuthnow, *The Good Life and Its Discontents* by Robert J. Samuelson and *Chasing After the American Dream* by Thomas Kerr. *Restoring the American Dream* was also the theme of the Republicans' 1996 San Diego convention and of Presidential candidate Bob Dole's speech.[53]

The mainstream media also promote the idea of work leading to success – and not only in the US is this a favoured theme. In 1999 the Australian version of *60 Minutes* did a follow-up on a 1990 story it had done on 'three young go-getters' who were making lots of money – an advertising executive, a real estate agent and a publisher. John McGrath, who presided over real estate interests worth some $50 million, the audience was told, came from a working-class suburb where his father was a publican. He said that the idea that only 1 or 2 per cent of people can make it and become rich was 'small poppy thinking'; instead, he believed, 'Everyone can be successful. There is enough money and food and wealth for everyone on the planet to live their dream.'[54]

Advertisers in many countries still reinforce this link between hard work and success in order to sell status consumer items. For example, Mitsubishi Motors advertises its Verada Car in Australia: 'It's the result of years of hard work. Yours. With success comes recognition and reward. And more responsibility. So as you're probably busier than ever, we'll get straight to the point. Your new car. It should be a car that reflects your status.... We simply suggest you reward yourself with a test drive. Haven't you earned it?'[55]

The myth of the self-made man is still promoted by businesspeople, despite decreasing social mobility and growing inequity. James Bell of Texas State University Business School told an audience in 1997 the story of a visit by the president of the railroad to one of the railway yards, where he chatted with a worker driving spikes into railroad ties. When asked how he knew the president of the railroad the worker told his workmate how they had both started work together 'twenty-five years ago out here in the yard'.

> 'You mean the president of the railroad started out here swinging a sledge hammer?' 'Yes,' was the reply. 'Then how come he's the president , and you're still out here in the yard?' The reply: 'Twenty-five years ago, I came to work for $1.25 an hour. But he came to work for the railroad!'[56]

Bill Gates, head of Microsoft is arguably the wealthiest man in history. His personal wealth is said to exceed 'the economic output of all but the 20 largest countries'.[57] His devotion to hard work is mythologised by business magazines. In an article in *Forbes* business magazine headlined 'Let 'em See You Sweat', managers are exhorted to inspire hard work amongst their employees by setting a good example as Gates does.[58] *Fortune*, another

78

business magazine, observed that Gates 'may be the hardest-working man in big business'. The article claimed that there is something of a personality cult amongst Microsoft employees: 'Gates clearly exploits this hero worship by setting a vivid and pragmatic example of what might be described as a Microsoftian work ethic. His grueling schedule is just one not-so-subtle hint of what he expects from employees.'[59]

Such stories keep the myth of the self-made man alive. David Griffiths in his book *Whither Work* explains the myth's durability:

There are real opportunities for some to succeed from poverty to wealth and from obscurity to prominence, but for the majority these opportunities are illusionary, peripheral and seductive. That these real opportunities are for the few is irrelevant to the fact that they are nonetheless real.[60]

BLAMING THE POOR (AGAIN)

Whilst the myth of the self-made man or woman has less credibility these days, the idea that the poor are responsible for their own fate maintains its widespread currency in many English-speaking countries. This is a key to understanding why people so readily accept the presence of poverty in wealthy countries.

Psychological studies in the US and the UK suggest that those who subscribe most strongly to a work ethic have the harshest, most unforgiving attitudes to the poor and unemployed.[61] Rather than blaming social institutions or government failures, they blame individuals for their own fate. They tend to agree with statements such as 'I can't understand why some people make such a fuss over the disadvantaged state of the poor, most of them could improve their condition if only they tried', or 'Although we don't like to face it, most people on welfare are lazy', or 'In this country, almost everyone can make it if he tries hard enough.'[62]

Although poverty is usually associated with unemployment, substantial numbers of people remain poor despite working hard in countries such as the UK, Australia and the US. In Australia 7.4 per cent of employees (460,000 adults) have incomes that are below the official Henderson poverty line. This compares with 3 per cent (139,000) in 1981. Some of these workers don't work enough hours to earn a living but increasingly full-time workers are falling below the poverty line because of low wages.[63] In Britain the likelihood that a family with a male breadwinner would be in poverty increased by nine times between 1979 and 1999.[64]

In the US, almost 60 per cent of families living below the poverty line have at least one member working.[65] Many workers barely earn enough to live on and are 'sinking into debt and poverty'. Between 7 and 9 million people who have jobs are classified by the US government as living in poverty. (Other estimates are considerably higher, as the definition of poverty varies.) The number of full-time US workers who earned less money than is considered necessary to live on rose between 1979 and 1992 from 12 to 18 per cent. During that time the number of young people (18–24) earning less than a living wage doubled to 46 per cent.[66]

Yet people in the US have traditionally held the same attitudes to the poor as to the unemployed. A 1970s study of the attitudes of Americans to the poor found that more than half of those surveyed blamed the individuals themselves. In particular, 58 per cent said that 'lack of thrift and proper money management by poor people' was a very important reason for poverty, while another 30 per cent said it was somewhat important. Similar percentages gave 'lack of effort by the poor themselves' as the reason. These reasons were closely followed by 'lack of ability and talent among poor people' and 'loose morals and drunkenness' (48 per cent and 31 per cent respectively).[67]

Stanley Feldman of the University of Kentucky had similar results with respect to the poor in his study: 58 per cent of people agreed that 'many poor people simply don't want to work hard' and a similar percentage agreed that 'maybe it's not their fault but most poor people were brought up without drive or ambition'.[68]

These people are at the bottom of the social hierarchy, and although they work hard they are held responsible for their failure to succeed in a society where there is supposed to be equality of opportunity and where anyone can make it if they work hard enough. Yet a study by Marlene Kim, published in the *Journal of Economic Issues*, found that 'few of the working poor would be able to work enough hours to earn their way out of poverty: most command wages that are so low that working full-time and year round would still leave them poor'.[69]

Increasingly, however, workers at the bottom of the occupational hierarchy are employed in temporary and insecure jobs (see Chapter 8) and find themselves rotating through periods of unemployment and low-paying jobs. This is a major reason for increasing levels of poverty and welfare dependence in modern societies. The community has even less sympathy for the unemployed, however, than for the working poor.

The perception of the unemployed as responsible for their own fate, as a corollary to the belief that those willing to work hard will find success, is reinforced by the corporate establishment and politicians. Politicians would rather the unemployed were blamed than governments that fail to provide economic conditions for job growth. Corporations, too, would prefer to draw attention away from their role in creating unemployment (see Chapter 8).

During times of 'full employment', officially defined as less than 1.5 per cent of the working population unemployed, it is widely assumed that anyone who is unemployed must have chosen to be so.[70] Yet the jobs may exist in areas where the unemployed don't live, or may require skills the unemployed don't have. Even employers of unskilled workers may find some of those applying for jobs undesirable for a variety of reasons ranging from appearance through to lack of work experience.

Even in times of high unemployment, a significant proportion of the community in English-speaking countries believe that unemployed people could get a job if they tried hard enough, if they really wanted one. Paradoxically, the community often expresses more hostility to welfare payments during times of recession when jobs are difficult to get and unemployment levels are high. Those with jobs find it more difficult to cope financially in such times and are even more resentful of the taxes they are paying towards welfare. Of course, the community is often primed to be unsympathetic to the unemployed by the media, the government and corporate propaganda.

In his book *In the Shadow of the Poorhouse* Jeffrey Katz claims: 'The availability of work for every ablebodied person who really wants a job is one of the enduring myths of American history.'[71] In the 1960s the city of Newburgh in New York became a model for other cities throughout the US for its programme of getting tough on welfare recipients and reducing their numbers through strict regulations. The city manager, Joseph Mitchell, described their reforms:

> We challenged the right of moral chiselers and loafers to squat on the relief rolls forever. We challenged the right of cheaters to make more on relief than when working. We challenged the right of those on relief to loaf by State and Federal edict. We challenged the right of people to quit jobs at will and go on relief like spoiled children.[72]

Senator Goldwater, in his presidential campaign of 1964, used welfare and poverty as a key issue: 'The fact is that most people who have no skill, have had no education for the same reason – low intelligence or low ambition.' The solution was to force those on welfare to work.[73] This is a solution that has become universally popular today (see Chapter 10).

Leading US Republican Newt Gingrich argues that the welfare system is based on a 'redistribution ethic that subsidizes idleness. Nothing could be less traditionally American than the modern welfare system. It violates the American ethic that everyone should work hard to improve both their own lives and the lives of their children.'[74] Robert Rector of the Heritage Foundation, a leading conservative think tank, claims that welfare 'rewards permissiveness' and that it is a 'liberal myth' that 'poverty is bad for kids'.[75]

False community perceptions about how easy it is to get a job are fed by anecdotal accounts put about by businesspeople with their own agendas, who allege they are finding it difficult to fill vacancies:

In a recent case of which I have personal knowledge, a large, centrally located Sydney corporation advertised for a young woman. The job advertised was in pleasant surroundings, the qualifications sought were modest and the pay was good. The advertisement evoked one response, and this is a city where allegedly numerous young people are unemployed seeking work.[76]

Gabrielle Lord, who worked as an officer in the Australian Commonwealth Employment Service (CES) in the 1970s, found that the unemployed themselves believed the media stories about jobs going begging and unemployed people not really wanting to work. They would say, 'But I really want to work. I'm not like the others.' [77]

An Australian government survey of the long-term unemployed at this time found that staff in employment offices tended to believe that people were unemployed due to a lack of motivation or other personal factors rather than external economic and structural factors. Yet describing the long-term unemployed as not wanting to work was 'an over-simplification in nearly every case, and altogether untrue in many'.[78] An American study similarly found that 84 per cent of people said that 'There are too many people receiving welfare money who should be working.'[79] It found that people's perceptions of welfare were grossly inaccurate.

Recent surveys confirm that those who have a strong work ethic tend 'to see those on social security as idle and dishonest'.[80] The unemployed tend to be blamed for their own plight by large sections of the community. In particular, welfare recipients are 'pictured as virtually irredeemable, lazy, dependent, living off the hard-earned money of others'.[81]

A 1997 Australian government report found that, despite public and employer perceptions, young unemployed people really do want to work. Such findings are outweighed, however, by media reports and business propaganda. In one case television current affairs programmes reported the lack of applicants for retail traineeships in Victoria 'with much enthusiasm, reinforcing the perception that unemployed people do not want to work. In fact, the newspaper and television coverage resulted in a massive response from people looking for work who had not been reached' by the earlier advertising efforts.[82]

In the US, even welfare workers often assume the unemployed are responsible for their own problems. In the office which she studied in the Midwest, Gale Miller found that workers assumed that their clients were socially incompetent and possessed 'personal and cultural traits which keep them from properly fulfilling their social obligations, the most important being finding and keeping jobs'. They encouraged the unemployed to see their problems as personal and not a manifestations of wider economic problems. They saw their own role as helping these people to change their attitudes, behaviour and way of life – and, if they would not change, stopping their welfare payments.[83]

THE ROLE OF EDUCATION

The question remains: why do the working poor and the unemployed themselves accept their situation to be fair, when they know by bitter experience that hard work does not bring status and success? When Robert Lane interviewed 'the common man' in the American town of Eastport he found that education was a key legitimator of differing pay rates and social status. The working-class and lower-middle-class men blamed their lack of social status and lower incomes on their lack of education, and accepted their relative success in school as a measure of their ability. Those with more ability who were willing to put in the effort got better educational qualifications and better-paying, higher-status jobs. This was seen as fair.[84]

> The concept of 'education' is the key to much of the thinking on social class and personal status. In a sense, it is 'natural' because it fits so neatly into the American myth of opportunity and equality, and provides a rationale for success and failure that does minimum damage to the souls of those who did not go to college.[85]

In many countries, schools provide a 'filter through which the young labour supply eventually reaches appropriate occupational destinations and place in the social structure'.[86] Schools label and stream children, sending some to the higher-status academic streams and others to the lower-status, more vocationally oriented streams. Education serves as 'an increasingly refined training and selection mechanism for the labor force'.[87]

The education system is supposed to be part of the social apparatus that ensures equality of opportunity, enabling those with ability and application to get good qualifications that give them entry into the best jobs. The use of educational qualifications to differentiate between job applicants serves to legitimise inequalities in the workplace, proving that the occupational hierarchy is based on merit.[88] Yet the selection process that is provided by the educational system is not independent of a child's background.

A child's experience at school affects not only job opportunities but also job aspirations. It influences 'his or her approach to employment and understanding of how the labour market operates'.[89] It has been found that children, particularly working-class children, who are assigned to lower streams in primary school tend to accept that they must be intellectually inferior, as do their parents, and their school work usually deteriorates from then on.[90]

Traditionally British schools have performed a socialising function, teaching leadership and conservative values in elite schools and 'submissive acceptance of the social order' in the schools where working-class children attended. Over time this socialisation has had to be less explicit, but the underlying assumptions are still there. In Britain today, students destined for the professional and managerial jobs are given a liberal education whilst vocational education is offered to working-class children.[91]

Ralph Miliband suggests in *The State in Capitalist Society* that working-class children are confirmed in their future status 'by virtue of the starved education' which they are given 'and by the *curtailment* rather than the "development" of further educational opportunities'.

> And the very fact that some working-class children are able to surmount these handicaps serves to foster the notion that those who do not are themselves, because of their own unfitness, the architects, of their lowly fate, and that their situation is of their own making. The educational system thus conspires to create the impression, not least among its victims, that social disadvantages are really a matter of personal, innate, God-given and insurmountable incapacity.[92]

In Britain, high social status, a public school education ('public' schools being the more prestigious private schools) and a non-technical degree from one of the more prestigious universities – such as Oxford or Cambridge – are better keys to top corporate jobs than a technical education, even at university level, or a postgraduate business qualification.[93] Sociologists Pierre Bourdieu and Luc Boltanski suggest that the use of the right educational qualifications is 'a method of class reproduction no less effective than the older mechanism of direct inheritance of wealth'.[94]

Schools in the supposedly more egalitarian countries of Australia and the US also perform a selecting role that is often influenced by the wealth of a child's parents. In Australia, private schools, particularly Protestant schools, have a greater intake of children from higher-status backgrounds and traditionally 'cater for an occupational and economic élite'. R. W. Connell in *Ruling Class Ruling Culture* observes that 'The structure of the school system thus serves as a streaming system on a grand scale, which sorts children in very large measure on class criteria.'[95]

Connell's interviews also showed that working-class Australian teenagers often recognised which jobs were the best ones but had disqualified themselves early on because they had decided they were not intelligent enough. The children were in fact of normal intelligence and school performance but they had 'working-class' expectations. Yet they explained their lower expectations to themselves in terms of whether or not they 'had the brains'.[96]

The Australian Council for Educational Research has found that students in government schools tend to be doing vocational subjects far more often than those attending private schools, and that the students doing vocational education had parents who were mainly in manual jobs: the establishment of vocational education in schools thus 'retains a social division'.[97] In the 1990s funding for government schools declined whilst government funding for wealthy private schools increased. The consequence has been falling school retention rates (Australia was the only country in the OECD to experience this) with only 60 per cent of boys in government schools finishing high school, and even fewer in the poorer government schools.[98]

A similar trend has been occurring in the US. In the twentieth century the US educational system, which previously had treated all children the same, evolved to provide different types and levels of education to children according to their expected occupational level. One school board president stated in the 1920s: 'For a long time all boys were trained to be President. Then for a while we trained them all to be professional men. Now we are training them to get jobs.'[99] David Sneddon, a Commissioner of Education, argued that some children should be trained to be leaders and others to be rank and file. Rank and file training should prepare individuals to be efficient in their work.[100] A school superintendent claimed in 1908:

> Until very recently [the schools] have offered equal opportunity for all to receive *one kind* of education, but what will make them democratic is to provide opportunity for all to receive such education as will fit them *equally well* for their particular life work.[101]

The idea was that students would be sorted in junior high school into different courses according to their 'probable destinies'. Some of these courses would provide 'prevocational training' in commercial subjects, industrial arts, agricultural arts and household arts.[102] Vocational education was supposed to ensure that those who were not so gifted academically still had an opportunity to succeed in a trade or vocation through hard work.[103]

Schools became part of a legitimation system that reinforced the supposed link between merit and well-paid jobs. In practice, however, children from different social backgrounds were treated in different ways. Although this differentiation was supposed to be on the basis of ability, studies showed that already in the 1920s the social status of a child's parents 'played an enormous role in determining entrance to secondary school, the likelihood of remaining in school, and the curricula pursued within schools'.[104]

IQ tests were introduced after the First World War to ensure that differentiation was on the basis of individual intelligence. Army tests, developed during the war, purported to show that there was a correspondence between intelligence, as measured in the tests, and occupational achievement. Educators used these IQ tests to stream students according to their 'intelligence' and therefore their predicted niche in the occupational hierarchy.[105]

Such tests were used in every major American school between the world wars and a new profession, educational psychology, was established. Although subsequent research on IQ tests has shown them to be biased in favour of certain types and classes of people, these tests were used to reinforce the idea of a society stratified on the basis of merit rather than class, race or gender.[106] Different groups of students were streamed superficially according to IQ tests, ability and grades, but essentially according to predicted occupational expectations and the behavioural norms that need to be instilled.[107]

Today in the US, although education is becoming a more important determinant of status than family background, 'children of white-collar workers are almost twice as likely to end up in white-collar jobs as are children of blue-collar workers. And children from disadvantaged families are clearly more likely to do poorly in life.'[108]

Students in the US are also treated differently in different types of schools, as they are in Britain. At the lower levels of the educational system and in schools where students are predominantly from poor and working-class backgrounds, obedience to rules and ability to follow instructions are stressed. These mirror not only the types of workplace conditions to which their parents are accustomed but also those they are likely to experience themselves. Their parents tend to prefer this type of education as it reflects their own experience in the workplace, where they have found submission to authority is 'an essential ingredient in one's ability to get and hold a steady, well-paying job'.[109] Because of the emphasis on discipline, school tends to be unpleasant for many working-class children and they are keen to leave early. They then blame themselves when, in later years, their lack of schooling prevents them from getting well-paid, higher-status jobs or promotions.

In contrast, in the more affluent suburbs, where students are expected to fill higher-level jobs in the occupational hierarchy, schools tend to be more progressive, employing 'relatively open systems that favor greater student participation, less direct supervision, more student electives, and, in general, a value system stressing internalized standards of control'.[110]

These differences are reinforced by financial inequalities, so schools in poorer areas have larger class sizes, fewer resources, fewer course choices and fewer specialised teachers with less discretionary time to devote to students.[111] Harold Wenglinsky, in his study of eighth-graders in the US, found that the amount spent on schools for teaching and administration, per student, correlated with achievement in those schools mainly because of class size. The smaller the class, the higher the achievement.[112]

Similar differences can be found as one goes up the levels of education, since 'different levels of education feed workers into different levels within the occupational structure'. Higher education, for example, tends to stress more independence and freedom.[113] Over time, however, increasing numbers of technically skilled workers have been required in the workplace who will not be amongst the managers and decision makers at the top of the work hierarchy. These people require a tertiary education but educational processes appropriate for the elite are not considered suitable for them. This has led to a number of tertiary institutions that are vocationally oriented, such as technical institutes and two-year colleges.[114]

> The student is allowed little discretion in selecting courses. Systems of discipline and student management resemble those of secondary education more than those of the elite universities; these colleges have been called 'high schools with ashtrays'. The social relations of the community-college classroom increasingly resemble the formal, hierarchical impersonality of the office, of the uniform processing of the production line.[115]

The educational system serves not only to promote work as a value (see Chapter 11) but also to justify occupational status and income by a system of selection that is seen to be based on merit rather than class, race, ethnic background or gender. Educational credentials appear to depend on individual achievement so that 'bitterness arising from one's job or one's income or status is often directed against oneself rather than against a social system or those whose "success" was facilitated – if not predetermined – by that system'.[116]

CONCLUSION

Self-identification with one's occupational role, so important to the work ethic, requires people to feel that their occupational position is one they deserve. The work ethic promotes the idea that success in life depends on individual character, effort and educational qualifications that are based solely on merit. The school education system reinforces the idea that the distribution of status and wealth in society is fair because it is a system open to all and supposedly based on merit. Those unable to gain good educational qualifications are therefore intellectually inferior or lazy.

This is in fact not borne out by the reality. Schwarz notes that in 1989, after seven years of record economic growth, 'more than two thirds of all workers employed in year-round full-time jobs paying less than the base-line wage had graduated from high school, and more than a third had completed at least some postsecondary education'.[117]

> Skeptics may claim that these men and women, of every race and level of education, could and should have tried still harder than they did. Their will-

power and effort are not the real issue, though. They encountered a severe shortage of opportunity, totalling in the millions of adequate jobs.... Given the scarcity of opportunity, steady full-time work sustained over many years, coupled with a decent level of education, is not necessarily enough in this country to enable people managing frugally to attain a mainstream standard of living.[118]

In *The Culture of Contentment* John Kenneth Galbraith asserts that 'The first and most general expression of the contented majority is its affirmation that those who compose it are receiving their just deserts. What the individual member aspires to have and enjoy is the product of his or her personal virtue, intelligence and effort.'[119] Robert Lane observed in his study that those at the bottom of the social hierarchy also want to believe that the system is fair:

> The greater the strain on a person's self-esteem implied by a relatively low status in an open society, the greater the necessity to explain this status as 'natural' and 'proper' in the social order. Lower-status people generally find it less punishing to think of themselves as correctly placed by a just society than to think of themselves as exploited or victimized by an unjust society.[120]

Attributing individual causes to poverty and unemployment, such as lack of effort and education, serves several purposes. First, it causes people to work harder for fear of failing themselves, since failure is not only unpleasant in itself but carries with it the shame of not having enough character and diligence to succeed. Second, it excuses poverty and counters arguments for institutional change. Poverty is supposed to be a temporary phenomenon which can be escaped, especially by each new generation, through education, hard work and character. If there are not enough opportunities, however, then the poor cannot be blamed for failing to take advantage of them.

Stigmatisation of the poor also provides working people with scapegoats that distract attention from their own situation and from the structural and inherent inequalities in the economic system.[121]

> By this means, anti-poor sentiments help legitimize the existing class structure.... Anti-poor views depoliticize the society and forestall conflict by concentrating the attention of workers on the poor at the bottom, diverting the animosity of the bulk of workers downward rather than upward.[122]

NOTES

1 Robert E. Lane, *Political Ideology: Why the American Common Man Believes What He Does* (New York: The Free Press, 1962), p. 70.

2 Quoted in *ibid.*, p. 250.

3 Daniel Yankelovich and John Immerwahr, 'Putting the Work Ethic to Work', *Society*,

Vol. 21, No. 2 (1984), p. 58.

4 Ely Chinoy, *Automobile Workers and the American Dream* (Urbana and Chicago: University of Illinois Press, 1992), pp. 3, 6.

5 John W. Sloan, 'The Reagan Presidency, Growing Inequality, and the American Dream', *Policy Studies Journal*, Vol. 25 (Fall 1997).

6 Edward M. Kennedy, 'Can Workers Reclaim the American Dream?', *USA Today*, Vol. 125 (September 1996), p. 22.

7 John E. Schwarz, *Illusions of Opportunity: the American Dream in Question* (New York: W. W. Norton, 1997), p. 12.

8 Charles J. Whalen, 'The Age of Anxiety: Erosion of the American Dream', *USA Today*, Vol. 125 (September 1996).

9 Schwarz, note 7, pp. 66–8.

10 Clinton E. Boutwell, *Shell Game: Corporate America's Agenda for Schools* (Bloomington, Indiana: Phi Delta Kappa Educational Foundation, 1997), p. 31.

11 Juliet B. Schor, *The Overworked American: the Unexpected Decline in Leisure* (New York: Basic Books, 1991), p. 81.

12 Desiree Cooper, 'Whistle While You Work', (Metrobeat, 1997). http://www.cln.com/charlotte/newsstand/c090697/metro.htm.

13 Boutwell, note 10, pp. 54–5; Sloan, note 5.

14 'UNDP: Runaway Consumption Widens Gap Between Rich, Poor', *Go Between* (October/November 1998), p. 16.

15 Edward N. Wolff, 'How the Pie Is Sliced', *New Prospect*, Vol. 22 (Summer 1995).

16 Ross Gittins, 'Wrong Side of Great Divide', *Sydney Morning Herald*, 10 November 1999.

17 Brian Dean, 'The Puritan Work Ethic' (Anxiety Culture, 1999) www.anxcult.dircon.co.uk/puritan.htm.; Wolff, note 15.

18 Whalen, note 8; Sloan, note 5; Kennedy, note 6.

19 Boutwell, note 10, p. 33.

20 'From Rich to Richer, They Bathe in New Guilded Age', *The Dominion* (8 October 1999).

21 Sloan, note 5.

22 Quoted in Anthony Sampson, *Company Man: the Rise and Fall of Corporate Life* (London: HarperCollinsBusiness, 1996), p. 253.

23 René Morissette, 'Why Has Inequality in Weekly Earnings Increased in Canada?' (Ottawa: Statistics Canada, 1995).

24 Tom Allard, 'Record Profit, Wages Rising, Jobs Better', *Sydney Morning Herald*, 21 May 1999; Paul Sheehan, 'Welcome to the Dog Years', *Sydney Morning Herald*, 4 September 1999, p. 3s; Adele Horin, 'All Work, Low Pay', *Sydney Morning Herald*, 27 December 1997, p. 6s.

25 Malcolm Brown, 'Young Men Poorer than Fathers Were', *Sydney Morning Herald*, 12 December 1998.

26 Elizabeth Sexton, 'Young, Hip and a Big Spender', *Sydney Morning Herald*, 4 September 1999, p. 65; Adele Horin, 'The Lucky (Few) Country', *Sydney Morning Herald*, 24 July 1999.

27 Michael Raper, 'State Isn't Doing a Good Job', *The Australian*, 4 August 1999, p. 13.

28 Department of Social Security, 'Opportunity for All: Tackling Poverty and Social Exclusion' (Department of Social Security, 1999), p. 1.

29 Alistair Darling, 'Speech at the Launch of the Government's First Annual Report on Tackling Poverty' (Department of Social Security, 1999). http://www.dss.gov.uk/hq/press/1999/sep99/povspeech.htm.

30 Suzanne Franks, *Having None of It: Women, Men and the Future of Work* (London: Granta

Books, 1999), pp. 41, 176.

31 Sloan, note 5.

32 Schwarz, note 7, p. 92; Boutwell, note 10, p. 32.

33 T. R. Martin, 'In Pursuit of Happiness: Sources of American Discontent', *Commonweal*, Vol. 123 (23 February 1996).

34 Boutwell, note 10, p. 61.

35 Sheehan, note 24; 'The State of Greed', *US News and World Report*, Vol. 120 (17 June 1996); 'Executive Decisions', *Multinational Monitor* (March 1998), p. 5; Joanna Coles, 'Corporate High-flyers in a League of Their Own', *Sydney Morning Herald*, 13 April 1998.

36 *Ibid.*

37 Padraic Flanagan and Brendan Berry, 'Boss Pockets $44m While Sacked Car Workers Face the Scrap Heap', *Sydney Morning Herald*, 2 February 1999.

38 'Executive Decisions', note 35, p. 5; 'The House of the Mouse', *New Internationalist* (December 1998), p. 19.

39 Chuck Colson and Jack Eckerd, *Why America Doesn't Work* (Dallas: Word Publishing, 1991), p. 23.

40 'Fat Cats of Business Lick up All the Cream', *Sydney Morning Herald* (24 July 1998).

41 Quoted in Gerard Henderson, 'The Taint of Class Is Back', *Sydney Morning Herald*, 7 April 1998.

42 Leon Gettler, 'Local CEOs Paid Well, but US Is Way Ahead', *Sydney Morning Herald*, 13 August 1998.

43 Tom Allard, 'Big Gulf between Rich and Poor', *Sydney Morning Herald*, 3 July 1998, p. 3.

44 Joseph L. DeVitis and John Martin Rich, *The Success Ethic, Education, and the American Dream* (Albany, NY: State University of New York Press, 1996), pp. 28–9.

45 *Ibid.*, p. 29.

46 FAIR, 'ABC News Gives up on Accuracy' (New York: FAIR, 1999).

47 United Nations Children's Fund report, 'The Progress of Nations', cited in DeVitis and Rich, note 44, pp. 173–4.

48 Tom Waters, 'Chesson's Choice', *New Internationalist* (March 1999), p. 16.

49 Whalen, note 8.

50 'The Mall of Dreams', *The Economist*, Vol. 339 (4 May 1996), p. 23.

51 *Ibid.*, p. 23.

52 Quoted in Newt Gingrich, 'Renewing America', *Newsweek*, Vol. 126 (10 July 1995).

53 Ray D. Dearin, 'The American Dream as Depicted in Robert J Dole's 1996 Presidential Nomination Acceptance Speech', *Presidential Studies Quarterly*, Vol. 27 (Fall 1997).

54 Bernard Woolley, 'Let the Good Times Roll', *60 Minutes*, 5 September 1999.

55 *Good Weekend*, 28 March 1998.

56 James D. Bell, 'Working and Living: What "Track" Are You On?', *Vital Speeches of the Day*, Vol. 63, No. 13 (1997).

57 Sheehan, note 24, p. 4s.

58 Bill Walsh, 'Let 'em See You Sweat', *Forbes* (5 December 1994). 15.

59 Brent Schlender, 'On the Road with Chairman Bill', *Fortune*, Vol. 135 (26 May 1997).

60 David Griffiths, *Whither Work* (Bundoora: Preston Institute of Technology Press, 1977), p. 1.

61 Adrian Furnham, *The Protestant Work Ethic: the Psychology of Work-related Beliefs and Behaviours* (London: Routledge, 1990), pp. 176–83.

62 *Ibid.*, p. 179.

63 Adele Horin, 'Working but Poor: How 460,000 Battle', *Sydney Morning Herald*, 25 July 1998.

64 Franks, note 30, p. 177.

65 Barrie Stevens and Wolfgang Michalski, 'Long-term Prospects for Work and Social Co-hesion in OECD Countries: an Overview of the Issues', in Stevens and Michalski, *OECD Societies in Transition: the Future of Work and Leisure* (Paris: OECD, 1994), p. 18.

66 Boutwell, note 10, pp. 51, 66.

67 Joe R. Feagin, *Subordinating the Poor* (Englewood Cliffs, NJ: Prentice–Hall, 1975), p. 97.

68 Stanley Feldman, 'Economic Individualism and American Public Opinion', *American Politics Quarterly*, Vol. 11, No. 1 (1983), p. 12.

69 Marlene Kim, 'The Working Poor: Lousy Jobs or Lazy Workers?', *Journal of Economic Issues*, Vol. 32, No. 1 (1998).

70 Brotherhood of St Laurence, 'Why So Harsh on the Unemployed? A Second Discussion Paper' (Fitzroy, Victoria: Brotherhood of St Laurence, 1974), pp. 1, 28.

71 Quoted in Lydia Morris, *Dangerous Classes: the Underclass and Social Citizenship* (London: Routledge, 1994), p. 58.

72 Quoted in Feagin, note 67, p. 3.

73 Quoted in *ibid.*, p. 4.

74 Gingrich, note 52.

75 Quoted in David Corn, 'Welfare, Inc.', *The Nation*, Vol. 264 (5 May 1997).

76 Alan Reid, 'Life of Ease on $51 a Week', *The Bulletin* (19 June 1979), p. 38.

77 Gabrielle Lord, 'Life in the CES Pool', *The National Times*, 30 December – 6 January 1984, pp. 12–13.

78 Alan Jordan, 'Long Term Unemployed People Under Conditions of Full Employment' (Canberra: Commission of Inquiry into Poverty, 1975), p. 36.

79 Feagin, note 67, p. 104.

80 Furnham, note 61, p. 182.

81 Quoted in Janice Peterson, "Ending Welfare As We Know It': the Symbolic Importance of Welfare Policy in America', *Journal of Economic Issues*, Vol. 31, No. 2 (1997).

82 Education and Training House of Representatives Standing Commitee on Employment, 'Youth Employment: a Working Solution' (Canberra: Parliament of the Commonwealth of Australia, 1997), p. 20.

83 Gale Miller, *Enforcing the Work Ethic: Rhetoric and Everyday Life in a Work Incentive Program* (Albany, NY: State University of New York Press, 1991), pp. 49–51, 53, 199.

84 Lane, note 1, pp. 69–71.

85 *Ibid.*, p. 70.

86 Cath Blakers, 'School to Work: Transition and Policy', in Milicent Poole (ed.), *Education and Work* (Hawthorn, Victoria: Australian Council for Educational Research, 1992), p. 56.

87 David K. Cohen and Marvin Lazerson, 'Education and the Corporate Order', in Michael B. Katz (ed.), *Education in American History: Readings on the Social Issues* (New York: Praeger, 1973), p. 319.

88 *Ibid.*, p. 321.

89 Shane J. Blackman, 'The Labour Market in School: New Vocationalism and Issues of Socially Ascribed Discrimination', in P. Brown and D. N. Ashton (eds), *Education, Unemployment and Labour Markets* (London: The Falmer Press, 1987), p. 29.

90 G. H. Elder, 'Social Class Influence 3', in Eric Butterworth and David Weir (eds), *The Sociology of Modern Britain* (London: Fontana/Collins, 1970), pp. 121–4.

91 Philip Cohen, 'Teaching Enterprise Culture: Individualism, Vocationalism and the New Right', in Ian Taylor (ed.), *The Social Effects of Free Market Policies: an International Text* (New York: Harvester Wheatsheaf, 1990), pp. 52–3.

92 Ralph Miliband, *The State in Capitalist Society* (London: Quartet Books, 1969), p. 216.

93 Tony Watson, *Sociology, Work and Industry* (London: Routledge and Kegan Paul, 1987), p. 190.

94 Cited in *ibid.*, p. 190.

95 R. W. Connell, *Ruling Class Ruling Culture: Studies of Conflict, Power and Hegemony in Australian Life* (Cambridge: Cambridge University Press, 1977), p. 158.

96 *Ibid.*, pp. 152–3, 163.

97 Nadia Jamal, 'Rich Avoid Work Subjects', *Sydney Morning Herald*, 28 December 1998.

98 Adele Horin, 'It's a Recipe for a Poorly Educated Underclass', *Sydney Morning Herald*, 16 October 1999.

99 Quoted in Cohen and Lazerson, note 87, p. 323.

100 Arthur C. Wirth, 'Issues in the Vocational–Liberal Studies Controversy (1900–1917): John Dewey vs The Social Efficiency Philosophers', in David Corson (ed.), *Education for Work: Background to Policy and Curriculum* (New Zealand: Dunmore Press, 1988), p. 57.

101 Quoted in Cohen and Lazerson, note 87, p. 331.

102 Wirth, note 100, p. 57.

103 DeVitis and Rich, note 44, p. 6.

104 Cohen and Lazerson, note 87, p. 331.

105 *Ibid.*, p. 321.

106 *Ibid.*, pp. 321, 332.

107 Samuel Bowles and Herbert Gintis, *Schooling in Capitalist America: Educational Reform and the Contradictions of Economic Life* (New York: Basic Books, 1976), p. 132.

108 Cynthia G. Wagner, 'Making It in America: Education Trumps Background in Determining Status', *The Futurist*, Vol. 32, No. 1 (1998), pp. 16–17.

109 Bowles and Gintis, note 107, pp. 132–3.

110 *Ibid.*, p. 132.

111 Bowles and Gintis, note 107, p. 133.

112 Harold Wenglinsky, 'How Money Matters: the Effect of School District Spending on Academic Achievement', *Sociology of Education*, Vol. 70, No. 3 (1997).

113 Bowles and Gintis, note 107, p. 132.

114 Samuel Bowles, 'The Integration of Higher Education into the Wage-Labor System', in Michael B. Katz (ed.), *Education in American History: Readings on the Social Issues* (New York: Praeger, 1973), p. 149.

115 *Ibid.*, p. 151.

116 *Ibid.*, p. 145.

117 Schwarz, note 7, p. 75.

118 *Ibid.*, p. 79.

119 John Kenneth Galbraith, *The Culture of Contentment* (London: Penguin, 1992), p. 18.

120 Lane, note 1, p. 79.

121 Feagin, note 67, pp. 120–1.

122 *Ibid.*, p. 121.

PART II

Motivating Work –
Coercion and Persuasion

✦6✦

Increasing Productivity

————

Now one of the very first requirements for a man who is fit to handle pig iron as a regular occupation is that he shall be so stupid and so phlegmatic that he more nearly resembles in his mental make-up the ox than any other type.
Frederick Winslow Taylor, 1911 [1]

Most people like hard work. Particularly when they're paying for it.
Franklin P. Jones [2]

The idea of work as virtue has had to be continually reinforced. The work of an industrial worker can be unpleasant, boring, repetitious, and even dangerous. George Orwell described the hell of working in a coal mine:

The time to go there is when the machines are roaring and the air is black with coal dust, and when you can actually see what the miners have to do. At those times the place is like hell. Most of the things one imagines in hell are there – heat, noise, confusion, darkness, foul air, and, above all, unbearably cramped space. Everything except the fire, for there is no fire down there except the feeble beams of Davy lamps and electric torches which scarcely penetrate the clouds of coal dust. [3]

Industrialisation required an obedient and hard-working labour force, yet factory routines and division of labour made work increasingly meaningless and unbearable, undermining the work ethic. Hours in factories were long and the work was tedious. Work for many people came to be seen as something to be endured in order to earn a living; a matter of serving time rather than producing finished goods. As work approximates slavery, the value of a work ethic declines. [4]

Factories facilitated the subdivision of work, which increased production. The example of pin manufacture used by Adam Smith in his *Wealth of Nations* (1776) is now well known. He argued that by dividing the task of producing each pin into a number of sub-tasks, ten men could produce 48,000 pins in the time that they would have produced 10 pins if they had been working individually.[5] In 1832 Charles Babbage wrote about how parts of a skilled job could be separated off and given to unskilled workers who required little training, leaving the skilled worker with a reduced task that could be done more quickly. This reduced labour costs since unskilled workers were paid less; it also reduced the employer's dependence on skilled workers, who had more bargaining power than the average worker.[6]

It was difficult to get any sense of satisfaction or feel any pride in work that was so reduced that the worker felt like little more than a cog in a machine. There was little scope for individual discretion or ability. Nineteenth-century office work was often little better and the bleakness has been described by numerous authors from Charles Dickens in *Sketches by Boz* to Herman Melville in *Bartelby The Scrivener*[7] and, in the early twentieth century, Sinclair Lewis in *Our Mr Wrenn*.[8]

Karl Marx described the way workers were alienated from their work:

> What constitutes the alienation of labour? First that the work is external to the worker, that it is not part of his nature; and that, consequently, he does not fulfill himself in his work but denies himself, has a feeling of misery rather than well-being, does not develop freely his mental and physical energies but is physically exhausted and mentally debased.... It is not the satisfaction of a need, but only a means for satisfying other needs. Its alien character is clearly shown by the fact that as soon as there is no physical or other compulsion it is avoided like the plague. Finally, the external character of work for the worker is shown by the fact that it is not his own work but work for someone else, that in work he does not belong to himself but to another person.[9]

Work, for the vast majority of people in the nineteenth century, offered neither intrinsic satisfaction nor a route to success. Salaries seldom depended on how hard a person worked and there was little chance of promotion out of the boredom of factory or lowly office work.

> Industrialization upset the certainty that hard work would bring economic success. Whatever the life chances of a farmer or shop hand had been in the early years of the century, it became troublingly clear that the semi-skilled labourer, caught in the anonymity of a late-nineteenth-century textile factory or steel mill, was trapped in his circumstances – that no amount of sheer hard work would open the way to self-employment or wealth.[10]

Despite all the reinforcement of the work ethic, workers in the late nineteenth and early twentieth centuries often displayed a healthy disrespect for their work, not turning up to work regularly, not staying at boring jobs for long, and not obeying orders. So employers, unable to rely on a work ethic to motivate workers, had to find other ways to get them to work hard. A variety of professionals offered solutions to this problem, especially engineers, psychologists and sociologists.

ENGINEERS AND SCIENTIFIC MANAGEMENT

As work in factories was becoming increasingly divided and fragmented and companies grew into large-scale joint stock companies, professional managers increasingly took over the running of the companies from the capitalist owners. These professional managers sought to rationalise production and increase the company's competitiveness. At the same time they had to deal with union disquiet and large numbers of untrained rural people pouring into the cities and into their workforces.[11]

The aim of engineers and industrial managers working for these firms in the later part of the nineteenth century and first part of the twentieth century was to find ways to control dissatisfied workers and ensure their productivity. Frederick Winslow Taylor was one of several engineers experimenting with ways of speeding up production. He invented scientific management, the 'most conscious and systematic expression of the existing trends in the organization of work'.[12] Taylor came from a well-to-do Quaker/Puritan family. He was well endowed with a Protestant work ethic, lived an ascetic lifestyle, and considered work 'as the greatest blessing which we have'. He applied to his own life the schedules, routines and scientific management that he sought to introduce into the workplace.[13]

Taylor's study of scientific management was aimed at overcoming the workers' lack of work ethic, which resulted in high rates of absenteeism and workers doing as little work as they could get away with. This was referred to as 'soldiering' in the US, 'hanging it out' in England and 'ca canae' in Scotland. Taylor claimed that 'this constitutes the greatest evil with which the working-people of both England and America are now afflicted'.[14] To combat it he sought to reduce the discretion available to workers about how they did their work and thereby increase their productivity.

The way that most managers at the time tried to increase productivity was to offer incentives to work harder, such as payment according to how much a worker produced (piece rates).[15] Taylor's scientific management was, he argued, a more certain way of improving productivity which did not rely on individual workers chasing incentives. Scientific management was based, according to Taylor in *Principles of Scientific Management* (1911), on four principles:[16]

1 The most efficient way of doing a task should be worked out scientifically using experiment and time and motion studies.
2 Workers should be carefully selected and trained to do the work in this way.
3 Workers should do their work under the close supervision and control of management and be paid a bonus for doing exactly as they had been told.
4 Management should take over the planning and thinking part of the work.

Scientific management could increase productivity by two or sometimes even three times, argued Taylor, requiring a smaller and therefore cheaper workforce.[17] There was at the same time a growth in clerks, office workers and lower levels of management to plan and schedule work, order and maintain equipment, and supervise the workers.[18] Taylor argued that the thinking part of the work could be better carried out by more intelligent and educated people sitting at desks and that the sort of person who did the planning and thinking should be a quite different sort of person from the one who actually did the work.[19] He said:

> The managers assume, for instance, the burden of gathering together all the traditional knowledge which in the past has been possessed by the workmen and then of classifying, tabulating, and reducing this knowledge to rules, laws, and formulæ which are immensely helpful to the workmen in doing their daily work.[20]

All the workers needed to do was follow instructions about what to do, how to do it and how much time to spend doing it. Their cooperation was enforced through close monitoring and control by management.[21] Taylor had little respect for the thinking abilities of the manual worker. He described the work of handling pig iron:

> This work is so crude and elementary in its nature that the writer firmly believes that it would be possible to train an intelligent gorilla so as to become a more efficient pig-iron handler than any man can be. Yet it will be shown that the science of handling pig-iron is so great and amounts to so much that it is impossible for the man who is best suited to this type of work to understand the principles of this science, or even to work in accordance with these principles without the aid of a man better educated than he is.[22]

Selecting the right sort of workers was an essential part of the scheme. Taylor managed to get a carefully chosen man to handle 47.5 tons of pig iron a day. Even using his scientific methods, however, seven out of eight of the men employed as pig-iron handlers could not meet this output and were shifted to other work or dismissed.[23] Taylor argued that the type of man who could shift this amount of pig iron in a day was 'no rare specimen of humanity, difficult to find and therefore very highly prized. On the contrary, he was a man so stupid that he was unfitted to do most kinds of laboring work, even.'[24]

When he applied his methods to a bicycle ball-bearing factory, Taylor admitted that this scientific management 'involved laying off many of the most intelligent, hardest-working, and most trustworthy girls merely because they did not possess the quality of quick perception followed by quick action'.[25] In this factory he eliminated the play and talk between the women, seating them out of talking distance from one another.

In reducing the activity of workers to the bare necessities of the task in hand and removing any thought or skill from that task, Taylor removed the more desirable and challenging parts of the work and made it monotonous, tedious and unremittingly boring. He recognised that 'The man who is mentally alert and intelligent is for this very reason entirely unsuited to what would, for him, be the grinding monotony of work of this character.'[26] But he argued that the unskilled worker was not harmed by the monotonous work because he was stupid. Not all engineers were convinced by this argument however. An editorial in *The Engineer* stated: 'We do not hesitate to say that Taylorism is inhuman. As far as possible it dehumanizes the man, for it endeavours to remove the only distinction that makes him better than a machine – his intelligence.'[27]

Scientific management was a key development leading to the eradication of the 'surviving remnants of ancient work values'.[28] As Ed Andrew points out in *Closing the Iron Cage*,

> The skilled artisan who had oiled and repaired his machine, tightened its belting, adjusted the speed and cutting angle of his machine and ground his own tools became, after Taylor's innovations, a semi-skilled machine operative mechanically executing the directions of the planning department.... Thus the varied work of skilled machinists who made their own tools and were attached to the machine whose operations they determined was transformed into a standardized function of a replaceable unit within the machine shop.[29]

Any pride that workers might have felt in their work was destroyed as tasks were broken up and any individuality removed from manual work. Taylor failed to recognise that this deskilling was a major reason for the industrial unrest scientific management was causing. He believed that scientific management could solve the conflict between employers and workers by maximising the profits for employers and raising the wages of workers, so that everyone would be happy.[30]

SCIENTIFIC MANAGEMENT WIDELY ADOPTED

At the time that 'The Principles of Scientific Management' was published in 1911, Taylor claimed that more than 50,000 workers were subject to scientific management in the US. The paper was translated into French, German, Dutch, Swedish, Russian, Lettish, Chinese, Hindi, Italian, Spanish and

Japanese within two years of publication. Owing to union resistance, however, scientific management did not flourish until the First World War, 'when restriction of output and class warfare were considered treasonable' and many non-unionised women were brought into the workforce to replace men away at war.[31]

Henry Ford, who introduced the mass production of cars, adopted Taylor's methods but took them further with the use of machines to replace some of the tasks performed by workers.[32] Most famous of these was the introduction of a moving conveyor belt in his factories which provided an extension to Taylor's methods. Instead of workers moving from car to car at their own pace, the belt moved the cars to the workers at a speed set by management, helping to speed up the flow of work and make it difficult for workers to 'soldier'. In this way Ford removed another element of discretion from workers' jobs and thereby reduced his reliance on workers' motivation.

Ford also broke jobs down into very small parts so that each worker only performed a few movements over and over. As one observer noted of a Ford factory in the 1930s:

> Every employee seemed to be restricted to a well-defined jerk, twist, spasm or quiver resulting in a fliver. I never thought it possible that human beings could be reduced to such perfect automats.
>
> I looked constantly for the wire or belt concealed about their bodies which kept them in motion with such marvellous clock-like precision. I failed to discover how the motive power is transmitted to these people and it don't seem reasonable that human beings would willingly consent to being simplified into jerks, I assume that their wives wind them up while asleep.[33]

Ford, like Taylor, had a rather low opinion of the worker on his assembly lines:

> The average worker, I am sorry to say, wants a job in which he does not have to think. Those who have what might be called the creative type of mind and who thoroughly abhor monotony are apt to imagine that all other minds are similarly restless and therefore to extend quite unwanted sympathy to the labouring man who day in and day out performs almost exactly the same operation.[34]

Taylor's innovations, together with those of Ford, destroyed the tradition of having pride in one's work for twentieth-century factory workers, and absenteeism and high worker turnover was the inevitable response to the unfulfilling boredom of work. During 1913, for example, 50,000 workers left Ford from a total workforce of 13,000–14,000.[35] So even though it was cheap to train an individual worker, the high turnover rate meant that total training costs were very high.[36]

To overcome this problem Henry Ford experimented with shorter working hours and extra pay, and had some success with decreasing the length of the work day from ten to nine hours and changing pay and promotion systems. In 1914 he more than doubled the pay of workers to $5 per day. The idea was to motivate the workers and ensure loyalty, since this was far more pay than other companies were paying at the time. Absenteeism and turnover dropped, the workers became much more docile and Henry Ford declared that the decision was 'one of the finest cost-cutting moves we ever made'.[37]

To ensure that workers did not use the extra money in a degenerate way, Ford established a 'Sociological Department' which consisted of 'investigators' who visited workers' homes 'to make sure that no one was drinking too much, that everyone's sex life was without blemish, that leisure time was profitably spent, that no boarders were taken in, that houses were clean and neat, and so on'. If the investigators were unsatisfied, the worker could lose his five dollars a day until he again qualified through 'proper living'.[38]

After the First World War former allies and foes alike sent deputations to the US to learn about scientific management. The Harvard School of Business Administration incorporated it 'as a central feature of its curriculum'.[39] Scientific management was adopted by companies throughout the US, Britain and Europe and even promoted in the Soviet Union by Lenin. It was taken up rapidly in France but adopted more slowly in Britain and Germany, where it met with union resistance and some management resistance. By the end of the 1930s, however, similar management strategies had been widely adopted in most European countries.[40] Australian employers implemented scientific management increasingly after the First World War and a delegation of employers and trade unionists, led by enthusiast Prime Minister Stanley Bruce, visited the US in 1926 to learn more about Taylor's methods.[41]

In the US, Westinghouse Electric became an enthusiastic promoter of scientific management, causing its adoption by companies that had business links with Westinghouse, including Siemens in Germany and Mitsubishi Electric in Japan. The spread of American multinational firms into other countries also aided the diffusion of scientific management. Ford, for example, set up subsidiaries in Britain, Germany and Japan. Car companies competing with Ford adopted his methods, including Citroën in France, Toyota in Japan and General Motors in the US, Britain, Germany and Japan.[42]

It was Taylor's separation of mental and manual labour that became characteristic of mass production methods in the twentieth century. The influence of Taylor and Ford is still evident in many factories today – particularly in mass production in the US and Britain. It is manifest in the job fragmentation, minimal skill and training requirements, maximum repetition, separation of thinking and doing, and the lack of variety in workers' jobs.[43] Observers at a Texas Levi Strauss jeans factory in 1995 reported: 'In our tour of the plant, we were struck by the minute segmentation of operations. Six different sewing machine operators, each doing one simple task, were needed to sew a pocket onto the pants. And most operators did the same task, hour after hour, day after day, year after year.'[44] In his book *The McDonaldization of Society*, George Ritzer argues that modern fast food restaurants operate in this way with work being 'highly rationalized, geared to discover the most efficient way to grill a hamburger, fry chicken, or serve a meal'. Workers repeat the same simple tasks over and over like robots, have no scope to show initiative or innovation, and utilise a small portion of their capabilities.[45]

SOCIAL SCIENTISTS

The success that Taylor had in demonstrating to managers the importance of the human element in productivity led to the entry of psychologists into the field who argued they could also help in raising productivity and increasing the efficiency of work. Thus the profession of industrial psychology was born.[46] Early industrial psychologists argued that they could help managers select workers with the appropriate qualities for a particular job and that they could also select those who would work harder – but early selection tests, developed before the First World War, were not particularly successful.[47]

Social scientists working for industry in the 1930s and 1940s advocated methods of motivating work values that focused on interpersonal relationships and morale – the 'Human Relations approach'.[48] Basically it was about being nice to workers on the assumptions:

1 That a certain *style* or *manner* of supervision and of reaching decisions with subordinates (variously called friendly, democratic, participatory, consultative, considerate, team-oriented, etc.) will greatly increase the moral and satisfaction of workers; and

2 That the happier, or more satisfied, a worker is (e.g., in his social relations with his work group) the harder he will work.[49]

Eminent sociologist Daniel Bell has called the work of Elton Mayo and the Human Relations school 'cow sociology' because it aims to make the workers content and satisfied so they will produce more.[50]

The idea of inducing hard work through gratitude was not new. Various corporations introduced 'welfare' programmes in the second half of the nineteenth century in Britain and in the early part of the twentieth century in Japan and many other parts of the world. In the US, companies such as Eastman Kodak, the National Cash Register Company, United States Steel, International Harvester and Sears Roebuck introduced such programmes,[51] sometimes alongside Taylor's scientific methods, sometimes as an alternative to scientific management.

The 'welfare' programmes were superficially aimed at taking care of workers and providing them with facilities and services, but their agenda was to get the workers to work harder and to counter the gains being made by the unions. The idea was to develop feelings of appreciation and loyalty in employees by looking after them so they would want to work harder. The programmes offered pension plans, medical services, libraries, gymnasiums and recreational activities, including classes in language and civics:[52] 'The content of these classes was mainly oriented towards industrial discipline.'[53]

Welfare capitalism had some limited success in increasing worker productivity.[54] Some workers saw through it as being just a means of buying them off with trivial benefits.[55] Another means of getting employees on side and countering unions was to have mechanisms for employee representation. Goodyear Tire and Rubber Company established a pseudo-parliamentary structure for employee representation which it then publicised heavily. Other schemes involved employee work councils and company-funded 'unions'. One estimate was that almost 500 companies in the US instituted some form of employee representation in the 1920s.[56] Such plans tended to be token gestures that had little to do with shared power or employer concessions and much more to do with gaining employee cooperation.

The Human Relations approach was given scientific recognition following a series of experiments carried out at the Hawthorn Works of the Western Electric Company in the 1920s. It had been commonly assumed at the time that the productivity of workers was influenced by the physical conditions in which they worked. In experiments on how lighting affected workers, however, it was found that whether the level of lighting was increased or decreased, the workers still increased their productivity.[57]

A subsequent set of experiments on a group of six female workers at the Hawthorn Works, under the direction of Australian Elton Mayo, found that every change – in rest breaks, working hours, pay regimes – produced increased productivity. The experiments caused the scientists to 'shift their attention away from the psycho-physical aspects of work towards social factors'. The reason for the workers' increased production was explained by the fact that the women had become a group, a cohesive and stable social unit that thought well of management because they had been specially selected by it and were consulted about the changes throughout the experiments.[58]

Further experiments confirmed the importance of group dynamics to individual worker productivity and indicated that this could be far more significant than the individual characteristics that industrial psychologists had been concentrating on.[59] Social rewards were seen to be more important than economic incentives in winning the cooperation of these informal groups. This finding brought sociologists into the service of employers.

Sociologists noted that whilst groups could work to benefit management they could also work against management goals. In particular the phenomenon of soldiering that Taylor had observed was enforced by groups. A study of telephone electricians revealed that they had worked out their own standard for what was a fair day's work and that this level was well below their full capacity. Their standard was enforced on all fourteen members of the group and those not adhering were ostracised and punished.[60]

The widespread practice of soldiering increased during the Depression, when workers tried to make their jobs last as long as possible for fear of being laid off. Soldiering was also a way in which workers could control their work in the face of management pressures to work as fast and hard as possible.[61] Social scientists sought to redirect group pressures to benefit management: 'People often expend more energy in attempting to defeat management's objectives than they would in achieving them. The important question is not how to get people to expend energy, but how to get them to expend it in one direction rather than another.'[62] Industrial psychologist Alex Carey claimed that 'Until at least 1955 the Human Relations movement consisted mainly of a search for techniques of persuasion through which … group pressures could be fostered and made to work in the service for management.'[63]

HUMAN RELATIONS AFTER THE SECOND WORLD WAR

After the Second World War worker morale seemed to be at an all-time low in the US and productivity had fallen: it was down 34 per cent at Ford Motor Company from 1941, and down 37 per cent at General Motors.[64] Surveys showed that large numbers of workers were not satisfied with their jobs. One showed that almost half of the factory workers surveyed were dissatisfied compared to a third during the Depression.[65] Fewer than half believed that the benefits of hard work were worth the effort and many 'who felt that they only received the "crumbs" had little incentive to work hard'.[66] The soul-destroying nature of work under scientific management often meant that workers were hostile to and distrustful of management, alienated from their work, and resentful of their situation. All this made control and discipline difficult to exercise and quality output difficult to achieve.[67]

Employers complained of increasing absenteeism and that workers didn't feel obliged to provide a 'fair day's work for a fair day's pay'. Managers believed that a lack of morale was affecting productivity and a number instituted attitude surveys to find the cause. Psychological testing made a big comeback and some common tests were mass-produced. Human relations approaches made an even bigger comeback, offering as they did a way to create more contented employees who would be more productive.[68]

Various business journals such as *Factory* and *American Business* advocated the Human Relations approach as the only way to get workers to cooperate. Courses and articles on Human Relations proliferated. Firms gave recognition to good employees with awards and prizes, and acknowledged individual workers with birthday cards.[69] Foremen were given leadership courses so that their relations with other workers could be improved and they could better motivate them. A 1951 study that showed that Human Relations was being taught in 96 per cent of US companies to foremen and that it was given primary emphasis in 57 per cent of these training courses.[70]

Unions remained somewhat cynical and, at Ford, downright satirical:

> The profit possibilities of human engineering, as it is called by Henry Ford II, are fantastic. As the result of this discovery, foreman are attending schools throughout the country to receive training in the art of convincing workers that they really are deeply beloved by the boss.
>
> Employers are trooping to special classes at Harvard, where they learn workers are not the least bit mercenary, and that while it is true that the boss is in business for an honest, or at least a fast, dollar, workers report to the plant each morning for love, affection, and small friendly attentions.[71]

Human relations became an important strategy in the battle to get the most out of workers and to combat the unions. According to Carey, 'vast amounts of money suddenly became available' for this sort of research.[72] Companies such as Esso embraced it: 'the biggest competitive advantage that Esso can gain lies in continuing to build initiative, cooperation, and the will to work within our people'. Whilst it would have been expensive for Esso to compete with other firms on the basis of worker benefits and wages, motivation by Human Relations seemed to offer 'limitless' possibilities for increased productivity and therefore competitive advantage.[73]

The Human Relations approach emphasised participation of employees, and worker democracy, because it was believed that participation would motivate workers to be better workers through increased morale, decreased resistance to company authority, and a fuller sense of involvement and belonging. And indeed many companies found that limited employee participation did result in increases in productivity, reductions in costs, more willingness to change, better acceptance of restrictions, and fewer grievances against management.[74]

> Atlantic Refining was most explicit. The advantage of participation, according to this company, was that an individual tended to accept the decisions of a group of which he was a member. Group pressures were so relentless that, regardless of personal convictions, conformity to a group decision was virtually guaranteed.[75]

Researchers Lester Coch and John French, who undertook some classic studies with women at Harwood Manufacturing Corporation in Virginia, argued that allowing workers to participate in designing their jobs overcame worker hostility toward management and made it 'possible for management to modify greatly or remove completely group resistance to change in methods of work and ensuing piece rates. This change can be accomplished by the use of group meetings in which management effectively communicates the need for change and stimulates group participation in planning the changes.'[76]

In Britain labour–management cooperation went under the title of 'joint consultation'. Committees of workers and management discussed working hours, holidays, dismissal procedures, safety and accidents, work conditions and – far less frequently – training and promotion prospects.[77]

In both the US and Britain worker participation tended to be illusory. Companies were reluctant to make any real changes or to restructure either the company organisation or the decision-making hierarchy. Often the 'participation' was limited to suggestion schemes or consultation with employees on decisions that affected them, so that they would feel as if their wishes and ideas had been taken into account.[78]

One academic who studied a company system of participation decided that the aim was 'to get the workers to accept what management wants them to accept *but* to make them feel *they* made or helped to make the decision'.[79] Another noted that 'the decisions to which the workers were said to have assented in democratic discussion had been reached by management in advance.... There is the danger of confusing democratic procedure with the manipulation of groups by persuasion that retains only the external forms of freedom.'[80]

The Human Relations approach was also aimed at ensuring workers were less vulnerable to persuasion by union organisers. Indeed, some firms were using foremen as a counter to union influence. Lukens Steel Company, for example, 'instructed foremen to compete with the union steward for worker allegiance by personally greeting each employee every day and by providing a sympathetic ear for on-and-off the job problems'. At other firms, foremen were given counselling instruction and at General Electric they were given a manual with answers to objections workers might raise to their working conditions.[81]

Peter Drucker stated in a paper to the American Management Association that 'Most of us in management' had implemented Human Relations reforms 'as a means of busting the unions.... They are based on the belief that if you have good employee relations the union will wither on the vine.'[82] In a 1953 book entitled *Motivation and Morale in Industry* a leading industrial psychologist, Morris Viteles, claimed that the three great needs of industry were to increase production, 'promote employee satisfaction and adjustment at work' and to 'prevent industrial strife'.[83]

The façade of participation that was part of the Human Relations approach was also thought to be an effective counter against unions. Viteles cited a study purporting to show that where foremen were active in involving the workers but the union stewards were not, the workers were more likely to take a management point of view, and vice versa. He concluded that 'any management which wants its employees to be management-minded must take steps to provide the opportunity for and to encourage active participation by workers in arriving at decisions pertaining to the work process and to the work situation'.[84] Some companies, such as a subsidiary of Bethlehem Steel, found that participation 'actually converted radical workers into "sound" management-oriented employees'.[85]

SIDING WITH MANAGEMENT

C. Wright Mills noted that social scientists readily took up the management viewpoint in their studies, applying their research to the problem of 'how to secure the cooperation of people in attaining' the purposes of the business or industry. Quoting from a major text of the time, he showed that their Human Relations approach was asymmetrical. Orders were to be transmitted down the organisation and information transmitted up. Therefore those at the bottom needed to 'understand the economic objectives of the top' and those at the top needed to 'understand the feelings and sentiments at the bottom'.[86] Mills concluded:

> there seems to be a technicalization of the manager, and a sentimentalization of the employee.... The problem is thus put in terms of technological advance-ment, as a problem of the engineer and the human being, rather than in terms of human beings in power and economic relations. The issue between manager and worker is thus seen as a vast misunderstanding, which perhaps accounts for the great emphasis upon 'open channels of communication'.[87]

He pointed out that whilst the Human Relations literature called for coopera-tion and collaboration, it really meant cooperation of workers with manage-ment since it was the cooperation between workers involved in soldiering that they sought to end. Nor did the scholarly literature discuss unions and shop stewards as promoting collaboration and fulfilling human relations needs.[88]

Mills also claimed that the aim of Human Relations studies was manipula-tion of the workers. The texts said that the supervisor, now a counsellor, should be non-authoritative, willing to listen and sympathetic – but 'this kind of non-authoritative agency serves to control and to direct those human processes within the industrial structure which are not adequately controlled by the other agencies of management'.[89]

By 1954 'social science research in industry had become a highly lucrative business' and many social scientists had no qualms about accepting employer goals as their own research goals, such as getting workers to work harder for the same or less money.[90] The American Psychological Association stated in a paper on 'The Psychologist in Industry' in 1962 that:

> while the psychologist's most basic interest is human behaviour, he can help with management's most basic aim, increasing profitability.... Essentially what the industrial psychologist attempts to do is to help the employee come to ... a recognition of how his interests and management's coincide ... [to] help the employee adjust to the requirements of a successful enterprise.[91]

In Britain, too, employers 'turned to social scientists for help' and after the Second World War many other countries, including Australia, relied heavily on American industrial sociology and psychology to motivate workers. A 1961 UNESCO report noted that 'in nearly every [country] the teacher of industrial sociology must depend quite heavily on material derived from research conducted by social scientists in the United States'.[92] The same was true for decades to come. In the 1970s Carey noted that 'one, primarily American, school of social and industrial psychology has dominated the field for some forty years'. The Human Relations school had provided 'the only ideas from the social sciences that many managers may have encountered' in Australia and in Britain.[93]

The Human Resources Movement in the 1960s was really an extension of the Human Relations approach, or 'a change in emphasis'. The idea of how to satisfy workers was expanded to include aspects of the job such as interest, variety, responsibility and self-direction. The problem was now to motivate a new generation of employees who seemed to be more self-centred and less willing to work hard for the sake of it.[94]

Recognising that the job fragmentation emphasised by scientific management might be undermining work motivation, various industrial psychologists advocated a reintegration of job tasks. This job redesign called for each job to be more varied and fulfilling, incorporating a measure of self-control and self-monitoring as well as self-regulation by the worker. The job was supposed to 'include all the tasks necessary to complete a product or process' so that the work would have 'intrinsic meaning and people can feel a sense of achievement'.[95]

Consultants such as Frederick Herzberg advocated 'job enrichment' as a way of getting workers to like their work and therefore put more effort into it. Herzberg built on Maslow's theories of motivation. Abraham Maslow had argued that humans were motivated by a hierarchy of needs and that once basic physiological needs were satisfied higher social needs became more important motivators of behaviour. Herzberg argued that whilst salary, adequate working conditions and security were necessary to prevent dissatisfaction, motivation required workers to feel a sense of achievement, advancement, recognition and responsibility.[96] To achieve this jobs had to be expanded, reintegrating tasks that had been fragmented off to suit a Tayloristic division of labour, and increasing the decision making necessary to do the job.

The London-based Tavistock Institute of Human Relations and others applied a systems approach to work, taking the view that the organisation was a socio-technical system and so job design needed to integrate social and technical components. Workers were put together in groups that had a whole task to complete. In this way the social and psychological needs of the worker could be met in a cooperative endeavour, and job satisfaction could be improved by seeing something more whole being achieved.[97]

In 1973 reports were published – in Britain, *On the Quality of Working Life*, and in the US, *Work in America* – promoting this job enrichment approach. It did not catch on in management circles, however, or in the workplace. In practice what management tended to do was merely to recombine several tasks, often to balance workloads rather than promote job satisfaction. According to one chemical worker: 'You move from one boring, dirty monotonous job to another boring, dirty monotonous job. And somehow you're supposed to come out of it all "enriched". But I never feel "enriched" – I just feel knackered.'[98]

Schemes for individual development were supplemented with organisational development schemes, including 'team building' to increase productivity through a more harmonious organisation. Team building also became popular in some large European corporations.[99] The goals remained the same, however: to get workers to work hard for the corporation. More recent management methods to motivate workers and increase their productivity are discussed in Chapter 8.

CONCLUSION

The irony is that having made work the centre of life, both material and spiritual, capitalism then proceeded to destroy work as a satisfying, meaningful activity for millions of people by fragmenting it and reducing some jobs to activities that were better suited for animals or machines to do. Unable to rely on a work ethic to motivate manual workers in such jobs, employers have used the services of engineers, psychologists, sociologists and others to find ways to increase productivity and motivate workers.

The focus through the nineteenth century was on increasing productivity and reducing labour costs, and engineers played a key role in this. Scientific management was the ultimate culmination of this trend, which sought to remove control of work and productivity from workers to management. It tried to make the work ethic irrelevant for unskilled workers. But scientific management further reduced work to a monotonous, unfulfilling exercise done merely for the purpose of making a living. This meant that workers were dissatisfied and resentful; they took lots of sick days and many could not stick at such demeaning jobs, so that turnover was high and quality of work low. It appeared that a work ethic was still necessary and other methods were sought to promote and encourage that ethic.

Welfare capitalism attempted to buy worker loyalty. Then social and behavioural scientists looked for ways to use non-material motivations to increase productivity, including the social pressure of the groups and teams where loyalty to other workers could substitute for the missing loyalty to the firm and its management.

> Through motivation studies, through counseling, through selection devices calculated to hire only certain types of people, through attitude surveys, communication, role-playing, and all the rest of their bag of schemes, social scientists slowly moved toward a science of behavior.... Authority gave way to manipulation, and workers could no longer be sure they were being exploited.[100]

The work of social scientists did not necessarily replace scientific management but augmented or 'improved' it.[101] Even efforts at job enrichment have often only expanded the size of the task and added some token monitoring responsibilities to it.

Methods of increasing productivity largely fall within a spectrum that ranges from directly controlling the worker to attempting to gain some sort of voluntary commitment to production goals through earning their gratitude and loyalty or helping to make work more pleasant.[102] Voluntary compliance is easier when workers identify with their work: this is the subject of the next chapter.

NOTES

1 Frederick Winslow Taylor, 'The Principles of Scientific Management', in *Scientific Management* (Westport, Connecticut: Greenwood Press, 1911), p. 59.

2 Quoted in John Wareham, 'Spotting the Hard Worker', *Across the Board*, Vol. 33 (January 1996), p. 49.

3 Quoted in David Bleakley, *Work: the Shadow and the Substance* (London: SCM Press, 1983), p. 37.

4 Robert Eisenberger, *Blue Monday: the Loss of the Work Ethic in America* (New York: Paragon House, 1989), pp. 10–11; David J. Cherrington, *The Work Ethic: Working Values and Values That Work* (New York: AMACON, 1980), p. 37.

5 Cited in David Dickson, *Alternative Technology and the Politics of Technical Change* (UK: Fontana/Collins, 1974), p. 50.

6 Craig R. Littler and Graeme Salaman, 'The Design of Jobs', in Craig R. Littler (ed.), *The Experience of Work* (UK: Gower Publishing, 1985), p. 85.

7 Herman Melville, 'Bartleby the Scrivener: a Story of Wall Street', in Wallace and Mary Stegner (eds), *Great American Short Stories* (New York: Dell Publishing, 1957).

8 Cited in Anthony Sampson, *Company Man: the Rise and Fall of Corporate Life* (London: HarperCollinsBusiness, 1996), pp. 52–3.

9 Karl Marx, quoted in Charles H. Anderson, *The Political Economy of Social Class* (Englewood Cliffs, NJ: Prentice-Hall, 1974), pp. 41–2.

10 D. Rodgers, quoted in Adrian Furnham, *The Protestant Work Ethic: the Psychology of Work-related Beliefs and Behaviours* (London: Routledge, 1990), pp. 5–6.

11 Tony Watson, *Sociology, Work and Industry* (London: Routledge and Kegan Paul, 1987), p. 32; Ed Andrew, *Closing the Iron Cage: the Scientific Management of Work and Leisure* (Montréal: Black Rose Books, 1981), p. 57.

12 Paul Thompson, *The Nature of Work: an Introduction to Debates on the Labour Process* (Hampshire, UK: Macmillan Education, 1983), p. 127.

13 Ed Andrew, note 11, pp. 58–61.

14 Taylor, note 1, p. 14.

15 *Ibid.*, p. 34.

16 *Ibid.*, pp. 36–7, 85.

17 *Ibid.*, p. 13.

18 Andrew, note 13, p. 79.

19 Taylor, note 1, p. 38.

20 *Ibid.*, p. 36.

21 *Ibid.*, p. 83.

22 *Ibid.*, pp. 40–1.

23 *Ibid.*, p. 61.

24 *Ibid.*, p. 62.

25 *Ibid.*, p. 90.

26 *Ibid.*, p. 59.

27 Quoted in Andrew, note 13, p. 72.

28 Paul Bernstein, *American Work Values: Their Origin and Development* (Albany, NY: State University of New York Press, 1997), p. 7.

29 Andrew, note 11, p. 90.

30 Taylor, note 1, p. 10.

31 *Ibid.*, p. 28; Andrew, note 11, pp. 58, 72.

32 Littler and Salaman, note 6, p. 87.

33 Quoted in Stuart Ewen, *Captains of Consciousness: Advertising and the Social Roots of the Consumer Culture* (New York: McGraw-Hill, 1976), pp. 11–12.

34 Henry Ford, quoted in George Ritzer, *The McDonaldization of Society: an Investigation into the Changing Character of Contemporary Social Life*, revised edn (Thousand Oaks, California: Pine Forge Press, 1996), p. 110.

35 Loren Baritz, *The Servants of Power: a History of the Use of Social Science in American Industry*, reprint (Westport, Connecticut: Greenwood Press, 1974), pp. 32–3.

36 Littler and Salaman, note 6, p. 88.

37 Baritz, note 35, pp. 32–3; Juliet B. Schor, *The Overworked American: the Unexpected Decline in Leisure* (USA: Basic Books, 1991), p. 62.

38 Baritz, note 35, p. 33.

39 Andrew, note 11, pp. 72–3.

40 Robin Theobald, *Understanding Industrial Society: a Sociological Guide* (New York: St Martin's Press, 1994), p. 97; Littler and Salaman, note 6, pp. 86–90; Thompson, note 12, pp. 128, 131.

41 Kevin Blackburn, 'Preaching "the Gospel of Efficiency": the Promotion of Ideas about Profit-sharing and Payment by Results in Australia, 1915–1929', *Australian Historical Studies*, No. 107 (1996).

42 Littler and Salaman, note 6, pp. 89–90.

43 Watson, note 11, pp. 32–3; Andrew, note 11, p. 75; Littler and Salaman, note 6, pp. 85, 87.

44 Quoted in 'Levi's and its Labor Unions', *Reputation Management* (1995). http://www.prcentral.com/rmmj95levis.htm.

45 Ritzer, note 34, pp. 25–6.

46 Baritz, note 35, p. 31.

47 *Ibid.*, pp. 37–9.

48 Bernstein, note 26, p. 10; Baritz, note 35, p. 90.

49 Alex Carey, *Taking the Risk Out of Democracy*, ed. Andrew Lohrey (Sydney: University of New South Wales Press, 1995), pp. 164–5.

50 Theobald, note 40, p. 100.

51 Alan Wolfe, 'The Moral Meanings of Work', *American Prospect*, Vol. 34 (September/October 1997); Roland Marchand, *Creating the Corporate Soul: the Rise of Public Relations and Corporate Imagery in American Big Business* (Berkeley: University of California Press, 1998), p. 17; Sanford Jacoby, 'Downsizing in the Past', *Challenge*, Vol. 41, No. 3 (1998).

52 Theobald, note 40, p. 91; Marchand, note 51, Chapter 1.

53 Ewen, note 33, p. 15.

54 Bernstein, note 26, p. 194; Sanford Jacoby, quoted in Wolfe, note 51.

55 Marchand, note 51, p. 21.

56 *Ibid.*, pp. 99–100, 116.

57 Baritz, note 35, pp. 78, 80.

58 *Ibid.*, p. 83–9; Theobald, note 40, p. 98.

59 Baritz, note 35, p. 94.

60 Theobald, note 40, p. 99.

61 Baritz, note 35, pp. 99–101.

62 Morris S. Viteles, *Motivation and Morale in Industry* (New York: W. W. Norton and Co., 1953), p. 441.

63 Carey, note 49, p. 163.

64 Viteles, note 62, p. 4.

65 Baritz, note 35, pp. 148–9.

66 Elizabeth A. Fones-Wolf. 'Beneath Consensus: Business, Labor, and the Post-War Order', PhD thesis, University of Massachusetts, 1990, pp. 47–8, 119.

67 Littler and Salaman, note 6, p. 92.

68 Fones-Wolf, note 66, pp. 119, 123–5; Baritz, note 35, pp. 148–9, 156.

69 *Ibid.*, pp. 125–6, 155.

70 Viteles, note 62, p. 445.

71 Quoted in Baritz, note 35, p. 183.
72 Carey, note 49, p. 36.
73 Baritz, note 35, p. 169.
74 *Ibid.*, p. 186.
75 *Ibid.*, p. 187.
76 Lester Coch and John R. P. French, 'Overcoming Resistance to Change', in Dorwin Cartwright and Alvin Zander (eds), *Group Dynamics: Research and Theory* (New York: Harper and Row, 1960), p. 341.
77 Viteles, note 62, p. 461.
78 Fones-Wolf, note 66, p. 151.
79 Quoted in *ibid.*, p. 152.
80 Quoted in Carey, note 49, pp. 148–9.
81 Fones-Wolf, note 66, pp. 123–5, 149–50.
82 Quoted in Carey, note 49, p. 150.
83 Viteles, note 62, p. ix.
84 *Ibid.*, pp. 454–5.
85 Baritz, note 35, p. 187.
86 Quoted in C. Wright Mills, 'The Contribution of Sociology to Studies of Industrial Relations', paper presented at the Proceedings of the First Annual Meeting of the Industrial Relations Research Association, December 1948, p. 209.
87 *Ibid.*, pp. 209, 210.
88 *Ibid.*, pp. 210–12.
89 Quoted in *ibid.*, pp. 214–16.
90 Baritz, note 35, pp. 171–3.
91 Quoted in Carey, note 49, p. 157.
92 Quoted in *ibid.*, p. 156.
93 Tom Lupton, quoted in *ibid.*, p. 162.
94 *Ibid.*, p. 165; Bernstein, note 26, p. 221.
95 Littler and Salaman, note 6, pp. 92–3.
96 Herzberg, cited in Watson, note 11, p. 35.
97 *Ibid.*, p. 181.
98 Littler and Salaman, note 6, pp. 92–3, 101.
99 Sampson, note 8, p. 1225.
100 P. D. Anthony, *The Ideology of Work* (London: Tavistock Publications, 1977), p. 209.
101 Thompson, note 12, p. 132.
102 *Ibid.*, p. 151.

⋄7⋄

Work and Identity

In a society whose value system is predicated upon the work ethic, people must work for their own psychological well-being.
Johnny Tolliver [1]

In the modern world we must *make* an identity for ourselves; we do not inherit one. We have outgrown the tradition that assigns one's way of life, one's station, and one's loyalties at birth ... it makes an identity something we must achieve.
Paul L. Wachtel [2]

To become a fully functional adult male, one prerequisite is essential: a job.
US President's Commission Report, 1964 [3]

The problems of motivating workers outlined in the previous chapter are considerably reduced if people have their lives oriented to their work and particularly if they identify with their work and with the company that employs them. In this way, instead of being forced to work hard through the threat of unemployment and strict workplace controls, they will do so voluntarily.

The identification of people with their work is a phenomenon that corporations and employers have consciously fostered. In part it is a consequence of the work ethic and the system of status based on occupation which replaced a feudal status system. In feudal societies identification is determined much more directly by birth. This was still the case in the southern states of America right up to the Civil War. In his novel *The Fathers*, Allen Tate's narrator illustrates the differing cultures when he says of the pre-Civil War South:

114

It was significant that we always spoke of the Carters of Ravensworth, the Carys of Vaucluse, the Buchans of Pleasant Hill. The individual quality of a man was bound up with his kin and the 'places' where they lived; thinking of a man we could easily bring before the mind's eye all those subtly interwoven features of his position. 'Class' consisted solely in a certain code of behavior. Even years later I am always a little amazed to hear a man described as a coal man or the steel man or the plate-glass man, descriptions of people after the way they make their money, not after their manner of life.[4]

The higher up in the occupational scale people are, the more likely they are to identify with their occupation and be self-motivated. The career structure fosters employees who demonstrate that they can be trusted to work unsupervised towards company goals. It encourages and rewards hard work, loyalty and commitment. Higher-level employees are expected to compete with each other for favour from their superiors rather than to act together against them.[5]

Jobs have a socialising effect, which employers are aware of and foster. Generally people find they have to adapt to a job, to make compromises and to see things in different ways, in order to gain promotions. Pyschologist Paul Wachtel claims that 'As one enters the job market and does what is necessary to get ahead, one accepts new responsibilities and commitments that bind one to the system and change one's point of view.'[6]

FOSTERING WORK IDENTITY

In the twentieth century corporations actively promoted the identification of workers with their work, particularly their place of work. They sought to raise what Elizabeth Fones-Wolf refers to as 'company consciousness':

> This involved convincing workers to identify their social, economic, and political well being with that of their specific employer and more broadly with the free enterprise system. A company conscious worker, rather like the idealized boy scout, was not only productive but took pride in his job and demonstrated loyalty and allegiance to the firm.[7]

Many of the public relations programmes, including corporate advertising, that the large corporations ran in the early part of the century were targeted not only at the wider public but also at employees, particularly when it was noted that such PR boosted the morale of employees and made them proud. Corporate advertising featuring employees was found to be particularly effective for this and the advertisements were made into posters and put up around the factories. It was probably the managerial staff, however, that got the biggest morale boost from corporate advertising: 'By presenting an idealized portrait of a cohesive, powerful, benevolent corporation to the public,' says Roland Marchand in *Creating the Corporate Soul*, 'the crucial managerial cadres' were offered 'an energizing vision of the corporation'.[8]

Advertisements that sought to humanise the corporation through the metaphor of the family also served to claim the loyalty of workers as members of the corporate family. The theme of family often featured in the titles of employee magazines (*RCA Family Circle, American Sugar Family,* etc.) as well as the text. The idea was, according to the president of Standard Oil, that a person would work harder as a partner — part of the family — than as a servant. *Ford Man* stated in 1917 that the factory belonged to workers as well as managers, and that, as members of the corporate family, workers should devote 'every ounce of loyalty we possess'.[9]

Ford Man was one of many employee magazines put out during the First World War and afterwards 'to bind employees more closely to the corporation'. As early as 1905 the Colorado Fuel and Iron Company, under the management of the Rockefeller family, distributed an employee magazine to 'help develop a strong esprit de corps among employees'. Such magazines used 'human interest' stories about employees and a folksy prose style to get workers to read them. The magazines tended to moralise, however, emphasising the value of loyalty, hard work and good attendance, and the benefits of free enterprise.[10] The idea was to give the worker a feel for the overall enterprise and where s/he fitted in. The magazines tried to replace the personal communication between the owner and the workers that the growing size of the corporation had made impossible.[11]

> Even more self-consciously than they cultivated family imagery, the employee magazines sought to enhance workers' morale by bolstering their sense of place within their own extensive factory and within the corporation as a whole.[12]

Employee magazines blossomed and by 1925 the majority of manufacturing companies published them.[13]

Welfare programmes, even as early as the turn of the twentieth century, also aimed to promote 'a feeling of unity and identity with the corporation' as a 'social secretary' for International Harvester noted of his employee athletic associations in 1903. Sports teams and activities, theatre groups, hobby clubs, singing choruses and summer camps all aimed to create a sense of community in the workplace.[14]

> Company-sponsored Sunday schools, churches, housing, recreation facilities and employee representation plans were supposed to show the worker that the manager cared for him as an individual as well as an employee. They would fend off unionism and also develop an improved worker: thrifty, clean, temperate, industrious and Americanized.[15]

After the First World War the 'leaders of giant corporations sought more systematic methods for achieving the tacit consent from employees necessary for teamwork'. As well as promoting better interpersonal relations with employees, they used employee stock ownership and personnel counselling to get workers to identify with the corporation.[16] According to one trade association: 'The employee must not be made to feel that he is merely a cog in the machine, but that he is part of a team that is working together for victory; that the success of his employer is his own success.'[17]

Giving stock to employees helped them to identify with and feel they shared in corporate success and, as Firestone Tire and Rubber Company claimed in an advertisement, take 'more than a wage interest' in the company.[18] Profit sharing was also promoted by employers and politicians in Australia during and after the First World War and into the 1920s as a way of ensuring that workers on a fixed wage under the country's industrial regulation system would be motivated to work harder.[19]

Similar strategies were used after the Second World War. In the US a Human Relations approach was combined with a conscious communications strategy aimed at creating a sense of belonging. This involved a barrage of literature: pamphlets, letters, comic books and magazines as well as bulletin boards, films and posters. By 1950 there were 6,500 company magazines in the US, distributed to some 80 million workers at a cost of over $100 million/year. By 1955, 82 per cent of firms were writing letters to individual employees, compared to 28 per cent in 1947.[20]

The aim of all this literature was to promote a sense of purpose in the worker's job, a feeling of pride in the company they worked for, a feeling of participation in the whole enterprise, a closer relationship with management and a sense of having shared goals.[21] An American Management Association (AMA) report of 1954 noted that company information programmes were undertaken because employers believed 'that the better informed an employee is about his company ... the more understanding, cooperative, and productive he will be'.[22] It went on:

> They want to integrate the employee with his work group, to develop his 'sense of belonging,' to get him to identify his own welfare with the company's. Some employers view this kind of program as a sort of 'battle of loyalties' with the unions. Other believe strongly that morale (and productivity) improves when the worker is sufficiently well motivated to want to expend personally the effort to achieve higher performance.[23]

Welfare capitalism was also revived after the Second World War to enhance the image of the beneficent corporation, to reinforce company consciousness and loyalty, and to head off moves toward a welfare state. Firms offered

117

employees pensions, vacations, educational assistance and health insurance to show how employers cared for their employees. Working conditions were improved, loans were made available for home purchase, recreational facilities were provided, and paid coffee breaks introduced. 'Employers tried to convince workers that their security depended not on union organization or the state, but on acceptance of a managerial-dominated social and political order.'[24]

Welfare capitalism – with its company recreational activities, clubs, parties and picnics – facilitated work-based friendships and drew families into a friendly company-based social setting. It was also hoped that such social occasions would improve relations with management and break down the 'class' barriers between workers and management that unions tended to exploit.[25]

Open days and plant tours were also aimed at families to help them identify more with their breadwinner's occupation and employer. Summer camps were run for employees' children.[26] One journal noted in 1954 that corporate-sponsored children's activities would not only ensure that those children would 'look upon the industry which has given them some of the best sports and recreational years of their life with a warmth and respect no company can buy' but that these children were potential future employees and it was a good investment 'to tie them to the company at an early age'.[27]

Providing recreational facilities for workers helped build teamwork on the job and gave 'alienated workers the individual recognition and sense of achievement lacking on the job'. It was also believed that such recreational activities would raise worker morale, thus ensuring lower absenteeism and worker turnover, and greater productivity.[28] Worker education programmes also sought to achieve a degree of company consciousness.

Various employers attested to the value of profit sharing in the US in the 1950s.[29] It aimed at not only ensuring employee loyalty but also enhancing the idea that the worker and the employer were in partnership to produce profits. In this way, workers would be in favour of any measures aimed at increasing productivity and would identify more closely with employers. Profit sharing is still promoted today as a way of ensuring that workers have a stake in company profitability. Between 5 and 10 per cent of US companies offer stock options to all employees, even manual workers. Many more offer stock options to executives. Stock options are used to align the interests of employees with those of shareholders and to motivate employees to work hard for company success.[30] *HR Magazine* argues that stock options 'help to create a company-wide "ownership" culture by focusing employees' attention on the employer's financial performance'.[31]

Today there is also a vast public relations effort targeted at getting employees to take management's point of view. Edelman Public Relations Worldwide has an area of practice 'dedicated to employee communication', earning $1 million per year, which it calls Employee Engagement. The aim is to 'align employee behaviour with organizational goals and objectives' and 'evoke a strong, positive connection with employees through unique and innovative tactics involving a variety of media, including print, broadcast, Internet, Intranet and face-to-face communication'.[32]

Employee magazines still aim to engender employee identification with the firm. Examples include SunAmerica's Employee Newsletter *Ray,* which answers 'the need to maintain a strong corporate culture';[33] Foodmaker's *Speaker Box,* which is used to instil 'in employees a greater sense of connection to, and understanding of, the company' and foster employee pride;[34] and Georgia Pacific's *New Opportunity.*[35]

Corporate universities (see Chapter 11) have become the modern way of instilling company consciousness and shared identity. Jeanne Meister, author of *Corporate Universities: Lessons in Building a World-Class Work Force,* suggests that the corporate citizenship taught in corporate universities is modelled on successful Japanese companies where production workers are given motivational courses to 'build employee pride and bonding between the employee and the company'. Corporate universities in the US and other parts of the world now also aim to promote a 'strong identification with one's company and its central values' and to inculcate 'all levels of employees to the culture, values, traditions, and vision of the company'.[36]

FOSTERING CORPORATE LOYALTY

The relationship between unskilled or semi-skilled workers and management tends to be marked by mutual distrust and therefore tasks have to be closely prescribed and supervised. At higher levels in the corporate hierarchy, however, employer/employee relationships are marked by a high degree of trust.[37] This provides an alternative means of control through the rewards and punishments of a career structure. Those who can be trusted to work hard towards company goals get promoted. The aim of managers of higher-level workers is to encourage workers to identify with the aims of the company so that they will be self-motivated and require less direct supervision. In return employees can expect better rewards and promotion prospects if they work hard and loyally.

Studies of engineers in their workplace have found that trust is an important element in the relationship between engineers and their employers. Engineers are promoted when they have proved their dependability and responsibility, and shown they can be trusted by their employers. In return the engineers receive a considerable amount of freedom to exercise discretion, that is, 'responsible autonomy'.[38]

Giving autonomy to skilled workers suits employers as it is 'the most efficient mode of deployment of skilled workers' in many circumstances.[39] Work is assigned in large chunks and the employee is able to decide how s/he will do it, given certain time and money constraints and performance specifications. Performance is judged by results. Company objectives are often internalised so that workers are self-motivated and self-disciplined.[40]

Authority is exercised in situations of loose supervision through selection, training and promotion. In engineering as in many other occupations, career success is entirely dependent on the salary grades and promotion levels established by management. In this way an engineer's career and thus personal success are completely determined by management; this constitutes a form of control over the engineer which can be more extensive and pervasive than direct supervision.[41]

Not only is close supervision unnecessary but, given that future managers are often chosen from these engineers, it is considered to be counterproductive to their training. Also, close supervision can undermine the trust that is so essential to the relationship.[42] Authority is very much behind-the-scenes and invisible, with job demands being seen in terms of company goals and profitability, goals that are accepted by engineers who are able to fit their job into a company context.

It is especially important to a company that its senior management and executives submit fully to the company goals and believe wholeheartedly in the company.[43] The route up the corporate hierarchy requires the employee to demonstrate that they 'subscribe to the company's values'.[44] The importance of loyalty, particularly amongst salaried white-collar employees, is recognised by employers, who urge their employees to identify their welfare with that of the company.

Clark Davis, in his research into corporations at the beginning of the twentieth century, found that 'Employers expected from employees nothing less than total commitment. Managers wanted employees to aggressively support their firms not only while at work but in their non-working hours as well – to act like limited partners, or stockholders.'[45] They recognised that it was employees who came into contact with the community and that contact could be vital in how the community felt about the corporation. For example, the Pacific Mutual Life Insurance Company told its employees in 1925: 'Happy is he who speaks, not of the boss's business, but of our business, who considers himself an integral part of the concern, who thinks not of personal gain or satisfaction but of the welfare and greater success of the organization.'[46]

Employers believed 'employees should identify so strongly with the company that promoting its products and services would be a logical part of every job description'. Employees were expected to take advantage of any opportunity to sell the company's products or stock to friends and family, and to set an example by using those products themselves. 'Leaders of oil companies asked employees to support new industries and technologies that would create a heightened demand for petroleum' by buying automobiles, sending letters airmail, and advocating these and other products such as asphalt and pesticides.[47]

During the Second World War, Shell Oil sent booklets to its workers featuring the following exhortation:

> If every member of the Shell family will make just a few good friends, and will have a good word for his associates and his company, within a year the Shell family will have thousands of new friends and supporters. And a good, strong, well-liked company is a mighty fine guarantee of a good, steady job.[48]

This identification with the company was supposed to encourage more than just voluntary salesmanship outside work hours and courteous service during work hours; it extended to political activism on behalf of the company's interests. Most firms tried to 'educate' their employees as to the correct political line they should take on matters concerning the company; some asked workers to 'become advocates of specific political issues and to canvass their friends, neighbours, and relatives for support'.[49] Also employees, particularly managers, were urged to 'represent the firm as a vital local institution' at meetings of professional societies, neighbourhood associations and with other community organisations such as the Boy Scouts, and to give speeches at schools, clubs and churches.[50] The ability of executives to mix socially with the community became an important element of their job.

The US private utilities were perhaps the earliest firms to expect their senior employees to join various community groups and activities, the rationale being that the company gained prestige and an opportunity to present its views in the community; it also increased its opportunity to distribute pamphlets, films and other PR material. In 1912 the *Electric Railway Journal* pointed out that executives who actively participated in community affairs were trusted more by the community when they made statements on behalf of the company. The utilities often paid membership dues to the various social, sporting, civic, scientific and professional organisations that executives joined. The Boy Scouts was a particularly favoured organisation.[51]

Such expectations became more common following the Second World War. For example, Sears Roebuck 'encouraged' its executives 'to participate in community activities, outside business hours and outside the relatively narrow circle of business acquaintances'. A 1954 American Management Association

121

report noted that 'No control or guidance is offered, except that in any local community the company would expect to find its senior personnel playing some part in such groups as Rotary, Chamber of Commerce, Community Chest, etc.'[52]

For white-collar salaried male corporate employees, employment at a particular company became a lifetime career. Employers offered rewards and lifetime security in return for lifetime loyalty:

> Corporations sought to craft a broad definition of corporate employment. Under this definition, employees would not only meticulously perform their specific duties over a lifelong career, but would also assume a sense of obligation to promote corporate prosperity.... The early years of most enterprises were dominated by efforts to implement programs and policies that would induce ambitious young people to tie themselves to a single firm and to view its interests as synonymous with their own.[53]

ORGANISATION MAN

In 1956 William H. Whyte wrote *The Organization Man,* which described how middle-level employees not only worked for organisations but belonged to them as well. He noted the disparity between the ideal of the individual in twentieth-century American life and the reality of the collective situation that most Americans found themselves in, where individuality was actually a handicap and conformity the way to get promoted in one's career.[54]

Whyte observed that young organisation men identified their own well-being with that of the company. He noted that, in those years of rapid expansion after the war, 'many a young man of average ability has been propelled upward so early – and so pleasantly – that he can hardly be blamed if he thinks the momentum is constant'.[55] Such men assumed that they would be with the organisation for their whole careers.

At the executive level, Whyte described men who worked long hours but didn't feel that it was a burden. They worked fifty or sixty hours a week, as well as doing after-hours, work-related entertaining, conferences and reading. They promoted those who followed their example. 'We have, in sum, a man who is so completely involved in his work that he cannot distinguish between work and the rest of his life – and is happy that he cannot.'[56] Sloan Wilson depicted a similar image in *The Man in the Gray Flannel Suit,* in which the main character described the 'bright young men in gray flannel suits rushing around New York in a frantic parade to nowhere.... pursuing neither ideals nor happiness – they were pursuing a routine'.[57]

The organisation men were influential in the communities in which they lived, organising committees, sitting on school boards, setting trends. Because they moved about so often with their work, Whyte argued that it was the organisation, generally a corporation, that determined a person's position in the community rather than birth or background, at least for the middle and upper classes. (It was still rare for working-class people and coloured people to reach the top levels of the organisation.)[58]

So important was the socialisation of the organisation man that personality tests were used regularly for management personnel, not just to select the right people but to decide on their promotions. Whyte claimed that the proportion of US corporations using personality tests had jumped from one-third to 60 per cent in two years (1952–4) and was still increasing. Unlike aptitude tests that attempted to find out about a person's skills, the personality test purported to find out more about the person: how well-adjusted he was and would be in future; how conservative he was, how stable; his 'potential loyalty' to the organisation.[59] According to Whyte, such tests were in reality tests of normality and conformity:

> Neither in the questions nor in the evaluation of them are the tests neutral; they are loaded with values, organization values, and the result is a set of yardsticks that reward the conformist, the pedestrian, the unimaginative.... [60]

Of course, anyone refusing to take a test automatically failed the test of normality, conformity and company loyalty. Whyte suggested that in order to 'cheat' on the tests so as to 'do well', one should pick 'the most conventional, run-of-the-mill, pedestrian' answers and if in doubt portray oneself as the sort of person who would have the following views:

> I loved my father and my mother, but my father a little bit more.
> I like things pretty much the way they are.
> I never worry much about anything.
> I don't care for books or music much.
> I love my wife and children.
> I don't let them get in the way of company work.[61]

Companies still use personality tests in hiring and promotion.[62] One of the favourites in the late 1990s was the Myers-Briggs Type Indicator which differentiates between types such as ENTJ – 'extroverted intuitive thinking judger, a born leader' and ISFP – 'introverted sensing feeling perceiver, a loyal follower'.[63]

In the 1980s Whyte revisited the organisation man and found little had changed: 'The United States continues to be dominated by large organizations, and they are run much as they were before.... The people who staff them are pretty much the same as those who did before.'[64] And a 1989 survey of middle managers in 20 well-known US corporations – including American Express, Dow Chemical, General Motors, Johnson and Johnson, Mobil and

Westinghouse – found that 76 per cent believed they would spend the rest of their career with the company they worked for, 80 per cent said they were deeply committed to the company because it had been good for them, and 77 per cent worked more than 50 hours in an average week (26 per cent worked more than 60 hours).[65]

Salaried employees are still required to put company interests first, both during and outside work time. Anthony Sampson notes in *Company Man* that 'Young American executives are expected to be still more thoroughly committed to their bosses, leaving still less time for hobbies or philosphical thoughts; while leisure-time is associated with failure or opting-out.'[66] American firms also still expect employees to be politically active on their behalf.[67] Ron McCallum, professor of industrial law at the University of Sydney, observes that 'not since the eighteenth century have employers been able to exercise such controls over the private lives of their workforces'.[68]

IDENTIFICATION AND BELONGING

Paid work has become essential for defining a person's individual identity. When asked who they are most people identify themselves by their occupations ('I am an engineer' … 'I am a secretary') or lack of paid occupation ('I am unemployed' … 'I am retired').

> For most of us the primary source of life's labels and ego boundaries is our work. In work we come both to know ourselves and orient ourselves to the external world. Work allows us to establish a 'coherent web of expectations' of the rhythm, direction, and definition of our lives.[69]

In earlier times, when most people were farmers, occupation did not differentiate one person from another. Today, occupation is more likely to say something special about a person and who s/he is. It says something about skills and inclinations. It has become a basis on which a person can build an identity.[70] Entry into the paid workforce marks the transition from childhood to adulthood. It provides 'the signal that young people have been accepted as adults and have been accorded place and status as member of the society…. To the young person leaving education, it is abundantly clear that the social recognition of adulthood depends on successful entry to the paid workforce.'[71]

Work provides people with a sense of belonging, a place in the order of things: 'A paid job has become a badge of membership in the larger society and an almost indispensable symbol of self-worth.'[72] It is through our work that we obtain a niche for ourselves in our society. It provides a sense of belonging through shared work experiences and understandings with others of similar occupations, as a member of a work organisation, and through the idea that one is contributing to a community through one's work.

Work provides the main source of social interaction outside of the family for many people, and a role and purpose within the community. Friends (and enemies) are made in the workplace, and people feel less isolated.

> For some people, work has been practically their only source of identity and companionship. Dulling as their tasks may be, they have prided themselves in doing the best they know how because the workplace has been not just a place to be but a community. On the job, they joke, complain, tell stories, recount baseball games, and do the many other small things that give them a better sense of belonging. Off the job, they use their economic rewards to win the esteem of others; money and the things it can buy sometimes bring recognition and even admiration.[73]

Work provides identity in terms of class and status within an established occupational hierarchy.[74] Traditionally even the lowliest worker has been accorded a measure of respect for being a worker, particularly if the worker is a male supporting a family: 'Their self-sacrifice was seen as a laudable effort to provide their families with opportunities and a standard of living that would have seemed impossible a few decades earlier.'[75] The breadwinner had a respected place in the family, made a recognised contribution to society, and had his masculinity affirmed.

The morality associated with the modern work ethic has more to do with social contribution than individual virtue. Each person is expected to contribute to the wealth creation activities of the society through work. To be a worthwhile person one must do one's share, and little besides paid work counts anymore. Over 80 per cent of Americans say that work gives them a sense of worth as a person and provides some sort of meaning to them.[76] Workers can get a sense of doing something for others and being part of a network of people working towards a goal.[77]

When David Cherrington and his colleagues conducted a survey of the attitudes and values of American workers some fifteen years earlier, they found strikingly similar results; 80 per cent of workers questioned sought intrinsic rewards such as feeling worthwhile and being recognised by others.[78] Wendy Lowenstein, who interviewed many Australian workers for her book *Weevils at Work*, states: 'Even in the worst jobs, workers console themselves that they contribute to society. "I still have a lot to give," says the fifty-year-old retrenched Ford worker.'[79]

Modern citizens 'regard wage-work as natural and necessary for human dignity'.[80] The value of work for the modern worker goes far beyond the pay cheque. It 'has become in large part the basis for the individual's own sense of place, identity self-respect and self-worth'.[81] It is for this reason that in surveys from the 1970s to the present, the vast majority of people claimed that that they would continue to work even if they had enough money to live as comfortably as they liked for the rest of their lives.[82] Similarly, large percentages of people in Britain and in Canada said they preferred working to not working.[83]

People work for more than the pleasure and pride it brings. Although Cherrington found that 86 per cent of people he surveyed said they sought pride and craftmanship in their work,[84] most people do not. 'In well over one hundred studies in the last twenty-five years, workers have regularly depicted their jobs as physically exhausting, boring, psychologically diminishing, or personally humiliating and unimportant.'[85] Despite this, most people prefer to work. Work is seen as 'a basic dimension of human existence' and many people feel they would be less than human if they did not work, no matter how tedious it is.[86]

It seems that although people may yearn for a different job, few would prefer not to work at all. As Gini and Sullivan conclude:

> What we think this data means is that for most men and for an increasing number of women there is no alternative to work, no other activity that absorbs time, uses energy, taps creativity, demands attention, provides regular social interaction, and is a source of status, identity, self-respect, and financial remuneration.[87]

CONCLUSION

Employers have fostered a sense of belonging and identification by workers with their work. They have also encouraged a total devotion by higher-level employees to their work that has gone beyond working hours. They have ensured that work is central and all-consuming to their employees.

> Corporate America has been telling us we build our character by working hard and doing 'productive' things in organizations. We have learned to define ourselves by our jobs. There is something seriously wrong with this: If we think we are what we do for a living, we have lost most of our character.[88]

The investment of social identity in paid work causes problems for those without it: the retired, the unemployed and the disabled. Many unemployed have 'the sense that the value of one's own personal time moves towards zero'.[89] An OECD report acknowledges that people who don't work for a living have major problems integrating into society because paid work is a key source of social recognition and status.[90]

The loss of a job can have consequences far beyond the loss of income. People will fight very hard to protect their jobs; in the face of such strong

126

psychological and personal needs, other social priorities, such as environmental protection, seem less pressing. 'The preservation of existing jobs has become for many *the* overriding social goal.'[91]

Alternative mechanisms for gaining a sense of belonging to society, such as church and community groups, have been declining, leaving work as a more important mechanism: 'traditional symbols of personal identification seem to be fading, leaving people with a strong sense of needing to "belong" and to participate, but with fewer means of expressing collective sovereignty, defining general interest, and structuring solidarity'.[92]

The irony is that at a time when most of the population in industrialised countries can conceive of no identity outside of work, corporations have been dramatically reducing their workforces, retrenching layers of management who had expected lifetime employment with their firms, and destroying the job security that had once formed the basis of employee loyalty. Millions of people around the world are finding themselve without identity and purpose. This is the topic of the next chapter.

NOTES

1 Johnny Tolliver, 'The Computer and the Protestant Ethic: a Conflict', in Walter Mathews (ed.), *Monster or Messiah? The Computer's Impact on Society* (University Press of Mississippi, 1980), p. 160.

2 Paul L. Wachtel, *The Poverty of Affluence: a Psychological Portrait of the American Way of Life* (Philadelphia, PA: New Society Publishers, 1989), p. 99.

3 'The Challenge of Crime in a Free Society', report of President's Commission on Law Enforcement and Administration of Justice (1964) quoted in J. Kraus, 'Juvenile Unemployment and Delinquency', paper presented at the Conference on Unemployment and Crime, University of Sydney, 19 July 1978, p. 21.

4 Allen Tate, *The Fathers* (Middlesex, England: Penguin, 1938), pp. 127–8.

5 Tony Watson, *Sociology, Work and Industry* (London: Routledge and Kegan Paul, 1987), p. 191.

6 Wachtel, note 2, p. 246.

7 Elizabeth A. Fones-Wolf. 'Beneath Consensus: Business, Labor, and the Post-War Order', Doctor of Philosophy, University of Massachusetts, 1990, p. 121.

8 Roland Marchand, *Creating the Corporate Soul: the Rise of Public Relations and Corporate Imagery in American Big Business* (Berkeley: University of California Press, 1998), pp. 83, 100, 162.

9 Quoted in *ibid.*, pp. 105–9.

10 *Ibid.*, pp. 16, 109–110.

11 *Ibid.*, p. 113.

12 *Ibid.*, note 8, p. 110.

13 Alan R. Raucher, *Public Relations and Business 1900–1929* (Baltimore: The Johns Hopkins Press, 1968), p. 69.

14 *Ibid.*, pp. 23, 116.

15 Richard S. Tedlow, *Keeping the Corporate Image: Public Relations and Business, 1900–1950* (Greenwich, Connecticut: Jai Press, 1979), p. 17.

16 Raucher, note 12, p. 68.

17 Quoted in *ibid.*, p. 68.

18 Marchand, note 8, pp. 24, 116.

19 Kevin Blackburn, 'Preaching "the Gospel of Efficiency": the Promotion of Ideas about Profit-sharing and Payment by Results in Australia, 1915–1929', *Australian Historical Studies*, No. 107 (1996).

20 Fones-Wolf, note 7, pp. 130–6.

21 *Ibid.*, p. 134.

22 Douglas Williams and Stanley Peterfreund, *The Education of Employees: a Status Report, Management Education for Itself and Its Employees* (New York: American Management Association, 1954), p. 29.

23 *Ibid.*, p. 29.

24 Fones-Wolf, note 7, pp. 187–8.

25 *Ibid.*, p. 203.

26 *Ibid.*, p. 208.

27 Quoted in *ibid.*, p. 209.

28 *Ibid.*, pp. 201–2.

29 *Ibid.*, pp. 192–4.

30 Theodore Kinni, 'Why We Work', *Training*, Vol. 35, No. 8 (1998); Edward O. Welles, 'Motherhood, Apple Pie and Stock Options', *Inc.*, Vol. 20 (February 1998).

31 Arthur H. Kroll, 'Exploring Options', *HR Magazine*, Vol. 42 (October 1997), p. 96.

32 Bob Reincke, 'Edelman Formalizes Commitment to Employee Communication' (enews@newsweb.edelman.com: Edelman Public Relations Worldwide, 1999).

33 'SunAmerica's Employee Newsletter' (Creativity in Public Relations Awards (CIPRA) 1998) www.prcentral.com

34 'Speaker Box: Foodmaker's Employee Magazine' (Creativity in Public Relations Awards (CIPRA) 1997) www.prcentral.com

35 'Selling Change, Solidifying Morale', *Reputation Management* (September/October 1996).

36 Jeanne C. Meister, *Corporate Universities: Lessons in Building a World-Class Work Force*, revised edn (New York: McGraw-Hill, 1998), p. 90.

37 Watson, note 5, p. 193.

38 *Ibid.*; Robert Zussman, *Mechanics of the Middle Class: Work and Politics Among American Engineers* (University of California Press, 1985); Peter Whalley, *The Social Production of Technical Work: the Case of British Engineers* (Basingstoke: Macmillan, 1986).

39 Whalley, note 38, p. 70.

40 Watson, note 5, p. 193.

41 Zussman, note 38.

42 Whalley, note 38.

43 John Kenneth Galbraith, *The Anatomy of Power* (London: Hamish Hamilton, 1984), p. 59.

44 Thomas H. Naylor, William H. Willimon and Rolf Osterberg, *The Search for Meaning in the Workplace* (Nashville: Abingdon Press, 1996), p. 56.

45 Clark Davis, '"You are the Company": the Demands of Employment in the Emerging Corporate Culture, Los Angeles, 1900–1930', *Business History Review*, Vol. 70 (Autumn 1996), p. 330.

46 Quoted in *ibid.*, p. 336.

47 *Ibid.*, pp. 342, 345.

48 Quoted in Tedlow, note 15, p. 137.

49 Davis, note 45, p. 346.

50 *Ibid.*, pp. 352, 9; Tedlow, note 15, p. 138.

51 Raucher, note 12, p. 88.

52 Robert G. Simpson, *Case Studies in Management Development: Theory and Practice in Ten Selected Companies, Management Education for Itself and Its Employees* (New York: American Management Association, 1954), p. 47.

53 Davis, note 45, pp. 361–2.

54 William H. Whyte, *The Organization Man* (Harmondsworth, Middlesex: Penguin, 1960), pp. 8–10.

55 *Ibid.*, p. 124.

56 *Ibid.*, p. 142.

57 Quoted in Anthony Sampson, *Company Man: the Rise and Fall of Corporate Life* (London: HarperCollinsBusiness, 1996), p. 97.

58 Whyte, note 54, p. 256.

59 *Ibid.*, pp. 161–2.

60 *Ibid.*, p. 170.

61 *Ibid.*, p. 184.

62 See for example, Kerri McCarthy, 'Psyched Out', *Sydney Morning Herald*, 10 November 1999.

63 Thomas A. Stewart, 'Gray Flannel Suit? Moi?', *Fortune* (16 March 1998).

64 Quoted in John A. Byrne, 'Is the Company Man Really a Goner?', *Business Week* (26 August 1991), p. 12.

65 Jerry Buckley, 'The New Organization Man', *US News and World Report*, Vol. 106 (16 January 1989).

66 Sampson, note 57, p. 261.

67 Sharon Beder, *Global Spin: the Corporate Assault on Environmentalism* (Melbourne: Scribe Publications, 1997), pp. 38–41.

68 Quoted in Ross Gittins, 'Bosses Take Over Our Not So Private Lives', *Sydney Morning Herald*, 22 August 1998.

69 A. R. Gini and T. J. Sullivan, 'A Critical Overview', in Gini and Sullivan (eds), *It Comes with the Territory: an Inquiry Concerning Work and the Person* (New York: Random House, 1989), p. 23.

70 Wachtel, note 2, p. 244.

71 Cath Blakers, 'School to Work: Transition and Policy', in Millicent Poole (ed.), *Education and Work* (Hawthorn, Victoria: Australian Council for Educational Research, 1992), pp. 54–5.

72 Daniel Yankelovich, 'The New Pyschological Contracts at Work', in Gini and Sullivan, note 69, p. 86.

73 Perry Pascarella, *The New Achievers: Creating a Modern Work Ethic* (New York: The Free Press, 1984), p. 17.

74 Adrian Furnham, *The Protestant Work Ethic: the Psychology of Work-related Beliefs and Behaviours* (London: Routledge, 1990), p. 148.

75 Daniel Yankelovich and John Immerwahr, 'Putting the Work Ethic to Work', *Society*, Vol. 21, No. 2 (1984), p. 59.

76 Robert Wuthnow, *Poor Richard's Principle: Recovering the American Dream Through the Moral Dimension of Work, Business and Money* (Princeton, NJ: Princeton University Press, 1996), p. 31.

77 Naylor, note 44, p. 49.

78 David J. Cherrington, *The Work Ethic: Working Values and Values That Work* (New York: AMACON, 1980), p. 44.

79 Wendy Lowenstein, *Weevils at Work: What's Happening to Work in Australia — an Oral Record* (Annandale, NSW: Catalyst Press, 1997), p. 4.

80 David Bleakley, *Work: the Shadow and the Substance* (London: SCM Press, 1983), p. 73.

81 Blakers, note 71, p. 55.

82 Michael Maccoby and Katherine A. Terzi, 'What Happened to the Work Ethic?', in Gini and Sullivan, note 69, p. 66; Seymour Martin Lipset, 'The Work Ethic, Then and Now', *Journal of Labor Research*, Vol. 13, No. 1 (1992).

83 Abbas J. Ali, 'Work Ethic and Loyalty in Canada', *Journal of Social Psychology*, Vol. 135, No. 1 (1995); Elizabeth Fenner, 'Take the Pizza, Shove the Job', *Money*, Vol. 23, No. 3 (1994), p. 82; Duncan Gallie, 'Are the Unemployed an Underclass?', *Sociology*, Vol. 28, No. 3 (1994).

84 Cherrington, note 78, p. 44.

85 Gini and Sullivan, note 69, p. 4.

86 *Ibid.*, p. 11.

87 *Ibid.*, p. 17.

88 Ernie J. Zelinski, *The Joy of Not Working: a Book for the Retired, Unemployed, and Over-worked* (Berkeley, California: Ten Speed Press, 1997), p. 41.

89 Barry Jones, *Sleepers, Wake! Technology and the Future of Work*: Oxford University Press, 1983), p. 200.

90 Barrie Stevens and Wolfgang Michalski, 'Long-term Prospects for Work and Social Cohesion in OECD Countries: an Overview of the Issues', in Stevens and Michalski, *OECD Societies in Transition: the Future of Work and Leisure* (Paris: OECD, 1994), p. 16.

91 Wachtel, note 2, p. 244.

92 Stevens and Michalski, note 90, p. 20.

✧8✧

Work Ethic in Crisis?

———

Don't tell me about the millions of new jobs
created – I've got four of them and I'm not all that
impressed.
Worker's response to President Clinton[1]

Part-time workers are second-class citizens entitled
to third-class benefits.
Barbara Castle[2]

For the first time since the Great Depression, the
well-educated, middle-managing, mostly white
middle class is now experiencing the chronic job
insecurity long familiar to the unskilled poor.[3]
Editorial, *America*[3]

Technological change in the 1960s and 1970s prompted optimistic predictions of a new era of reduced working hours and increased leisure, as machines
did more of the work. What has happened is very different. It is true that
many corporations have drastically reduced their workforce, but for those
who remain the work has increased; for many others, work is now sporadic,
insecure and badly paid.

The changing global climate for business in the 1980s and 1990s has led to
changes in corporate attitudes towards employees. The perceived need for
global competitiveness and a lean, efficient company structure has taken
precedence over the need for employee loyalty attained through the promise
of secure employment and steady advancement.

Permanent full-time jobs have declined. Jobs are becoming more insecure.
Temporary, contract, and part-time work with no future is increasing. Work
remains central to status and identity, but these developments, together with

131

the lack of commitment of employers to lifetime employment, have created new problems of morale and motivation for employers who want a loyal, committed, hard-working workforce. Today there are endless books and journal articles on human resources management and how to get the most productivity out of workers in the new circumstances.

DOWNSIZING AND JOB INSECURITY

During the 1980s and 1990s there was a massive wave of restructuring in industrialised countries. Mergers and downsizing amongst corporations have led to large numbers of lay-offs, including many of the organisation men and women. Between 1979 and 1992 the Fortune 500 companies decreased their workforces by over four million workers.[4] The biggest 100 US companies reduced their workforces by 22 per cent in the years between 1978 and 1996. During the early 1990s a million workers were laid off in the US per year.[5] In 1998 the downsizing was still going strong, with the highest number of lay-offs by US corporations in five years.[6]

Lay-offs have been a major cause of unemployment in Australia, too. Hundreds of thousands of Australians lost their jobs in this way each year during the 1980s and more than half a million per year in the early 1990s.[7] This included 30,000 banking and 50,000 manufacturing jobs that were downsized out of existence in the first half of the 1990s.[8] Downsizing continues in Australia: 60 per cent of firms reduced staff numbers in 1997 and 1998. Sixty-four per cent of them had downsized more than once in two years.[9]

By 1988 some 300,000 professional and managerial people were out of work in Britain.[10] In the early 1990s 35 million people were unemployed in OECD countries, more than ever before.[11] This amounted to an average 8.5 per cent of the workforce and represented an upward trend in Europe, Australia and New Zealand.[12] As a result, unemployment has become institutionalised in modern societies. OECD reports suggest that 'high unemployment could be here for the foreseeable future'.[13]

Labour force cuts have not been forced by tightened economic circumstances but have been occurring at times of record company profits. Lay-offs are now seen as an expedient means of increasing profits and share value.[14] Companies such as IBM, which announced massive lay-offs (60,000 jobs), saw their share prices rise phenomenally (30 per cent). When Boeing announced 21,000 job losses, its stocks went up 31 per cent.[15] Clearly investors felt that downsizing was good for business. In Australia, highly profitable companies are as likely to downsize as those that are not very profitable.[16]

Downsizing has been accompanied by an increase in temporary and part-time jobs in many countries. Temporary jobs are increasing more quickly than any other category of work. Temporary workers, apart from being cheap, enable firms to expand and contract their workforces easily as determined by production requirements at any particular time. This is supposed to help the firms be competitive as they don't have to pay for employees when they don't have work for them. For the same reason many firms rely on contractors, who do chunks of work for them as it becomes necessary. These contractors mainly use temporary workers, hiring them and firing them as they get each contract.[17]

Millions of people who lost their jobs during the 1980s and 1990s, many of them middle-class, did not find equivalent jobs to replace them. It was often the well-paying, high-quality jobs that were cut in the downsizing fever. A 1994 US Department of Labor study found that fewer than a third of those laid off had returned to full-time jobs with as much pay as in their previous job. On average their wages dropped more than 20 per cent.[18] An Australian survey found that only 55 per cent of workers retrenched between 1995 and 1997 had found new jobs by 1999.[19]

Jobs are now far more insecure than they used to be. In *The Loyalty Effect* (1996) Frederick Reichheld says that the average US firm loses half its employees every four years.[20] Turnover rates for jobs in the service sector can be as high as 500 per cent.[21] In the US 8 million people changed jobs in the year 1997 compared to 3.8 million people in 1965. One in four workers in one survey had held their jobs for a year or less.[22] It has been estimated that the average American starting work in the 1990s could expect to change jobs 10 or more times during the length of a career.[23] Many highly trained workers, as well as recent university graduates, now find themselves working at jobs, often part-time or temporary, that use few of their skills.[24]

Between 1970 and 1990, when employment grew by 54 per cent in the US, the number of people working in part-time work whilst wanting full-time work increased by 121 per cent and the number of temporary workers increased by 210 per cent.[25] Whilst temporary agencies provided 5 per cent of workers in the US in the 1980s, they now provide 15 per cent and one of them, Manpower Inc., is the largest employer in the US and worldwide.[26] The US economy has created many new jobs but they are often low-wage, low-skilled, part-time, temporary or contingent jobs with few benefits and little security.[27] Today it is estimated that some 28 per cent of the US workforce (35 million people) are employed as part-time, temporary or contract workers.[28]

One in three Australian jobs is now either part-time or casual (temporary) compared with one in twenty in the 1970s.[29] Men have been hardest hit with the number of men in full-time employment falling from 67 per cent in 1966 to 50 per cent in 1997.[30] The number of casual full-time jobs increased ten times between 1990 and 1997.[31] More than one in four workers (27 per cent) is now employed on a temporary basis (the second highest percentage of all OECD nations),[32] double the proportion in the early 1980s.[33] More than 80 per cent of them would prefer to have permanent jobs.[34] As in the US, firms like Manpower Services Australasia are booming. It is doubling in size every five years and the number of other employment agencies established to provide contract labour trebled between March 1994 and September 1997.[35]

In Europe casual work is referred to as 'precarious' work and in France the growth of precarious work was such a problem that a major election platform of the winning Socialist government in France in 1997 was to deal with the growth of precarious jobs and create hundreds of thousands of permanent jobs.[36] In Britain the proportion of the workforce in part-time work is approaching one-third, compared to 5 per cent in 1951 and 15 per cent in 1971.[37] Only half the families in Britain include a full-time worker, compared to two-thirds in 1979.[38] In 1995 1.5 million workers were in temporary jobs, up 50 per cent on 1985. The increase has been even more rapid since 1995.[39]

In all these countries, jobs have become temporary or casual so that employers can avoid paying benefits to which permanent employees are entitled, and can terminate employees without cost or obligation.[40] Those working for labour-hire firms and work contractors, or self-employed, are twice as likely to be killed on the job as those who are regularly employed.[41] Temporary workers can be terminated with as little as an hour's notice.[42] In Britain, some firms 'will even insist on specific waiver clauses [in the contracts of temporary workers] renouncing rights to compensation for redundancy or unfair dismissal'.[43] Some US companies, such as Tupperware in Hemingway, South Carolina, have sacked their workers and then re-employed them as temporary workers without benefits.[44]

People in casual and part-time jobs seldom have sick pay, holiday leave or superannuation entitlements. They get very little training. And they are unable to get a bank loan with this sort of insecure employment.[45] Inevitably, such jobs have lower status as well as lower pay rates than full-time permanent jobs. In Australia a quarter of casual workers say they do not 'get enough work to support themselves and their family'.[46]

In Britain, outsourcing of work, where an organisation gets an outside organisation to do work previously done in-house, was encouraged by successive Conservative governments as a way of cutting costs and improving efficiency in government departments and agencies.[47] In Australia private firms and government departments have contracted out sections of their operations previously done in-house, such as cleaning, maintenance, security, catering and information systems. Occasionally companies have outsourced their whole labour force, handing them over to firms such as Manpower to manage.[48] The amount of outsourcing is expected to double over the next five years – and the more work is outsourced, the more jobs are casualised.[49]

Outsourcing, or contracting out, has the same advantages as hiring temporary workers. One firm, Australian Contracting Solutions (ACS), advertises its services, according to the *Sydney Morning Herald*, by informing employers that

> by using contractors, companies do not have to pay award wages, annual leave pay and loading, penalty rates, sick leave, public holidays, workers' compensation, superannuation, payroll tax, fringe benefits, redundancy and severance packages. Neither will a company be caught by unfair dismissal rules, equal opportunity legislation, industrial relations legislation, preference to unionists, demarcation disputes, seniority or parental leave.[50]

Outsourcing can lead to the sweatshop conditions found in various industries in the US, Australia and elsewhere. A good example is the garment industry where immigrant workers, unaware of their rights, work long hours for little pay and no security of employment. They receive neither benefits nor overtime rates; often don't receive the minimum wage; and sometimes even have to give their children work to help them meet deadlines. Often they are employed by firms that are contracted to do the work by big-name companies. The products of this sweated labour can be sold for large prices in the top fashion shops.[51]

In Australia the Textile Clothing and Footware Union (TCFU) estimates there are 329,000 garment 'outworkers' with some 70,000 children involved in working in these sweatshop conditions as part of contracting out in the garment industry. The children work before and after school and during holidays to help their parents, who are paid as little as $2 per hour.[52]

The erosion of work conditions in recent years has also meant that working hours have become more irregular and unpredictable for workers. People can be asked to work at all hours, and on weekends, without getting extra or overtime pay as they had previously. A person's working hours are tailored to meet the needs of employers rather than the needs of workers.[53]

The new system of 'enterprise bargaining' in Australia has enabled employers to institute 12-hour work periods (43 per cent of wholesale and retail trade agreements include this provision), to reduce meal breaks and stagger them so the workers don't all have lunch together, and to average working hours over one-month or even three-month periods. As a result, only a third of the workforce regularly works standard hours. Additionally, working hours can change from week to week. This causes problems for childcare, coordinating family activities, and commitments to sports and other activities outside work.[54]

The combination of downsizing and temporary work has enabled employers to keep wages down, as we saw in Chapter 5. Because of the loss of well-paid, full-time jobs, it now takes two people working in a family to bring in the amount of money one salary used to bring in in 1973: 'one well paid smoke-stack job with health insurance has been replaced by two service jobs without benefits'.[55] In Canada, more than half a million people have taken on a second job.[56] The percentage of workers who officially took on second jobs in the US increased from 5.7 million workers in 1985 to 7.7 million in 1997. Many more took on unofficial second jobs which they did not report for taxation or other reasons.[57]

The loyalty of a few lucky people with skills that are in demand is bought with high salaries, bonuses and stock options. Those who have done well in the new circumstances include those who work as public relations executives, investment bankers, lawyers, real estate developers, financial consultants, systems analysts and those who have creative talents that are in demand in the commercial world of video, film and the media.[58] Their wages have increased dramatically. But for those who work in 'routine production services' or in the routine service industry jobs, the situation is very different.[59]

The restructuring of workplaces has created two different classes of workers: those who form part of the essential core of company staff and have full-time permanent jobs that are well paid with various associated benefits, and those at the periphery who have temporary, casual, part-time work and few benefits. Some are highly skilled and do freelance work that is highly paid. Most are low-skilled jobs that are poorly paid.

BREAKING THE EMPLOYMENT CONTRACT

Corporate downsizing has involved the retrenchment of 'entire layers of middle managers and whole categories of professional staff', in other words the organisation men and women.[60] In Britain restructuring – eliminating management layers – had become the norm for corporations in the 1980s.[61] The 1980s left British middle managers insecure and unsure of promotion prospects.[62] The same occurred in the US. The middle manager of the 1990s was often a 'frustrated, disillusioned individual … with no real hope of career progression'.[63] A survey of 13,000 executives by St Vincent's Private Health Assessment Centre in Sydney found that 'stress levels had increased dramati-cally among executives' during the 1990s because of job insecurity and fear of retrenchment.[64]

Traditionally there has been an unstated understanding in most Western countries between employers and employees, particularly those employed in management and skilled positions, where good work and loyalty on the part of the employee were rewarded by job security and promotion. That under-standing was basically an unwritten employment contract which stated:

- Employees would put in a reasonable work effort for a company and show loyalty.

- Employers, in return, would pay fair wages and provide reasonable working conditions, promotions based on merit, and job security to the extent that their financial situation made it possible.[65]

The employment contract has been eroded by the downsizing of recent times. Whilst in the past firms had reduced the workforce in times of recession when sales were down and they could not afford the extra employees, the new cycle of downsizing has occurred when many corporations were making big profits. Before, unemployment had been temporary and depended on the health of the economy; now unemployment is a more permanent feature of booming economies.[66] Before, the social contract between worker and company had been broken reluctantly, when there was no choice. Now, it is a simple matter of economic calculation and employees are just another variable in the calculation.

In the past, employers have absorbed some of the economic consequences of fluctuations in market demand and production by keeping most middle- and upper-level employees on although they didn't have enough work for them. Now, employees are the first cost to be cut[67] and the economic conse-quences of those fluctuations are being borne by individuals who lose their jobs when production is reduced and have to go without wages for that time.[68] The risks and costs of economic cycles have been transferred to the workforce but the profits have been kept by the employers.

Job insecurity has made people frightened and those who are left have to do more work to make up for the smaller workforce.[69] The obvious message that employees have received from the massive lay-offs has been that if you want to keep your job you have to work harder and make yourself more valuable. Yet the profound effect of the downsizing on employee morale has not produced, in many cases, the increases in productivity hoped for.[70]

The aim of downsizing, according to British management consultant Charles Handy, was 'to employ half as many people, pay them twice as much and increase output by three times as much ($1/2$ x 2 x 3).[71] But in reality lay-offs have often resulted in lower productivity and lower profits because they have demoralised surviving employees, whose commitment to the company is weakened. Less than half of the US firms that downsized between 1990 and 1996 reported an increased profit in the year following the lay-offs, and an American Management Association survey found that less than half of the companies surveyed reported an increase in productivity three years after downsizing.[72]

A survey of corporate communications people at over 250 of the largest firms in the US, by Hill and Knowlton and Yankelovich Partners, found that over half believed that morale had declined as a result of organisational changes and lay-offs.[73] Trust has been another casualty of downsizing, with three-quarters of executives surveyed in another survey saying that trust had declined.[74]

An Australian survey by academics at the Melbourne Institute found that there was no evidence that downsized companies made greater profits in the following two years, but that downsizing caused a considerable decline in morale, loyalty and job satisfaction – as well as productivity losses and increased workplace injuries.[75] John Buchanan, deputy director of the Australian Centre for Industrial Relations Research, observes a culture of 'high-stress, low trust' amongst those remaining in jobs following retrenchments.[76] And a British study found that the number of males in the workforce suffering depression had doubled in the last few years to 9 per cent.[77]

A research team has investigated the phenomenon of falling productivity in the face of job cuts and found that moderate levels of job insecurity resulting from lay-offs can lead to increased work effort, especially when surviving workers are the breadwinners for their families, but if survivors experience either high or low levels of job insecurity then they will not work harder, because they don't believe it will make much difference. They recommend to employers planning the lay-offs that they need to 'create moderate levels of job insecurity' in order to get the most work out of the remaining workers.[78]

As corporations downsize and demonstrate their lack of loyalty to their employees, some employees feel a declining sense of loyalty in return. A 1996 survey of employees found that 'nearly 80 per cent of employees are "inactive" – just doing their jobs and unwilling to expend any more energy than is absolutely necessary' – and that this is a consequence of downsizing which left employees 'disengaged, uncommitted and unwilling to give 110 per cent'. Some 60 per cent feel that their companies don't value them.[79] In a recent *Fortune* magazine article on 'The New Organization Man' Nina Munk observes: 'New young workers know that loyalty is for suckers; a company can get rid of them at will.'[80]

In an effort to get people to think differently about jobs, the 1990s management literature attempted to redefine and reconceptualise jobs. Companies claimed that what they offer in place of lifetime employment is marketable skills and interesting work.[81] Workers were expected to move from job to job and team to team, garnering skills and knowledge and managing their careers to ensure that they had the experience and skills to remain an attractive proposition to employers.[82]

A whole new rhetoric has been developed to convince professional workers and middle management that the new insecurity works in favour of those who maintain a work ethic. Job security and long-term employment is supposed to have been replaced by 'long-term employability'.[83]

> Job security no longer comes from sticking with a single company but from maintaining a portfolio of job-related skills. This shift signals a 'new psychological contract' between employer and employee. Under the terms of this new contract, employers provide learning in place of job security.[84]

In the journal *Across the Board*, A. J. Vogl notes that 'some corporations are encouraging their workers to think of themselves as "employables" rather than employees' and to build their self-esteem around their work rather than the company.[85] Similarly, Charles Handy has coined the term 'portfolio workers' to cover the same idea of workers with portable skills that they sell to successive employers.[86] Ken Ferguson of Business in the Community, an Australian business-sponsored organisation, talks about the need for workers to develop 'enterprise' values and is teaching school students the concept of 'self-managed employment' where they learn how to present themselves to clients.[87]

REINFORCING THE WORK ETHIC

The dispiriting of workers forced to work in dead-end, temporary jobs without any future has led some writers to claim a decline in the work ethic,[88] but what is really happening is that these workers are unable to express their work ethic in such jobs without feeling exploited.

In particular, the 1990s generation of new job seekers – variously referred to as Slackers, Twentysomethings, or Generation X – were accused of having no work ethic and being lazy.[89] For example, a 1996 Christian Broadcasting Network programme began: 'If you think service has gotten worse and then worse in America, you're probably right. Increasing numbers of employees and managers say the problem is today's young worker, Generation Xers who just don't have a strong work ethic.'[90] The expert interviewed for the programme, a consultant for fast-food chains, said that these young people were

> selfish, get bored easily, and don't know the meaning of loyalty and commitment.... Our generation, my generation, was a generation that looked upon work as the be all, end all. This generation, for them, it's just a means to an end, to their free time, their leisure, and their money to have fun.[91]

Yet research does not seem to back up these perceptions that young people have less work ethic than previous generations. Surveys by both the Roper Center for Public Opinion Research and the Gallup organisation have found that the work ethic is just as important for younger people as for older generations.[92] Bob Filipczak, a self-proclaimed member of Generation X, suggests that they seem to have a different attitude to work because most positions available to them have no future: they are 'McJobs', that is 'temporary, dead-end jobs in the service sector'.[93] Young people feel no loyalty to employers in such jobs and tend to job hop. It also means they don't look to work for their fulfilment and do not willingly work overtime:

> Why put in lots of overtime and bust butt for a McJob? If even well-paid, challenging work is seen as a temporary assignment, it's hard to argue that young workers should go the extra mile in the name of future promotions or job security that most companies can't deliver.[94]

Young people still feel the need to give of their best but are not doing so because they do not feel they will be the beneficiaries of their work given the structure of the societal reward system that sees fewer benefits of increased productivity going to workers.

It is the perceived decline in the work ethic, particularly amongst the young, and the demoralisation of older workers that has prompted a resurgence in advocacy of the work ethic in recent years. President Clinton named the work ethic as one of the traits that need national encouragement.[95] In this he was in agreement with Speaker of the House Newt Gingrich, who listed the work ethic as one of the key factors 'at the heart of the successes we Americans have had as a people'.[96] Jesse Jackson promoted the work ethic as an essential character trait that blacks need to adopt if they are to achieve equality with whites.[97]

Various states in the US have programmes for instilling a work ethic in minor offenders. In Washington State a sentencing judge may recommend that an offender serve his/her sentence at a work ethic camp which lasts 120–180 days. Each day of confinement at the camp is considered to be the equivalent of three days of standard confinement.[98] In Tennessee judges can use, as an alternative to prison sentencing, community correction programmes which include a vocational component aimed at instilling a work ethic.[99] In Spokane, Washington, a community policing demonstration project aims to instil a conventional work ethic in youths thought to be 'at risk of abusing alcohol or illegal drugs or of joining a criminal gang'.[100]

The media also reinforce the work ethic, not only in news and editorial content but also through advertising.

> Prime-time beer commercials are mythic playlets, romanticizing and idealizing the Herculean efforts of men at work. They depict men pouring molten ingots

in factories, spanning huge chasms with cables of steel, cutting down tall trees in the midst of a rain forest, blasting tunnels through mountains of solid granite.... And through all the grit of these various scenarios the participants are, to a man, grinning from ear to ear at both their accomplishments and their camaraderie. After all of this the worker-warriors retire to a local saloon where they consume large quantities of iced beer and debrief one another in a warm sundown glow of work well done and worth doing.[102]

Writing in *Newsweek,* Robert Samuelson labelled preferences for more leisure time as 'fundamentally un-American'. He proudly pointed out: 'Ours has always been a hurried society, brimming (perhaps excessively) with ambition. We crowd more things into already-crowded schedules. We are uneasy with ease.'[101]

Business leaders often emphasise the importance of a work ethic. Peter Du Pont wrote in the *National Review* that

[t]he work ethic is at the core of a healthy society, and the individual responsibility of doing a job, earning a living, and striving for improvement is crucial to restoring opportunity and self-respect to underclass Americans.[103]

Even sports people are lauded for their work ethic. For example, basketball players Michael Jordan and Karl Malone describe their 'nose-to-the-grindstone work ethic' which they claim younger players lack. 'It's hard to suit up every single night and play when you don't feel like playing,' says Malone. 'Young players coming in have got to learn the work ethic we've had. If they can't take the lessons we've learned, the game of basketball is going to take a hit,' says Jordan.[104] Cal Ripken Jr was praised by President Clinton after playing 2,131 consecutive games and the ABC television commentator called him 'a paragon of the work ethic'.[105] In the same vein, Olympic gold medallist Lisa Leslie, also a basketballer, told *Seventeen* magazine that the reason for her success was a strong work ethic.[106]

MOTIVATING WORKERS IN THE TWENTY-FIRST CENTURY

Downsizing and the growth of insecure jobs has clearly created a problem for employers in terms of motivating employees and ensuring that they work hard on the job even though it may be temporary. One response has been to use new technologies to intensify the monitoring of workers, particularly low-level unskilled workers. Computers enable close and immediate monitoring and evaluation of job performance.[107] Millions of employees today are subject to some form of electronic surveillance of their work, such as counting key strokes or keeping track of time spent on telephone calls.[108] Such monitoring is just as intimidating, persistent and stressful as an assembly line.

In Australia workplace surveillance is big business, and miniaturisation of camera equipment is making it easier and cheaper. One survey by Price Waterhouse-Coopers found that half of Australia's top 65 companies said they used video equipment to monitor the workplace. Most, but not all (85 per cent) told their employees they were doing it. Six per cent admitted to regularly monitoring email.[109]

One of the booming industries of the 1990s was call centres. Many companies and government agencies are contracting out their telephone answering services. Dozens of workers spend all day in a large open-plan office answering the phone, up to 100 calls a day:

> New technology is making possible an old-style of autocratic control of workers that some thought dead and buried. Every little move they make is monitored. If phone agents fail to process calls fast enough, or stray from the prescribed script, or fail to convert enough calls into sales, the electronic monitoring and the audio tapes will expose them.... For almost half the workers in the industry take-home pay can be affected if they fail to meet targets for calls taken or made. This is performance assessment on a minute-by-minute basis.[110]

Increasingly employers are seeking information about employees including their shopping habits, attitudes to unions and living arrangements. In the US,

> [f]or less than $100, employers can purchase packages of detailed personal information that can include a criminal history, driving records, credit histories and workers' compensation records, as well as more subjective information on character and reputation gathered during interviews with former employers and even neighbors.[111]

In Britain the *Sunday Times* reported on a proposal to implant microchips in workers to keep track of them. Cybernetics expert Kevin Warwick told the paper: 'It is pushing at the limits of what society will accept, but in a way it is not such a big deal.... Many employees already carry swipecards.' Perhaps more palatable is the 'smart badge' being developed by AT&T Laboratories in Cambridge, which uses ultrasound to keep track of an employee's whereabouts.[112]

In Japan Hitachi is marketing a cellphone-based tracking device that will inform employers not only where workers are but whether they are standing, walking, running or lying down. Originally developed to keep track of family members with dementia, it is too expensive for most families and is now being offered to employers who want to catch workers who sneak out of the office for a coffee break or a nap.[113]

An alternative approach to increasing work productivity, particularly for work that requires skill and discretion and therefore the willing effort of employees, has been to encourage a new work ethic and elicit loyalty through management techniques. The business management literature of the 1990s told a story of a completely redesigned workplace 'where hierarchy is dead and partners engage in meaningful but often fast-paced and stressful work in a collaborative environment of mutual commitment and trust'.[114] These texts are sometimes idealistic rhetoric about how things are, sometimes exhortations and predictions about how things should be or will be.[115] What is being described, however, is an extension of earlier Human Relations and Human Resources approaches and the goal is clearly to get greater productivity from workers.

In these new management structures many of the middle levels of management have been removed as a result of downsizing. For example, when Xerox restructured in 1993 it eliminated 9,500 jobs and reduced the 18 pay levels to only three.[116] The flatter structures that remain are no longer described in authoritarian terms. Instead of bosses there are 'coaches' and 'leaders' and the remaining middle managers have become 'team leaders', 'facilitators', 'mediators', etc. Workers have become 'partners' and 'associates'.[117]

The idea is that traditional workers were treated as mindless bodies who had to be told exactly what to do and closely supervised to ensure they worked hard. The new worker is part of a team of people committed to company goals, contributing ideas and suggestions about how they can improve productivity and solve problems, coaxing each other to work hard, and supported and aided by the leaders and coaches. Leadership is now supposed to be inspirational rather than autocratic.[118]

The aim is to ensure workers work harder and longer, supervised by each other, utilising group pressure to ensure performance and undertaking some of the information processing tasks that were once undertaken by the missing layers of middle management. The commitment and loyalty that are necessary for this to work are supposed to come from visionary and inspirational company leadership and/or a company culture that promotes certain well-defined core values, 'a sense of purpose beyond just making money'.[119]

Such core values are felt to be necessary to elicit loyalty and commitment in the absence of the traditional workplace contract of secure employment in return for loyalty. Team loyalties are another way of substituting for lost company loyalty and keeping temporary workers in line through group pressure. One way to accomplish this is to replace individual performance bonuses with team bonuses, shared equally between team members, and to get teams to compete with each other. This engenders a team spirit but also the coercive team pressures that discipline individual team members.[120]

Team discipline is also necessary to make up for the eradication of layers of middle management and supervisory staff. The new system, rather than assuming that workers have no interest in their work and need to be closely supervised, hopes to improve motivation by enriching jobs through making teams of workers responsible for their own performance and quality control.[121]

The rhetoric of lessened managerial control in the modern workplace is belied by the fact that the new monitoring technologies are often utilised in the same workplaces as the new management strategies. The only difference is that both the bosses/leaders and the workers themselves have access to the monitoring data.[122] 'Worker participation' and 'democracy' are other ways, in the new circumstances, to engender commitment to the task and to the firm in the absence of employer commitment to the worker. The new 'participative management' claims to empower and involve workers using 'quality circles, project teams, task forces, and work groups'.[123] This worker democracy is being promoted globally 'in the popular mass media, the popular management books which can be found in airport bookstores and in universities among business school academics and organisational theorists'.[124]

But the participation is token rather than real. It is not the workers who decide the company core values and goals, nor are they supposed to question them. Rather, they are supposed to suggest better ways of achieving them. 'As a result, the necessity of allegiance to a set of ends over which one has little control can become a recipe for a dangerous corporate intrusiveness that produces not autonomy and freedom, but enforced conformity, not genuine participation, but a kind of high-touch coercion.'[125]

James Paul Gee, Glynda Hull and Colin Lankshear, in *The New Work Order*, studied an award-winning firm in Silicon Valley, with a good reputation for high-quality work, that was pioneering the new type of management which is supposed to empower workers and create an 'enchanted' workplace of the future, giving the worker a sense of 'ownership, responsibility and pride'.[126] The company was progressively training and establishing some 200 'self-directed work teams' to improve productivity and quality control. The aim was to create a new culture in the workplace.[127] The training sought to help workers understand why they were in teams and how they could solve problems and improve productivity.[128]

Gee and his colleagues sat in on some of the training sessions and found the classes were extremely patronising and involved little participation. The teacher stood at the front and the workers sat in rows, in a traditional school classroom set-up. The interaction often involved inviting students to offer the 'right' answers to questions posed by the teacher, or getting people to read aloud from the course manual. Writing activities involved filling in blank spaces with the 'correct' words or summarising what they had learned in a 'pearls of wisdom' section of their workbooks.[129] The researchers noted:

Not once in all the classes that we observed were participants ever invited to respond critically to reading material – by contrasting their own experiences with examples provided, by revealing what seemed particularly apropos and what wrongheaded, by offering additional topics to be discussed or covered.... We would argue that the message sent here is 'don't question', 'listen carefully', and 'follow directions'.[130]

Indeed in practice the teams accepted directions from engineers and others above them in the hierarchy unquestioningly, even when they knew they were wrong.[131] They had enough sense to see that, despite the rhetoric, nothing had really changed in terms of power differentials in the areas they worked in.[132] What had changed was that they now had extra things to do, such as attending team meetings and filling out more forms, whilst they were also expected to increase production.[133]

There is nothing special about the training programme described by Gee and his colleagues. The curriculum materials used were standard materials produced by outside specialists who produce them for a range of companies.[134] Worker empowerment is little more than rhetoric and manipulation and the last thing that employers want is critical thinking or questioning from employees. Therefore the training that accompanies the new work arrangements has to be closer to indoctrination or propaganda than real education that requires a deeper understanding and questioning of grounds and reasoning.[135]

Laurie Graham, a sociologist who worked on the assembly line at a Subaru-Isuzu plant in the US, found that the façade of teamwork could be even more oppressive than an openly autocratic model because peer pressure replaced discipline from the boss, and was continually present. The rhetoric of teamwork was used to keep unions out and to prevent individuals from complaining about being worked too hard. Such complaints indicated that a person was not being a good team player.[136]

CONCLUSION

The idea that hard work provided an increasing income and social mobility over one's lifetime has been dealt a severe blow by the corporate restructuring of the 1980s and 1990s and the new relationship with employees that offered little to peripheral employees apart from low wages that might end at any time. For millions of people in precarious employment, the old rhetoric of the self-made man and work leading to success has little grounding in the reality of their experience.

The age-old problem of how to get workers to work long and hard and yet produce high-quality output has become a pressing issue. One way to solve it has been to increase surveillance of employees. Another has been to introduce the façade of participatory democracy. The technical content of work has changed little and the degree of worker autonomy is purposely kept limited.

While position titles may have changed, hierarchies remain and production goals are set by those at the top of the hierarchy.[137]

Thomas H. Naylor and his colleagues note in their book on the meaning of work that in fact 'American companies are among the least democratic institutions in the world.' Not only is there no freedom of speech, assembly or the press, but a small group of people make all the significant decisions, including those that have most impact on the majority of workers such as working hours and conditions.[138]

In an effort to ensure that precarious, low-paid jobs are preferable to unemployment, politicians and businesspeople have adjusted the work ethic to emphasise the morality of contributing to society through work. They have also ensured that welfare is more difficult to get, more temporary, and more unpleasant so as to ensure that the fear of job loss keeps productivity high. This strategy is discussed further in the next two chapters.

NOTES

1 Quoted in Charles J. Whalen, 'The Anxious Society: Middle-class Insecurity and the Crisis of the American Dream', *The Humanist*, Vol. 56 (September/October 1996).

2 Quoted in Suzanne Franks, *Having None of It: Women, Men and the Future of Work* (London: Granta Books, 1999), p. 80.

3 'Laying off the American Dream', *America*, Vol. 174 (March 1996).

4 Paul Bernstein, *American Work Values: Their Origin and Development* (Albany, NY: State University of New York Press, 1997), p. 187.

5 Whalen, note 1.

6 Daniel McGinn and John McCormick, 'Your Next Job', *Newsweek (in the Bulletin)* (2 February 1999), p. 58.

7 Social Justice Consultative Council, 'Social Justice: Economic Restructuring and Job Loss', (Melbourne: Social Justice Consultative Council, 1992), p. 9.

8 Sue Lecky, 'The Failure of Slash and Earn', *Sydney Morning Herald*, 4 July 1998, p. 83.

9 Ross Gittins, 'When Downsizing Backfires on the Bosses', *Sydney Morning Herald*, 6 October 1999, p. 21.

10 Anthony Sampson, *Company Man: the Rise and Fall of Corporate Life* (London: Harper-CollinsBusiness, 1996), p. 256.

11 OECD, *The OECD Jobs Study: Evidence and Explanations*, 2 vols, Vol. I (Paris: OECD, 1994), p. 1.

12 Barrie Stevens and Wolfgang Michalski, 'Long-term Prospects for Work and Social Cohesion in OECD Countries: an Overview of the Issues', in Stevens and Michalski, *OECD Societies in Transition: the Future of Work and Leisure* (Paris: OECD, 1994), p. 7.

13 *Ibid.*, p. 7.

14 Murray Weidenbaum, 'A New Social Contract for the American Workplace', *Challenge!* Vol. 38, No. 1 (1995).

15 *Ibid.*

16 Gittins, note 9, p. 21.
17 James Paul Gee, Glynda Hull and Colin Lankshear, *The New Work Order: Behind the Language of the New Capitalism* (Sydney: Allen and Unwin, 1996), p. 78.
18 Whalen, note 1.
19 Cited in Gittins, note 9, p. 21.
20 Cited in Chris Lee and Jean Bethke Elshtain, 'Trust Me', *Training*, Vol. 34, No. 1 (1997).
21 Barbara Whitaker Shimko, 'Pre-Hire Assessment of the New Work Force: Finding Wheat (and Work Ethic) Among the Chaff', *Business Horizons*, Vol. 35, No. 3 (1992).
22 McGinn and McCormick, note 6, p. 49.
23 Bruce Nussbaum, 'I'm Worried about My Job', *Business Week* (7 October 1991), p. 94.
24 Clinton E. Boutwell, *Shell Game: Corporate America's Agenda for Schools* (Bloomington, Indiana: Phi Delta Kappa Educational Foundation, 1997), pp. 30–1.
25 Whalen, note 1.
26 *Ibid.*; Barry Bluestone and Stephen Rose, 'Overworked and Underemployed: Unravelling an Economic Enigma', *The American Prospect* (March–April 1997); Chris Bullock, 'A Flexible Future', *Background Briefing, ABC Radio*, 25 October 1998.
27 Boutwell, note 24, pp. 30–31.
28 JoAnn Lum, 'Sweatshops Are Us', *Dollars and Sense* (Sept–Oct 1997), p. 7.
29 Nikki Barrowclough, 'They Get What?!' *Good Weekend* (6 June 1998), p. 18.
30 Paul Cleary, 'Casual Work Boom Hits Job Security', *Sydney Morning Herald*, 26 May 1998.
31 *Ibid.*
32 ACTU, 'Working People Want a Balanced and Secure Working Life: ACTU Survey Reveals Many Don't Have One' (ACTU, 1999), http://www.actu.asn.au/national/media/media99/990902survey.htm.
33 Bullock, note 26.
34 Clive Hamilton, 'Winners and Losers from Globalisation', *Australasian Science* (July 1998), p. 42; Cleary, note 30.
35 Diana Bagnall, 'All Work No Jobs', *Bulletin* (2 February 1999), p. 14.
36 Bullock, note 26.
37 Franks, note 2, p. 80.
38 *Ibid.*, p. 85.
39 *Ibid.*, p. 91.
40 George J. Church, 'The Work Ethic Lives! Americans Labor Harder and at More Jobs than Ever', *Time*, Vol. 130 (7 September 1987); Juliet B. Schor, *The Overworked American: the Unexpected Decline in Leisure* (New York: Basic Books, 1991), p. 31; Whalen, note 1.
41 Michael Quinlan, Professor of Industrial Relations, quoted in Chris Richards, 'Dying to Work', *Background Briefing, ABC Radio*, 8 June 1997.
42 Bullock, note 26.
43 Franks, note 2, p. 92.
44 Adele Horin, 'All Work, Low Pay', *Sydney Morning Herald*, 27 December 1997, p. 6s.
45 Barrowclough, note 29, p. 18.
46 ACTU, note 32.
47 Peter Reilly and Penny Tamkin, 'Outsourcing: a Flexible Option for the Future?' (Brighton: Institute for Employment Studies, 1996), p. 2.
48 Bullock, note 26.
49 *Ibid.*
50 Helen Trinca, 'Reinventing the Worker as Contractor', *Sydney Morning Herald*, 1 June 1999.

51 Lum, note 28, p. 7.
52 Gerard Ryle and Gary Hughes, 'Pocket Money That Comes at a Price', *Sydney Morning Herald*, 26 October 1998, p. 5.
53 Ron Callus, 'Employers Flex Their Muscle on Hours', *Sydney Morning Herald*, 3 August 1999.
54 *Ibid.*
55 Marilyn French, quoted in Franks, note 2, p. 176.
56 Michael Posner, 'Whatever Happened to Spare Time: 'The Protestant Ethos in Turmoil', or Why We Cannot Stop Working', *World Press Review*, Vol. 38 (September 1991), p. 26.
57 Church, note 40; Schor, note 40, p. 31; Whalen, note 1.
58 Boutwell, note 24, pp. 43–4.
59 *Ibid.*, p. 51.
60 Nussbaum, note 23, p. 94.
61 Sampson, note 10, p. 254.
62 *Ibid.*, p. 255.
63 A study by Sue Dopson and Rosemary Stewart quoted in Sampson, note 10, p. 254.
64 Madeleine Coorey, 'Overweight, Stressed Out, the Puff Goes Out of Executives', *The Australian*, 19 August 1998, p. 6.
65 Adapted from Weidenbaum, note 14.
66 Whalen, note 1.
67 McGinn and McCormick, note 6, p. 48.
68 Franks, note 2, pp. 94.
69 Sue Lecky, note 8, p. 87.
70 Weidenbaum, note 14.
71 Cited in Franks, note 2, p. 67.
72 Lee, note 20; 'Fortune 1000 Companies Treating Employees Better', *Inside PR* (2 December 1996).
73 'Employee Issues Top Corporate Agenda', *Inside PR* (31 October 1996).
74 *Ibid.*
75 Gittins, note 9, p. 21.
76 Bagnall, note 35, p. 14.
77 Bullock, note 26.
78 Joel Brockner, Steven Grover, Thomas F. Reed and Rocki Lee Dewitt, 'Layoff and Surviving Employees – the Relationship Between Job Insecurity and Work Effort', *Stores*, Vol. 76, No. 1 (Section 1) (1994).
79 'The Legacy of Downsizing: Dispirited Workforce', *Inside PR* (13 January 1997).
80 Nina Munk, 'The New Organization Man', *Fortune* (16 March 1998).
81 Thomas A. Stewart, 'Gray Flannel Suit? Moi?', *Fortune* (16 March 1998).
82 Gee, Hull and Lankshear, note 17, p. 30.
83 Bullock, note 26.
84 Jeanne C. Meister, *Corporate Universities: Lessons in Building a World-class Work Force*, revised edn (New York: McGraw-Hill, 1998), p. 9.
85 A. J. Vogl, 'Soul Searching: Looking for Meaning in the Workplace', *Across the Board*, Vol. 34, No. 9 (1997).
86 Cited in *ibid.*
87 Bagnall, note 35, p. 15.
88 For example, Abbas J. Ali, Tomas Falcone and A. A. Azim, 'Work Ethic in the USA

and Canada', *Journal of Management Development*, Vol. 14, No. 6 (1995); Chuck Colson and Jack Eckerd, *Why America Doesn't Work* (Dallas: Word Publishing, 1991); Larry Reynolds, 'America's Work Ethic: Lost in Turbulent Times?', *Management Review*, Vol. 81, No. 10 (1992); Kevin Blackburn, 'Does the West Need to Learn "Asian Values"?' *IPA Review*, Vol. 47, No. 2 (1994); Seymour Martin Lipset, 'The Work Ethic, Then and Now', *Journal of Labor Research*, Vol. 13, No. 1 (1992); John Graham, 'The End of the Great White Male', *USA Today*, Vol. 122 (November 1993); David T. Bottoms, 'Dominate or Die: Can American Industry Survive in the '90s?', *Industry Week*, Vol. 241 (7 September 1992); Bob Yandle, 'Does Anyone Still Care?' *Supervision*, Vol. 53, No. 9 (1992); Diane Stafford, 'Instilling the Work Ethic', *Kansas City Star*, 20 October 1995.

89 Catherine Romano, 'Generation X's Horoscope', *HR Focus*, Vol. 71, No. 8 (1994), p. 22.

90 Jennifer Robinson, 'Generation X: 'What's a Work Ethic?'', *Christian Broadcasting Network*, 24 April 1996.

91 *Ibid.*

92 James Aley, 'Slacker Myths', *Fortune*, Vol. 129 (21 February 1994), p. 24.

93 Bob Filipczak, 'It's Just a Job: Generation X at Work', *Training*, Vol. 31, No. 4 (1994).

94 *Ibid.*

95 Richard Todd, 'All Work, No Ethic', *Worth Magazine* (December/January 1996).

96 Newt Gingrich, 'Renewing American Civilisation', *Futurist*, Vol. 29, No. 4 (1995).

97 A. R. Gini and T. J. Sullivan, 'A Critical Overview', in A. R. Gini and T. J. Sullivan (eds), *It Comes with the Territory: an Inquiry Concerning Work and the Person* (New York: Random House, 1989), p. 12.

98 Washington State, 'RCW 9.94.137 Work Ethic Camp Program', (Washington State, 1995). http://www.leg.wa.gov/pub/rcw/title_09/chapter_094a/rcw_9_94a_137

99 Kirby Logan, 'Fifth Work Ethic', *Training and Development*, Vol. 49, No. 3 (1995), p. 2.

100 Quint C. Thurman, 'Cops, Kids and Community Policing: an Assessment of a Community Policing Demonstration Project', *Crime and Delinquency*, Vol. 39, No. 4 (1993).

101 Robert J. Samuelson, 'Overworked Americans?', *Newsweek*, Vol. 119 (16 March 1992), p. 50.

102 Gini and Sullivan, note 97, p. 13.

103 Quoted in Todd, note 95.

104 Tom Enlund, 'Jordan, Malone Preach Work Ethic', (NBA Features, 1997). http://cgi2.nando.net/newsroom/sports/bkb/1997/nba/chi/feat/archive/060497/chi34823.html

105 Todd, note 95.

106 Carmen Renee Thompson, 'Lisa Leslie: Center of Attention', *Seventeen*, Vol. 56 (June 1997), p. 116.

107 Gee, Hull and Lankshear, note 17, p. 38.

108 Colson and Eckerd, note 88, p. 22.

109 Joanne Painter, 'Crackdown on Workplace Spying', *Sydney Morning Herald*, 25 January 1999.

110 Adele Horin, 'Working the Phones', *Sydney Morning Herald*, 19 September 1998, p. 6s.

111 'Technology Raises New Employee Privacy Concerns', *Reputation Management* (November/December 1995).

112 Stephan Bevan, 'Companies Seek Chip Implants to Control Staff', *Sunday Times*, 9 May 1999.

113 Peter Hadfield, 'You Can Run, but You Can't Hide', *New Scientist* (21 August 1999), p.12.

114 Gee, Hull and Lankshear, note 17, p. 25.

115 *Ibid.*, p. 24.

116 Meister, note 84, p. 3.

117 Gee, Hull and Lankshear, note 17, pp. 26, 31.

118 Meister, note 84, p. 3.

119 Quoted in Gee, Hull and Lankshear, note 17, p. 32.

120 *Ibid.*, pp. 107–8.

121 Paul Ransome, *The Work Paradigm: a Theoretical Investigation of Concepts of Work* (Aldershot: Avebury, 1996), pp. 154–5.

122 Gee, Hull and Lankshear, note 17, p. 38.

123 Robert W. Lear, 'Whatever Happened to the Organization Man? Speaking Out', *Chief Executive*, Vol. 95 (June 1994), p. 8.

124 Fazal Rixvi and Bob Lingard, 'Foreword' in Gee, Hull and Lankshear, note 17, p. ix.

125 Quoted in *ibid.*, p. 34.

126 *Ibid.*, p. 73.

127 *Ibid.*, p. 84.

128 *Ibid.*, p. 87.

129 *Ibid.*, pp. 96–9.

130 *Ibid.*, pp. 98–9.

131 *Ibid.*, p. 122.

132 *Ibid.*, p. 101.

133 *Ibid.*, pp. 101–2.

134 *Ibid.*, p. 88.

135 *Ibid.*, pp. 102–3.

136 Cited in Richard Sennett, *The Corrosion of Character: the Personal Consequences of Work in the New Capitalism* (New York: W. W. Norton, 1998), pp. 112–13.

137 Paul Thompson, *The Nature of Work: an Introduction to Debates on the Labour Process* (Hampshire, UK: Macmillan Education, 1983), p. 142.

138 Thomas H. Naylor, William H. Willimon and Rolf Osterberg, *The Search for Meaning in the Workplace* (Nashville: Abingdon Press, 1996), pp. 69–70.

9

Keeping the
Unemployed Down

Hunger will tame the fiercest animals, it will teach
decency and civility, obedience and subjection to
the most perverse....
William Townsend [1]

In place of disenfranchisement and the workhouse,
there was the means test and the inspecting officer
policing the management of the family economy. In
theory, the bureaucratisation of welfare promoted
access and justice, in practice it engendered alienation and fear.
David Vincent [2]

Work sucks, but I need the bucks.
Bumper sticker [3]

There is nothing like hunger or the fear of starvation to motivate people to
work, even in the most unpleasant jobs. Providing income security for the
unemployed undermines that motivation. Today some still argue that the
able-bodied who cannot support themselves should go hungry (and this
seems to be the approach taken in the US to the long-term unemployed without dependent children). *Director* magazine noted approvingly the excellent
work ethic of Singaporeans and attributed it in part to 'the absence of welfare,
so if you don't work, you're in trouble'.[4]

Throughout the twentieth century, welfare was characterised as creating
dependency and eroding the work ethic.[5] Just as in sixteenth-century England,
modern governments differentiate between the 'deserving' and the 'undeserving' poor. The 'deserving' are those in need who are unable to work because
they are too old, disabled, or too sick. The 'undeserving' are people who

151

don't want to work and often it is assumed that all able-bodied unemployed people fit into that category.[6]

Welfare has often been provided, not only for compassionate and humanitarian reasons, but also in response to a fear that hunger and dispossession would lead to social disorder, including crime and even rebellion, by those who were thus cut off from society and a means of sustenance.[7] Yet the problem for governments has always been how to confine welfare to those who are unwillingly unemployed or unable to work.

The introduction of unemployment benefits in Britain was accompanied by the 'search for the scrounger'.[8] In 1905 the Birmingham Chamber of Commerce proposed a system of labour registries to differentiate between the deserving and temporarily unemployed and the undeserving malingerer:

> it is essential that permanent machinery be constructed for obtaining reliable information as to the number of persons out of work who are entitled to be classed as bona fide unemployed, that is to say, men who, through some cause over which they have no control, are temporarily out of work.... With regard to the other class, the unemployable, the wastrel and the loafer, the sternest measures are necessary....[9]

These distinctions between deserving and undeserving have been reflected in differences in treatment of welfare recipients by governments. Welfare benefits accorded to pensioners (aged and disabled) are generally significantly higher and less conditional than those given to unemployment beneficiaries. Such distinctions are thought necessary to preserve the work ethic and to signify to the wider community 'what behaviours are deemed virtuous or deviant'.[10]

Even today the quality of service and degree of assistance provided to the unemployed is kept inadequate to ensure that only the most deserving cases take advantage of it. The quality of shelter provided to the homeless is uniformly bad in the UK[11] and it is almost always in short supply. In Australia people are often turned away from hostels for lack of room. Some hostels are full by 9 a.m.[12]

FEAR OF SOCIAL DISORDER

During the sixteenth century, when many of the unemployed became 'wanderers, vagrants, or vagabonds', they 'struck fear into village and town as they wended their way on the road to nowhere'.[13] The ruling and middle classes associated these wandering labourers with crime and social disturbance. They were an underclass outside the normal social control mechanisms. They did not fit into the rigid social hierarchy and answered to no master. There were also occasional riots amongst the poor that exacerbated the fear of revolt.[14]

Governments therefore made provision for such people through local poor taxes levied on householders.[15] Yet they were careful to do this in a way that 'deterred all but the most desperate' from taking up help in the poor-houses. It was necessary to ensure that such 'welfare' kept the unemployed in a poorer and more miserable state than the lowliest worker in order to ensure that there remained an incentive to work at even the worst of jobs.[16]

In nineteenth-century Britain 'the lumpenproletariat, the street folk, the social outcasts, the residuum, and the dangerous classes' were still viewed with a mixture of fear, contempt and suspicion.[17] And even in the twentieth century welfare measures were in part a reaction to this fear of the under-classes.

Unemployment insurance was first introduced in Britain in 1911 but was limited to tradespeople.[18] After the First World War, 'fear of social disorder, guilt about those who had fought for their country, and a reluctance to return to the Poor Law prompted the extension of the insurance scheme to "uncovenanted workers"'. Insurance still did not cater for long-term unemployment, however, and large numbers of people without employment during the Great Depression found themselves without any income. In 1934 the Unemployment Assistance Act provided a means-tested benefit that came into effect after contributory benefits had run out.[19]

Unemployment insurance was introduced in the US in the 1930s for similar reasons, particularly fear of social disorder.[20] In the early years of the Depression, a strong belief in individualism in the US made governments reluctant to intervene to alleviate the distress of the unemployed.[21] Businessmen also argued against the government providing relief.[22] For example, the President of the National Association of Manufacturers (NAM) stated that 'such a system of doles, from the economic value-point, is an unwarranted weakening drain on industry, a deterrent of individual initiative, and a menace to our competing strength in the marts of the world'.[23]

The bankruptcy of private charities and the inadequacy of local relief agencies, however, together with the threat to social order posed by congregations of strong yet unemployed men, caused the government to act.[24] One of Roosevelt's advisers claimed that society was on the brink of rebellion when Roosevelt took office in 1933: 'we were confronted with a choice between an orderly revolution – a peaceful and rapid departure from the past concepts – and a violent and disorderly overthrow of the whole capitalist structure'.[25]

When Roosevelt established public assistance for families with dependent children he did not extend it to the unemployed generally, who were supposed to be covered by short-term contributory insurance. They were not 'deserving' of public welfare. The distinction between the deserving and the non-deserving poor meant that welfare in the form of Assistance to Families with Dependent Children (AFDC) was restricted to single women and families of unemployed men.[26]

Joe Feagin, in *Subordinating the Poor*, argues that the main goals of welfare in the US were:

1 To relieve the suffering of the destitute poor (usually at minimum cost);
2 To maintain existing political and economic order (a) by expanding public relief somewhat in times of protest and (b) by utilising public assistance to encourage or ensure maximum work effort from key groups among the very poor;
3 To reform the work attitudes and morals of the very poor.[27]

Governments in the UK have also tried to strike the right balance between providing enough welfare to prevent political protest and other disturbances and yet keeping it low enough to ensure unemployed people will take low-income unpleasant jobs. The British Employers Confederation stated in 1942 that welfare benefits 'should not be such as to weaken the incentive of the population to play their full part in maintaining the productivity and exporting ability of the country'.[28]

Following the Second World War, the United Nations, in its Universal Declaration of Human Rights, included the guarantee of protection and security in the event of unemployment (articles 23 and 25). This was in large part a response to the belief that the rise of Hitler in Germany and of extreme political movements in general had been facilitated by the presence of widespread unemployment and disaffection.[29] Various countries, including Australia and Britain, introduced a welfare safety net to cover everyone, including unemployment benefits as a conditional right for the able-bodied.

MODERN UNDERCLASSES

The need to make unemployment as unpleasant as possible within the humane limits of a society was thought to be necessary to maintaining a subdued and obedient workforce. In order to preserve work incentives, unemployment benefits had to be kept at low levels. As a result those receiving such benefits in most English-speaking countries tend to live in poverty.

Often poor people tend to congregate. This can happen because they live in areas where housing is cheaper or where the government provides cheap public housing. It can also happen where key industries move out of an area leaving many of the residents without jobs. The problem for those concerned with social order and protection of property comes when the poor are concentrated in particular neighbourhoods and when the opportunities for social mobility, 'the solvent for discontent', are cut off. When the 'underclass has become a semipermanent rather than a generational phenomenon they can pose a threat as they turn to other means to earn a living and develop an alternative culture of their own'.[30]

A number of studies have linked unemployment rates with criminality, delinquency, drug addiction and various forms of deviance. For example a World Health Organisation (WHO) report in 1975 stated:

> The poverty and frustration caused by unemployment debilitates, predisposes to fatigue and apathy, engenders despair, and increases not only pyschological and bodily illness, but also crime, violence, drug abuse and other forms of deficient behaviour to which people resort when they reject society or are rejected by it.[31]

Such views not only suggest that work is necessary for happiness and fulfilment but cast aspersions on poor and unemployed people as likely to turn to crime, violence and other deviancy. This is the basis of the fears associated with an underclass. The unemployed, who have plenty of time on their hands and resentments to match, are perceived as a threat to the society.[32]

In the 1980s the formation of an underclass came to be the focus of a considerable debate in the US. Various writers argued that provision of AFDC was creating 'the danger of permanent segregation of a class of unemployed from the rest of society'.[33] Poverty and perceived reliance on welfare in black communities in particular caused concern amongst conservatives. Mickey Kaus, in an article in *The New Republic*, referred to 'a culture of poverty' and described:

> a 'community' where 90 per cent of the children are born into fatherless families, where over 60 per cent of the population is on welfare, where the work ethic has evaporated and the entrepreneurial drive is channeled into gangs and drug-pushing.[34]

In 1984 Charles Murray's book *Losing Ground* argued that welfare encouraged young single women to become unmarried mothers and men to remain unemployed. Such arguments do not stand up to examination. In Europe, where single mothers get much higher welfare benefits, teenage childbearing is much lower than in the US.[35]

Kaus put a less extreme spin on the problem. He claimed that although welfare didn't cause unemployment and sole parenthood, it did allow such lifestyles to be lived without too much hardship – so that a girl who becomes pregnant, for example, might find the option of keeping the baby a more desirable one. Similarly, the option of remaining unemployed was made more congenial to a person who has lost his/her job or been unable to find one: 'welfare might not *cause* the underclass, it *sustains* it.... Welfare, as the umbilical cord through which the mainstream society sustains the isolated ghetto society, permits the expansion of this single-parent culture.'[36] Neither author recognised that it might be a lack of money, rather than a surplus of money, that pushed people into this so-called 'culture of poverty', forcing many young unemployed men into crime to support themselves and excluding people from the opportunities available to others in American society.

The view that welfare led to a culture of poverty persisted into the 1990s and was argued by conservatives and their think tanks. Robert Rector, senior analyst for welfare and family issues for the Heritage Foundation, claimed in 1996 that 'children are suffering because the liberal welfare state has carpet-bombed the moral foundations of the inner city, toppling marriage, gutting the work ethic, and leaving a rubble of social pathology in its wake'. He argued that children were at greater risk growing up under welfare than under poverty, which he suggested wasn't a big problem. On the other hand, growing up dependent on welfare, he argued, reduces a child's IQ, 'triples the level of behavioural and emotional problems … and doubles the probability a boy will engage in criminal activity and wind up in jail'.[37]

In the US, welfare has been characterised as responsible for creating an underclass of mainly black mothers who have many children so as to receive welfare benefits for most of their lives and avoid work, and whose children grow up to become welfare recipients. In fact the average family size of welfare recipients is no larger than the American norm. Only 15 per cent of AFDC recipients receive welfare continuously. And not only did most women on welfare not receive it as children but 'a majority of daughters who grew up in highly dependent homes did not share the fate of their parents'. Forty per cent of mothers receiving AFDC worked while on welfare but did not earn enough to support their families.[38] The problem was not their lack of a work ethic but their inability to keep a job or earn enough to get out of poverty.[39]

Despite its inaccuracy, the conservative view of welfare has been widely accepted, particularly in government circles. As a result, the Clinton Administration dismantled AFDC in 1996, in an effort to reform welfare and rid America of the culture of dependency (see next chapter).

The concern in the US about the culture of poverty has also been taken up in the UK, encouraged by Charles Murray in a recent book, *The Emerging British Underclass*. In his first speech as Prime Minister, given on a poor housing estate, Tony Blair spoke of 'an underclass of people cut off from society's mainstream, without any sense of shared purpose'. He described 'households where three generations have never had a job', 'estates where the biggest employer is the drugs industry', 'an economy built on benefits, crime, petty thieving and drugs', and people who have become 'detached, not just from work, but also from citizenship in its wider sense'.[40] Like Clinton, he has reformed the welfare system in an effort to get rid of this underclass.

More recently the Australian government has started to take up the rhetoric of an underclass. Senator Jocelyn Newman, minister responsible for welfare, speaks of 'the transfer of welfare dependency across generations' and 'an entrenched culture of welfare dependency'.[41] She argues that it isn't fair to ask 'hard-working' Australians 'to underwrite what can only be described as a destructive and self-indulgent welfare mentality' when jobs are available, even if such jobs are undesirable.[42] The Minister for Employment Services, Tony Abbott, has justified moves to 'crack down' on dole recipients in terms of wiping out the 'culture of welfare dependency' and the rise of the 'job snob'.[43] Even Aboriginal activist Noel Pearson has argued that welfare dependency is to blame for the plight of Aboriginal people and the loss of traditional culture.[44]

In Canada, too, moves are being made to deal with the welfare culture. In Alberta, Social Services Minister Mike Cardinal has cut welfare benefits and services in an effort to make welfare less attractive. 'The goal is not to make welfare unbearable,' he said, 'but it has to be uncomfortable enough that people will try to find an alternative way of living.' As a result of government efforts, he claims, 'the vast majority of freeloaders have already left the rolls'. Those remaining need to be taught a work ethic: 'the key for many of these people is just to get back into a routine – to get up every morning, to go to work or classes ... they have lost that fundamental sense of routine which is necessary to keep a job'.[45]

It is not only a work ethic that welfare workers seek to embue in welfare recipients but what some may refer to as a realistic view of their own worth. Gale Miller, in her study of a Midwest American Work Incentive programme (WIN), found that welfare workers tend to employ an inferiorization strategy that they believe will make recipients more employable and willing to take undesirable jobs. This involves ensuring that these people will 'accommodate and subordinate themselves to the interests of institutional elites who control access to jobs and other opportunities'.[46] The values and life experiences and interests of recipients are devalued and ignored. They are taught to 'accept prevailing social relations and practices' and to gain employment by taking on the values of those whom they want to get jobs from – to fit in.[47]

The welfare workers believed that welfare recipients were too choosy about what jobs they would take and too unwilling to submit to the authority of the employer.[48] 'Specifically, they sought to teach clients realistic employment expectations by instructing them on their "true" value in area labor markets, including instructing them on their subordinate position in dealing with employers.'[49] They taught them that they should do whatever their employers asked, 'including tasks that they might find unpleasant or degrading'.[50]

SEARCHING FOR THE SCROUNGER

Methods of finding the undeserving welfare recipient who is unwilling to work have been introduced into all English-speaking countries, and some form of work test seems to be common. The work test generally involves the person being offered a job. If they do not take the job they are deemed to be unwilling to work and taken off benefits. The work test is often, in effect, 'really a form of conscription into poorly paid and unpleasant occupations'.[51] In fact, in some places resigning from a job because of low pay, long hours or dangerous work can be taken as a failure of the work test, and this can delay the payment of benefits.[52]

> The work test was conceived of as a means of distinguishing deserving claimants from the undeserving, who were destitute through their own fault.... [T]here was fairly clearly a basic assumption that the claimant for relief was a probable malingerer, and that the onus of proving he was not a malingerer was on him. There was no presumptive right to support. Behind it all was a lurking fear that if people could live without work, even on a miserably low level, many would choose to do so.[53]

It is for the same reason, fear of encouraging idleness, that governments have generally avoided giving benefits above the poverty line. Attempts to relax the work test and make unemployment benefits livable on have been opposed strongly by the establishment in both Britain and Australia. One attempt was made in Australia after the Labor Government came to power at the end of 1972. It was effectively countered by the strong opposition of employers, a barrage of political comment and a media campaign to portray a paradise for 'bludgers' (scroungers).

In 1973 the Whitlam government raised unemployment benefits and relaxed the work test to be more compassionate.[54] In response the media reported employers' claims that they couldn't fill job vacancies because welfare was too easy to get and enabled those who did not want to work to be too comfortable. The *Sydney Morning Herald* told the story of a clothing factory that was offering 30 jobs and had no takers; the paper also found a farm manager who couldn't get enough asparagus pickers at harvest time.[55]

It also ran a story implying that hundreds of people who had registered as unemployed on the sunny Gold Coast of southern Queensland 'simply do not want to work'. It quoted a small businessman who claimed the wages he could offer could not 'compete with Government handouts to teenage girls'.[56] At the time there were over fifteen hundred registered unemployed people in the region and only 136 jobs on offer.[57]

There was 'a perfect blizzard of denunciations of "loafers" (Leader of the Opposition), "bludgers" (Victorian Premier), "drop-outs, no hopers and hippies" (Victorian Labor Minister), "slackers" and "work-dodgers".' The *Sydney Morning Herald* concurred with these sentiments: 'The general, and eminently justified, view is that people have a right not to work, but no right to taxpayers' support in choosing idleness.'[58]

In 1974, at the height of a media campaign against unemployed welfare recipients, a government survey found that very few unemployed people had anti-work attitudes – yet this survey was not published. (Similar studies in the UK and the US in the early 1970s came to the same conclusion.) Instead the media portrayed the unemployed as lounging on the beach and having a good time at taxpayers' expense.[59]

The media campaign was very influential. A Morgan Gallup poll found that the percentage of people who thought a main cause of unemployment was 'people not wanting to work' in 1975 was 48 per cent, compared with 30 per cent the previous year. The new level remained fairly steady for the following decade.[60]

As a result of business-inspired, media-led public opinion the government was forced in 1974 to announce its intention to take a tougher approach with the unemployed and to tighten the work test. The Minister of Labour, Clyde Cameron, stated:

> I have no sympathy for people who can be described as professionally unemployed, who treat the benefits as a satisfactory alternative to working. We are looking at whether the formula or the criteria attached to the test can be tightened. I am not satisfied that there are not some who are just remaining on unemployment benefits rather than accepting work – especially young people. I want to get rid of slackers who are on unemployment benefits and who just won't work.[61]

The work test was tightened to ensure that unemployed people had to accept job offers anywhere in Australia and that leaving a job voluntarily or moving to an area of high unemployment could constitute a failure of the work test.[62] After the Liberal/National Government came to power at the end of 1975 it moved to further tighten conditions for receiving the dole.

Between 1976 and 1979, as unemployment levels rose, the work test was tightened. People could be forced to move their place of residence so as to find a job. If the government officials thought the person's dress and appearance were unsuitable they could fail the work test. People had to accept short-term, part-time and temporary work as part of the test.[63]

The work test remained stringent in the following years. In both Australia and Britain people were required to prove they had been looking for work, giving full details of employers approached.[64] Today Australia has one of the 'most tightly targeted welfare systems in the OECD – and one of the stingiest', spending a significantly lower proportion of GDP on welfare than the average OECD country.[65]

A work test has also been incorporated into US welfare schemes. In 1967 the Social Security Act was amended to incorporate the Work Incentive Program – the subject, as we have seen, of Gale Miller's *Enforcing the Work Ethic*. 'One purpose of WIN,' she explains, 'is to identify and eliminate clients who have chosen welfare dependence as a way of life.'[66] Welfare recipients who are identified as being unwilling to look for jobs or to undertake assignments or training, which are supposed to make them more employable, can have their welfare payments withheld or reduced. In the WIN office which Miller studied, some clients had to report their job-seeking efforts (names of employers approached, for example) every day and were expected to undertake a daily quota of job inquiries or applications. Others were required to do volunteer work for local non-profit organisations.[67]

The aim of welfare workers, according to Miller, was to force a work ethic on to recipients through the threat of discontinued payments and the tactic of making welfare an unpleasant experience. One welfare worker in Miller's study stated: 'Well, I think we should make it tough on 'em. People don't change if they don't have to, why should they? I think we should make them uncomfortable and this should be an unpleasant experience.'[68]

In *Dangerous Classes* (1994) Lydia Morris takes the view that requiring unemployed people to search continually for work when they are unlikely to find it merely causes 'unnecessary demoralisation.... [T]he right to benefit is increasingly dependent upon a discouraging, demoralising and humiliating procedure in which claimants are called upon to prove their worth.'[69]

The work test is not only demoralising for welfare recipients but also serves the purpose of deterring dissatisfied workers from leaving their jobs. Graeme Brewer notes in his book *Rough Justice* that 'The work test acts as an intimidatory device in locking vulnerable workers into unsatisfying (and perhaps dangerous and noxious) jobs.'[70] In particular the assumption that those who resign from a job are not 'deserving' of immediate benefits and the requirement that unemployed people take any job offered ensures that such jobs are filled.

In recent years work tests have been tightened and extended in many countries. The New Zealand work test has recently been revised to include widows and sole parents whose children are school age. They are also looking for ways to get invalid beneficiaries into the workforce by 'testing their capacity to do tasks rather than their incapacity'. Social Welfare Minister Roger Sowry has observed bluntly: 'I think we're in a national mood that says Look, you know, these people, we shouldn't allow people to malinger on a benefit.'[71]

In Britain the Blair government has introduced a bill supposed to challenge the 'something for nothing culture' of the old welfare state. The bill provides for welfare beneficiaries, including sole mothers and disabled people, to be cut off benefits if they fail to turn up to job interviews.[72] Whereas once only single mothers with children over five were required to go for job assessment (back-to-work) interviews, all single mothers, no matter how young their children, are required to attend such interviews regularly or lose their benefits. In announcing these welfare 'reforms', the Secretary of State for Social Security, Alistair Darling, stated: 'There is no unconditional right to benefit.'[73] (Similar reforms are being carried out in Canada where single mothers are having to look for a job when their children are as young as six months old.[74])

STIGMATISING THE UNEMPLOYED

To make sure there is no desirable social identity outside of employment, the unemployed are stigmatised. They tend to be portrayed in the media as either frauds, hopeless cases or lazy bludgers who are living it up at taxpayers' expense. 'As a result of their jobless status, they are subject to a range of economic and social discriminations, including stigmatization, economic and social invisibility, stereotyping, denial of authority, and exclusion from the job market.'[75]

Discrimination on the basis of work status is not treated seriously as a form of discrimination in the way that discrimination on the basis of gender, race and disability are, but it is just as real.[76] It extends to retired people, homemakers and students, but is particularly targeted at 'unemployed' people. The need to stigmatise the unemployed as an example to others goes back at least to the seventeenth century when attempts were made in England to get people receiving poor relief to wear badges on their sleeves. Those receiving poor relief in many of the American colonies were also required to wear badges sewn onto their clothing.[77] 'Stigma was an overt and integral part' of poor relief in both countries: 'The physical appearance of inmates was altered, by compulsory wearing of institutional dress and hair-cropping, so as to illustrate and emphasise the changed status of those in occupation.'[78]

Today much of the stigma comes from media portrayals. The unemployed are depicted as remaining so as a result of their lack of worth and motivation rather than as a consequence of corporations sacking large numbers of workers and moving operations to Third World countries. Welfare recipients and their advocates are seldom given the opportunity to counter such portrayals in the media – in the US they are used as sources only 9 per cent of the time for stories on welfare, according to a study by Fairness and Accuracy in Reporting (FAIR).[79]

Newspapers love headlines such as 'Luxury Life on the Dole: Two Homes, a Car and a Private Pool',[80] or 'Teenagers Make a Living on the Dole'. The latter story from an Australian newspaper told of Keith (no surname supplied) 'a smart and artistic youth' who gave up a trainee job after three weeks 'because I've decided to go up to the Gold Coast, laze about the beaches and live on the dole'.[81] People are both shocked and fascinated by such stories; their prejudices are confirmed and they can feel indignant rather than sympathetic.[82]

Through the 1970s in Britain conservatives did their best to characterise the unemployed as lazy scroungers. Iain Sproat, a backbencher, claimed that half those receiving unemployment benefits weren't really looking for work and Robert Adley, another conservative politician, argued that people were 'sick and tired' of having their taxes 'squandered on people who would not know what a day's work looked like if it stared them in the face'.[83] The media amplified such comments with stories of their own about individuals who had been convicted of welfare fraud. In 1975, when asked 'What is the one thing you would most like to change to improve the quality of life in Britain today?' people expressed welfare concerns – like 'make people work' and 'stop social security abuses' – more frequently than all other concerns except crime and world peace.[84]

In the 1970s an Australian media campaign against welfare recipients was also particularly effective at stigmatising them. The *Daily Mirror* reported:

> Weed Out the Dole Cheats! It is patently obvious that there are people in this community who don't give a damn about their mates. They laughingly laze on beaches, frequent pubs and clubs, indulge themselves all day, living as parasites on the community. They are the dole bludgers.[85]

The respected *Age* newspaper also ran a story entitled 'Jobless Who Cop It Sweet' in which its economics writer stated: 'There are two classes of cheats – the criminal variety (working and also collecting the dole) and malingerers (collecting the dole and making no attempt to gain a job).'[86] Commenting on the media coverage at the time, Keith Windschuttle argued that the press had given up any pretence of objective, detached reporting: 'The dole bludger has aroused the media to undertake a moral crusade and any sense of objectivity – even in the simple way the media interpret that term by giving "both sides" of a question – is thrown out the window.'[87]

The media coverage succeeded in stigmatising the unemployed. A survey by academics and students at Monash University found that the majority of those surveyed felt that unemployment benefits were too easy to get and 72 per cent believed that there was widespread abuse of the benefits system.[88]

162

The role of the government in portraying a picture of fraud has been self-serving. Alec Pemberton, in his article on dole cheating, noted that the government had employed a scapegoating strategy of 'blaming the victim' to avoid blame being put on the government and that 'what the Government has done is to create a climate of mistrust and alienation at the very time the unemployed really need our support and sympathy'.[89]

The distorted media portrayal of the unemployed continued in Australia through the 1990s. In November 1997 the Australian *Bulletin* published a front cover showing a surfer, emblazoned with the headline 'Dole addicts. He plays, we pay ... how many more like him?' The surfers interviewed for the story were unemployed people who were unable to get work and therefore filled in their time at the beach. The reporter noted, unselfconsciously, that the media 'habitually trawled' the beaches 'looking to record the indolent thoughts of "career" surfers' as a way of stigmatising the unemployed.[90]

Stories of lazy dole bludgers are used by the media to exploit the prejudices of the public to sell papers or get ratings. People who work at jobs they don't like can be envious of those who get by without having to work. They don't like to see other people getting something for nothing when they have to work so hard. And it especially gets people mad to see unemployed people enjoying themselves on the beach rather than sitting at home feeling miserable. A worker's precarious work ethic can be threatened by the thought that they too could give up work. And in a society that relies on a work ethic to keep people in boring, unfulfilling jobs the spectacle of hundreds of thousands of people able to survive without doing any work at all threatens to undermine the work ethic.

Very occasionally newspapers give the other side of the picture. For example, in January 1998 the *Sydney Morning Herald* reported that 1,500 people had queued for hours in the hot sun in the hope of getting a job at the supermarket chain Coles. One of these people, a 53-year-old, told the reporter he had travelled from Canberra to Sydney and waited more than five hours in the heat to get a job packing shelves.[91] Nevertheless, even today 66 per cent of Australians say that they think the welfare system makes people unwilling to look after themselves. This is even true of the young who have the highest rates of unemployment. Over half of the 14–17-year-olds surveyed said unemployment was due to 'personal unwillingess to work'.[92]

Even when the media is supposedly sympathising with the unemployed it tends to paint an undesirable caricature of despondent souls who have given up the effort:

> They congregate in milk bars, pool rooms, pinball parlours, on street corners, in pubs, and when the little money they have in their pockets runs out they wander home to stare at television.[93]

You don't feel like getting up off the chair, but every night, you feel tired. You don't have showers. I watched TV from practically 10 am till night.... I used to go to bed as early as I could because I'd feel tired from just watching TV.... My backside gets sore from sitting all the time. You feel rotten, but you get used to it.[94]

Perhaps nowhere have welfare recipients been so vilified as in the US, where they are characterised as: 'the greedy lazy Welfare Queen with six children and a freeloading boyfriend'.[95] From the 1970s conservative think tanks have played an important part in building resentment amongst workers against welfare recipients in the US. For example, both the Heritage Foundation and the Cato Institute have claimed that welfare recipients could get more income through various benefits than workers got from working.

In 1995 the Cato Institute manipulated the figures, by including benefits that most AFDC families don't get and ignoring benefits workers do get, to claim that welfare paid more than low-wage jobs in every state. A later Center on Budget and Policy Priorities (CBPP) critique found that actually the typical welfare family had an average income of $9,000 a year, not the $17,500 estimated by the Cato Institute.[96] The Cato report was given wide coverage in the media, however, despite its distortions.[97] It enabled conservatives to argue that there is no incentive for welfare recipients to get work because welfare benefits are too high and there is too much incentive for low-waged workers to become welfare recipients. (The Cato Institute did not consider the question of whether low-waged workers should be paid more.)

The resentment against unemployed people whipped up by conservatives goes far beyond the costs to the taxpayer of maintaining welfare which in the 1980s, when it came under sustained attack in the US, made up only about 1 per cent of the federal budget. The indignation about money spent on welfare has not been matched by a similar concern by the same people for the money spent on corporate welfare, including subsidies, tax breaks, and other financial incentives. Corporate welfare, or 'wealthfare', is estimated to cost the US government seven times more than welfare spent on the poor.[98]

The US General Accounting Office reported that 'in each year between 1989 to 1995, a majority of corporations, both foreign- and US-controlled, paid no US income tax'. Almost a third of the large corporations, some of them doing billions of dollars' worth of business, paid no taxes.[99] The mainstream media, however, focus on welfare to the unemployed as the big problem.

At a time when dole cheating was making big headlines in the news in Australia, tax evasion was costing the government many times more than dole fraud. As Robin Anne Bright pointed out in her paper on 'Dole Bludgers or Tax Dodgers', 'the honest citizen has more to gain from a crackdown on tax dodgers than on dole bludgers.... At a purely economic level, an investigator working on unemployment benefit fraud would not solve enough cases to pay his wages, whereas a tax investigator would do so many times over.'[100]

In Britain, too, welfare fraud receives far more media attention and public opprobrium than tax evasion, which deprives the government of money more effectively. And although unemployment benefits make up a small proportion of the total social welfare bill (9 per cent) those concerned about the size of the welfare bill tend to focus on the unemployed rather than pensioners, who receive the greatest proportion of the total welfare payments.[101]

There is little evidence that welfare spending harms economic growth. Anthony Atkinson, in an article in *American Economics* on 'The Economics of the Welfare State', found nine studies on this topic. Four concluded that high social security spending was correlated with less economic growth, two that it had an insignificant effect, and three that it tended to result in more economic growth. Atkinson argued, therefore, that the empirical evidence for negative economic impacts of welfare spending was not 'compelling'. Despite this he found that economists tended to dwell on the negative economic effects of the welfare state, ignoring the benefits of welfare such as the way a welfare net enables people to change jobs and take risks in their careers, both necessary elements of a vibrant economy.[102]

In Europe there has been debate about whether welfare reduces work incentive. The editors of *Welfare and Work Incentives: a North European Perspective* conclude that 'for each country dealt with, there is only limited evidence of a relationship between labor supply and welfare state taxes and transfers'.[103] In Denmark one in five people live off government wages or benefits and well over four million of the country's five million people get some sort of transfer payment from the government. Yet the government claims this welfare is affordable and that the economy and government finances are healthy. And far from this putting people off participating in the labour force, in Denmark labour participation is higher than in most other countries, 84.4 per cent in 1994 compared with 76.8 per cent in the US.[104]

FRAUDS, CHEATS AND DEVIANTS

In English-speaking countries campaigns against welfare have often focused on dole cheats and frauds as a way of stigmatising recipients. Government officials often feed such campaigns. In 1998, for example, the Australian government released a report claiming that a crackdown on welfare fraud had resulted in $230 million being paid back. The Australian Council of Social Service (ACOSS) pointed out, however, that much of the recovered overpayment resulted from administrative errors and people wrongly estimating their future incomes for the purpose of family payment.[105] It pointed out that in 1996/7 overpayment went up by 24 per cent but underpayment by 36 per cent, while fraud accounted for less than 0.5 per cent of welfare spending.

ACOSS accused the government of distorting the picture and overemphasising fraud for political reasons.[106] The *Herald*'s Paul Cleary pointed out that welfare fraud attracts more auditing than taxation fraud and yet taxation audits result in the need for adjustments in 83 per cent of cases audited: 'But the government does not put out statements every six months on tax cheats. It seems happy to hound welfare recipients because there are votes in it.'[107]

A similar pattern has occurred in the US. The media plays a role in stigmatising welfare recipients, often as frauds. During the 1960s and 1970s, studies found between 5 and 6 per cent of people ineligible for their welfare – but in each case the majority of mistakes were made by the agencies rather than the recipient, and even where recipients had made errors they mostly 'could not be construed as intentional fraud'. Prosecutions amounted to less than 1 per cent of cases. Yet at the time 71 per cent of Americans surveyed agreed that 'Many people getting welfare are not honest about their need.'[108]

In 1992 an ABC *Prime Time Live* show on welfare fraud involved interviews with anonymous welfare recipients who told of how they cheated the system. Host Diane Sawyer suggested to the audience that 'with so much money up for grabs' welfare fraud could be 'even better than robbing a bank'. *Progressive* magazine pointed out that Los Angeles had spent more than $2 million on a fingerprinting system in 1991 but only caught 11 people cheating. More taxpayers' money was lost through Medicaid fraud by doctors, it claimed, than welfare fraud.[109]

Joe Feagin found in his book on welfare and American beliefs that 'one would be hard pressed to find a group of American citizens who have received more hostility and criticism than have welfare clients in the last few decades'. He noted that whilst 'sensational and grossly exaggerated stereotypes' of other minority groups, such as black and Jews, had become unacceptable, 'this was not the case for welfare recipients'.[110]

Perhaps the most common sort of fraud in most countries is where welfare recipients do some casual 'off the books' work to supplement their benefits without reporting it for fear of losing those benefits, particularly such entitlements as medical insurance.[111] The same is true in the UK and Ireland, where it is referred to as 'doing the double'. People who find it difficult to survive on benefits supplement them with this sort of casual work which itself is not enough to live on.[112]

Employers are able to pay very low wages for these 'junk jobs' because they know that people are also getting welfare payments. The work is usually insecure, low-paying, exploitative and sometimes dangerous. It seldom constitutes any real competition to real jobs, which are not available to these people.[113] For those on welfare, however, such jobs help ends meet. Ironically, the existence of this informal work indicates that those on welfare are not work-shy at all, but are doing what they can to cope with a situation where there are not enough jobs to go around.

Yet such coping behaviour is portrayed as criminal. In his 1998 speech on welfare reform, the UK welfare minister Frank Field stated that the welfare system 'promotes fraud and deception, not honesty and hard work'.[114] And a green paper produced by the Department of Social Security, in a considerable departure from the style of the rest of the paper, relied on anecdote rather than documented evidence when it claimed that 'One in four people say they know someone who has defrauded the social security system.'[115]

In Canada the wider community often associates welfare recipients with fraud. But, as in the UK, the US and Australia, overpayments tend to be the result of bureaucratic errors rather than cheating. As elsewhere, however, the media play up the fraud angle. In 1993 the *Alberta Report* conjectured that 'only a small fraction of such abusers might be apprehended' without providing any evidence for this.[116] In 1995 *Maclean's* magazine reported that Ontario had saved $66 million by cracking down on cheats. Although only 0.4 per cent of 266,000 recipients surveyed had been found guilty of cheating, *Maclean's* used anecdotal evidence to spread the guilt to many more recipients. It stated that it had 'inadvertently discovered three examples over a three-week period' and that 'although such cases are rare, almost every Canadian seems to know someone who, in turn, knows someone who is ripping off the system'.[117]

Closely related to the issue of fraud is the depiction of unemployed people as having criminal or delinquent tendencies. Whilst there may be a higher proportion of crimes committed by unemployed than employed people, this is because criminals often do not have day jobs and juvenile delinquents do badly at school and find it difficult to get jobs. The stigmatising of all unemployed people as likely to turn to crime or drug addiction is unwarranted. However, the unemployed sometimes make a convenient scapegoat. For example, police and public officials blamed the 1980 Bristol riot on unemployment and job discrimination against blacks. Those involved argued that the riot was against police harassment.[118]

There is also a trend to stigmatise unemployed people, particularly those who are homeless, as having mental problems. This has been reinforced by the use of unemployment as a symptom for some psychiatric disorders in the Diagnostic and Statistical Manual of Mental Disorders (DSM IV) published by the American Psychiatric Association. DSM IV states that a mental disorder is a condition that 'causes clinically significant distress or impairment in social, occupational, or other important areas of functioning'. In particular, occupational dysfunction is a symptom of schizophrenia.[119] Indeed, dissident psychiatrist Thomas Szasz argues that Western societies have been using 'psychiatric diagnoses to validate idleness as illness' since the nineteenth century. Szasz suggests that people are either producers or parasites and that schizophrenia is a label used to explain people who are idle and lazy and who want to lie in bed all day.[120]

The unemployed in Australia are also increasingly being given psychiatric labels. The Australian Labor government introduced a system of privatised case management in 1994 that was continued by the Liberal government when it came to power. It provides for psychological assessment of long-term unemployed people who are perceived to have 'low work motivation and negative orientations to labour market participation', who have 'unrealistic work expectations', who have low self-esteem, who have become discouraged in their search for work, and who have 'poor presentation and grooming skills' or interpersonal difficulties such as shyness.[121]

One of the options available to the case manager who finds an unemployed person has such psychological problems is psychiatric referral. Indeed there is an incentive to refer as case managers get paid for each person they get into a job placement. Those that they cannot place can be removed from their case load by referring them to a psychiatrist, making room for someone with better prospects.[122]

CONCLUSION

Welfare is necessary to protect social order and prevent property crimes but it is also threatening to employers and to the capitalist order because it erodes the work ethic, provides alternatives to low-paying, unpleasant jobs, and creates a class of people who do not have to submit to employers.

One might have thought that it was in the ordinary working person's interests to know that those who are on unemployment benefits are happy and contented, when there aren't enough jobs for everyone. Not only would it mean that there was less competition for those workers who wanted to hold on to their jobs, but it would be reassuring to know that it would not be so terrible if they did lose their jobs. Yet the community expression of the work ethic in modern society is loudest and clearest in attitudes to the unemployed, and logic does not prevail.

The social benefits of treating unemployed people humanely have been hidden behind a screen of propaganda aimed at stigmatising the unemployed. It is in the interests of governments and employers to reinforce prejudices against the unemployed. The government would rather people blamed the unemployed for high levels of unemployment than government policies. The efforts to make sure recipients continue to look for jobs benefits employers who want maximum competition for the jobs they offer. Labelling welfare recipients as bludgers and scroungers, cheats, delinquents, and deviants also 'works to make the unemployed feel guilty and humble instead of angry and indignant'.[123]

In recent years, however, the humbling and impoverishment of the unemployed have not been enough for those employers who rely on a ready supply of desperate workers to fill low-paid, unpleasant jobs. This is because the jobs they offer are just as humbling and badly paid as welfare and they are unwilling to compete. Under pressure from the business community and the think tanks they finance, governments in English-speaking countries have introduced welfare reforms that further deter people from seeking welfare, limit the time they can be on welfare, and prevent them from receiving benefits without working for them. These reforms are described in the next chapter.

NOTES

1 Quoted in Daniel Bell, 'Work and Its Discontents (1956)', in A. R. Gini and T. J. Sullivan (eds), *It Comes with the Territory: an Inquiry Concerning Work and the Person* (New York: Random House, 1989), p. 122.

2 Quoted in Lydia Morris, *Dangerous Classes: the Underclass and Social Citizenship* (London: Routledge, 1994), p. 41.

3 Daniel Yankelovich and John Immerwahr, 'Putting the Work Ethic to Work', *Society*, Vol. 21, No. 2 (1984), p. 65.

4 Stuart Rock, 'Another Country', *Director*, Vol. 45, No. 8 (1992).

5 Lucy A. Williams, 'Rethinking Low-wage Markets and Dependency', *Politics and Society*, Vol. 25, No. 4 (1997).

6 Brotherhood of St Laurence, 'Why So Harsh on the Unemployed? A Second Discussion Paper' (Fitzroy, Victoria: Brotherhood of St Laurence, 1974), p. 1.

7 Morris, note 2, p. 34.

8 *Ibid.*, p. 38.

9 Quoted in J. R. Hay, *The Development of the British Welfare State, 1880–1975* (London: Edward Arnold, 1978), p. 32.

10 Janice Peterson, '"Ending Welfare as We Know it": the Symbolic Importance of Welfare Policy in America', *Journal of Economic Issues*, Vol. 31, No. 2 (1997).

11 Ruby Chau, 'The Functions of Negative Aspects of Welfare in Capitalist Societies: a Case Study of Temporary Accommodation for the Homeless in Britain and Housing Policy for Small Households in Hong Kong', *International Social Work*, Vol. 38, No. 1 (1995).

12 Malcolm Brown, 'Homeless Turned Away', *Sydney Morning Herald*, 25 June 1998, p. 5.
13 Paul Bernstein, *American Work Values: Their Origin and Development* (Albany, NY: State University of New York Press, 1997), p. 2.
14 *Ibid.*, p. 102; Joe R. Feagin, *Subordinating the Poor* (Englewood Cliffs, NJ: Prentice-Hall, 1975), p. 17.
15 Feagin, note 14, p. 19.
16 Morris, note 2, p. 35.
17 *Ibid.*, p. 2.
18 *Ibid.*, p. 37.
19 DSS, 'New Ambitions for Our Country: a New Contract for Welfare' (Department of Social Security, 1998), appendix. http://www.dss.gov.uk/hq/wreform/
20 Bernstein, note 13, p. 187.
21 Feagin, note 14, p. 40.
22 Stuart Ewen, *PR! A Social History of Spin* (New York: Basic Books, 1996), p. 234.
23 Quoted in *ibid.*, p. 235.
24 Feagin, note 14, p. 40.
25 Quoted in Ewen, note 22, p. 237.
26 Morris, note 2, p. 63.
27 Feagin, note 14, p. 52.
28 Quoted in Hay, note 9, p. 48.
29 Richard Gosden, 'Punishing the Unemployed', *AES Report* (May 1991), p. 10.
30 John Kenneth Galbraith, *The Culture of Contentment* (London: Penguin, 1992), p. 38.
31 Quoted in Milton Luger, 'Delinquency and Unemployment', paper presented at the Conference on Unemployment and Crime, Institute of Criminology, University of Sydney, 19 July 1978, p. 10.
32 Paul L. Wachtel, *The Poverty of Affluence: a Psychological Portrait of the American Way of Life* (Philadelphia, PA: New Society Publishers, 1989), p. 245.
33 Keith Ogborn, *Workfare in America: an Initial Guide to the Debate* (Woden, ACT: Department of Social Security, 1986), p. 4.
34 Mickey Kaus, 'The Work Ethic State: the Only Way to Break the Culture of Poverty', *The New Republic* (7 July 1986), p. 22.
35 Derrick Jackson, 'Why Do Stereotypes and Lies Persist?', *Nieman Reports*, Vol. 51 (March 1997).
36 Kaus, note 34, p. 24.
37 Robert Rector, 'Really Stand for Children: Fix Welfare' (The Heritage Foundation, 1996). http://www.heritage.org
38 'Dethroning the Welfare Queen: the Rhetoric of Reform', *Harvard Law Review*, Vol. 107 (1994), pp. 2021–3; Katha Pollitt, 'Just the Facts', *The Nation*, Vol. 262 (24 June 1996), p. 9.
39 Morton S. Baratz and Sammis B. White, 'Childfare: a New Direction for Welfare Reform', *Urban Studies*, Vol. 33, No. 10 (1996), p. 1938.
40 Tony Blair, 'Welfare Reform: Giving People the Will to Win', *Vital Speeches of the Day*, Vol. 63, No. 18 (1997).
41 Jocelyn Newman, 'The Future of Welfare in the 21st Century' (Department of Family and Community Services, 1999), http://www.facs.gov.au/dss/newman.nsf/v1/sdiscusswelfare.htm.
42 *Ibid.*
43 Tom Allard, 'Dole Crackdown on 300,000', *Sydney Morning Herald*, 8 July 1999, p. 1.

44 Peter Botsman, 'Give Them a Stake in Society', *The Australian*, 28 July 1999.

45 Christopher Serres, 'Social Services Lead the Way', *Alberta Report*, Vol. 21 (31 January 1994).

46 Gale Miller, *Enforcing the Work Ethic: Rhetoric and Everyday Life in a Work Incentive Program* (Albany, NY: State University of New York Press, 1991), p. 39.

47 *Ibid.*, pp. 38–9.

48 *Ibid.*, p. 55.

49 *Ibid.*, p. 56.

50 *Ibid.*, p. 196.

51 Alan Jordan, quoted in Keith Windschuttle, 'Dole Bludgers: How the Media Created a Phoney Scandal', *New Journalist* (December–January 1975–6), p. 22.

52 Morris, note 2, p. 52.

53 Alan Jordan, *Long Term Unemployed People under Conditions of Full Employment* (Canberra: Commission of Inquiry into Poverty, 1975), p. 45.

54 Windschuttle, note 51, pp. 18–19.

55 *Herald* Investigation Team, '6 Months Paid Holiday – Who Wants to Work?', *Sydney Morning Herald*, 10 December 1974.

56 Herald Investigation Team, 'Teenagers Make a Living on the Dole', *Sydney Morning Herald*, 9 December 1974, p. 1.

57 Trevor Hawkins, 'Where the Jobs Are', *The National Times*, 18–23 November 1974, p. 1.

58 *Sydney Morning Herald,* quoted in Jordan, note 53, p. 47.

59 Brotherhood of St Laurence, note 6, pp. 11–14; Windschuttle, note 51.

60 Morgan Gallup, 'Better Outlook for Unemployment' (Sydney and Melbourne: Morgan Gallup, 1985), p. 1.

61 Quoted in Brotherhood of St Laurence, note 6, p. 16.

62 *Herald* Investigation Team, note 55.

63 'The "Work Test": Meat in the Sandwich', *Australian Social Welfare: Impact*, Vol. 9 (July 1979), pp. 19–20.

64 Ann Harding and Bob Mills, 'The Attack on the Unemployed', *The National Times*, 1 September 1979, p. 28.

65 Adele Horin, 'Farewelfare', *Sydney Morning Herald*, 8 May 1999, p. 36.

66 Miller, note 46, p. 36.

67 *Ibid.*, pp. 36–7, 46–7.

68 Quoted in *ibid.*, p. 56.

69 Morris, note 2, p. 53.

70 Quoted in 'The "Work Test"', note 63, p. 23.

71 Gareth Robinson, 'The Needy not the Greedy – the Future of Welfare', *Background Briefing*, ABC Radio, 11 October 1998.

72 Philip Webster, 'Welfare Reform Is Top Cabinet Priority', *The Times*, 24 November 1998, p. 1.

73 Quoted in Bettina Arndt, 'Blair Faces Party Rebellion over "Harsh" Welfare Bill', *Sydney Morning Herald*, 13 February 1999, p. 24.

74 Bettina Arndt, 'A Debt to Society', *Sydney Morning Herald*, 13 February 1999, p. 4s.

75 'Finding a Place for the Jobless in Discrimination Theory', *Harvard Law Review*, Vol. 110 (1997), p. 1609.

76 *Ibid.*

77 Feagin, note 14, pp. 23, 26.

78 Matthew Colton, Ferran Casas, Mark Drakeford, Susan Roberts, Evert Scholte and

Margaret Williams, *Stigma and Social Welfare: an International Comparative Study* (Aldershot, UK: Avebury, 1997), p. 15.

79 Jackson, note 35.

80 Pictured in Windschuttle, note 51, p. 23.

81 *Herald* Investigation Team, note 56, p. 1.

82 Windschuttle, note 51, p. 22.

83 Alan Deacon, 'Scrounger Bashing', *New Society* (17 November 1977), p. 355.

84 *Ibid.*

85 Quoted in Windschuttle, note 51, p. 18.

86 Tony Thomas, 'Jobless Who Cop It Sweet', *The Age*, 2 October 1975.

87 Windschuttle, note 51, p. 18.

88 Russell Lansbury and Barry Guy, 'Attitudes to Employment', *National Bank Monthly Summary* (January 1977), p. 5.

89 Alec Pemberton, 'Doing Something About Nothing', *Social Alternatives*, Vol. 2, No. 1 (1981), p. 61.

90 Damien Murphy, 'Life's a Beach and Then You … Um', *The Bulletin* (18 November 1997), pp. 24–5.

91 Tim Jamieson, '1,500 Wait for Hours in Heat for Chance of a Job at Coles', *Sydney Morning Herald*, 16 January 1998, p. 2.

92 Arndt, note 74, p. 4s.

93 Tim Colebatch, Eric Beecher and Greg McKenzie, 'Broke and Bored…', *The Age*, 29 November 1976.

94 Paul Heinriches, John Hurst, Sue Cram and Alix Macdonald, 'On the Edge of the Bay: Living without Work in Frankston', *The National Times*, 2–8 November 1980, p. 31.

95 Katha Pollitt, 'Just the Facts', *The Nation*, Vol. 262 (24 June 1996), p. 9.

96 Seth Ackerman, 'Cato Pads the Poor', *Extra!* (January–February 1998), p. 22.

97 Williams, note 5.

98 Jackson, note 35.

99 Quoted in Robert Weissman, 'Corporate Tax Freeloaders', *Multinational Monitor* (April 1999), p. 6.

100 Robin Anne Bright, 'Dole Bludgers or Tax Dodgers: Who Is the Deviant?', in Paul R. Wilson and John Braithwaite (eds), *Two Faces of Deviance: Crimes of the Powerless and the Powerful* (Brisbane: University of Queensland Press, 1978), p. 167.

101 BBC, 'The Thorny Question of Welfare Reform' (BBC News, 1998). http://news. bbc. co.uk hi/english/uk/politics/newsid_69000/69873.stm.

102 Anthony Barnes Atkinson, 'The Economics of the Welfare State', *American Economist*, Vol. 40, No. 2 (1996).

103 Quoted in Robert Hutchens, 'Welfare and Work Incentives: a North European Perspective', *Journal of Economic Literature*, Vol. 33, No. 2 (1995).

104 Leif Beck Fallesen, 'Welfare Changes', *Europe* (June 1995).

105 Tom Allard, 'Benefit Cheats: $230m Paid Back', *Sydney Morning Herald*, 8 April 1998.

106 Robinson, note 71.

107 Paul Cleary, 'If They're Calling It Fraud, Why So Few Prosecutions?', *Sydney Morning Herald*, 8 April 1998.

108 Feagin, note 14, pp. 103, 108.

109 'Welfare Sleaze', *Progressive*, Vol. 56 (November 1992).

110 Feagin, note 14, p. 115.

111 'Welfare Sleaze', note 109.

112 Madeleine Leonard, 'The Long-term Unemployed, Informal Economic Activity and the "Underclass" in Belfast: Rejecting or Reinstating the Work Ethic', *International Journal of Urban and Regional Research*, Vol. 22, No. 1 (1998).

113 *Ibid.*, pp. 50, 53.

114 Frank Field, 'A New Contract for Welfare' (Minister for Welfare Reform, British Government, 1998). http://www.dss.gov.uk/hq/press/speeches/ff26398.htm.

115 DSS, note 19, chapter 1.

116 Patty Fuller, 'Fed Up with Frauds', *Alberta Report*, Vol. 20 (1 November 1993).

117 Mary Janigan, 'Wading into the Welfare Mess', *Maclean's*, Vol. 108 (4 December 1995).

118 Tim Jones, 'Pressure Mounting for Public Inquiry into Bristol Riot', *The Times*, 5 April 1980; John Young, 'Anger over Unemployment at Root of Bristol Riot, Council Chief Says', *The Times*, 8 July 1980.

119 American Psychiatric Association, *Diagnostic and Statistical Manual of Mental Disorders*, fourth edn (Washington, DC: American Psychiatric Association, 1994), pp. 7, 22.

120 Thomas Szasz, 'Idleness and Lawlessness in the Therapeutic State', *Society*, Vol. 32, No. 4 (1995).

121 Education and Training, Department of Employment, 'Special Intervention Programme (SIP) Tender Specification – Psychological Assessment and Intervention Services', (ACT/ Illawarra Office: DEET Programs Business Unit, 1995).

122 Richard Gosden, 'Shrinking the Dole Queue', *Arena Magazine,* No. 29 (June–July, 1997), pp. 31–41.

123 Bright, note 100, p. 164.

✦10✦

Welfare to Workfare

———

[T]o get people to go on doing work that does not make them happy requires social arrangements that either imbue productive toil with a false grandeur or punish with destitution those who do not play the game.
Joshua Rey[1]

[The welfare system] doesn't work; it defies our values as a nation. If we value work, we can't justify a system that makes welfare more attractive than work.
Bill Clinton[2]

Conservatives see the welfare system as encouraging unemployment and poverty when it should be pushing recipients into work.[3] Employers are concerned that a long period on welfare payments, especially for young people, undermines the work ethic and deprives them of 'experience with the satisfactions and disciplines of work'.[4]

Work-for-benefit schemes are becoming more prevalent in the English-speaking world. Whilst forcing welfare recipients to work for welfare payments has always been popular in theory amongst conservatives, it has not been adopted much because it tends to cost more money in supervision and administration than it saves.[5] One US study found that workfare, the American version of work-for-benefit, cost between $1,000 and $7,000 more per recipient than straight welfare.[6]

Nor is work-for-benefit designed to increase employment opportunities. Rather, it is in part a deterrent to those who would choose an 'easy' life on welfare, and in part designed to teach and promote a work ethic and work habits. Welfare recipients who are made to work for their benefit have to get up early, arrive at work on time, work with and for others, and acquire work skills.[7]

It is believed that welfare recipients who don't work not only lose the work ethic themselves but bring up children without a work ethic because their children lack a positive role model. It is also thought that requiring work for benefits is important to signal national priorities, goals and values.[8] One advocate openly states: 'The point is to enforce the work ethic. This is a long-term cultural offensive, not a budget-control program or an expression of compassion.'[9]

WORK AS RESPONSIBILITY

In Australia, the US and the UK the language of welfare reform clearly demonstrates a new form of work ethic: work as responsibility. The moral obligation to work comes not from God, nor from a desire to succeed, but is the obligation to contribute to the wealth creation of the nation and the maintenance of one's family. Those receiving welfare are described as 'dependent' because they are not fulfilling this responsibility. Writing in an Australian business magazine in 1979, Peter Samuel argued:

> Work is, after all, service to our fellow citizens and should be celebrated as an essential contribution to the community. It is giving as well as taking. Dependency in the form of living off the dole is taking without giving. It is 'parasitism'.[10]

Terms such as 'mutual obligation' have come into fashion. The idea of mutual obligation or 'reciprocal obligation' replaces the concept of welfare being a right or an entitlement with the concept that such benefits should be earned.[11] Such terms have think-tank origins. Lawrence Mead, author of a number of books including *The New Paternalism: Supervisory Approaches to Poverty* (published by the Brookings Institute), claims to have first used the terms 'mutual obligation' and 'social contract' with respect to welfare.[12]

Associated terms are 'personal responsibility' or 'reciprocal responsibility'.[13] The Heritage Foundation argues for workfare as a way to 'convert welfare from a one way hand-out into a system of mutual responsibilities'.[14] These terms imply that welfare recipients haven't been fulfilling their moral duties in the past and have been irresponsible. The assumption is that people on welfare do not want to work and have to be made to work so they can fulfil their responsibilities.[15]

Such language has been taken up by politicians in all English-speaking nations. According to the Department of Social Security the UK welfare reforms were based on 'nothing less than a change of culture among benefit claimants, employers and public servants – with rights and responsibilities on all sides'.[16] British MP Patricia Hewitt claimed that the main principle behind the welfare reforms in Britain is 'to rebuild the benefit system around the work ethic, transforming passive support into active support'.[17]

In Australia the Work for the Dole scheme is framed in terms of 'the mutual obligation principle: that it is fair and just that people receiving unemployment benefits from the community be asked to make a contribution to the community in return'.[18] Shortly after Jenny Shipley became Prime Minister in New Zealand she announced her intention to reform welfare and introduce the idea of reciprocal responsibilities in order to 'reverse the socially and economically damaging trend of long-term benefit dependency'.[19]

The use of the term 'dependency' in relation to welfare originates in American politics. Its roots go back to Roosevelt, who argued that 'continued dependence on relief induces a spiritual and moral disintegration fundamentally destructive to the national fiber'.[20] The idea of dependency was later promoted by Senator Patrick Moynihan in the 1960s[21] and by conservatives ever since. It is language President Clinton used extensively in the 1990s: '[H]ow can we help people who have been trapped in a culture of dependence and poverty to move to a culture of independence, family, and work?'[22]

In 1996 US welfare reforms replaced Aid to Families with Dependent Children (AFDC) with Temporary Assistance for Needy Families (TANF). The change in name reflected the aim of limiting the time that anyone could be 'dependent' on welfare. The name of the act that affected this change was also carefully chosen – the Personal Responsibility and Work Opportunity Reconciliation Act. It was approved by both Republicans and Democrats and requires that welfare recipients get cut off welfare after five years, even if they have attended all the training programmes and done the work for benefit that has been required of them.[23] In fact, the legislation includes a two-year limit for receiving assistance without working.[24]

The legislation enables states to reduce the maximum period on welfare to less than five years,[25] and several have. In Connecticut, where the limit is 21 months, welfare benefits have been stopped for 15,000 families, and homeless shelters and free food pantries are facing increased demand. Various other states have shorter limits than the five years.[26] In New York City, the Mayor, who has been taken to court for a policy that discourages poor people from applying for welfare, has stated that New York 'had become a city of mass dependency'. To destroy that culture of dependency, city officials turn applicants away on their first effort to apply for welfare and don't offer them the opportunity to apply for food stamps and Medicaid.[27]

Mary Jo Bane, former assistant secretary for children and families in the

US Department of Health and Human Services, who resigned over welfare reform, argues that the 'political rhetoric supporting the new law, unfortunately, made the concept of federal entitlement synonymous with irresponsibility and lifelong dependency'.[28]

The rhetoric about dependency is just that. Women who do not have jobs because they are supported by their husbands to raise children and take care of their homes are not stigmatised. In fact, feminists and others have done much to gain recognition for these activities as work, and hard work at that. Yet women who do the same work of bringing up young children, but are supported by benefits rather than a husband, are labelled 'dependent' and lazy. In an obvious double standard, people who decry middle-class mothers leaving their children in care from an early age to pursue a career sometimes demand that welfare mothers should be made to work.[29]

Suzanne Franks claims that the British government is willing to spend extra money to get poor mothers back to work because it considers paid work, such as washing up for McDonalds, 'a more valuable activity for a mother than being at home with her children'.[30] The difference is, however, that a pay cheque from McDonald's is earned whereas a welfare cheque is not, even if a woman works just as hard at home looking after her children.

The language of 'dependency' and the 'culture of poverty' are not restricted to the conservatives any more. President Clinton happily uses these terms[31] as does Britain's Labour Prime Minister Tony Blair. And the terms are also current in Canada.[32] Australian Labor politicians such as their spokesman on community services Wayne Swan and backbencher Mark Latham have also spoken of welfare dependency and mutal responsibility in support of Work for the Dole.[33]

The OECD rhetoric centres on creating an 'active society'. The welfare state is seen as creating 'a problem of large-scale inactivity' and welfare recipients as 'inactive'. The solution is to promote activity – that is, paid employment in the workforce. The rhetoric behind the active society concept is that human fulfilment results from paid employment and this is what everyone aspires to, or should aspire to. Whilst former welfare systems attempted to integrate non-working people into society through the payment of benefits, the 'active society' integrates everyone through making them undertake work.[34] In its 1990 *Employment Outlook* the OECD stated: 'The basic thrust of the "Active Society" is to foster economic opportunity and activity for everyone in order to combat poverty, dependence and social exclusion.'[35]

'Social exclusion' is a term that has gained currency in the UK, where the government has set up a 12-person Social Exclusion Unit. Ironically, representatives of the socially excluded are excluded from their unit.[36] The unit plans to initially focus on school drop-outs and homelessness.[37] Geoff Mulgan is a member of the unit and special adviser to Tony Blair. He describes social exclusion very much in terms of exclusion from the world of work:

> We at the moment have about one in five working age households in which no-one has a job. That means a third of all children are being brought up in a house in which no-one has a job, no-one has to get up in the morning to go to work, no-one is, in a sense, living in the disciplines, the structures of working life.[38]

Mulgan says the term social exclusion, which comes form the French term *l'excluse*, is used rather than underclass, as in the US, because underclass has 'very misleading implications about moral failure'. Nevertheless, when the new term is used in combination with others like dependency and mutual obligation, welfare recipients don't escape moral judgement.

WORK FOR BENEFIT

As early as 1967 US legislation was amended to include work requirements for women receiving AFDC through the introduction of 'workfare'.[39] 'Workfare' referred to a number of programmes aimed at getting welfare recipients back into the workforce. It included training programmes, work testing, subsidised childcare and job seeking assistance, as well as working for benefits.[40]

Working for benefits was reintroduced in the 1980s under Ronald Reagan's conservative government.[41] Reagan enabled individual states to require welfare recipients, even sole parents of young children (over three years), to work in public service jobs to earn their payments. Congress repeatedly blocked attempts by the Reagan administration to make the scheme compulsory in all states but it was taken up by many of them, although not in any comprehensive manner because of the cost.[42]

When Bill Clinton came to power in 1993 he promised to 'end welfare as we know it'. The new US welfare reforms require that, by the year 2002, 50 per cent of those receiving benefits will be doing work or training in return.[43] By the end of 1998 working for benefits was a major component of welfare in New York, California, Ohio, Florida, Massachusetts, Wisconsin, New Jersey, and Colorado.[44]

One of the most celebrated experiments in working for benefits in the US was that of Wisconsin. Governor Tommy Thompson became a hero of the conservative think tanks and politicians championing welfare reform. In 1996 he introduced 'Pay for Performance', which required a minimum number of hours of work or training in return for benefits.[45] Then in 1997 Thompson introduced 'Wisconsin Works' (W2) with the aim of abolishing cash benefits altogether, replacing them with payments for hours worked.[46]

Whilst some of the thousands cut off the Wisconsin welfare rolls have found jobs, what has become of the rest no-one really knows. And Thompson certainly doesn't seem to want to know, since he cut funding for tracking such people. Some may have moved in with relatives or moved to another state. The homeless shelters in Milwaukee have reported large increases in people using their facilities.[47] The number of families in shelters in the winter of 1997 rose by 25 per cent, according to the *New York Times*.[48] Jason Turner, who has overseen the welfare 'reforms', claimed there was 'no evidence' connecting 'large numbers of new people in homeless shelters' with Wisconsin welfare reforms.[49]

In Australia, work-for-benefit schemes were traditionally targeted at Aboriginal communities (about 10 per cent of all Aboriginal people in Australia are in such schemes).[50] In 1997 the Howard government introduced 'Work for the Dole' for young people aged 18–24 who had been unemployed for more than six months. Its purpose was to 'raise young unemployed people's work ethic, through fostering appropriate work habits and attitudes, and improving self esteem'.[51] Work habits the scheme is expected to foster include being able to work as part of a team and take directions from a supervisor; motivation and dependability are supposed to improve.[52] The Minister for Employment David Kemp said, in a statement that showed the effect of media-reinforced prejudices about the unemployed, that the scheme would make it clear to young people 'that the dole is not an alternative lifestyle'.[53]

The government claimed 'overwhelming community support' for the scheme and has been progressively expanding it.[54] In July 1999 Work for the Dole was extended to cover 25–34-year-olds at a cost of $100 million over four years.[55] More than 40 per cent of young people who work on such projects are conscripted – they don't have a choice if they don't want to lose part of their allowance.[56] They work 2–2.5 days per week in return for the unemployment allowance plus $10 for expenses. As an adjunct to this scheme, in 1998 the government cut welfare benefits to unemployed people under 25 whose parents earned more than $23,400 and who couldn't prove financial independence by having had a full-time job for at least 18 months or a part-time job for two years.[57]

In Britain, the New Deal for Young People, which the Labour Government introduced after it came into office in 1997, gives young unemployed people four choices: working for an employer who would get a £60 per week subsidy; working for a voluntary sector organisation; working on an Environmental Taskforce; or full-time education and training. The green paper on welfare reform made it clear there would be 'no 'fifth' option' of simply remaining on benefit' and those 'who unreasonably refuse an offer or fail to take up a place will be sanctioned'.[58]

179

Work for benefit has also been increasing in Canada. In June 1996 Ontario Works was launched. It requires welfare recipients to work up to 17 hours a week on community projects in return for their benefits.[59] A key part of Ontario Premier Mike Harris's election platform was his promise to make able-bodied welfare recipients either work or do training in return for benefits.[60]

DETERRING WELFARE

Forcing welfare recipients into low-paying jobs or government created make-work schemes is supposed to give them the right 'work attitude'. According to Kaus, the 'whole problem is that there are people who won't climb up a "ladder of opportunity" even when the economy or the government dangles it in front of their noses', so the solution is to '"make" people do things they might not do if they have a check coming every month'.[61]

Working for benefits is rationalised as helping the unemployed, the argument being that the unemployed are better off working than not working and that earning their payments will give them more self-esteem and community respect. In this way the welfare state is transformed into the 'Work Ethic State, in which status, dignity, and benefits flow only to those who work'.[62]

Such work, however, has a secondary status in the workforce. In this way recipients remain marginal to the workforce.[63] The low wages are necessary to ensure that real jobs are always more attractive, so that the incentive to find a real job remains and there is always a reserve of workers available for private employers.[64] Workfare jobs are not real jobs in the sense that there is no career ladder extending from them, and people doing them can't be promoted for showing skill and initiative. The work that recipients are given may be not very useful. Alternatively, if it is valued work it may displace workers already in the workforce with welfare recipients who are paid considerably less. And there is some doubt as to whether this forced work under degrading conditions offers status and dignity.

Those who do take part in workfare programmes in the US often work under awful conditions. In 1997 a group of New York workfare participants took the Mayor to court for failing to provide decent working conditions (Capers v. Giuliani). Workfare workers lacked access to protective clothing, toilets, drinking water and safety training, and often had to work in dangerous situations. In an affidavit Tamika Capers, who was required to clean highways and their verges, stated:

> If we need to urinate or move our bowels, we have to squat behind a tree or bush or ask one of our co-workers to hold up a plastic bag to shield us from the passing cars. We have not been given insect repellent, and I am afraid to

180

relieve myself outdoors, because I will be exposed to the many biting insects flying and crawling around us. My stomach cramps from holding my urine. During my menstrual period, there is no place to go to change my pad. I have to wait until the end of our shift, and by then my clothes are soaked with blood.[65]

Anastacio Serrano, who sweeps streets, stated in her affidavit: 'Because I have no dust mask or eye protection, I suffer from the dust that blows up in my face while I am sweeping. I have glaucoma … the dust gets in my eyes and dries up the solutions. I can hardly see by lunchtime.'[66] Mery Meijia's experience differed only in the details:

There are also all sorts of plants, maybe poison ivy, that give me rashes…. The only things we get for protection are an orange vest, a pair of cotton gloves, and a hard hat. The gloves and the hard hat are filthy, but I am not allowed to take anything home to wash it. They gave out boots for one week in February, but they were all size 12 and did not fit me…. When I work, the dust gets in my clothes, in my eyes, and in my nose. When I blow my nose during work the mucus is dark brown because I don't have a dust mask.[67]

Omar Torres has scars on her legs where she was burned by the splashing of graffiti-cleaning fluid. She was not provided with protection, not even goggles, whilst using this fluid. Workers are not provided with lockers to store personal items or food, so many go without lunch rather than carry it on their dustbins and garbage cans. Often they are unable to wash their hands before lunch despite having handled garbage all morning.[68] Sylvia Ruff (age 57) stated in her affidavit:

I always worry about the germs and often I do not eat. And now the weather is hot, I get terribly thirsty on the job, but there is no bathroom to use and I am afraid of having to urinate with nowhere to go. Even if I dared to drink, there is nowhere at the worksite to get water…. [69]

Such treatment hardly builds self-esteem and confidence, and is clearly punitive. The State Supreme Court ruled that the city was obliged to supply the 5,000 workfare people working for the departments of Sanitation and Transportation with training, protective clothing, toilets and drinking water, and it stopped welfare recipients being required to do this work until these basics were provided. This ruling was overturned on appeal in 1998, however, following the introduction of legislation ensuring that workfare workers have the same protections and complaint procedures as public employees. Workfare workers are appealing this latest ruling.[70]

Work-for-benefit programmes are in reality meant to deter people from being attracted to the 'good life' of the welfare recipient:

[W]hat's important is not whether sweeping streets or cleaning buildings helps Betsy Smith, single teenage parent and high school dropout, learn skills that will help her find a private sector job. It is whether the prospect of sweeping streets and cleaning buildings for a welfare grant will deter Betsy Smith from having the illegitimate child that drops her out of school and onto welfare in the first place – or, failing that, whether the sight of Betsy Smith sweeping the streets after having her illegitimate child will discourage her younger sisters and neighbours from doing as she did.[71]

Work-for-benefit schemes are therefore punitive to victims of unemployment, blaming them and their supposed lack of a work ethic for their inability to get jobs, rather than fixing the structural problems that lead to unemployment in the first place. It assumes that the reason they are unemployed is that they are 'bludgers', 'scroungers' or 'freeloaders' who are happy to be dependent on the welfare system.

The deterrence value is also acknowledged by Australian employment services minister Tony Abbott, who says: 'If work for the dole is a condition of unemployment benefits, work for a wage suddenly starts to look … more attractive.'[72]

Workfare is also supposed to help the unemployed become more attractive to employers, and give them a chance to prove themselves on the job. This reasoning is often subscribed to by the unemployed themselves.[73] However, the work provides little training. Australian Kirsty Newton described her experience on Work for the Dole which involved 'sanding the rust off memorial cannons at the Wollongong Lighthouse'.[74] Karl Gerber, an American welfare recipient points out: 'They call it a work experience program, but you don't need experience to go out and sweep the streets…. It's not a training programme at all. It's a kind of slave labor.'[75]

A coalition of churches, synagogues and non-profit groups in New York has stated that they will not take part in the work-for-benefit scheme because of its similarity to slavery.[76] Yet despite opposition from some religious groups and progressives, work-for-benefit schemes tend to find favour in the broader community.[77]

Forcing the unemployed to work for their benefits makes welfare payments more acceptable to taxpayers, who believe they are then getting something for their money – even though it is actually costing them more.[78] In Canada a 1994 Gallup poll found that 86 per cent of Canadians surveyed thought it was a good idea to force people on welfare to work.[79] Another 1994 survey found that 84 per cent of Americans believed that the welfare system discouraged recipients from finding jobs; 92 per cent said able-bodied people should have to work.[80] Three-quarters of Australians surveyed favoured the Work for the Dole scheme.[81]

EFFECT ON THE LABOUR MARKET

US businesses are helping to ensure that welfare reform is a success because surplus labour is of little value to them unless it is desperate to work. Being able to draw on a large pool of unemployed, who want to work because of punitive welfare conditions, gives employers a huge advantage in their dealings with employees because they are easily replaceable. Polish economist Michal Kalecki points out that fierce competition for jobs strengthens the authority of the employer:

> [U]nder a regime of full employment, 'the sack' would cease to play its role as a disciplinary measure. The social position of the boss would be undermined and the self assurance and class consciousness of the working class would grow.... [C]lass instinct [of business leaders] tells them that lasting full employment is unsound from their point of view and that unemployment is an integral part of the normal capitalist system.[82]

What is more, without quantities of unemployed people keen to get jobs it becomes more difficult to find experienced, suitably trained workers, and because demand outstrips supply the price of labour increases. On the other hand a surplus of labour in a deregulated labour market ensures a downward push on wages, while in a more regulated market it slows increases in wages.

> The quality of life and attitudes of people who represent surplus labour, i.e. the unemployed, therefore are essential elements in the scheme to push wages down through labour market deregulation. The surplus labour must be kept in a stressed and anxious state of mind so that they will compete and under-bid for jobs on the labour market.[83]

Some jobs are hard to fill because they are dangerous, dirty, distressing or dead-end, and such jobs can either be filled by paying high wages or by requiring people to do those jobs for low wages because they won't get welfare benefits if they don't. Employers don't want welfare payments to give unemployed people an alternative. Those who choose welfare over low-paid, dirty and demeaning jobs are called work-shy, or labelled bludgers.[84]

John Kenneth Galbraith pointed out in *The Culture of Contentment* that people who have the most enjoyable jobs also have the highest pay. This system is justified, as has been seen in earlier chapters, by the idea that those who are paid more have achieved their positions through merit and hard work. Yet the boring, tiring and demeaning jobs have to be done by someone: the existence of an underclass will supply these workers, provided they are given no choice.[85]

In some European countries foreigners are given working visas to fill such jobs. In other countries, such as Australia, new migrants often fill them. In countries like the US and Britain, and to some extent Australia, an underclass of citizens provides a reservoir of workers for these undesirable and low-paid jobs. But only if welfare does not provide a more desirable alternative. This is the real rationale behind recent welfare reforms.

The more people who are available to do an undesirable job, either because they are desperate for work having been cut off benefits or because it is a condition of their welfare benefits, the less the employer will have to increase the wages and ensure that their workplaces are safe and healthy to attract workers.

> From its start, welfare was a safety net that enabled many job seekers to refuse some of the worst jobs offered.... Since millions of recipients did not compete for jobs at whatever rock-bottom terms employers were offering, the labor market was not flooded with every single, desperate parent of a young child, displacing workers and driving down the earnings of the working poor and near-poor.[86]

In some countries such as the US,[87] Australia and Canada,[88] welfare can offer more income for families than low-paid jobs, particularly when health and housing benefits are taken into account, as many low-paid jobs do not offer health insurance. For employers wanting to get workers into these jobs without raising wages, welfare provides direct competition. They therefore lobby governments to lower welfare benefits and to make recipients uncomfortable on welfare. Even the International Monetary Fund (IMF) advocates reductions in welfare as a way of promoting economic growth. It advised the Australian government in 1998 to cut welfare spending and to put a time limit on unemployment benefits as has happened in the US.[89] It also urged the government to do away with minimum wages and benefits.[90]

The reduction of the welfare safety net and abolition of mimimum wages would ensure that wages for unskilled workers would go down even further, removing any industrial bargaining power workers at the bottom of the hierarchy might have. In one US case welfare workers were sent to a hotel to train as maids, paid only their benefit plus $30 a week by the hotel, in the midst of a labour dispute.[91]

Elaine McCrate, from the University of Vermont, found that in states where welfare benefits were higher, so was women's pay: 'Statistically, an additional $100 [per month] in benefits was associated with women's wages that were 2.5 per cent higher.'[92] And the Economic Policy Institute estimates that Clinton's welfare reform measures will lower the wages of the bottom 30 per cent of wage earners by almost 12 per cent. Another study by the Russell Sage Foundation found that 30,000 workfare placements in New York alone would cause 20,000 job losses and reduce the wages of the bottom third of wage earners by 9 per cent.[93]

The jobs that former welfare recipients have been forced into as a result of the welfare reforms in the US tend to be low-paid jobs in wholesale/retail (including food) and in service industries. For example, in Texas 41 per cent were employed in restaurant/fast food, clerical, or retail/sales jobs.[94] Researchers from the Employment Policy Foundation have reported that the actual earnings of former welfare recipients, when they get a job, tend to be between $9,000 and $12,000 per year which leaves them below the poverty line if they have one or more children. They tend to remain in these low-paid jobs for long periods of time. The researchers argue that taxpayers should take responsibility for assuring workers a minimum standard of living, not private employers.[95]

Workfare also enables public works projects to be undertaken cheaply with compulsory labour. In Baltimore, a campaign to raise the wages of city workers was immediately undermined by the new welfare reforms. Workers watched in horror as welfare recipients were brought on the job, working 30 hours a week for their $350 a month benefit, a rate of about $3 per hour. Because the state pays the benefit, the city council gets these welfare workers for free and regular workers are likely to be displaced.[96]

The story is being repeated all over the country from New York to Los Angeles, where tens of thousands of welfare workers do public workfare jobs.[97] In a 1997 submission on the Work Experience Program (WEP) in New York, the Migrant Employment Taskforce stated:

> While the program's rules clearly state that WEP participants are trainees to be assigned work that city workers normally would not do, WEP assignees frequently do some of the work once done by employees who have retired, quit, been laid off.... [T]hey are prominent in those areas which have suffered the greatest job cutbacks.[98]

Benjamin Duchin, for the Fifth Avenue Committee, claimed that same year:

> Workfare takes away the entry level jobs that people used to get. There is now a hiring freeze in New York City. Why? Because WEP workers are doing the jobs. You go to the Parks Department and they have lost 2,000 jobs in the last couple of years but they have 6,000 WEP workers.... There has been massive displacement – around 21,000 workers....[99]

The payment of minimum wages to welfare recipients also undermines the position of those doing similar work whose wages are above the minimum wage. In the case of Brukhman v. Giuliani the calculation of workfare hours based on minimum wages, rather than the normal wage for the type of work being done, was challenged. The case was won in the NY State Supreme Court in 1997 but lost on appeal after the state changed the legislation to say that workfare should be calculated on the basis of minimum rates.[100] In Ohio, welfare recipients were being asked to work for below the minimum wage rate. The policy was rescinded after the threat of legal action by the Welfare Law Center and the Equal Justice Foundation.[101]

In this climate a US Labor Department ruling has come as a major blow to proponents of work-for-benefit schemes as a way of ensuring a downward pressure on wages. The ruling states that people on welfare who have to work for their benefits are entitled to the same labour protection as other workers, including minimum wages, unemployment insurance, workers' compensation and perhaps even overtime pay in some circumstances. Michael Tanner from the Cato Institute called this 'the end of welfare reform as we know it'.[102]

Australian legislation specifically excludes Work for the Dole participants from the entitlements workers normally enjoy, such as superannuation, workers' compensation, occupational health and safety, and industrial relations protections. The legislation makes it clear that participation in Work for the Dole does not 'create an employment relationship at common law'.[103] Instead, the unemployed people are covered by public liability and insurance organised by the federal government.

The benefits of welfare reform to business are so overwhelming that many companies have clubbed together to ensure its success. A grouping of 500 companies, Welfare to Work Partnership, has been organised by the White House to assist with this process.[104] The Partnership was founded in 1996 by the CEOs of United Airlines, Burger King, Sprint, Monsanto and United Parcel Service of America (UPS). It points out to employers that 'by recruiting welfare recipients, companies can greatly enlarge their pool of potential entry-level workers'.[105] The chairman of this group is Gerard Greenwald of United Airlines, which pays wages so low (barely above the minimum wage) for jobs such as ticket agent, gate agent and reservations representative that it has difficulty attracting people, even welfare recipients, to apply for jobs.[106]

United Airlines is not unique. Two-thirds of employers pay entry-level workers less than $6 an hour, which is not enough to support two children above the poverty line. In addition, 25 per cent of employers offer these workers no benefits at all and 83 per cent pay no sick leave. What is more, 36 per cent of entry-level positions cannot be reached by public transport and two-thirds of them are part-time.[107]

The US Small Business Administration (SBA) has also established a 'Welfare to Work' initiative to help 'small business gain access to a new pool of potential workers'. The SBA promotes Welfare to Work by showing employers how 'by hiring former welfare recipients, small business owners can tap into significant wage subsidies and tax breaks as well as gain access to new workers'. This is a particularly revealing initiative at a time when unemployment is relatively low in the US and many businesses are having trouble finding workers to suit them.[108]

Work Not Welfare, another of these pressure groups, is an alliance of corporate employers who are lobbying to ensure that legislation which offers them free or heavily subsidised welfare workers is not overridden. The alliance includes Pizza Hut, J. C. Penny and various hotel and retail chains.[109]

CONCLUSION

Within a year the welfare reforms in the US were being hailed as a great success. Success was defined in terms of reducing the welfare rolls and delivering cheap workers to employers. The average employee did not benefit, as the impact of welfare reform was to make jobs more insecure and to put downward pressure on wages through an increased supply of people desperate for work.

In an upbeat article in *Newsweek* proclaiming the success of welfare reform, Jonathan Alter admitted: 'Yes, homelessness and visits to the food banks are rising a bit in areas with the toughest new laws. But if the economy holds up and the private sector does its part, we're on the threshold of the greatest social-policy achievement in a generation.'[110]

The new welfare reforms, including compulsory work-for-benefit schemes, are premised on the idea that unemployment has been caused, or at least exacerbated, by the welfare system rather than factors such as the massive corporate and government downsizing that occurred during the 1980s and 1990s (see Chapter 8). The assumption was that if people left welfare, or didn't apply because of tough new rules, then they couldn't have really needed it.[111] Yet the reality was that many people were forced into taking demeaning jobs at pay levels that left them in poverty, enabling employers to keep wages at these unreasonably low levels.

It is evident that jobs have been created and unemployment has been reduced in the US by limiting welfare, enabling employers to offer ever lower wages to unskilled workers. This has created millions of 'working poor' and has been accompanied by slums, homelessness, crime and drugs.[112] It is not a particularly attractive policy prescription, except for businesspeople and those who serve them. Yet the US policy prescription of low wages and a much-reduced safety net for those who do not accept them is being successfully promoted in many English-speaking countries.

In Europe welfare has come under attack from business leaders and conservative politicians who wish to emulate the US 'success'. They argue that the welfare state makes labour too costly, labourers too lazy and taxes too high. Efforts to cut back on welfare in Europe have met with stiff public opposition, however, including 'violent labor protests in Italy and massive demonstrations in Germany'.[113] In Sweden, where there is an extensive and generous welfare system, the Social Democrats won another term of government in 1998 after promising to expand welfare, after widespread protest against welfare cuts in their previous term of office.[114]

The US reforms and their proclaimed success reinforce the wider community perception that people are unemployed as a result of their own deficiencies rather than economic problems created by others. It 'shifts the blame for unemployment away from the economy and the Government by placing it firmly on the shoulders of those who are in fact victims of unemployment'.[115] As a spokesperson for the Australian welfare organisation the Brotherhood of St Laurence said of the Australian government's Work for the Dole scheme:

> The government's programs represent and promote the belief that unemployment is a problem because of deficiencies in individuals, like being unmotivated or lacking a work ethic, rather than recognising that there is insufficient demand or growth in the economy to employ those who want to work.[116]

It has been suggested that the work ethic has been replaced by a new ethic 'that requires one to have enough resources, financial resources, not to be a burden on other people' but in fact this is really another expression of the work ethic.[117] Work is imbued with a moral value through an emphasis on responsibility and contribution. Work-for-benefit schemes are one of the most recent political expressions of work ethic promotion. And, as we shall see in the next chapter, the work ethic continues to be inculcated in schools.

NOTES

1 Joshua Rey, 'Give Us a Break', *New Statesmen and Society* (22 November 1991), p. 17.

2 Quoted in 'Dethroning the Welfare Queen: the Rhetoric of Reform', *Harvard Law Review*, Vol. 107 (1994), p. 2016.

3 Paul Bernstein, *American Work Values: Their Origin and Development* (Albany, NY: State University of New York Press, 1997), p. 255.

4 Keith Ogborn, *Workfare in America: an Initial Guide to the Debate* (Woden, ACT: Department of Social Security, 1986), p. 3.

5 *Ibid.*, p. 1.

6 'Working for Whose Welfare?', *Canada and the World Backgrounder*, Vol. 62 (October 1996), p. 22.

7 Mickey Kaus, 'The Work Ethic State: the Only Way to Break the Culture of Poverty', *The New Republic* (7 July 1986), p. 27.

8 Ogborn, note 4, p. 15.

9 Kaus, note 7, p. 33.

10 Peter Samuel, 'The Real Story of Unemployment', *The Bulletin* (6 November 1979), p. 21.

11 Senate Community Affairs Legislation Committee, 'Social Security Legislation Amendment (Work for the Dole) Bill' (Canberra: Parliament of the Commonwealth of Australia, 1997), Minority Report; Helen Trinca, 'Forced Labour', *Sydney Morning Herald*, 17 January 1998.

12 Bettina Arndt, 'A Debt to Society', *Sydney Morning Herald*, 13 February 1999, p. 1s.

13 'Working for Whose Welfare?', note 6.

14 Quoted in 'Dethroning the Welfare Queen', note 2, p. 2027.

15 *Ibid.*, p. 2028.

16 DSS, 'New Ambitions for Our Country: a New Contract for Welfare', (Department of Social Security, 1998), Chapter 3. http://www.dss.gov.uk/hq/wreform/

17 Quoted in 'What Should We Do with the Welfare State?', *Prospect* (March 1998), p. 37.

18 DEETYA, 'Work for the Dole: Sponsor Handbook', (Canberra: Department of Employment, Education, Training and Youth Affairs, 1998), p. 1.

19 Jane Dunbar, 'Shipley to Sink Welfare Dependency', *Sydney Morning Herald*, 18 February 1998.

20 Quoted in Lydia Morris, *Dangerous Classes: the Underclass and Social Citizenship* (London: Routledge, 1994), p. 63.

21 Derrick Jackson, 'Why Do Stereotypes and Lies Persist?', *Nieman Reports*, Vol. 51 (March 1997).

22 William J. Clinton, 'Remarks in a Roundtable Discussion on Welfare Reform in New York City', *Weekly Compilation of Presidential Documents*, Vol. 33 (24 February 1997).

23 David R. Riemer, 'Viewpoint', *Planning*, Vol. 62, No. 11 (1996), p. 42.

24 Daniel Casse, 'Why Welfare Reform Is Working', *Commentary*, Vol. 104, No. 3 (1997).

25 Lucy A. Williams, 'Rethinking Low-wage Markets and Dependency', *Politics and Society*, Vol. 25, No. 4 (1997).

26 Richard Wolf, 'Welfare Cutoffs Defy Dire Forecast', *USA Today*, 17 November 1998.

27 Rachel L. Swarns, 'US Inquiry Asks if City Deprives Poor', *The New York Times*, 8 November 1998, p. 39.

28 Mary Jo Bane, 'Welfare as We Might Know It', *American Prospect*, Vol. 30 (January/February 1997).

29 Margaret Carlson, 'Home Alone', *Time*, Vol. 150 (10 November 1997), p. 30.

30 Suzanne Franks, *Having None of It: Women, Men and the Future of Work* (London: Granta Books, 1999), p. 216.

31 William J. Clinton, 'Remarks of the Business Council', *Weekly Compilation of Presidential Documents*, Vol. 33 (3 March 1997), p. 263.

32 Christopher Serres, 'Social Services Lead the Way', *Alberta Report*, Vol. 21 (31 January 1994).

33 Greg Roberts, 'Too Much Charity in Welfare: Labor MP', *Sydney Morning Herald*, 27 July 1999; Wayne Swan, 'Two-way Street to End Poverty Traps', *Sydney Morning Herald*, 6 May 1999.

34 William Walters, 'The 'Active Society': New Designs for Social Policy', *Policy and Politics*, Vol. 25, No. 3 (1997), pp. 225, 230.

35 Quoted in *ibid.*, p. 224.

36 Tom Morton, 'Social Exclusion', *Radio National, ABC*, 7 February 1999.

37 DSS, note 16, Chapter 8.

38 Quoted on Morton, note 36.

39 Williams, note 39.

40 Ogborn, note 4, p. 5.

41 Kaus, note 7, p. 25.

42 Ogborn, note 4, pp. 7–8.

43 Casse, note 24.

44 Low Income Networking Communications Project, 'Organizing and Litigation' (Low Income Networking Communications Project, 1998). http://www.lincproject.org/hotnews.htm.

45 Robert Klara, 'Working off Welfare', *Restaurant Business*, Vol. 95, No. 18 (1996); Casse, note 24.

46 J. Jean Rogers, 'Making Welfare Work', *New Statesman* (29 August 1997).

47 'Ending Welfare: Were We Wrong?', *The Progressive*, Vol. 61 1997); David Corn, 'Welfare, Inc.', *The Nation*, Vol. 264 (5 May 1997)

48 Cited in Kenneth L. Deavers and Anita U. Hattiangadi, 'Welfare to Work: Building a Better Path to Private Employment Opportunities', *Journal of Labor Research*, Vol. 19, No. 2 (1998).

49 Quoted in Corn, note 47.

50 Deborah Cameron, 'Land Where Pensions Are as Poisonous as Grog', *Sydney Morning Herald*, 8 May 1999.

51 Senate Community Affairs Legislation Committee, note 11.

52 DEETYA, note 18, p. 2.

53 Laura Tingle, 'Young Jobless Have Work Cut Out for Them', *Sydney Morning Herald*, 27 July 1998.

54 Minister's Foreword in DEETYA, note 18, p. I.

55 Peter Reith and Jocelyn Newman, 'Strengthening and Extending Mutual Obligation', (Canberra: Government Press Release, 1999).

56 Jodie Brough, 'Work-for-Dole Conscription a "Shambles"', *Sydney Morning Herald*, 15 January 1998.

57 Adele Horin, 'Why the New Dole Rules Are Treating This Bouncer Like a Child', *Sydney Morning Herald*, 13 July 1998.

58 DSS, note 16, Chapter 3.

59 'Working for Whose Welfare?', note 6, p. 20.

60 Mary Janigan, 'Wading into the Welfare Mess', *Maclean's*, Vol. 108 (4 December 1995).

61 Kaus, note 7, p. 26.

62 *Ibid.*, p. 31.

63 Ogborn, note 4, p. 2.

64 Kaus, note 7, p. 31.

65 Quoted in 'Welfare as They Know It', *Harper's*, Vol. 295 (November 1997).

66 Quoted in *ibid.*

67 Quoted in *ibid.*

68 *Ibid.*

69 Quoted in *ibid.*

70 Welfare Law Center, 'Litigation Docket' (Welfare Law Center, 1999). http://welfarelaw.org/MarchDocket.htm.; Low Income Networking Communications Project, note 44.

71 Kaus, note 7, p. 27.

72 Jonathan Singer, 'Why More Australians Are Getting Poorer', *Green Left Weekly*, 25 August 1999, p. 3.

73 Ogborn, note 4, p. 14.

74 Kirsty Newton, 'Work for the Dole?', *Tertangala*, November 1999, p. 28.

75 Quoted in Evette Porter, 'Work Ethic', *Village Voice*, 6 May 1997, p. 53.

76 Casse, note 24.

77 Ogborn, note 4, p. 14.

78 *Ibid.*, p. 2.

79 'Working for Whose Welfare?', note 6, p. 20.

80 Bernstein, note 3, p. 255.

81 Arndt, note 12, p. 4s.

82 Quoted in Juliet B. Schor, *The Overworked American: the Unexpected Decline in Leisure* (New York: Basic Books, 1991), p. 75.

83 Richard Gosden, 'Punishing the Unemployed', *AES Report* (May 1991), p. 9.

84 Brotherhood of St Laurence, 'Why So Harsh on the Unemployed? A Second Discussion Paper' (Fitzroy, Victoria: Brotherhood of St Laurence, 1974), pp. 9–10.

85 John Kenneth Galbraith, *The Culture of Contentment* (London: Penguin, 1992), p. 33.

86 Elaine McCrate, 'Hitting Bottom: Welfare "Reform" and Labor Markets', *Dollars and Sense* (September/October 1997).

87 Morton S. Baratz and Sammis B. White, 'Childfare: a New Direction for Welfare Reform', *Urban Studies*, Vol. 33, No. 10 (1996), p. 1938.

88 Mary Janigan, note 60.

89 Adele Horin, 'Ignore IMF's "Cure"', *Sydney Morning Herald*, 21 November 1998.

90 Paul Cleary, 'Push to Curb Wages', *Sydney Morning Herald*, 31 October 1998.

91 Marc Cooper, 'When Push Comes to Shove', *The Nation*, Vol. 264 (2 June 1997).

92 McCrate, note 86.

93 Cited in *ibid*.

94 Sarah Brauner and Pamela Loprest, 'Where Are They Now: What States' Studies of People Who Left Welfare Tell Us' (Urban Institute, 1999). http://www.urban.org/

95 Deavers and Hattiangadi, note 48.

96 Cooper, note 91.

97 *Ibid*.

98 Quoted in Senate Community Affairs Legislation Committee, note 11.

99 Quoted in Eleanor J. Bader, 'Unfair Workfare', *Dollars and Sense* (September/October 1997).

100 Welfare Law Center, note 70.

101 Low Income Networking Communications Project, note 44.

102 Michael Tanner, 'Ending Welfare Reform as We Know It', *Human Events*, Vol. 53 (22 August 1997).

103 Senate Community Affairs Legislation Committee, note 11.

104 John Greenwald, 'Off the Dole and on the Job', *Time*, Vol. 150 (18 August 1997); 'The Muddled Maths of Welfare to Work', *The Economist*, Vol. 342 (8 March 1997), pp. 25–6.

105 The Welfare to Work Partnership, 'The Welfare to Work Partnership' (The Welfare to Work Partnership, 1999), http://www.welfaretowork.org/wtwpapps/WTWPHOME.nsf.

106 'United Recruiting Welfare Recipients: Low Entry-Level Pay Deters Some Applicants', *Denver Post,* 19 August 1998.

107 Urban Institute, 'Good News for Entry-Level Workers', (Urban Institute, 1998). http://www.urban.org/

108 Small Business Administration, 'Welfare to Work@SBA' (US Small Business Adminis-

tration, 1999). http://www.sba.gov/welfare.

109 Cooper, note 91.

110 Jonathan Alter, 'A Real Piece of Work', *Newsweek*, Vol. 130 (25 August 1997), p. 32.

111 Alberto Martini and Michael Wiseman, 'Explaining the Recent Decline in Welfare Caseloads: Is the Council of Economic Advisers Right?' (Urban Institute, 1997). http://www.urban.org/

112 Jay Branegan, 'Farewell to Welfare', *Time*, Vol. 142 (22 November 1993).

113 *Ibid.*

114 Warren Hoge, 'Swedish Party Pledging Expanded Welfare Gains Slim Victory', *The New York Times*, 21 September 1998, p. 3.

115 Australian Democrats in Senate Community Affairs Legislation Committee, note 11.

116 Quoted in *ibid.*

117 P. Kelvin quoted in Adrian Furnham, *The Protestant Work Ethic: the Psychology of Work-Related Beliefs and Behaviours* (London: Routledge, 1990), p. 202.

PART III

Motivating Work – Conditioning

Teaching
Work Values

Kids are tomorrow's labor force or tomorrow's
social problems.
Alan Deutschman[1]

Since its inception in the United States, the public-
school system has been seen as a method of
disciplining children in the interest of producing a
properly subordinate adult population.
Samuel Bowles and Herbert Gintis[2]

A large part of the school's job is to motivate children not only to want to work but also to accept the
dominant place of work in their future lives.
John White[3]

The prime purpose of education since the nineteenth century has been to provide a workforce
appropriately graded and trained for the needs of
the labour market.
Cath Blakers[4]

The desire of employers for well-trained employees with a good work ethic
put pressure on schools throughout the twentieth century to produce children
who fit employer requirements. If schools provided the appropriate skills and
behaviour, they argued, then the nation would gain prosperity and competitiveness from having a more productive workforce.

Throughout the history of school education there has been a struggle
between a utilitarian approach that attempts to shape school education to meet
practical purposes such as equipping children to be workers and the view that

school education should develop the human potential of individual children without reference to what might be expected of them as workers in the future.[5] In the latter view an education that prepares children to be workers restricts the potential of tomorrow's citizens to a narrow economic role and deprives future generations of other qualities that could otherwise be more fully developed, such as creative and critical faculties.

Despite this conflict of philosophies, business leaders have ensured that a primary purpose of schools has been to prepare students to be productive workers: 'The schools' role has been to socialize economically desirable values and behavior, teach vocational skills, and provide education consistent with student's expected occupational attainment.'[6]

A work ethic is what employers want most in terms of work preparation from the educational system.[7] A survey of 1,900 US personnel officers found that they were more concerned that applicants had a good attitude, were dependable when it came to turning up to work and were unlikely to steal or be dishonest, than they were with school grades.[8] Countless other surveys show that the work ethic is a major attribute that American employers look for when recruiting employees.[9]

- A survey of 150 human resource managers from the largest US companies found that the work ethic was the most cited quality that employers looked for in employees.[10]

- A survey of 3,000 employers by the Commission on the Skills of the American Workforce found that 80 per cent of those interviewed were most concerned with 'finding workers with a good work ethic and appropriate social behaviours'.[11]

- A survey of US employers by Towers Perrin found that a lack of appropriate work attitudes and behaviours was the most common reason, after lack of prior work experience, for not hiring applicants.[12]

Similarly in Australia a government report on youth employment found that employers place a high value on work attitudes such as 'willingness to work, a desire to learn, punctuality, honest and appropriate personal behaviour and presentation'.[13] These attitudes were found to be more important to employers than skills because skills can be learned on the job or through company training if the person has the right attitude to start with.[14] A similar survey in Canada found that almost 40 per cent of managers cited a work ethic as the main quality they looked for in employees.[15]

In France, employers have dwelt on the lack of work skills, practical training and 'ignorance of working conditions'. In Britain the most important deficiency noted by employers was 'pupil attitudes toward work' and the Association of British Chambers of Commerce has argued for preparation for work to become an integral part of the secondary school curriculum.[16]

INSTILLING WORK VALUES

Puritans tended to consider children to be 'ungodly, altogether too playful, lacking in seriousness and ill-disposed toward work'.[17] They had to be taught a work ethic. Ministers, writers and educators in the seventeenth and eighteenth centuries promoted work and industry as qualities children needed to acquire. Anglican minister Samuel Johnson claimed in the 1760s that it was 'indispensably necessary that they [children] be inured to industry and diligence'.[18]

Not all parents could be trusted to counter the playful tendencies of their children; schools were necessary to ensure this was done. Yet most children did not receive schooling prior to the mid-nineteenth century. Even then, in England only two million out of five million children went to school. In poorer families children had to work for wages from an early age to supplement the family income.[19]

Many children were left free to do what they liked and the numbers of children roaming the streets without restraint or discipline alarmed middle-class leaders who were concerned it could lead to adults who were discontented and insubordinate. Education was seen as a way of instilling the discipline these children lacked and preparing them for the world of work. Children were taught the three Rs and inculcated with 'habits of obedience, punctuality, personal cleanliness and respect for authority'.[20]

As time went by educators and others increasingly saw families as inadequate to the task of properly socialising children and urged schools to take over the task. Throughout the nineteenth century, schools were seen as having the role of instilling proper values and morals where families failed to do so, or when families from different backgrounds and cultures, particularly immigrant families, became part of the community. Educational leaders in 1874 stated that 'In order to compensate for lack of family nurture, the school is obliged to lay more stress upon discipline and to make far more prominent the moral phase of education. It is obliged to train the pupil into habits of prompt obedience to his teachers and the practice of self control in its various forms.'[21]

Nineteenth-century children's books, as noted in Chapter 3, promoted the work ethic and the myth of the self-made man. Nineteenth-century schools tended to operate like factories where the children were products proceeding along a production line of instruction. Such schools were described by the Boston School Committee in 1828 as effectively disposing young minds 'to industry, to readiness of attention, and to subordination, thereby creating in early life a love of order, preparation for business'.[22] By 1909 the committee was specifying with even greater explicitness how an elementary school was expected to produce factory workers: 'Everything must conform as closely as possible to actual industrial work in real life.'[23]

Popular articles on the work ethic between 1900 and 1940 stressed the need to teach children to work. Some argued that the work ethic 'should be an integral part of the educational curriculum',[24] others that 'the elementary school could be used to break the labouring classes into those habits of work discipline now necessary for factory production.... Putting little children to work at school for very long hours at very dull subjects was seen as a positive virtue, for it made them "habituated, not to say naturalized, to labour and fatigue".'[25] William Bagley's book on *Classroom Management*, which was a standard teacher training text early in the twentieth century, approached education as a method of building good work habits and ensuring future assembly line workers would be efficient and productive.[26]

Against voices such as Bagley's other voices have been raised that argued that education has a value in its own right that is separate from economic values. The twentieth century therefore saw a struggle over the purpose and meaning of schools that continues today. This struggle manifests in the tension between work and play in schools. Some educators have argued that children learn better in an environment that 'stresses self-expression, independence, and spontaneity' and that learning is more likely if it happens naturally – for example, in games, songs and stories, or as a result of a child's curiosity. Such ideas, however, made little headway in schools. Kindergartens, where this sort of play was encouraged, were often criticised as undisciplined and providing inadequate preparation for school.[27]

The shift from play to work has also been evident in institutionalised after-school activities. There is an increasing trend for middle-class American children to be sent to some organised activity after school rather than coming home to play freely in the neighbourhood. Such activities, including sporting activities, are often competitive, particularly as the children get older and more involved, and incorporate 'performance criteria' into their play. Patricia and Peter Adler note in *The Sociological Quarterly* that children 'encounter the up-or-out dilemma' which means that over time the recreational versions of their activities are phased out and they have to either get serious and committed or drop the activity. 'Play becomes transformed into games, and games into work.'[28]

> These adult-structured activities encourage professionalization and specialization, opposing children's unorganized tendencies toward recreation and generalism....

[This] organizational framework ... encompasses an implicit ascension into the ladder of adult, corporate-style norms, values and structures.... Obedience, discipline, sacrifice, seriousness, and focused attention are valued; deviance, dabbling, and self-indulgence are not.... they are steered away from goal-setting, improvisation, and self-reliance toward the acceptance of adult authority and adult pre-set goals.[29]

In Australia, too, the work ethic in sport is encouraged in schools. In the lead-up to the Olympic Games the Australian Olympic team placed various half-page advertisements in the *Sydney Morning Herald*, with one stating: 'I used to swim for fun. Then I heard Sam Riley [Olympic Gold medal winner] speak at school. Now I swim for gold.'[30]

Childhood experts are fairly unanimous about the value of play for a child's development. It is how children explore the world and experiment with relationships and learn about themselves. If it is unstructured it fosters independent thinking. According to paediatrician Berry Brazleton from Harvard Medical School, 'If we don't pay attention to this, we're going to create obsessive-compulsive people.'[31] The view that schools should transform childish playfulness into the material of 'a stable quiescent labor force' prevailed, however, and schools not only promoted the virtues of work but also aimed to internalise work as 'a pattern of behaviour' rather than as a means to an end.[32] Homework ensured that school work went beyond school hours and that after-school hours would also be productive. In his history of education in the US, Joel H. Spring claims: 'To a great extent children became a form of natural resource that was to be moulded by the schools and fed into the industrial machine.'[33] David Cohen and Marvin Lazerson concur:

> Typically, school officials stressed that classroom activities should inculcate the values thought to make good industrial workers – respect for authority, discipline, order, cleanliness, and punctuality – and the schools developed elaborate schemes for grading, reporting, and rewarding student behavior.[34]

Schools condition children to accept authority and the exercise of power over them. They teach children that 'the acceptance of leadership – the contented submission to the will of others – is a normal and commendable thing'. In indirect, and sometimes direct, ways children are also taught to accept the current power structure of the society.[35]

BUSINESS INVOLVEMENT IN EDUCATION

One reason that the utilitarian approach has come to dominate, despite the opposition of many educators, is the strong influence of business in school education. The business community began taking an active interest in

199

education early in the twentieth century, as they realised their own interest in assuring suitable training for future employees.

Andrew Carnegie, who was involved in the use of strikebreakers and the National Guard to subdue workers, later decided that education was a better, more subtle way of approaching labour problems. He founded the Carnegie Foundation for the Advancement of Teaching which played an influential role in the shaping of education in the US.[36]

Control of schools shifted as businesspeople, and therefore business ideology, came to dominate boards of education throughout the US. One study by Scott Nearing of 104 schools systems in 1916 found that businessmen made up more than half the total number of board members. Another by George Counts ten years later found that school boards were dominated by proprietors, professionals and business executives. In rural areas farmers made up 95 per cent of the boards.[37]

Author Upton Sinclair also wrote about the domination of the American education system by business interests in the 1920s. He told of how business interests took over the National Education Association and John D. Rockefeller established the General Education Board with an endowment of $125 million 'for the purpose of exercising supervision over American education'. Sinclair described this board as 'without doubt the most powerful single agency now engaged in keeping our schools subservient to special privilege'. The board supplied expert educators to run schools all over the country free of charge.[38]

Business leaders called for schooling that more directly prepared children to become workers, with particular emphasis on vocational education and guidance, whilst unions opposed vocationalism which, they argued, was aimed at producing docile employees.[39] The unions, however, were much less influential than business when it came to education.

In the 1930s the Depression undermined business influence as corporate funding of schools dropped off and some business organisations in the US actually advocated the reduction of public funding of schools. In the 1940s the National Association of Manufacturers tried to repair some of the damage and to regain the trust of school teachers and administrations. Whilst it remained opposed to federal government funding of schools, it attempted to get corporations to donate money to schools and win alliances with school administrators in the process.[40]

The US Chamber of Commerce established hundreds of committees of education (1,300 by 1949) and individual employers established relationships with local schools. As well as financial support, they sponsored vocational guidance programmes and provided teaching materials. Employers asked in return that students be trained with the 'correct attitudes' for the workplace.

They also wanted students to be taught about the benefits of the American system of free enterprise.[41]

Business–education partnerships were encouraged intermittently over the following decades in the US, as they were in other countries. In the 1960s Industry–Education Councils were set up in some states such as California, New York and Ohio. Each council was made up of 'leaders in business, public education, labor, government and the professions' and had a full-time executive director, support staff and a budget. Their tasks included provision of teacher training, revision of curricula, upgrading instructional materials and equipment, and more efficient educational management.[42]

During the 1980s President Reagan proclaimed 1983/4 as the National Year of Partnerships in Education and urged businesses to form partnerships with schools and community colleges across the country.[43] A report commissioned by the Reagan administration, *Nation at Risk*, argued that the public school education system was in a bad way, threatening economic growth in the US. American children were said to be falling behind their counterparts in other industrialised countries and a shortage of skilled labour was forecast for the future. This report 'provided the underlying justification for over a decade of corporate involvement in the reform of America's public schools'.[44]

In 1989 two hundred company CEOs on the Business Roundtable decided 'to help produce systemic change in the way teaching and learning are practiced in the nation's elementary and secondary schools'.[45] As a result various business alliances were set up, such as the Business for Education Coalition in Connecticut, the Partnership for Kentucky School Reform and a West Virginia Business and Education Alliance. The goal of the latter was to 'recruit and support a businessperson for each of the thousands of school improvement councils in the state'. By 1990 51 per cent of schools had become involved in partnerships with businesses.[46]

> Soon, it seemed no area of school life was beyond corporate scrutiny or without business involvement. Corporations helped train teachers and administrators, offered scholarships to deserving students, provided instructional materials, subsidized school programs, and cosponsored the activities of professional organizations. Businesspeople toiled as tutors, served as mentors, and offered their organizational knowledge to schools willing to learn the lessons of the corporate management 'revolution'.[47]

Yet despite all this business involvement, funding of schools remained inadequate. Corporations preferred to give small amounts of money through gifts and sponsorships and be seen as benefactors, than to pay the taxes required to fully fund the schools. Alex Molnar, author of *Giving Kids the Bu$iness*, estimates that the total amount donated by corporations to US schools would run the schools in the US for less than two hours a year.[48] The supposed largesse of corporations is further reduced by the fact that these donations are generally tax-deductible. One US Senator, Howard Mertzenbaum, observed:

> In speech after speech, it is our corporate CEOs who state that an educated, literate work force is the key to American competitiveness. They pontificate on the importance of education. They point out their magnanimous corporate contributions to education in one breath, and then they pull the tax base out from under local schools in the next.[49]

In 1995 the National Center on the Educational Quality of the Workforce found that 'most partnerships have diffuse and unquantifiable goals, and, in the worst cases, are exercises in public relations'.[50]

Businesspeople today still advocate education, and business involvement with it, as a way of ensuring business prosperity. George Kaplan wrote in the educational magazine *Phi Delta Kappan*: 'Much of American business views the schools as a farm system designed to fill roster slots in its plants and offices. Students are seen as future employees and customers.'[51]

Joseph A. Miller, senior vice-president for research and development of Du Pont Corporation, urged educators in 1995 to 'adopt two concepts from business: first, the idea of education as a supply chain, with linkages from primary education through secondary and higher-level institutions and on into the workplace; and second, the formation of strategic partnerships all along it'.[52] Robert Kennedy, CEO of Union Carbide, told an audience of Connecticut businesspeople that 'school reform is the business of Union Carbide. And I hope you'll make it your business, too.'[53]

Grand Metropolitan (a British food corporation incorporating Burger King amongst other food outlets) has developed a multimillion-dollar elementary education programme in the US called Kapow (Kids and the Power of Work). The programme fosters partnerships between elementary schools and businesses and provides a curriculum that involves specially trained business volunteers visiting schools to teach them about the world of work.[54]

By 1997 Kapow had achieved Grand Metropolitan's dream of becoming 'a large-scale national movement' and was being used in over a hundred elementary schools by 12,000 students. It focuses particularly on schools in disadvantaged areas. It is aimed at 'helping kids develop positive work attitudes and habits, increasing their awareness of the spectrum of occupations, and getting them to understand the importance of teamwork'. There are also hands-on projects such as inventing new Haagen-Dazs icecream flavours.[55]

An example of Kapow in action is the partnership of Cutler Ridge Elementary School in Miami, Florida with Burger King. Volunteers teach children at the school about 'interdependence' and 'positive work habits'. Children at the school visit Burger King headquarters to 'see and experience the wide range of jobs that are available in the fast-food industry'. They are also taken to the quality control department where they do 'taste tests' on French fries. What is achieved by this, apart from good PR for Burger King? According to *Principal* magazine, 'KAPOW's lessons reinforce school ideals, such as working together to achieve a common goal, and provide a concrete way to connect children to the world of work.'[56]

Individual companies also foster partnerships with schools so as to influence the curriculum and ensure students are being prepared for the world of work. Ashland Oil's activities have included classroom materials on self-esteem distributed to more than 7,000 elementary schools, providing speakers for career days, taking part in educational alliances, and encouraging its own staff to volunteer as adult leaders for youth organisations and mentors for students.[57]

Business organisations in Britain and Europe have also urged companies to make alliances with schools and provide educational materials to teachers about work and business, making clear to them what educational characteristics they look for in new employees. Since the 1980s business organisations have been more assertive in their efforts to influence school curricula, in part prompted by worsening economic conditions that they believe could be alleviated by improving the quality of the workforce.[58]

An example is the Personal Effectiveness Programme Initiative (PEPI) introduced by the Wellcome Foundation. The foundation found that school graduates lacked 'essential workplace skills such as time management, punctuality, presentation, self-awareness, working in a team and problem-solving'. The PEPI scheme aims to provide some of these skills and has been introduced into over a hundred schools in Britain and also into schools in Europe with the help of the European Secondary Heads Association. PEPI encourages business/school links where companies send their employees into schools to tell pupils about what would be required of them in particular jobs.[59]

Writing in *People Management* in 1996 David Warwick, 'an adviser to schools, colleges and employers on links between education and industry', noted that a third of all British companies have educational links of some kind but argued that work experience, workplace visits and teacher placements were not enough. What was needed was a whole curriculum approach. Examples of this he cited were British Telecom's links with schools and also the 'whole-school planning' model developed by Parker Hannifin Kodak and the former British Gas Eastern.[60] According to Harold Noah and Max Eckstein, 'Business/industry has contributed to new thinking and practice in general education, has expanded its training activities, and has participated in revisions of examinations and proposals to introduce new credentials and new forms of assessment.'[61]

In Canada, 97 per cent of the largest firms provide some sort of support, usually donations, scholarships and sponsorships, for schools and tertiary institutions. In an article in *Marketing* magazine entitled 'Educational Assistance: School Support Programs Can Do Wonders for Corporate Image', Jeffrey Crelinsten notes that not only is such support good for public relations but it also creates 'a pool of well-trained talent from which to draw upon in the future'.[62]

SCHOOLS PARALLELING THE WORKPLACE

One way of inculcating a work ethic at school is to demand a full work schedule from children. Diane Fasel in her book on work addiction blames institutions such as schools for nurturing that state of mind: 'The processes in many of our educational systems are such that they require children either to work addictively or to fail.' She notes that children have almost every hour of the school day and often hours after school scheduled for them: 'The result is that children never learn to organize their own time, nor to respect their own preferences and rhythms.'[63]

> The processes of external pressures, comparison, more work than is possible in the time allotted, and adult models who are frantic and harried – all of these educational characteristics tell children that work addiction is to be imitated. Moreover, it gives the impression that workaholism is normal.[64]

Yet advocates of the work ethic argue that North American children do not work hard enough. Writing in the Canadian magazine *Maclean's*, Ross Laver argues that Japanese and German schools do a much better job of instilling the work ethic. He describes the situation for a typical Japanese child:

> As a Grade 6 pupil in Tokyo, 11-year-old Tadayoshi Sasaki attends classes each weekday from 8.50 am until 3 pm. But unlike his counterparts in Canada, Tadayoshi has little time after school to play with friends or watch television. As soon as he gets home, he begins his homework – an average of two hours a day. Then, from 6 pm until 9 pm, four times a week, he studies math and Japanese at one of Japan's famous jukus, privately run cram schools that offer students extra tutoring. Even his weekends are not entirely free: on most Saturdays, public school classes throughout Japan run from 9 am until shortly after noon.[65]

This demanding schedule, Laver argues, is a main reason why Japanese children are better at maths and science than Canadian children, why more

Canadian children drop out of school, and why Canadian children do not learn the value of hard work.[66]

Similarly, Chuck Colson and Jack Eckerd, in their book *Why America Doesn't Work*, argue that short school days and long vacations send students the wrong message, both about the value of schooling and the need for hard work.[67] And the CEO of Union Carbide criticises the short time children spend at school as an anachronism from the past.[68]

In their book *Schooling in Capitalist America*, Samuel Bowles and Herbert Gintis claim the social relations 'between students and teachers, students and students, and students and their work' are similar to those in the workplace. In this way students learn how they should behave in the workplace:

> The conditions of the office or factory are reflected in the student's lack of control over his or her education, in the irrelevance of school work to the student's interests, in the motivation of work by a system of grades and other external rewards rather than by the student's interest in either the process of production (learning) or the product (knowledge), in the persistent and ostensibly objective ranking and evaluation of students, in the emphasis on discipline and acceptance of authority, and in the supremacy of strict and unvaried routine.[69]

Bowles and Gintis point out that not only does the American school system accustom young people to the discipline of the workplace, but it also 'develops the types of personal demeanor, modes of self-presentation, self-image, and social class identifications which are crucial ingredients of job adequacy'.[70] John White claims that, in Britain, 'Part of Conservative educational policy since 1979 has been to make schools more work-like' and that this has involved ensuring that school activities are 'directed towards end products' rather than being child-centred and spontaneous.[71]

The correlation between school grades and work performance is important to employers who use the education system as a means of selecting employees. Cath Blakers notes of the Australian system:

> Reinforcing the established practices of stereotyping and grading in school processes, there are again the familiar demands from employers, politicians and others for more of those practices most likely to ensure conformity and to discourage individual initiative and the enquiring mind: more external examinations; national testing of basic skills; centrally designed common curricula; ranking of students for the convenience of employers.[72]

During the twentieth century the aim of educators went beyond merely discipline and obedience to 'behaviour modification', a way of internalising values, so that external control is less necessary. One way of doing this was through grades and a system of rewards which reinforced particular behaviours. Bowles and Gintis, who surveyed many of the studies which attempt to link personality traits to grades, found that 'Students are rewarded for exhibiting discipline, subordinacy, intellectually as opposed to emotionally oriented behavior, and hard work independent from intrinsic task motivation.'[73]

Whilst cognitive performance is a major determinant of grades, for students of similar cognitive performance various work-related characteristics are also a major predictor of grades. According to Bowles and Gintis various studies demonstrate that the school system rewards conformity and submission to authority and 'inhibits those manifestations of personal capacity which threaten hierarchical authority'. They argue that this is no accident, moreover, since in the context of corporate capitalism schooling is aimed at 'integrating young people into adult work roles' rather than personal development which would not fit with the requirements of those roles.[74] As we saw in Chapter 5, this tendency of rewarding submission and crushing creativity is more pronounced in working-class schools. Elite schools, which are preparing students to be managers and professionals, tend to encourage a wider range of personal qualities, whilst still placing emphasis on a work ethic.

In another study student-peer ratings (based on classroom observation) of 42 common personality traits were correlated with school success. Only those traits in the category of 'work orientation' were related to school success. This category was also three times more successful at predicting post-high-school academic performance than other variables, including verbal and maths test scores or class rank. Another study of Boston area workers found that traits rewarded in school are the very ones valued in the workplace by supervisors, whilst traits such as creativity and independence were equally disliked in schools and at work.[75]

Despite this bias in school grading, businesspeople in many countries are still very critical of the ability of schools to provide appropriate work attitudes and skills to students.[76] A 1991 survey by the Committee for Economic Development found that US employers felt 'dedication to work and discipline in work habits' were the major characteristics lacking in high school graduates applying for jobs.[77] The CEO of Union Carbide claims that business spends $50 billion a year 'to remediate the new workforce to make up for skills not acquired in public education'.[78] A 1995 editorial in *National Review* decried the failure to promote in schools values such as 'high standards, hard work, and discipline'. And a 1992 article in *Fortune* magazine stated:

> Kids across the socioeconomic spectrum are not learning the qualities they'll need in the workplace: patience, perseverance, and a positive attitude. Aside from their teachers, the only working adults that children really get to know are their parents. And in some underclass families, no one works, and in certain neighbourhoods some of the most visible adults are not engaged in legal occupations.[79]

Colson and Eckerd denounce the move away from teaching moral values that occurred in the 1960s in US schools:

> With the removal of prayer from the classroom and the purging of America's religious history and heritage from school textbooks, education has been 'freed' from the 'oppressive' influences of the Judeo-Christian tradition. Unfortunately individual accountability, personal achievement, and the work ethic fall squarely within that tradition.... As a result of this, the attitudes of students, even subconsciously, are affected. They simply no longer work as hard or, evidence shows, as long.[80]

The work ethic, they say, needs to be applied to school students: 'If young people don't see the tangible results of their work, or lack of work, in the form of grades and awards, they will be completely unprepared if we begin demanding excellence in the workplace.' They argue that students in other countries do better than American students because they work harder: 'Knowledge is not acquired by osmosis, but by discipline and hard work.' Vocational students in particular, they argue, need 'a solid education that teaches diligence, productivity, and the dignity of honest labor'.[81]

INCORPORATING WORK EXPERIENCE AT SCHOOL

The more that schools can be persuaded to take over the training role, the less employers have to pay to train the workers they hire. And their success is evident in the increasing vocational content of school and university education. The vocational content of schools has been beefed up in the name of preparing children for transition to the workforce. This goes beyond inculcating a work ethic in schools and is often little short of job training.

In a 1993 article in *Chief Executive* entitled 'Education is Everyone's Business', John R. Hall, CEO of Ashland Oil, said supporting education was good business for Ashland Oil because they needed highly trained employees and it was not economical for Ashland to train them itself. It was far better to aid schools 'with resources and expertise' to train students to be productive employees. 'We in business must roll up our sleeves and get involved wherever educational decisions are being made.... The push for educational excellence should be considered a crusade. As a business, it is in our self-interest to lead the charge.'[82] Ashland Oil planned 'to devote its corporate regional advertising campaign solely to promoting quality education' for a whole decade.

Today there are a variety of methods used for introducing work-related activities into schools. Apart from actual work experience, which involves spending time in the workplace, work situations can be set up at school.

Students may become involved in taking on the running of the school restaurant, shop, crèche or some other mini-enterprise. Alternatively such business experiences can be simulated using games and artificial projects. Also students can be involved in studying work situations by shadowing real workers in the workplace.[83]

In some countries a separate system of vocational schools exists, whilst others incorporate vocational elements into general schools. In the last part of the nineteenth century the National Association of Manufacturers pushed for separately run vocational schools in the American system, as in Germany. They felt that America was less effective economically than Germany without such schools.[84] Leading educators in the first part of the twentieth century also supported the idea of vocational schools. David Sneddon, Commissioner of Education, believed that what was good for business was good for America and he argued that the aim of education was national economic efficiency. He appointed Charles Prosser to develop vocational schools that would replace 'general education' with vocational training aimed at equipping students to get a job, hold it and advance in it. Prosser said of vocational education that it 'must establish habits: habits of correct thinking and of correct doing'.[85]

Some companies actually maintained their own schools. For example Colorado Fuel and Iron Corporation ran schools in all its major mining towns. N. O Nelson Company and Ludlow Manufacturing Associates 'supported school systems specifically designed to produce workers for their companies'. Boys from kindergarten to 12 years old, at the Nelson-supported schools, were taught regular studies as well as vegetable growing and manual arts. From the age of 12 they spent an hour a day at the factory or on the company farm, and each successive year they spent more time working and less time studying until they reached 18 and went to work at the factory full-time.[86]

Those at the Ludlow schools spent half the day at school and the other half at the factory. Children at the National Cash Register Company's kindergarten were taught order and neatness and 'the discipline of regulated play'.[87] At International Harvester Company plants English lessons included tracts such as this:

> I hear the whistle. I must hurry.
> I hear the five-minute whistle.
> It is time to go into the shop....
> I change my clothes and get ready to work....
> I work until the whistle blows to quit.
> I leave my place nice and clean.[88]

The push for separate vocational schools was opposed by other educators proposing reforms of the school system such as John Dewey, who preferred a more integrated model:

Instead of trying to split schools into two kinds, one of a trade type for children whom it is assumed are to be employees and one of a liberal type for the children of the well-to-do, it will aim at such a reorganization of existing schools as will give all pupils a genuine respect for useful work, an ability to render service, and a contempt for social parasites whether they are called tramps or leaders of 'society'....[89]

At Dewey's school, students as young as four had to prepare their own lunches and older children played at running a dry goods store.[90]

The push for integrated vocational education was resurrected in the US in the 1970s. The Commissioner of Education, Sidney Marland, supported the concept of 'career education' which would combine academic and vocational material in the school curriculum to ensure that school leavers were prepared for either higher education or useful employment. Career education would 'shore up and rationalize the Protestant work ethic' and provide a proper understanding of the free enterprise system and the 'opportunities and obligations' that it implied. Students would be shaped 'to function efficiently' by improving the preparation of children from the first years of school through to the world of work. To achieve this an alliance between schools and business was required, he argued.[91] Such advocacy of integrated vocational education continued through to the 1990s. In 1994 the *State Legislatures* journal reported that some schools were developing a work ethic in their students by lacing vocationally oriented programmes into their curricula.[92]

In 1994 the US Congress passed the School to Work Opportunities Act which enables the government to provide seed money for school-to-work programmes that involve partnerships between business leaders, labour representatives and school teachers. Hundreds of millions of dollars have been given out to some two thousand schools for this purpose. The aim of these programmes is to make sure school graduates are prepared to go into the workforce by incorporating work-related skills into the classroom, training teachers about the workplace and providing workplace experiences to school students. 'Under this model,' *Workforce* magazine notes, 'career orientation would be presented to all students, eventually as early as kindergarten and elementary grades.'[93]

The advantage to employers in terms of savings in job training is obvious. Training can be a huge cost to firms. For example, Procter and Gamble estimate that it spends \$15–20 million on training and workforce development each year; it is naturally very supportive of the school-to-work programmes.[94]

Round-table discussions between the business community and teachers have 'explored the necessary skills, personalities, attitudes, and various levels of careers students need to know about to successfully prepare for the work world and provide the business community with what it needs'.[95] *Workforce* magazine observes that 'For employers, at least, the real prize will come when, somewhere down the road, a new crop of graduates reports to work with the skills and attitudes necessary to make them successful, productive employees.'[96]

In Britain, the 'understanding of and preparation for the so-called world of work' became 'an important educational aim' in the 1980s with bipartisan political support. Traditionally, education in Britain has not been oriented towards vocational training and was criticised for its inability to prepare students for work. It was felt that Britain's economic decline was partly attributable to the weakness of its educational structure in preparing students for the modern world of work, industry and commerce. In various documents in the 1970s the Department of Education and Science (DES) had reiterated the need for education to be more relevant and for the involvement of industry and commerce in curriculum planning to enable this to happen.[97]

In 1982 a Technical and Vocational Educational Initiative (TVEI) was set up to provide schooling in the interests of employers and industry. The Manpower Services Commission was to run the initiative. Its chairman, noting how unprepared most school students were for the labour market, said of students in the TVEI pilot programme that 'By the time they leave, our youngsters will be highly employable.' In 1986 the initiative went national, to be embraced by all schools.[98]

Philip Cohen, from the Institute of Education, University of London, observes that a consensus formed during the 1980s in Britain that schools should prepare children for the world of work:

> The test of the relevance of any subject, its place in the hierarchy of classroom knowledge, depends not on the insight it gives into the fundamental workings of nature or culture, nor the extent to which it develops particular creative or critical sensibilities, but how far it contributes to the formation of general dispositions for manual or mental labour in capitalist or bureaucratic organizations.[99]

The Blair government is currently taking advice from Tom Bentley, director of the think tank Demos Foundation, on education for the twenty-first century; this includes an emphasis on the school-to-work transition. Bentley's book *Learning Beyond the Classroom* advocates using schools as 'agencies for young people's part-time employment and work-based learning'.[100] He visited Australia in 1999 to promote school-to-work programmes there.[101]

In Australia the 1980s saw a shift away from liberal education towards more vocationally oriented education. As in Britain the motivation was to improve Australia's economic position and global economic competitiveness. Millicent Poole observes in her book *Education and Work* that the idea of knowledge for its own sake was replaced by an instrumental view which saw education as a means to gain economic goals – wealth and productivity. This shift in educational priorities and values was promoted, according to Poole, by the coalition of conservative interest groups and businesspeople that make up the New Right.[102]

In New South Wales the government introduced a pilot programme in 1988 that would allow school students in Sydney's disadvantaged western suburbs to go to work for a day or two a week and earn credit for their Higher School Certificate in the process. A 1995 Australian government report on the workforce of the future argued the 'need for a convergence between general education and vocational training'. It claimed that rather than trying to get students to stay longer at school the goal should be to ensure that all teenagers 'have sufficient education or training to make a successful transition to full-time employment'. It noted approvingly that '[m]ore structured vocational training has already been introduced in some States in the final years of secondary school'.[103]

In Victoria school students are now able to incorporate part-time work at McDonald's restaurants as part of their studies towards their high school graduation certificate, the Victorian Certificate of Education, and get an enhanced Tertiary Entrance Rank mark as well. The 'Certificate II in Food Retail (McDonald's)' consists of 300 hours of on-the-job training at McDonald's and 294 hours of study on topics like interacting with customers, balancing a cash register and performing routine housekeeping duties. McDonald's is responsible for selection, training and assessment, even though it is for a state educational certificate, and these matters are not open to public scrutiny so as to protect McDonald's 'commercial secrets' and 'competitive advantage'.[104]

This initiative is part of Victoria's Vocational Education and Training in Schools programme, introduced in 1993, which seeks to prepare students for work whilst in school, through enabling them 'to develop skills and approaches to work most valued by employers'. According to the Victorian Board of Studies, the programme is beneficial to employers because it 'enables industry to influence educational programmes in schools', 'enables employers to use the programme for selection purposes' and provides training not only for future employees but also supervision experience for their own employees.[105]

Workplace learning is also being promoted at the national level in Australia as part of the curriculum for school students where 'substantial learning and assessment would occur in the workplace', reflecting industry requirements. The government report, *A Working Solution*, stated that workplace education had a place in schools because it helped young people 'to align' their attitudes 'with those of employers' and it strongly recommended extending workplace education, such as McDonald's, into the early years of high school:[106]

> McDonald's training is so successful in developing positive work related attitudes in young people that its employees are universally valued by other employers. McDonald's employs thousands of inexperienced young people, teaches them skills, builds their self-confidence and instils self-discipline as it motivates them to become the world's most productive hamburger vendors.[107]

CORPORATE UNIVERSITIES

University education is also being increasingly turned into vocational training and infiltrated by corporations. 'Corporate universities' are competing with real universities for students and funds and forming partnerships with them. These developments, together with funding cuts to higher education, have ensured that the content of university courses is increasingly influenced by employer needs. Universities are providing more and more training for specific sets of employees.

In the US there are over 1,600 corporate training institutions, euphemistically called universities, including McDonald's Hamburger University, Motorola University, Volvo University and Disney University. In reality they are training schools which aim to 'ensure that their own particular culture and winning ways percolate through the organisation'.[108]

There has been a huge increase in the number of corporate universities, particularly in the US, where they increased from 400 to 1,600 in a decade. Forty per cent of the Fortune 500 companies run a corporate university and it is expected that within another decade the number of corporate universities will exceed the number of real universities. The average operating budgets for these universities has also been increasing and now stands at $17 million per year. The aim of these universities is to increase employee productivity and performance.[109]

Motorola is the largest of the corporate universities, with 400 full-time faculty, 800 part-time teachers in 19 countries and over 100,000 students a year, one in five of whom are from other companies. It even offers an international MBA programme, although it is not accredited. Motorola spends about $200 million each year on its 'university' and claims that each dollar spent on training is worth $33 in company profits in the long term.[110]

Although most corporate universities do not offer degrees yet, some do. One that does is the Arthur D. Little School in Boston, formed by consulting firm Arthur D. Little, which offers a one-year master of science in management. Nintendo University is able to offer a Bachelor of Science degree in 'Real Time Interactive Simulation', or video game programming.[111]

Many corporate universities, including Motorola, aspire to offer accredited degrees in future. In an effort to have their qualifications more widely recognised many corporate universities are forming alliances with real universities. A 1999 worldwide survey of corporate universities found that more than 50 per cent of these institutions were planning to use existing or future partnerships with accredited universities to enable them to grant degrees in the business/management, engineering/technical, finance/accounting and computer science fields. About two-thirds of those surveyed already had some sort of alliance with an undergraduate college.[112]

Often partnerships are international. In 1998 Daimler Chrysler was planning partnerships with various universities worldwide, including Harvard in the US, Insead in Paris, Hong Kong University, and the Institute for Management Development in Lausanne.[113] Whirlpool has links to business schools at Michigan and Indiana Universities in the US as well as to Insead.[114]

Corporate universities are also growing in the UK. British Aerospace is one of the most ambitious of these, proposing to spend over £2 billion over the next decade, which would make it one of the country's richest universities. This virtual university (without a campus or buildings) was launched in 1998 and involves partnerships with established universities such as Oxford, Cambridge and York, and with business schools at Lancaster University and the Open University.[115] Accounting firm Ernst & Young, meanwhile, has teamed up with Henley Management College to create a Virtual Business School.[116]

Partnerships enable corporations to offer accredited degrees that have more value to employees than corporate training normally would. This helps to make a corporation a desirable employer, able to attract the best people to work for them. But the corporations, unresponsive to deeper intellectual currents and traditions, have extensive control over what is taught; they can also use the courses to instil a corporate culture and to further business strategy. Judy Irwin, acting director of the Business-Higher Education Forum, an arm of the American Council of Education which is promoting meetings between business and universities, explains the business view: universities aren't preparing graduates adequately for the workforce and recent graduates 'don't have the same work ethic as they have seen in prior years'.[117]

Corporate universities are established when companies are merging or changing direction to reinforce a new corporate culture. John Authers, who writes regularly about corporate universities in the *Financial Times*, points out that drawing up 'a common curriculum for all staff helps set out the values and strategy of a newly merged company, or any other company trying to enforce a significant shift in strategy'.[118] A 1998 survey of US corporate universities found that 22 per cent aimed at driving change and modernisation. Another 22 per cent sought to link education to business goals.[119] For example, a major goal of Daimler's university was to ensure that there was a common culture throughout Daimler Chrysler after the merger.[120]

Jeanne Meister, a consultant on setting up corporate universities, claims that corporate universities offer advantages to employers over normal university education because they can achieve 'tighter control and ownership over the learning process by more closely linking learning programs to real business goals and strategies'.[121] She points out that the goals of a corporate university include inculcating workers with the corporation's values, beliefs and culture:

> Regardless of the name or how the course is designed or delivered, the goal is similar in many of these organisations: to inculcate everyone from the clerical assistant to the top executive in the culture and values that make the organization unique and special and to define behaviours that enable employees to 'live the values'.[122]

According to Meister, a key objective of corporate universities is to ensure that a worker doesn't just perform the job that s/he is paid to do but goes beyond this to behave like an owner of the company in terms of doing what is best for the company.[123] The partnerships between corporate universities and regular universities are carefully selected to ensure that corporations can still dictate content and ensure corporate culture is instilled.

> [B]usinesses are now spelling out the specific skills, knowledge and competencies needed for success in an industry and in the process creating joint, accredited programs…. For companies, they meet the need to infuse the curriculum with their own corporate culture, use company-specific case studies, and emphasize a common language for jobs across the organization. For universities, they bring in large amounts of revenue.[124]

This revenue has become important to universities, particularly government-supported universities which have had their funding cut over the last few years in the US and Australia. In the US the proportion of university operating funds coming from state governments dropped 56 per cent between 1980 and 1993. 'To fill the gap, colleges are selling chunks of the curriculum to corporations which contribute relatively modest sums in order to obtain trained workers.'[125]

In Australia, government funding of the public universities has been cut and industry partnerships encouraged. In particular, universities increasingly offer postgraduate course work on a fee basis and inevitably such courses must cater for those who can pay, which usually means employers. This has led to the demise of academic courses, particularly in the arts, and the proliferation of short, practical, vocationally oriented courses that are 'easier to get into and have less of a disciplinary core' – in other words, are less academic.[126]

Corporate universities can pose a threat to universities, particularly business schools, as rivals for students. Even though many don't accept external students, the number of students getting their business education from corporate universities rather than business schools is making major inroads into the business school market. It is because of these pressures and government funding cutbacks that business schools worldwide are seeking to offer courses tailored to particular firms, or forming partnerships with corporate universities.[127]

One development worldwide has been the emergence of MBAs which are company-specific or industry-specific, rather than the generalist degrees traditionally favoured by business schools.[128] There are now MBAs in church management (Lincoln University), MBAs in luxury brand management (École Supérieure des Sciences Économiques et Commerciales), MBAs in customer insight (University of Texas), and MBAs in football industries (Liverpool University).[129] MIT's business school runs a course for Siemens-Nixdorf entitled 'Change Agent Program' which includes Outward Bound programmes and, according to the London *Financial Times*, 'being taught to chant like American military recruits'.[130]

In the US, business executive education programmes, including the 94,000 MBA programmes, earn universities $3 billion per year. Forty per cent of this corporate money is spent on customised offerings: curricula to suit specific job categories or companies. It is this sector that is growing fastest.[131]

Such developments are occurring worldwide. British Airways has teamed up with Lancaster University's Management School to offer an MBA for British Airways executives.[132] T. Eaton, a large Canadian retailer, has joined with Rerson Polytechnic to create a degree in retail management because there were no existing unversity courses that provided graduates with 'the unique set of skills needed to be successful in retail selling and management'.[133]

A close relationship between the University of Wollongong in Australia and two corporations, BHP and Telstra, enables the corporations to have input into the content of master's degree courses in education, engineering and informatics to suit the needs of company employees.[134] Sydney University has allowed Banker's Trust (BT) to suggest modules to be incorporated into its Master of Information Technology in return for $92,000 a year for a professorship and a flow of BT employees as students.[135]

Mairead Browne, dean of graduate studies at the University of Technology, Sydney (UTS), says that he does not approve any new postgraduate courses unless the relevant industry has had a chance to comment on it.[136] UTS has formed a partnership with insurance giant AMP, for whom UTS will tailor postgraduate qualifications to meet AMP needs, including work-based learning. 'The difficulty for AMP,' noted *The Australian*, 'was that universities would not allow the insurer to set the curriculum for its employees. All that is changing.'[137]

Such moves have full government backing. A federal government paper, 'Research Training for the Twenty-first Century', extends this principle to postgraduate research education, arguing that 'Universities must continue to adapt to the training needs of industry.' It argues that postgraduate research students should be made to do skills courses so that they will be more useful to future employers.[138]

Nor has industry's influence been confined to postgraduate studies. Petroleum company Santos recently pledged $25 million to the University of Adelaide to fund a school of petroleum engineering for the next 20 years, including staff, building and equipment. The school will have a board of management with 'significant representation from the petroleum industry'. The federal government has blessed this deal with a million dollars of its own money.[139]

Deakin University in Australia has teamed up with the Coles supermarket chain, establishing the Coles Institute to train all levels of a 55,000 workforce, from checkout scanners to executives, with subjects ranging from shelf stacking to full MBAs. The Coles Institute will have official Deakin University accreditation which means that the qualifications, including postgraduate degrees, will, in theory, be transferable to other jobs. The Minister for Education, Training and Youth Affairs has praised the initiative as 'the way of the future' and Deakin is hoping to form similar joint ventures with insurance, automobile and oil industry companies.[140]

Deakin also runs corporate courses for over 30 other corporations in Australia and the US, such as BHP, Alcoa, Coca-Cola, Du Pont, Ford, and the ANZ Bank. It has over 40,000 enrolments in corporate courses (not counting the Coles Institute), compared with 28,000 in its regular courses. The university's Vice-Chancellor, Geoff Wilson, puts Deakin's success in attracting corporate customers down to its ability to cater to corporate requirements: 'The secret of our success is unbelievably simple. It's customisation.' Deakin is now expanding its customised education programmes into the US and the UK.[141]

Another ubiquitous model is the university consortium, particularly for executive education. Those set up in the US include the Emory University Consortium, initiated by the CEO of Southern Company.[142] Another example is Melbourne University Private, established by Melbourne University. It is run as a private company, with funding from companies such as Ford

Australia, Mobil Oil, Shell Australia and WMC (previously Western Mining Corporation). Melbourne University Private will be relying on the reputation for academic excellence of Melbourne University to ensure its degrees and certificates are of value: 'The quality and integrity of the Melbourne brand is one of our greatest assets.'[143] One wonders how intellectually rigorous its courses on the environment will be, however, if they are tailored to corporate requirements.

In 1998 Ron Dearing, chair of the UK Review of Higher Education and also a member of the University of Melbourne council, told an Australian audience that universities needed 'to find ways of reducing dependence on the state' through partnerships with industry and business.[144]

> I believe the optimum approach often will be in partnership, a partnership in which the university is the prime partner, but one in which the client company also is a partner, with much to offer in shaping learning programmes and in providing learning opportunities.[145]

He argued that there were big opportunities for those willing 'to be responsive to the needs of the employer'.[146] He told the *Australian* newspaper that this partnering was necessary for universities to survive, particularly given that multinational companies were setting up their own universities that would compete with traditional universities.[147]

Others believe that this trend is not helping universities to survive; instead, it is destroying them. Lawrence Soley, author of *Leasing the Ivory Tower*, suggests that it is getting to the stage where state facilities are being provided to private companies to train future employees and that these companies could in future be deciding which classes should be taught.[148] Writing in *Dollars and Sense* magazine, Stanley Aronowitz argues: 'As long as they get the cash, desperate administrators are eager to have their university reflect the whims of individuals and the interests of corporations. They will train corporate America's workers and conduct its research.'[149]

CONCLUSION

The importance of schools in ensuring that future workers have a strong work ethic is evident to employers:

> Certain basic components of the work personality appear to be laid down in the early school years – the ability to concentrate on a task for extended periods of time, the development of emotional response patterns to supervisory authority, the limits of cooperation and competition with peers, the meanings and values associated with work, the rewards and sanctions for

achievement and non achievement, the effects (both positive and negative) which become associated with being productive.

School is thus a precursor of adult work and provides a set of models for it.[150]

It is the perceived failure of many schools to promote proper work attitudes and provide work skills that has caused businesses to become involved in school education, seeking a more direct say in how schools cater to their needs for future employees. The deliberate influence that business people have had on schools and on top educational bureaucrats has meant that schools and universities increasingly cater to the needs of business, inculcating work values and teaching work skills rather than educating citizens.

Whilst work-based learning in schools and universities has obvious benefits for employers, the benefits to students themselves and the society are more ambiguous. A major difference between training and education is that training is aimed at shaping a person towards a specific end, whereas education is aimed at giving people choices in life. Ideally education avoids behavioural objectives, aiming to equip people to make their own decisions.[151] As Noam Chomsky has argued:

> the purpose of education, from this point of view, cannot be to control the child's growth to a specific predetermined end, because any such end must be established by arbitrary authoritarian means; rather the purpose of education must be to permit the growing principle of life to take its own individual course, and to facilitate this process by sympathy, encouragement, and challenge, and by developing a rich and differentiated context and environment.[152]

Whilst there is inevitably some overlap, training is about giving a person the skills and knowledge to carry out a particular occupation or type of occupation; education is more about helping people to attain an understanding of the world they live in and their relationship with it.[153] It is supposed to foster independent learning and critical thinking, which are often inimical to employers. It is unlikely that vocational training gives children the opportunity to analyse the role of work in society critically, or even to know their rights as workers.

Education seeks to provide a 'breadth and depth of understanding'[154] as compared to the knowledge required for training which is limited to what enables a person to competently fulfil a function. Education is about understanding 'the reasons behind things', something training not only fails to provide but can sometimes 'obscure'.[155] The propensity to question and show initiative, which a good education breeds, may be quite unsuitable for some jobs, particularly those at the bottom end of the occupational hierarchy where intellect just gets in the way of operating a machine.[156]

The more employers influence and shape education the more it will tend

218

towards worker training and away from citizen education. Yet work is so central to most people's lives that it seems perfectly reasonable to many people that schools should spend a great deal of their time preparing children to be future workers. In the next chapter the role of consumerism in ensuring work remains central is discussed.

NOTES

1 Alan Deutschman, 'Why Kids Should Learn About Work', *Fortune*, Vol. 126 (10 August 1992).

2 Samuel Bowles and Herbert Gintis, *Schooling in Capitalist America: Educational Reform and the Contradictions of Economic Life* (New York: Basic Books, 1976), p. 37.

3 John White, *Education and the End of Work: a New Philosophy of Work and Learning* (London: Cassell, 1997), p. 17.

4 Cath Blakers, 'School to Work: Transition and Policy', in Millicent Poole (eds), *Education and Work* (Hawthorn, Victoria: Australian Council for Educational Research, 1992), p. 55.

5 Clinton E. Boutwell, *Shell Game: Corporate America's Agenda for Schools* (Bloomington, Indiana: Phi Delta Kappa Educational Foundation, 1997), p. 1.

6 David K. Cohen and Marvin Lazerson, 'Education and the Corporate Order', in Michael B. Katz (ed.), *Education in American History: Readings on the Social Issues* (New York: Praeger, 1973), p. 319.

7 Diane Stafford, 'Instilling the Work Ethic', *Kansas City Star*, 20 October 1995.

8 Jonathan Marshall, 'The Book of No Job', *Mother Jones*, Vol. 18, No. 5 (1993).

9 Roger B. Hill and Gregory C. Petty, 'A New Look at Selected Employability Skills: a Factor Analysis of the Occupational Work Ethic', *Journal of Vocational Education Research*, Vol. 20, No. 4 (1995).

10 'Work Ethic Top Job Skill', *The CPA Journal*, Vol. 64 1994); Gillian Flynn, 'Attitude More Valued than Ability', *Personnel Journal*, Vol. 73, No. 9 (1994), p. 16.

11 Marshall, note 8.

12 Peter Cappelli, 'Is the "Skills Gap" Really About Attitudes?', *California Management Review*, Vol. 37, No. 4 (1995).

13 House of Representatives Standing Commitee on Employment, Education and Training, 'Youth Employment: A Working Solution', (Canberra: Parliament of the Commonwealth of Australia, 1997), p. xv.

14 *Ibid.*, Chapter 1.

15 'Trade in Your Credentials for Hard Work and Computer Skills', *CA Magazine*, Vol. 127 (1994), p. 9.

16 Harold J. Noah and Max A. Eckstein, 'Business and Industry Involvement with Education in Britain, France and Germany', in Jon Lauglo and Kevin Lillis (eds), *Vocationalizing Education: an International Perspective* (Oxford: Pergamon Press, 1988), p. 49.

17 Bowles and Gintis, note 2, p. 37.

18 Quoted in Paul Bernstein, *American Work Values: Their Origin and Development* (Albany, NY: State University of New York Press, 1997), p. 132.

19 *Ibid.*, p. 99; Bowles and Gintis, note 2, p. 37; Robin Theobald, *Understanding Industrial*

Society: a Sociological Guide (New York: St Martin's Press, 1994), p. 90.

20 Theobald, note 19, pp. 90–1.

21 Quoted in Bowles and Gintis, note 2, p. 38.

22 Quoted in Joel H. Spring, *Education and the Rise of the Corporate State* (Boston: Beacon Press, 1972), p. 46.

23 Cohen and Lazerson, note 6, p. 320.

24 David J. Cherrington, *The Work Ethic: Working Values and Values That Work* (New York: AMACON, 1980), pp. 85–6.

25 Juliet B. Schor, *The Overworked American: the Unexpected Decline in Leisure* (New York: Basic Books, 1991), p. 61.

26 Spring, note 22, p. 46.

27 Cohen and Lazerson, note 6, p. 325.

28 Patricia A. Adler and Peter Adler, 'Social Reproduction and the Corporate Other: The Institutionalization of Afterschool Activities', *The Sociological Quarterly*, Vol. 35, No. 2 (1994), p. 324.

29 *Ibid.*, p. 324.

30 *Sydney Morning Herald*, 8 September 1999.

31 Nadya Labi, 'Burning Out at Nine?', *Time* (23 November 1998), p. 86.

32 Cohen and Lazerson, note 6, p. 330.

33 Spring, note 22, p. xii.

34 Cohen and Lazerson, note 6, p 320.

35 John Kenneth Galbraith, *The Anatomy of Power* (London: Hamish Hamilton, 1984), pp. 32–3.

36 Bowles and Gintis, note 2, pp. 18–19.

37 Cited in Spring, note 22, pp. 126–131.

38 Upton Sinclair, *The Goslings: a Study of the American Schools*, 1st edn (Pasadena, California: Upton Sinclair, 1924), pp. 263, 291–2.

39 Elizabeth A. Fones-Wolf, *Selling Free Enterprise: the Business Assault on Labor and Liberalism, 1945–60* (Urbana and Chicago: University of Illinois Press, 1994), p. 190.

40 *Ibid.*, pp. 190, 199.

41 *Ibid.*, pp. 200–1.

42 Donald M. Clark, 'The Trouble with Business–Education Partnerships', *Techniques*, Vol. 71, No. 9 (1997), p. 70.

43 *Ibid.*, p. 70.

44 Alex Molnar, *Giving Kids the Bu$iness: the Commercialisation of America's Schools* (Boulder, CO: Westview, 1996), Chapter 1.

45 John R. Hall, 'Education is Everyone's Business', *Chief Executive* (May 1993).

46 Robert D. Kennedy, 'Let Candles Be Brought: the Case for Business Involvement in Education', *Vital Speeches*, Vol. 60, No. 8 (1994); Hall, note 45; Molnar, note 44, p. 2.

47 Molnar, note 44, p. 2.

48 *Ibid.*, p. 8.

49 Quoted in *ibid.*, p. 7.

50 Quoted in Clark, note 42, p. 70.

51 George R. Kaplan, 'Profits R Us: Notes on the Commercialization of America's Schools', *Phi Delta Kappan*, Vol. 78, No. 3 (1996).

52 'Teaching Economic Competitiveness', *USA Today*, Vol. 124 (August 1995), p. 8.

53 Kennedy, note 46.

54 Deutschman, note 1; Beulah Richards and Amy Merker, 'What Do You Want to Be

When You Grow Up?', *Principal*, Vol. 77, No. 2 (1997).

55 Alan Deutschman, *ibid*.

56 Richards and Merker, note 54, p. 44.

57 Hall, note 45.

58 Noah and Eckstein, note 16, pp. 50–2.

59 Dorothy Lepkowska, 'Confidence-builders at Work Worldwide', *The Times Educational Supplement*, 9 June 1995, p. 4.

60 David Warwick, 'Industry as a Cog inside the Education Machine', *People Management*, Vol. 2 (7 March 1996), p. 39.

61 Noah and Eckstein, note 16, p. 56.

62 Jeffrey Crelinsten, 'Educational Assistance: School Support Programs Can Do Wonders for Corporate Image', *Marketing (Maclean Hunter)*, Vol. 102 (29 September 1997), p. 29.

63 Diane Fasel, *Working Ourselves to Death: the High Cost of Workaholism, the Rewards of Recovery* (San Francisco: HarperCollins, 1990), p. 113.

64 *Ibid.*, p. 115.

65 Ross Laver, 'Giving Kids a Head Start: What Canada Can Learn from Other Countries', *Maclean's*, Vol. 105 (9 November 1992).

66 *Ibid.*

67 Chuck Colson and Jack Eckerd, *Why America Doesn't Work* (Dallas: Word Publishing, 1991), p. 67.

68 Kennedy, note 46.

69 Samuel Bowles and Herbert Gintis, *Schooling in Capitalist America: Educational Reform and the Contradictions of Economic Life* (New York: Basic Books, 1976), p. 143.

70 *Ibid.*, p. 131.

71 White, note 3, p. 16.

72 Blakers, note 4, p. 64.

73 Bowles and Gintis, note 2, pp. 39–40.

74 *Ibid.*, pp. 42, 126.

75 *Ibid.*, pp. 135–9.

76 Noah and Eckstein, note 16, pp. 45–9.

77 Cappelli, note 12.

78 Kennedy, note 46.

79 Deutschman, note 1.

80 Colson and Eckerd, note 67, pp. 65, 67.

81 *Ibid.*, pp. 103, 107.

82 Hall, note 45.

83 Glen Evans and Millicent Poole, 'Experiencing Work: Bridges to Adulthood', in Poole, note 4, pp. 117–18.

84 Arthur C. Wirth, 'Issues in the Vocational–Liberal Studies Controversy (1900–1917): John Dewey vs the Social Efficiency Philosophers', in David Corson (ed.), *Education for Work: Background to Policy and Curriculum* (New Zealand: Dunmore Press, 1988), p. 55.

85 Quoted in *ibid.*, p. 58.

86 Spring, note 22, pp. 31, 36–7.

87 *Ibid.*, p. 37.

88 Quoted in Cohen and Lazerson, note 6, p. 328.

89 Quoted in Wirth, note 84, p. 64.

90 Spring, note 22, p. 52.

91 Robert Sherman, 'Vocational Education and Democracy', in Corson, note 84, pp. 67–8.

92 'Shaping Schools for the World of Work', *State Legislatures*, Vol. 20 (1995), p. 7.

93 Stephen Dolainski, 'Partnering with the (School) Board', *Workforce*, Vol. 76 (May 1997); Leo Giglio and Lawrence Bauer, 'School-to-Work Programmes and Partnerships', *Educational Horizons*, Vol. 76, No. 2 (1998).

94 Dolainski, note 93.

95 Giglio and Bauer, note 93.

96 Dolainski, note 93.

97 Colin Wringe, 'Education, Schooling and the World of Work', in Corson, note 84, p. 33; Gary McCulloch, 'Technical and Vocational Schooling: Education or Work', in Corson, note 84, p. 115.

98 *Ibid.*, p. 116.

99 Philip Cohen, 'Teaching Enterprise Culture: Individualism, Vocationalism and the New Right', in Ian Taylor (ed.), *The Social Effects of Free Market Policies: an International Text* (New York: Harvester Wheatsheaf, 1990), p. 51.

100 Demos Foundation, 'Publications' (Demos Foundation, 1999). www.demos.co.uk/B_pubs.htm

101 ABC Television, 7.30 Report, July 1999.

102 Millicent Poole, 'Changing Policy Perspectives', in Poole, note 4, pp. 1–3, 7.

103 House of Representatives Standing Committee on Long Term Strategies, *Report of the Inquiry into the Workforce of the Future* (Canberra: Australian Government Publishing Service, 1995), pp. 60, 67.

104 Board of Studies, 'VET in Schools Retail Operations' (Victoria: Board of Studies, 1997); Jane Kenway and Lindsay Fitzclarence, 'Consuming Children? Public Education as a Market Commodity', in Alan Reid (ed.), *Going Public: Education Policy and Public Education in Australia* (Deakin West, ACT: Australian Curriculum Studies Association and Centre for the Study of Public Education, University of South Australia, 1998), p. 47.

105 Board of Studies Victoria, 'VET in Schools' (Board of Studies, Victoria, 1996). http://www.bos.vic.edu.au/vce/vet/

106 House of Representatives Standing Commitee on Employment, Education and Training, note 13, pp. xvii, 39.

107 *Ibid.*, p. 16.

108 Leon Gettler, 'School's In!', *Management Today* (June 1998), p. 16.

109 Jeanne C. Meister, 'Survey of Corporate University Future Directions: Executive Summary' (Corporate University Xchange, 1999). http://www.corpu.com/newsletter/survey.htm

110 John Authers, 'Motorola Leads the Way in the Corporate University Sector', *Financial Times* (London), 18 June 1998, p. 7; Jeanne C. Meister, *Corporate Universities: Lessons in Building a World-class Work Force*, revised edn (New York: McGraw-Hill, 1998), p. 19; Stuart Crainer, 'Battle of the Business Schools', *Management Today* (September 1998).

111 Bruce Gottlieb, 'Game Brains', *The Australian*, 25 August 1999.

112 John Authers, 'Universities Spot a Business Opportunity', *Financial Times* (London), 16 March 1998, p. 15; Jeanne C. Meister, 'Forging Partnerships with Institutions of Higher Education', *Technological Horizons in Education*, Vol. 26, No. 3 (1998); Meister,

note 109.

113 Tom Lester, 'The In-house Campus', *The Times* (London), 26 November 1998.

114 Authers, note 110, p. 7.

115 Simon Targett, 'BAe's "Virtual University" Is Set for Take-off', *Financial Times* (London), 30 April 1998; Crainer, note 110.

116 Authers, note 110, p. 7.

117 Quoted in Mark Luce, 'Ivory Tower: Bartering Brains for Bread', *Salon Magazine* (6 January 1999).

118 John Authers, 'Extending the Learning Curve', *Financial Times* (London), 22 September 1997, p. 15.

119 'Companies Go Back to School', *Sales and Marketing Management*, Vol. 150 (September 1998).

120 John Authers, 'A World of Opportunities', *Financial Times* (London), 5 October 1998, p. 7.

121 Meister, note 110, p. ix.

122 *Ibid*, p. 39.

123 *Ibid.*, p. 93.

124 Meister, note 112.

125 Stanley Aronowitz, 'The New Corporate University: Higher Education Becomes Higher Training', *Dollars and Sense* (March–April 1998).

126 Rebecca Scott, 'A Question of Balance', *Sydney Morning Herald*, 30 September 1999.

127 Authers, note 110, p. 7.

128 Authers, note 112, p. 15.

129 Adam Eisenstat, 'Corporate Universities: Pioneers in Market-Driven Education', (*Fortune* Magazine, 1999). http://www.fortune-sections.com/corporateu1999/; Crainer, note 110.

130 Authers, note 120, p. 7.

131 Meister, note 112.

132 Crainer, note 110.

133 John Craig Eaton, quoted in Meister, note 110, p. 191.

134 Matthew Spencer, 'Niche MBAs at Wollongong's Sydney Centre', *The Australian*, 18 March 1998, p. 39.

135 Gareth Cosslett, 'Market Courses', *Sydney Morning Herald*, 30 September 1999.

136 *Ibid.*

137 Jane Richardson, 'Courses Now Made to Order', *The Australian*, 23 June 1999.

138 Jane Richardson, 'Research Should Cater to Industry', *The Australian*, 7 April 1999.

139 Patrick Lawnham, 'Santos Jump-starts School of Petroleum Engineering', *Sydney Morning Herald*, 18 August 1999.

140 Christopher Richards, 'New Era of Corporate Learning Begins', *The Age*, 14 April 1999; Dean Ashenden and Sandra Milligan, 'Best Sellers', *The Australian*, 1 September 1999, p. 42.

141 Ashenden and Milligan, note 140, p. 43.

142 Meister, note 112.

143 Gettler, note 108, pp. 17–18; Melbourne University Private, 'Melbourne University Private' (Melbourne University Private, 1999). www.muprivate.edu.au/Welcome/welcome.html

144 Ron Dearing, 'The Full-On University', *The Australian*, 14 October 1998, p. 34.

145 *Ibid.*

146 *Ibid.*

147 Guy Healy, 'Big Business Links Inevitable: Dearing', *The Australian*, 14 October 1998.

148 Cited in Luce, note 117.

149 Aronowitz, note 125.

150 W. Neff, quoted in Adrian Furnham, *The Protestant Work Ethic: the Psychology of Work-Related Beliefs and Behaviours* (London: Routledge, 1990), pp. 146–7.

151 Wringe, note 97, p. 44.

152 Noam Chomsky, 'Toward a Humanistic Conception of Education and Work', in Corson, note 84, p. 20.

153 Wringe, note 97, p. 41.

154 Colin W. Evers, 'A Philosophical Perspective', in Poole, note 4, p 47.

155 Corson, note 84, p. 52.

156 Blakers, note 4, p. 65.

✧12✧

Work, Consumption
and Status

I owe, I owe, so off to work I go.
Bumper sticker[1]

The job admits one to the high tables of the
economic system where goods are made. Money
tokens are received by those who labour, so ensuring a place at the consumer counter.
David Bleakley[2]

Our jobs may be boring, empty, and futile, but we
have been indoctrinated to believe that compact
discs and Armani suits can somehow fill the void.
Michael Posner[3]

Perhaps the most effective tool for motivating people to work has been consumerism. Once people were persuaded that they needed the many goods
that were being produced, they had a reason to want to earn money beyond
what was necessary to provide an adequate standard of living. People who
hated their work, who had little chance of being promoted up the corporate
hierarchy, now had their own reason to work long hours. Where the work
ethic failed to motivate workers, the consumer ethic stepped in.

Ironically, the expansion of consumption that was necessary to create
markets for the fruits of rising production 'required the nurture of qualities
like wastefulness, self-indulgence, and artificial obsolescence, which directly
negated or undermined the values of efficiency' and the Protestant ethic that
had originally nurtured capitalism.[4] Traditional patterns of consumption and
habits of thrift had to be overcome. Advertisers sought to redefine people's
needs, encourage their wants and offer solutions to them via goods produced

by corporations rather than allowing people to identify and solve their own problems, or to look to each other for solutions.[5]

Consumerism has also played a major role in legitimating a social system which rewards businessmen and top corporate executives with incomes many times greater than those of ordinary workers. The consumer society gives ordinary workers some access to the good life. Surrounded by the bounty of their work – the television set, stereo, car, computer, white goods – they are less likely to question the conditions of their work, the way it dominates their life, and the lack of power that they have as workers. Advertisers constantly tell them that these are the fruits of success, that this is what life is all about. To question a system which delivers such plenty would seem perverse. As we have seen in previous chapters, those without access to this world of goods – because they are unemployed or have such low-paid jobs – blame themselves just as others blame them.

OVERPRODUCTION AND THE SHORTER WORKING WEEK

The growth in production in the late nineteenth and early twentieth centuries required growing markets and this meant expanding the consuming class beyond the middle and upper classes to include the working classes. Production between 1860 and 1920 increased 12 to 14 times in the US, while the population increased only three times.[6] Supply outstripped demand and problems of scarcity were replaced by problems of how to create more demand.

By the early 1920s, when American markets were reaching saturation, 'overproduction' and lack of consumer demand were blamed for recession. More goods were being produced than a population with 'set habits and means' could consume.[7] There were two schools of thought about how this problem should be solved. One was that work hours should be decreased and the economy stabilised so that production met current needs and the work was shared around. This view was held by intellectuals, labour leaders, reformers, educators and religious leaders. In America and in Europe it was commonly believed that consumer desires had limits that could be reached and that production beyond those limits would result in increased leisure time for all.[8]

The opposing view, mainly held by business people and economists, was that overproduction could and should be solved by increasing consumption so that economic growth could continue. Manufacturers needed to continually expand production so as to increase their profits. Employers were also afraid of the alternative because of its potential to undermine the work ethic and encourage degeneracy amongst workers who were unable to make proper use of their time. Increasing production and consumption guaranteed the ongoing centrality of work.[9]

Keen to maintain the importance of work in the face of the push for more leisure, businessmen extolled the virtues and pleasures of work and its necessity in building character, providing dignity and inspiring greatness. In a best-selling book, *The Man Nobody Knows*, Bruce Barton, like Luther, portrayed work as a spiritual activity and an end in itself. Other businessmen, too, promoted work as an 'intrinsically rewarding experience that developed the personality and provided workers with a purpose in life and a place in the community'.[10]

Nor was there a shortage of economists ready to argue that the creation of work was the goal of production. John M. Clark, in a review of economic developments, stated: 'Consumption is no longer the sole end nor production solely the means to that end. Work is an end in itself....' Creating work, and the right to work, he argued, had a higher moral imperative than meeting basic needs. Work was the foundation of social well-being and provided people with purpose and meaning. Others agreed that meeting basic needs was not enough; people needed to be working and progressing to a higher standard of living.[11]

Manufacturer H. C. Atkins, along with the president of the National Association of Manufacturers John E. Edgerton, warned that a five-day week would undermine the work ethic by giving more time for leisure.[12] If work took up less of the day it would be less important in people's lives. Edgerton observed: 'I am for everything that will make work happier but against everything that will further subordinate its importance.... [T]he emphasis should be put on work – more work and better work, instead of upon leisure.'[13]

Most prominent business leaders opposed a five-day work week. George Markland of the Philadelphia Gear Works argued that 'any man demanding the forty hour week should be ashamed to claim citizenship of this great country' and that a five-day week represented 'decay' and the degeneration of Americans into a 'race of softies and mollycoddles'. In particular, employers were concerned that letting the workers have Saturday off would allow them to take their minds off the job for a significant period of time.[14]

Businesspeople argued that they could not afford shorter work weeks, that they would become uncompetitive and go bankrupt. They feared that, given extra free time, people would spend it in unsociable ways; they might turn to crime, vice, corruption and degeneracy – and perhaps even to radicalism. 'The common people had to be kept at their desks and machines, lest they rise up against their betters.'[15] In Edgerton's view of the world, 'nothing breeds radicalism more quickly than unhappiness unless it is leisure. As long as the people are kept profitably and happily employed there is little danger from radicalism.'[16]

227

Henry Ford represented a much smaller group of employers who believed that shorter working hours and higher wages were a way of increasing productivity. Workers with more money and time would buy more goods, Ford argued, and this would solve the problem of overproduction by creating extra demand. Rather than undermining the work ethic, he argued, the desire for these consumer goods would bind workers to their jobs even more tightly. A shorter working week would also raise consumption by increasing the time available for spending.[17]

Most businesspeople, however, believed that shorter hours meant less production and that this would limit the growth of America's business enterprise. They sought to expand markets without reducing working hours. Those who went along to some extent with Ford's argument drew the line at reducing the working week to forty hours over five days. They feared economic stagnation which, to them, represented an unpalatable alternative.[18]

Unions initially argued for shorter hours on the grounds that long hours were unhealthy and, because of fatigue, unsafe. Once the eight-hour day began to be established they then argued for a five-day week as a way of ensuring that jobs were maintained.[19] One American labour leader, Samuel Gompers, stated that 'As long as there is one man [sic] who seeks employment and cannot find it, the hours of work are too long.'[20] Shorter hours also increased wages because more overtime would be paid.

Other unions, including some in Britain and France as well as in the US, demanded higher wages and more free time as their share of raising productivity and as compensation for the degrading conditions of work. Nevertheless trade unions still conceived of work as the central organising principle and the most important aspect of the worker's life.[21]

Various attempts at using strike action to shorten the working week had mixed success after the First World War in the US and Britain. Workers in the clothing industry in the US, which employed a high proportion of Jewish workers whose Sabbath fell on the Saturday, won a five-day week in most factories during the 1920s.[22] American steel workers continued to work 12-hour shifts, however, and the coal miners won wage rises rather than a shorter day. British coal miners actually saw their working day increase. As real wages fell in Britain and France during the 1920s, the dream of leisure time faded.[23]

In Europe employers preferred the paid vacation as an alternative to the shorter working week. Wages remained lower than in the US and purchasing power did not increase as fast. Although mass consumption came much later to Britain and Europe, Ford's theory that higher wages and shorter weeks would avoid market saturation found agreement amongst industrial engineers there.[24]

In the US consumption rates were increasing in the mid-1920s and the 'new economic gospel of consumption' gained many adherents.[25] The idea that there were limits on consumer wants began to be eclipsed by the idea that such wants could be endlessly created. In 1929 the President's Committee on Recent Economic Changes stated that 'wants are almost insatiable; that one want satisfied makes way for another ... by advertising and other promotional devices, by scientific fact finding, and by carefully predeveloped consumption, a measurable pull on production ... has been created'.[26]

The public was urged by the National Association of Manufacturers to 'end the buyers' strike'.[27] The desire to consume did not come naturally, however; it had to be learned: 'People had to move away from habits of strict thrift toward habits of ready spending.'[28] From the 1920s corporations began advertising to the working classes in an effort to break down these old habits of thrift and encourage new consumerist desires. At the same time they sought to counter anti-corporate feelings generated by the conditions of work in their factories.[29]

Higher wages helped in this shift from the Protestant ethic of asceticism to one of consumerism that fitted with the need to create markets for mass production.[30] In boom times, workers were given increased wages rather than increased leisure. Between 1910 and 1929 the average purchasing power of workers in the US increased by 40 per cent.[31] With these rising wages they bought more and the upward spiral of production and consumption was maintained. In earlier times higher wages might have encouraged workers to work shorter hours, but once workers had been coached into becoming consumers there was little danger of this. With the help of marketers and advertisers, workers could be trusted 'to spend more rather than work less'.[32]

In this context it was important that leisure was not an alternative to work and an opportunity to reflect on life, but rather a time for consumption. In this way the forty-hour week, rather than threatening economic growth, would foster it. Leisure goods such as radios, phonographs, movies, clothes, books and recreational facilities all benefited from increased leisure time.[33] At the same time leisure had to be subordinated to work and importantly, to a strong, well-recognised reason for working.

Businesspeople still wanted to limit the reduction of working hours and believed that by 'educating' workers to become consumers, the demand from workers for reduced working hours would also be limited.[34] Manufacturers expanded markets by expanding the range of goods they produced, moving from the basic requirements of living such as food, clothing and building materials to items such as cars and radios that provided entertainment and recreation.[35]

Businesspeople and advertisers who were well steeped in the Protestant work ethic, yet at the same time were promoting a consumer ethic to get business, consoled themselves that far from undermining the work ethic, they were persuading families to work harder than ever so as to afford the extra commodities, the luxuries and the stylish replacements to perfectly functional products. 'Advertising has stimulated more work,' claimed one agency.[36]

US unions fell in with the consumption solution to overproduction in the late 1920s and concentrated on fighting for higher wages, in the cause of which union leaders promoted increased production and economic growth. It was not until the Great Depression of the 1930s that they again fought for a shorter working week as a solution to unemployment.[37]

The Depression enforced unwanted leisure on many people who had no money to spend and whose 'free' time was spent at home, hidden away from social stigma. Some people came to dread free time.[38] Bertrand Russell, in his 1932 essay 'In Praise of Idleness', claimed that the choice not to go for shorter working hours after the war had 'insured that the unavoidable leisure shall cause misery all round instead of being a universal source of happiness'.[39]

Those whose work was irregular wanted long hours when they did work to make up for when they didn't. Gary Cross argues, in *Time and Money: the Making of Consumer Culture*, that it wasn't so much consumer culture as 'the whip of job and wage insecurity and the absence of a viable alternative' that drove workers to prefer higher wages over increased leisure time. 'Depression diminished the value of leisure time for wage-earners' whilst increasing the value of an income.[40]

Many people, when they could not afford it, maintained consumption and therefore their status in the community by means of hire purchase schemes or payment by instalments. By 1932, more than half the furniture, cars and household appliances and three-quarters of the radios in the US were bought using hire purchase. Fifteen per cent of goods were purchased on instalment plans.[41]

The topic of shorter working hours as a solution to unemployment again took centre stage as increased consumption seemed an unlikely solution when so many people couldn't even afford life's necessities. US unions argued for a 30-hour week and some large firms such as Kellogg's, Sears Roebuck, General Motors and Standard Oil introduced it voluntarily at some of their plants.[42]

Legislation in the US during the Depression set the standard working week at 40 hours over five days. Nevertheless long hours through the use of overtime continued. A plan to introduce a 30-hour week in order to spread employment was passed in the US Senate but business interests were outraged, 'barraging the Roosevelt administration with pressure and threats'. Business-people, even those who had reduced working hours voluntarily, were afraid that such legislation might institute the 30-hour week as a permanent feature.[43]

For them recovery from the Depression entailed a return to business as usual, with long working hours and increased consumption. The President was forced to withdraw his support for the thirty hour week and it was never introduced. In its place, Roosevelt introduced work creation schemes.[44]

After the Second World War the idea of solving unemployment by reducing working hours disappeared from mainstream thinking. During the war a demand for consumer goods had built up and following it workers tended to prefer wage rises to shorter hours.[45] The unions no longer pressed for shorter working hours and workers themselves became wedded to a consumer lifestyle that required long hours to support. Thus many union gave up their fight for control of production in favour of a share of the fruits of production and 'ever-increasing levels of material well-being for their workers'.[46]

The promise of full employment assuaged fears that long work hours might create unemployment. Leisure became consumer-oriented, revolving round the home with its entertaining and convenience goods and the vacation where workers could enjoy living in luxury for a short time.[47] As Cross notes: 'The identification of leisure with consumption won many to hard and steady work in disagreeable jobs.'[48]

The issue of working fewer hours instead of getting extra wages was seldom discussed after the war and was off the agenda for several decades – a non-issue, despite its high priority before the 1940s. As a result, working hours stabilised at 40 per week in the US until the 1970s, when they started to increase again (see next chapter).[49]

Juliet Schor observes in her book *The Overworked American* that productivity in the US has been increasing steadily since the 1940s: '[W]e could now produce our 1948 standard of living (measured in terms of marketed goods and services) in less than half the time it took in that year. We could actually have chosen the four-hour day. Or a working year of six months....' Instead, workers work more hours now than in 1948 and consume more than twice as much.[50]

It suited employers to maintain long working hours, just as it suited them to increase consumption. Employers prefer fewer workers who work longer hours to having more employees working shorter hours. The reason is that each worker today involves overheads such as training, paid vacations, superannuation contributions, health and life insurance. The fewer the workers, the lower the overheads of this nature.[51]

Longer hours meant higher wages for each worker. The extra income enabled a higher standard of living and consumer expenditure. This meant the employee came to rely on the extra income and therefore became more dependent on his/her job – which suited the employer, who preferred a low turnover of workers.[52] For higher-paid employees, the 'golden handcuffs' are a way of ensuring company loyalty. By paying their executives well they become accustomed to a continually rising lifestyle that is dependent not only on keeping their jobs but getting promotions and raises.[53]

It was the 'social decision to direct industrial innovation toward producing unlimited quantities of goods rather than leisure' that created the foundation for our modern consumer culture, 'a culture of work and spend'. The movement for more free time for workers, and for leisure time free of market forces, was defeated by the middle of the century when mass consumer culture took off.[54] The consumer culture, rather than eroding the work ethic, tied people even more closely to working long hours in order to earn the money for their consumer desires.

CONSUMERISM AS OPIATE OF THE MASSES

Stuart Ewen, in *Captains of Consciousness: Advertising and the Social Roots of the Consumer Culture,* shows that advertising for mass consumerism was not only aimed at increasing markets for goods but also at shifting the locus of discontent from people's work to arenas that advertisers could promise would be satisfied by consumption. Their frustrations and unhappiness could then be directed towards buying rather than political protest against working conditions or other elements of industrial society.[55]

Ewen claims that consumerism, 'the mass participation in the values of the mass-induced market', was not a natural historical development but 'an aggressive device of corporate survival'. Discontent in the workplace could lead to a challenge to corporate authority but discontent in the consumer sphere provided an incentive to work harder and reflected an acceptance of the values of the capitalist enterprise.[56]

Similarly Robert Lane claims in his book *Political Ideology* that:

> The more emphasis a society places upon consumption – through advertising, development of new products, and easy installment buying – the more will social dissatisfaction be channeled into intraclass consumption rivalry instead of interclass resentment and conflict ... the more will labor unions focus upon the 'bread and butter' aspects of unionism, as contrasted to its ideological elements.[57]

If people were dependent on the products of the factories they were less likely to be critical of the appalling working conditions within them. The good life attained through this consumption also compensated for the unpleasantness of work and distracted attention from it. Advertisements were careful not to depict people working in factories. A leading copywriter in the 1920s, Helen Woodward, advised that consumption could help to sublimate and redirect urges that might otherwise be expressed politically or aggressively. 'To those who cannot change their whole lives or occupations,' she argued, 'even a new line in a dress is often a relief.'[58]

Department store merchant Edward Filene, a spokesperson for industrialists in the 1920s and 1930s, spoke frankly about the need for social planning in order to create a consumer culture where industry could 'sell to the masses all that it employs the masses to create' and the need for education to train the masses to be consumers in a world of mass production. He argued that consumer culture could unify the nation and, through education, social change could be limited to changes in the commodities that industry produced.[59]

Consumption allows people at the bottom of the social hierarchy to feel that they have some measure of access to the good life for all their troubles. The escape from real life provided by leisure activities allows people to continue what might otherwise be a dreary and downtrodden existence. Lisa Macdonald and Allen Myers of *Green Left Weekly* claim workers attempt to gain ownership of what they produce and overcome their alienation through consumption: 'it is only as purchasers, "shoppers", that we are treated with the courtesy worthy of a human being'.[60]

Employers encouraged workers to think of consumerism as the rationale for their work and so measures of success were moved from the realm of production and work to the realm of consumption. Advertising messages affected people's aspirations. They portrayed a bounty of consumer goods as the fruits of the American Dream. Rather than aspiring for their children to become leading businessmen or top executives or political leaders, consumers were courted by advertisements offering messages such as 'Some Day Your Boy Will Own a Buick'.[61]

Advertisers also undermined the nineteenth-century 'culture of character' which was the basis of the myth of the self-made man, someone who succeeded as a result of hard work, morality and discipline. In its place a 'culture of personality' evolved which promoted the importance of presentation and appearance, things that advertisers were so helpfully offering to assist with. What mattered in getting ahead and influencing people was the impression a person made on others. Things like their clothes, their home furnishings, their personal cleanliness were all used by others to judge their character.[62]

Advertising and consumerism also played a major role in the acceptance of the capitalist vision and its associated inequalities. Roland Marchand argues in *Advertising the American Dream* that advertisers repeatedly used 'the parable of the democracy of goods' to sell products to the middle classes. In this parable, although there was a social hierarchy with wealth concentrated at the top, ordinary people could enjoy the same products and goods that the people at the top did. Joe Bloggs could drink the same brand of coffee as the wealthiest capitalist. Mary Jane could buy the same soap as the lady with the maid in waiting. The most humble of citizens (although not the poor who were not the targets of these advertisements) could afford to purchase the same quality products as a millionaire.[63]

> The social message of the parable of the Democracy of Goods was clear. Antagonistic envy of the rich was unseemly; programs to redistribute wealth were unnecessary. The best things in life were already available to all at reasonable prices.... Incessantly and enticingly repeated, advertising visions of fellowship in a Democracy of Goods encouraged Americans to look to similarities in consumption styles rather than to political power or control of wealth for evidence of significant equality.[64]

According to Filene, the process of buying goods was a means by which people were supporting industry and thereby electing the manufacturers, who made the goods, to a government which would satisfy their needs. They were voting industry leaders into positions of leadership in society. In this way 'the masses have elected Henry Ford. They have elected General Motors. They have elected the General Electric Company, and Woolworth's and all the other great industrial and business leaders of the day.'[65]

Not only was the desire for social change displaced by a desire for changes in commodities, but political freedom was equated with consumer choice and political citizenship with participation in the market through consumption. Consumption was promoted as democratising at the very time it was being used to pacify the political unrest of workers.[66] According to well-known sociologist Daniel Bell:

> If the American worker has been 'tamed' it has not been through the discipline of the machine, but by the 'consumption society', by the possibility of a better living which his wage, the second income from his working wife, and easy credit all allow.[67]

DEBT AS AN INCENTIVE TO WORK

The advantages to employers of having employees who want to save money to buy things, or who need to pay off debts from purchases already made, are that those employees will be more willing to please. In his 1982 study of BHP workers in Whyalla, South Australia, R. J. Kriegler found that the company encouraged workers to buy goods on credit or hire purchase. The workers then had to do overtime and shift work to pay off these debts. When BHP reduced production and overtime was cut for a long period of time, some families had to sell their cars, freezers or television sets.[68]

Kriegler noted: 'One cannot stress enough the indirect industrial control that an employer can have over a work-force that is deeply entrenched in time payments of one kind or another. Strikes, lay-offs, lock-outs, or simple cutbacks in overtime loom as serious threats to the livelihoods of workmen's families and they are easily encouraged to join the ranks of the other hard-working, obedient and industrially docile instruments of production.'[69]

As 'Tennessee' Ernie Ford's song 'Sixteen Tons', says:

You load sixteen tons, and what do you get?
Another day older and deeper in debt
St Peter don't you call me, 'cause I can't go
I owe my soul to the company store.

Hire purchase and instalment selling went against traditional values of thrift and frugality. There was an odium attached to debt. In order to get middle-class consumers to take advantage of such schemes the salespeople used the word 'credit' instead of 'debt'. Debt was associated with usury and poverty and lack of thrift. Getting credit was a mark of respect and esteem and a sign of confidence in one's ability to make good money in the future.[70] Billing was made by way of a mailed invoice each month and the whole thing took on the flavour of a business transaction. Later, in the 1960s, banks made overdrafts available to these customers so they didn't have to worry about cheques bouncing.[71]

The availability of consumer credit, particularly credit cards, which enable people to spend beyond the money they actually have available, was a huge inducement to spending. It enabled consumers to make purchases easily without worrying about the consequences which seemed to be far off. Credit was used as 'an active sales tool'. Those buying on credit were less indecisive and less concerned about the price tag.[72]

Bell noted that the instalment plan was 'the most "subversive" instrument that undercut the Protestant ethic':[73]

Aided and abetted by advertising and the installment plan, the two most fearsome social inventions of man since the discovery of gunpowder, selling has become the most striking activity of contemporary America. Against frugality, selling emphasizes prodigality; against asceticism, the lavishness of display.[74]

By 1960 credit (debt) was becoming 'a way of life' in the US. Consumer debt had increased three times as fast as personal income during the preceding decade.[75] Between 1950 and 1990 consumer debt had increased by 3,400 per cent from $23 billion to $794 billion, much of it instalment payments.[76] The total household debt in the US at the beginning of the 1990s was 10 per cent higher than the total household income. A decade earlier it had been 20 per cent lower.[77]

The demand for consumer credit was still rising rapidly in the late 1990s: in the UK it rose by 16.3 per cent in the financial year 1997/8 to £1.33 billion.[78] In Australia total household debt (including home loans) increased by 136 per cent in the same year to $290 billion.[79] Debt had been made easier by low interest rates, easy access to credit, higher limits on credit cards, bigger personal loans and more use of overdrafts. Most credit cards today also offer loyalty points which provide 'rewards' according to how much consumers spend on their cards.[80]

Along with increased debt there have been more bankruptcies. In 1997 well over one million Americans were unable to meet their debts and became bankrupt, three times the figure in 1981.[81] In Australia bankruptcies, after reaching a record high in the financial year ending 1997, were up 13 per cent in 1998 and another 8.5 per cent in 1999. Eighty per cent of these bankruptcies are the result of personal rather than business-related debt, and almost half of the bankrupted individuals are under 35 years of age.[82]

John Kenneth Galbraith has noted that indebtedness provides the means for those who cannot afford coveted goods to keep up with those who can, and that it is in the interests of marketers to encourage them to do so.

> With those who lack the current means it is a brief and obvious step from stimulating their desire by advertising to making it effective in the market with a loan.... The process of persuading people to incur debt, and the arrangements for them to do so, are as much a part of modern production as the making of the goods and nurturing of the wants.[83]

PRODUCTION, CONSUMPTION AND STATUS

Vance Packard argued in *The Status Seekers* that the use of consumer goods as status symbols was a deliberate strategy of advertisers, or 'merchants of discontent', who took advantage of the 'upgrading urge' that people felt. The message that workers could improve their status through consumption was particularly aimed at people who had little chance of raising their status through their work because opportunities for promotion were slim.[84] Employers sought to divert the dissatisfaction of workers with the nature of their work into a more personal dissatisfaction that could be fed with consumer goods: 'offering mass produced visions of individualism by which people could extricate themselves from the mass'.[85]

The advertiser offered workers the possibility of gaining social status through buying goods that were better than those displayed by their neighbours. With the help of instalment plans and credit, they could purchase the signifiers of success even if they weren't achieving that success in their workplace. This was not something that came naturally to working people who were, for the most part, resigned to their position in life. According to Packard 'they need prodding and "educating" to desire many of the traditionally higher-class products the mass merchandisers desire to move in such vast numbers, such as the electric rotating spits or gourmet foods'.[86]

Car manufacturers, particularly, exploited people's desire for status, spending 'small fortunes exploring the status meaning of their product'. They found, for example that people in housing developments, where all the houses looked similar, were most likely to leave their large new cars parked on the street in front of the house rather than in the garage where no-one would see them. Plymouth advertisements pictured a family in front of their car saying 'We're not wealthy ... we just look it!' Dodge advertisements featured a man saying to a Dodge car owner 'Boy, you must be rich to own a car as big as this!' And Ford advertisements showed the back of one of their cars and stated 'let the people behind you know you are ahead of them!'[87] Such advertising was so successful that people began diverting funds from other purchases into the purchase of a car that would enhance their status, and by the end of the 1950s Americans 'were spending more of their total income on the family chariot than they were in financing their homestead, which housed the family and its car or cars'.[88] Not to be outdone, home builders and sellers ensured that the home became a status symbol that rivalled the motor car.

Chinoy observes that consumption provided automobile workers in the 1950s with a way of rationalising their failure to advance in their work: 'Advancement has come to mean the progressive accumulation of things as well as the increasing capacity to consume.... If one manages to buy a new car, if each year sees a major addition to the household – a washing machine, a refrigerator, a new living-room suite, now probably a television set – then one is also getting ahead.'[89] Rather than question the American Dream, workers would either blame themselves for their failure to live up to it, or find other ways to interpret it.

Such trends were not confined to the US. The consumerism that proliferated in the US in the 1920s and 1930s spread to other industrialised nations after the Second World War, particularly in the 1950s.[90] Greg Whitwell describes the rise of a consumer society in Australia:

> The ownership of certain sorts of consumer goods, each ranked according to brand names, came to be seen as guides to an individual's income which in turn, so it is believed, said something about his or her inner worth. Consumer goods became external signs, used to give a sense of hierarchy by members of a society characterized by an emphasis on change and on social and geographical mobility.[91]

In a British study of the working class in the 1950s Ferdynand Zweig found 'a steep rise in acquisitive tendencies and pre-occupation with money in work attitudes'. There was far less difference between middle-class and working-class purchase of consumer durables (cars, white goods, electrical appliances) than previously, and class self-identification had come to depend more on factors such as house ownership than type of work. In fact Zweig found workers impatient with questions about class. They were more interested in status as a way of organising the social spectrum.[92]

Increased consumerism led to an increased emphasis on the importance of pay. Many people work so as to earn the money to buy consumer goods and some measure of status that accompanies them. A European study by the Henley Centre in 1991 found that 'better pay' was the priority for new jobs for 70 per cent of those surveyed, compared with enjoyable work, which was a priority for 58 per cent.[93]

A US study found that those who believed 'having lots of money' was 'extremely important' had gone up to almost two-thirds in 1986 from less than half in 1977. It ranked higher than any other of goal in life.[94] Americans born since 1963, those referred to as Generation X, are more likely to agree that 'the only really meaningful measure of success is money' than any previous generation. They spend more money on stereos, mobile phones, beepers and cars than older people and are more likely to take a less interesting job if it pays well.[95]

Jimmy Carter, when President of the US, noted that 'Human identity is no longer defined by what one does, but by what one owns.'[96] Consumption has become a more important source of self-identity and status than work for many people. Compton Advertising undertook a survey of public attitudes to the economic system in 1974 and found that two-thirds of those surveyed identified their role in the economic system as that of 'consumers and spenders of money' rather than workers or producers. This included one-half of those in the labour force.[97] More recent opinion surveys also show that in countries like the US and Japan, 'people increasingly measure success by the amount they consume'.[98]

In a society where people don't know each other very well, appearances are important and social status, though more securely attained through occupation, can be attained with strangers through consumption. When people are uprooted and move to the cities they are strangers to each other. Previously everyone knew everyone else's business and the status that should be accorded to each person. In an anonymous city one can adopt a certain lifestyle (clothes, car) that is higher up the status ladder than one's occupation would indicate, particularly if one is willing to go into debt to do it. Consumption is used as an indicator of achievement.[99]

CONCLUSION

Consumer values have come to replace the work ethic for many people as a motivator for work and as a primary source of identity. This shift was most fully realised after the Second World War in the US, when Daniel Bell observed that 'the culture was no longer concerned with how to work and achieve, but with how to spend and enjoy'.[100] Towards the end of the twentieth century, he noted, there had been a 'shift from production to consumption as the fulcrum of capitalism.... Marketing and hedonism became the motor forces of capitalism.'[101] People came to regard their jobs as means to getting the money necessary to pay for the consumer items that were being marketed to them. 'Demand for goods and services became the flywheel that kept the economic engine running fast and smooth. The spiritual dimension, meanwhile, faded as a justification for the accumulation of wealth.'[102]

Today, rather than being concerned about social mobility through work, an avenue that is still unavailable for many workers, people seek material satisfactions and work for them. They cope with the disparity between the myth of social mobility and the reality that no amount of hard work is going to help them advance in their careers by displacing their ambition to the world of consumer goods. In a modern consumer society the search for status is often expressed through consumer goods and people are judged by the goods they possess. The essential benefit of increasing production is no longer questioned and the idea that there are limits on consumption is not taken seriously, except by some of the more radical environmentalists. Galbraith has observed that the 'paramount position of production' has provided corporate leaders with huge financial rewards and influence over policy decisions.[103]

> Society will accord him prestige appropriate to the role he plays; what may well be less important, he will be able, without difficulty or criticism, to command an income that is related to his prestige. As production has increasingly monopolized our economic attitudes, the business executive has grown in esteem.[104]

The revolutionary potential of the 'class-conscious radical' driven to protest by the conditions of his/her work has been subverted by the material rewards of consumerism.[105] For the working classes, the instalment plan and credit schemes ensure that the worker commits future time and money to present consumption.[106] The embracing of consumerism has ensured that working hours have increased, as will be seen in the next chapter. More importantly work, production and consumption have remained the primary elements of modern societies, the central aspects of our culture, at a time when the overproduction and overconsumption of goods are threatening the environment on which we all depend.

NOTES

1 Robert Wuthnow, *Poor Richard's Principle: Recovering the American Dream Through the Moral Dimension of Work, Business and Money* (Princeton, NJ: Princeton University Press, 1996), p. 25.

2 David Bleakley, *Work: the Shadow and the Substance* (London: SCM Press, 1983), p. 75.

3 Michael Posner, 'Whatever Happened to Spare Time: "The Protestant Ethos in Turmoil", or Why We Cannot Stop Working', *World Press Review*, Vol. 38 (September 1991), p. 27.

4 Roland Marchand, *Advertising the American Dream: Making Way for Modernity, 1920–1940* (Berkeley: University of California Press, 1985), p. 158.

5 Stuart Ewen, *Captains of Consciousness: Advertising and the Social Roots of the Consumer Culture* (New York: McGraw-Hill, 1976), pp. 70, 108.

6 David J. Cherrington, *The Work Ethic: Working Values and Values That Work* (New York: AMACON, 1980), p. 37.

7 Gary Cross, *Time and Money* (London: Routledge, 1993), p. 38; Rodney Clapp, 'Why the Devil Takes Visa', *Christianity Today*, Vol. 40, No. 11 (1996).

8 Cross, note 7, pp. 7–8, 28.

9 *Ibid.*, pp. 7, 9, 39; Benjamin Kline Hunnicutt, *Work Without End: Abandoning Shorter Hours for the Right to Work* (Philadelphia: Temple University Press, 1988), pp. 42, 67.

10 Hunnicutt, note 9, pp. 47–50.

11 *Ibid.*, pp. 62–3.

12 Paul Bernstein, *American Work Values: Their Origin and Development* (Albany, NY: State University of New York Press, 1997), p. 157.

13 Cross, note 7, p. 16.

14 Hunnicutt, note 9, p. 40.

15 Juliet B. Schor, *The Overworked American: the Unexpected Decline in Leisure* (New York: Basic Books, 1991), p. 74.

16 Quoted in Hunnicutt, note 9, p. 41.

17 Cross, note 7, pp. 11, 37–9.

18 Hunnicutt, note 9, pp. 41–2.

19 *Ibid.*, p. 68; Cross, note 7, p. 31.

20 Quoted in Anders Hayden, 'The Price of Time', *New Internationalist* (November 1998), p. 17.

21 Cross, note 7, pp. 31–5.

22 Hunnicutt, note 9, pp. 70–71.

23 Cross, note 7, pp. 131–3.

24 *Ibid.*, pp. 43, 95, 134.

25 Hunnicutt, note 9, p. 42.

26 Quoted in Cross, note 7, p. 41.

27 Quoted in *ibid.*, p. 38.

28 Clapp, note 7.

29 Ewen, note 5, p. 19.

30 *Ibid.*, p. 29.

31 Cross, note 7, p. 7.

32 Hunnicutt, note 9, p. 43.

33 *Ibid.*, p. 45.

34 *Ibid.*, pp. 46–7.

35 Robert Eisenberger, *Blue Monday: the Loss of the Work Ethic in America* (New York: Paragon House, 1989), p. 11.

36 Marchand, note 4, p. 162.

37 Hunnicutt, note 9, p. 79.

38 Cross, note 7, pp. 137–53.

39 Bertrand Russell, 'In Praise of Idleness (1932)', in Vernon Richards (ed.), *Why Work? Arguments for the Leisure Society* (London: Freedom Press, 1983), p. 28.

40 Cross, note 7, pp. 132–7.

41 *Ibid.*, p. 148.

42 Hunnicutt, note 9, p. 148.

43 *Ibid.*, p. 157.

44 *Ibid.*, pp. 157, 191; Cherrington, note 6, p. 3; Schor, note 15, p. 75.

45 Cross, note 7, p. 85.

46 Schor, note 15, p. 78; Daniel Yankelovich and John Immerwahr, 'Putting the Work Ethic to Work', *Society*, Vol. 21, No. 2 (1984), p. 59.

47 Cross, note 7, p. 155.

48 *Ibid.*, p. 153.

49 Charles Siegel, 'The End of Economic Growth: the Limits of Human Needs', *Earth Island Journal*, Vol. 13, No. 4 (1998/9).

50 Schor, note 15, p. 2.

51 *Ibid.*, pp. 3, 66–7.

52 *Ibid.*, p. 64.

53 Wuthnow, note 1, p. 24.

54 Cross, note 7, pp. 5, 9.

55 Ewen, note 5, pp. 43–5.

56 *Ibid.*, pp. 54, 109.

57 Robert E. Lane, *Political Ideology: Why the American Common Man Believes What He Does* (New York: The Free Press, 1962), p. 80.

58 Ewen, note 5, pp. 77–8, 85–6.

59 *Ibid.*, p. 54.

60 L. Macdonald and A. Myers, 'Malign Design', *New Internationalist* (November 1998), p. 21.

61 Marchand, note 4, pp. 162, 222.

62 *Ibid.*, pp. 209–10.

63 *Ibid.*, p. 218.

64 *Ibid.*, pp. 220, 222.

65 Quoted in Ewen, note 5, p. 92.

66 *Ibid.*, pp. 89, 91.

67 Daniel Bell, 'Work and Its Discontents (1956)', in A. R. Gini and T. J. Sullivan (eds), *It Comes with the Territory: an Inquiry Concerning Work and the Person* (New York: Random House, 1989), pp. 122–3.

68 R. J. Kriegler, 'Workers and Bosses', in Craig R. Littler (ed.), *The Experience of Work* (UK: Gower Publishing, 1985), p. 160.

69 *Ibid.*, p. 160.

70 Earl Shorris, *A Nation of Salesmen: the Tyranny of the Market and the Subversion of Culture* (New York: W. W. Norton, 1994), p. 220.

71 Daniel Bell, *The Cultural Contradictions of Capitalism* (London: Heinemann, 1976), pp. 69–70.

241

72 David Kiron, 'Perpetuating Consumer Culture: Media, Advertising, and Wants Creation. Overview Essay', in Neva R. Goodwin, Frank Ackerman and David Kiron (eds), *The Consumer Society* (Washington, DC: Island Press, 1997), p. 229; Vance Packard, *The Waste Makers* (Harmondsworth, Middlesex: Penguin, 1960), p. 141.

73 Daniel Bell, 'The Protestant Ethic', *World Policy Journal*, Vol. 13 (Fall 1996).

74 Bell, note 67, pp. 122–123.

75 Packard, note 72, pp. 140–2.

76 Shorris, note 70, p. 114.

77 Wuthnow, note 1, p. 25.

78 Anne Segall, 'Demand for Credit Continues to Grow', *Electronic Telegraph*, 30 June 1998.

79 Paul Sheehan, 'Welcome to the Dog Years', *Sydney Morning Herald*, 4 September 1999, p. 1s.

80 Sean Aylmer, 'Consumer Debt Hits $61 Billion', *Sydney Morning Herald*, 2 June 1998; Sean Aylmer, 'Credit Splurge Blamed for Soaring Debt Levels', *Sydney Morning Herald*, 1 October 1998.

81 Mara Shurgot, 'The Goods Life', *Sierra*, Vol. 82 (1 July 1997); 'The Sorry State of Saving', *The Economist* (30 August 1997).

82 Sharon Verghis, 'Young Take Bankruptcy to Beat Debt', *Sydney Morning Herald*, 11 October 1999.

83 John Kenneth Galbraith, *The Affluent Society*, 2nd revised edition (Great Britain: Penguin, 1970), pp. 166–7.

84 Vance Packard, *The Status Seekers: an Exploration of Class Behaviour in America* (Harmondsworth, Middlesex: Penguin, 1961), pp. 269–70.

85 Andrew Hornery, 'Family Pack Aims for the Children', *Sydney Morning Herald*, 24 September 1998, p. 45.

86 Packard, note 84, p. 271.

87 *Ibid.*, pp. 273–4.

88 *Ibid.*, p. 274.

89 Ely Chinoy, *Automobile Workers and the American Dream*, 2nd edn (Urbana and Chicago: University of Illinios Press, 1992), p. 126.

90 Stewart Lansley, *After the Gold Rush: the Trouble with Affluence: 'Consumer Capitalism' and the Way Forward* (London: Century Business Books, 1994), p. 85.

91 Greg Whitwell, *Making the Market: the Rise of Consumer Society* (Melbourne: McPhee Gribble Publishers, 1989), p. 7.

92 Ferdynand Zweig, *The New Acquisitive Society* (Chichester: Barry Rose, 1976), pp. 15, 21–2, 26–7.

93 Cited in Lansley, note 90, p. 136.

94 Alan Thein Durning, *How Much Is Enough: the Consumer Society and the Future of the Earth*, ed. Linda Starke, Worldwatch Environmental Alert Series (London: Earthscan, 1992), p. 34.

95 Dan Zevin and Carolyn Edy, 'Boom Time for Gen X', *US News and World Report* (20 October 1997).

96 Quoted in Thomas H. Naylor, William H. Willimon and Rolf Osterberg, *The Search for Meaning in the Workplace* (Nashville: Abingdon Press, 1996), p. 69.

97 Compton Advertising, *National Survey on the American Economic System* (New York: The Advertising Council, 1974), p. 17.

98 Durning, note 94, p. 22.

99   Bell, note 71, p. 68.
100 Quoted in Andrew Bard Schmookler, *The Illusion of Choice: How the Market Economy Shapes Our Destiny* (Albany: State University of New York Press, 1993), p. 149.
101 Bell, note 73.
102 Perry Pascarella, *The New Achievers: Creating a Modern Work Ethic* (New York: The Free Press, 1984), p. 31.
103 AAP, 'Australians Working Longer Hours as They Earn Less Pay', *Sydney Morning Herald*, 7 September 1998, p. 155.
104 Galbraith, note 83, p. 154.
105 Bell, note 67, p. 123.
106 Sebastian de Grazia, *Of Time, Work and Leisure* (New York: Anchor Books, 1964), p. 202.

·13·

Long Hours
and Little Leisure

There is no more fatal blunderer than he who con-
sumes the greater part of his life getting his living.
Henry David Thoreau[1]

Everywhere I go it seems people are killing themselves with work, busyness, rushing, caring, and
rescuing. Work addiction is a modern epidemic and
it is sweeping our land.... [W]hen work is the sole
reservoir for your identity, you are addicted. Work
has you, you don't have it.
Diane Fasel[2]

The best test of the quality of a civilization is the
quality of its leisure.
Irwin Edman[3]

The large increases in productivity since 1945 have not provided increased
leisure time for full-time workers as was once predicted. Instead they have
resulted in many unemployed and underemployed people.[4] Those who have
full-time jobs still work at least 40 hours a week but a significant proportion
of them work even longer hours. There is in fact much evidence to suggest
that people in English-speaking countries such as the US, Britain, Canada and
Australia are working harder than they have for decades.[5]

> Generally speaking, active people in the 20–50 age bracket constitute a group
> whose discretionary time is being squeezed.... They stand in sharp contrast to
> those in the population who, because of unemployment, underemployment,
> disability or early retirement, find themselves with a lot of free time but not
> necessarily the means to translate that into self-development and self-fulfilment
> on the basis of leisure activities.[6]

244

WORKING HARDER

An OECD survey in 1996 found that working hours in the US are rising and that white-collar workers, especially middle managers, are working harder than before. Indeed, working hours have not decreased for Americans since the 1940s. This is the trend for men and women, working-class and professional people, and a wide range of income levels and industries. US workers work an average of one month a year more than European workers. Manufacturing employees work two months each year more than manufacturing workers in West Germany or France.[7] Also leisure time is shrinking: 'According to a Harris survey, the amount of leisure time enjoyed by the average American shrank 37 per cent since 1973.'[8]

In the early 1990s the average American full-time worker was working 140–163 more hours each year (equivalent to an extra month a year) than in the 1970s. This extra work included an average extra hour a week on the job and more weeks per year. One in four full-time workers works 49 hours or more per week; one in eight spends 60 hours or more working. This is partly because of overtime and partly because some people work more than one job. Whilst European workers have been getting longer vacations, US workers have been getting fewer days off in terms of sick leave, holidays and other paid time off.[9]

Women are particularly hard hit by increasing work trends. Not only are they working an extra 305 hours per year on the job compared with twenty years ago but they tend to be responsible for household duties as well. Juliet Schor has calculated that mothers who are employed work an average of 65 hours a week. At the same time their husbands tend to be working increasing hours at their jobs and are less available for help in the home. About two-thirds of married women in the US have paid jobs.[10]

Workers spend additional time getting to and from work, getting ready for work, talking about their jobs, worrying about their work and also about losing their jobs, and looking for other jobs. American workers are spending an extra 23 hours per year commuting.[11] A recent survey of workplace trends in the US found that nearly 40 per cent of workers do extra work during their lunch hour. About 14 per cent of office workers take no lunch break at all and on average they take only 36 minutes. Apart from office work and eating and shopping, workers run errands and take clients to lunch and otherwise fill up their break with activities.[12]

In Canada working hours have also been increasing whilst wages have been decreasing.[13] And in Britain working hours increased during the 1980s so that the average working week for men is now 45 hours, more than anywhere else in Europe. In 1998 it was estimated that 4.5 million workers in

Britain were working more than 48 hours per week, up 600,000 since 1992. [14]

The Japanese work hardest of all, working 10 weeks a year more than Europeans and five and a half weeks more than American workers. They take less than eight days annual holiday, although they are officially entitled to more. Extracurricular activity includes entertaining customers and clients by playing golf with them and accompanying them to karaoke bars. And this is on top of a routine 60–70-hour work week.[15] Stewart Lansley in his book *After the Gold Rush* observes that Japanese walk faster than any other people. Americans walk next fastest, followed by the English, Taiwanese and Italians.[16]

In Australia hours are rising, as in the US. A 1998 study found that only 24 per cent of workers work a standard 40-hour week, compared with 44 per cent twenty years ago. The difference could be attributed mainly to overtime, often unpaid, with 30 per cent working more than 49 hours per week compared with 19 per cent in 1978.[17]

A government survey found that Australian workers today 'endure more stress, work faster and more intensively, and put more effort into their jobs than they used to'.[18] A 1998 survey of 19,000 people carried out by the Department of Industrial Relations found that 60 per cent of people said their work effort had increased over the previous year and half said they were more stressed.[19] A 1999 Australian Council of Trade Unions (ACTU) survey confirmed these findings.[20]

Decreasing wages have been a major cause of rising work hours. To maintain a family's standard of living individuals have to work longer and more members of the family have to work. Indeed, for families headed by less educated workers, family income has dropped whilst workloads have increased.[21] A 1995 survey found that economic circumstances had forced 40 per cent of American families to send an extra family member out to work or to get an extra job since 1979. As a result, the combined working hours of working couples in 1990 amounted to an average four months more per couple than in 1970.[22] In another survey 46 per cent of those who worked long hours said that they did so because they needed the money, 20 per cent said they did so because their employers required it and 16 per cent said they did so to help the company.[23]

Temporary and contract workers are particularly pressured to work long hours as employers want to get the most out of them whilst they have them, and they are often employed to get an urgent job done. Because of their lack of security such workers are keen to please employers in order to be kept on or given future assignments.[24] Growing competition, especially with firms based in nations where wages are lower, has also increased pressure on workers to produce more.

A number of new trends in management require more work from

employees: performance-related pay; outsourcing, where work is put out to contract and those who can achieve more for a given payment win the contracts; re-engineering, which requires fewer workers to be more flexible and cover more tasks; and 'stretch management', which involves 'setting goals just beyond a worker's previous limits'.[25]

Job insecurity is a major reason behind the rising working hours of middle managers. Two top business schools, Harvard and Stanford, have made their management courses shorter because 'potential customers are fearful of spending too many weeks away from their jobs'.[26] A study by Northwestern National Life Insurance found that almost half of workers surveyed were concerned about losing their jobs and 65 per cent said they suffered from stress-related health problems.[27]

Rising levels of consumerism have also increased working hours by increasing the consumer goods necessary to attain a normal and respectable standard of living, and therefore the hours of work necessary to earn an income to attain them. Those unable to afford these goods, even though people in previous generations happily did without them, feel that they are socially excluded and poor. A fairly basic example is a television. Those without a television in a modern industrialised society are excluded from a common form of communication and shared entertainment, and consequently feel that they are outsiders in the community. A television has become a necessity in such communities.[28]

Children are also working more than they used to. In poorer families they work to help support the family; in middle-class families they work to be able to consume. They want to buy fashionable clothes, music, cars. 'A New Hampshire study found that 85 per cent of the state's tenth-to-twelfth-graders hold jobs, and 45 per cent of them work more than twenty hours a week.'[29]

A 1997 survey by University of Michigan researchers found that American children between the ages of three and twelve are spending more hours in school (eight more than in 1981), more hours doing chores at home, and more time in organised activities (sports, music, clubs etc.) than fifteen to twenty years ago. They have much less time to themselves for fun and play and their leisure time (time outside of school or daycare, sleeping, eating, personal hygiene) has fallen from 40 per cent in 1981 to 25 per cent in 1997. They even have less time for watching television – which on average occupies about a quarter of their leisure time.[30]

HISTORICAL TRENDS

Although many people imagine that pre-industrial people worked harder to supply themselves with their needs than people in affluent countries today, this is not the case. In most pre-industrial societies, life was slow and leisurely and the hours of work required to meet their simple needs were far fewer than we spend today.[31] According to anthropologists, hunter-gatherer societies were able to meet their needs and enjoy an adequate diet in a few hours each day, working 20–35 hours per week.[32]

For example, Aborigines in Arnhem Land, Australia were observed in 1948 to spend an average of four or five hours a day collecting food and to occupy the rest of their time resting, socialising and in other leisurely activities. The same was true of !Kung Bushmen in the Kalahari Desert, Botswana. Whilst they occasionally went hungry for short periods, so too do significant numbers of people in modern industrial societies.[33]

Ancient Roman and Greek workers apparently had abundant holidays.[34] And in medieval society, scholarly studies show, people not only worked fewer days per year but their eight-hour day was carried out at a much more relaxed pace. Nor did medieval workers work any more than was necessary for their subsistence. If a worker could support his family by working three days a week, it was unlikely he would work any more days.[35]

Often work was seasonal or intermittent. Peasants engaged in agriculture worked according to growth cycles and seasons and were thought to have worked perhaps 120–150 days in a year, although some of these days would have been long. Those engaged in handicrafts were notorious for the slow start to their weeks. Having Mondays off was such a tradition, enabling workers to recover from their weekend activities, that it became known as St Monday.[36]

The calendar was controlled by the Church and included numerous saints' days and occasions for worship as well as longer periods of holidays (holy days) for Christmas and Easter. There were also rest days and time off to mark events such as weddings and wakes and fairs. Altogether these non-working days accounted for about one-third of the year in England and more in other parts of Europe such as France and Spain, where it is thought five months of the year were devoted to such religious and festive activities.[37]

All these non-work days posed a problem for the pioneering capitalists and for Protestant leaders such as Luther, who saw them as opportunities for 'carousing, idleness, gambling, and gluttony'. They campaigned for reductions and in the sixteenth century the 'Puritans launched a holy crusade against holidays, demanding that only one day a week be set aside for rest.' By the nineteenth century many workers in both the US and England were working a six-day week with only Good Friday and Christmas as holidays, and some workers worked 70 hours a week.[38]

There was a big incentive for industrial employers to increase the hours that workers worked because they tended to pay them by the day or week and so extra hours worked in this time did not cost the employer any more. Firms that were able to get more hours out of their workers for a given wage became more competitive and other firms were forced to follow. Even where piece rates were used, they tended to be so low that workers had to work long hours to earn sufficient income to live on. Since workers had few alternatives apart from the poorhouses or starvation, they were unable to oppose these trends. Hours rose steadily in the nineteenth century, reaching 75–90 a week in factories in the US.[39] Indeed, the working week for most occupations was over 60 hours.[40]

It was not until the workers organised into unions to fight long hours that they won the principle of being paid according to the number of hours they worked, but this did not lead automatically to shorter hours. Although unions did manage, through a long and concerted campaign, to bring hours down towards the end of the nineteenth century,[41] the average number of working hours per week remained over 50 until Henry Ford reduced it to 40 hours (see Chapter 12).

It suited employers to have their employees work long hours for several other reasons which Juliet Schor outlines in *The Overworked American*. First, firms increasingly borrowed money for expensive equipment and repayment could be completed more quickly (and therefore at less cost) if the equipment was used around the clock. Second, employers preferred to have fewer employees working longer hours because it was easier to find and train a smaller number of quality employees with suitable work experience.[42]

In modern times workers have continued to work long hours whilst others are unemployed. Indeed it is the presence of unemployment that enables employers to demand longer hours from those who feel they are lucky to have a job. In the 1980s it was estimated that overtime in the US steel industry cost workers about ten thousand jobs. In the automobile industry it was over eighty thousand jobs, and in the mining industry the situation was similar.[43]

Today it is still more economic for employers to have workers doing overtime, even if they have to pay double or triple rates, than to hire new employees because of insurance, benefits, 'high fixed costs of recruitment, training, and possibly the underwriting of future severance pay'.[44] In a recent court case the Massachusetts Supreme Court 'sided with a company that fired a single mother for refusing to work more overtime – even though she had been putting in long hours for many weeks'.[45]

White-collar and professional workers are usually paid a fixed daily, weekly or even annual salary that leaves them vulnerable to employer demands for longer hours, and provides employers with a strong incentive to demand them. Approximately 40 per cent of the US workforce is paid in this way. Not surprisingly, these people tend to work the longest hours.[46] In Australia 43 per cent of full-time workers work overtime and 65 per cent of these do not get paid for their overtime.[47] In a British study by the group Parents at Work, 64 per cent of those questioned said that they worked longer hours than were specified in their work contracts either because that was the only way to get the work done or because of the 'culture of long hours' at their workplace.[48]

Some professional groups and management executives work 70–80 hours per week, with extra work in times of heavy demand. Over 80 per cent of professional scientists and engineers surveyed by the Association of Professional Engineers, Scientists and Managers of Australia (APESMA) said they regularly worked unpaid overtime.[49] Even in Europe business executives work long hours, with more than four out of five working at least 50 hours a week and a significant number (18 per cent in Germany and 17 per cent in the Netherlands) working more than 65 hours a week.[50]

In such situations those who refuse to work these hours will be passed over when it comes to promotions, because refusal is taken as an indicator of lack of commitment to the company: 'For every aspiring manager determined to limit his or her hours, there are usually many more willing to give the company whatever time it demands.' And such jobs often carry such high salaries, benefits and status that they are in demand, so employers have most of the bargaining power.[51]

Stella Fearnley, an accountant turned academic, left public practice after more than 15 years when she realised that it had taken over her life:

> The profession has developed a work ethic and an organisational structure built around the way men work. There is this overwhelming view that in order to succeed in the profession you have to work yourself stupid, that it has to be the one and only focus in your life, and that if you are not prepared to do that, you are not a real professional.[52]

Business Ethics magazine reported in 1998 that expecting overtime to be done by waged workers for no extra pay has become standard practice in the US. A few years earlier the Employment Policy Foundation had estimated that the value of unpaid overtime was $19 billion each year. Here we are not talking about professionals on salaries who work long hours but secretaries, sales assistants and technicians who have a right to overtime pay.[53]

LOST LEISURE

Industrial societies define leisure by distinguishing it from work.[54] Leisure is time off the job. For this reason it is often equated with the term 'free time'. It is also usually assumed that leisure time does not include time spent on necessary or obligatory activities such as sleep, washing, household chores, and looking after children. There is an element of choice in leisure. One feels that one is doing something that one wants to do.

The experience of leisure in an industrial society is even more specific than the above definitions indicate. First and foremost leisure is a means of recovery from work and replenishment for further work. The most obvious need is to recover from physical fatigue. This is achieved through sitting and lying around, general inactivity and relaxation. Relaxation also helps the recovery from stress and tension. 'Tension management', according to Edward Gross,[55] comes about through the cathartic effects of some forms of leisure, including humour and spectatorship. Work colleague relationships are also important to tension management in some professions where failure and emotional stress are part of the job.

As long as leisure's status remains much inferior to that accorded work, the full potential of leisure activities will remain unexploited. 'Because America has a working tradition rather than a leisure tradition, leisure to corporate America has been a time for relief and escape, to recharge one's batteries for the work ahead.'[56] Entertainment enables recovery from boredom and concentration. It may provide a diversion from the workaday world into something quite different in terms of place, pace and style, or it may provide an escape into the realms of imagination and fantasy. Hobbies and 'do-it-yourself' activities are undertaken in an effort to compensate for the fragmented nature of modern work and the activity is often reminiscent of pre-industrial forms of work.[57] Edward Gross uses the term 'adaptation' here to describe leisure's role in answering the need for restoration from boredom, compensation for the deadening effect of work, and relief from the strain of 'work's purposefulness'.[58]

The value of leisure has become further circumscribed and stunted by the efforts of marketers to turn leisure into consumption. The consuming that people do during their free time is now essential to the continuation of industrial culture as we know it: 'leisure becomes the time when money is spent to keep the economy going'.[59] In earlier times the games which workers used to play – such as quoits, bowls or rabbit coursing – were free.[60] Today, much of our leisure comes prepackaged and is limited to that which is commercially exploitable. People are conditioned to consume by advertising and their leisure activities reflect that conditioning. Leisure has become concerned with commodities more than activities. Television, video recorders, boats and stereos become the basic requirements of the good life. Leisure activities such as reading, visiting friends, going to social clubs, and community activities have declined.[61]

The nature of modern leisure is dictated by work patterns. It is segmented and structured around work hours. Because free time falls outside of work hours, leisure comes in short bursts and 'inconvenient batches'.[62] For working people it comes at the end of the day and at weekends, with three or four weeks of holiday a year. This limits the sorts of activities that can be undertaken as leisure. Activities must be short or be able to be divided into short bursts. They must not affect a person's work performance or their ability to turn up on time for the job. They must be close to home, except for holiday periods and during retirement.[63] These short bursts of free time are the same for a majority of workers: Saturday and Sunday and evenings. This causes what Harold Wilensky calls the 'bunching' of leisure, which creates crowding and congestion, queuing and service overload: as a result, an enormous amount of free time is wasted in waiting and frustration.[64]

The work ethic makes us suspicious of anything that looks like laziness or idleness and Kenneth Roberts suggests that industrial success depends on the devaluation of spare time.[65] The more obvious effect of the work ethic on leisure is the compulsion to be doing something, preferably something productive. Many people feel compelled to spend their leisure time making additions to their house, gardening, tinkering with 'do-it-yourself' kits or doing handicrafts. It would be shameful to admit that one spent one's time doing nothing – lounging around, contemplating....

> In North America, the traditional vacation is, more often than not, another tightly scheduled week with an itinerary resembling a week at the office....
>
> Weekends are used to attend to miscellaneous chores and personal business. Time is spent on repairing houses, mowing lawns, and caring for children. Weekend busyness adds to the burnout already experienced during the work-week.[66]

Leland Ryken, author of *Work and Leisure in Christian Perspective*, claims that 'People who overvalue work tend either to be passive and lethargic in their leisure or to work at their play, carrying over the intensity and competitiveness of their work into their leisure....'[67]

Work has become so central to most people's lives that they would have difficulty knowing what to do with themselves without it. Many people do not know how to relax and find leisure time unsatisfactory. A study by the US Department of Commerce found that only six out of ten people said they got 'a great deal' of satisfaction from their leisure time. Many people fear retirement and some find they have difficulty coping with it: 'Death or senility is common within two years of retirement; suicide is also a possibility.' One study found that more than half of those who had accepted early retirement packages were wanting to return to work within three months. Similarly, the authors of *Suddenly Rich* found that those who win or inherit large amounts of money and leave their jobs often find it difficult to get used to the lack of routine and purpose that those jobs had given them.[68]

Nevertheless, workers are not particularly happy about the long hours they work. In Australia nearly half of those surveyed feel 'pressed for time', according to the Bureau of Statistics.[69] In the ACTU survey over half the workers surveyed said they were unhappy with the balance of work and family life.[70] In Canada, 90 per cent of people interviewed in an Ontario government survey said they did not have the time or the energy they would like to take part in leisure activities. Forty per cent of Canadians say they sleep less to make more time. And almost half would happily forgo a day's pay if they could have an extra day of free time.[71]

In Britain some 80 per cent of parents with young children wish they could spend more time with their children.[72] A study of British workers found that six in ten don't like their jobs, feel insecure and stressed about their work, are exhausted after a day's work, and don't feel the work is of any use to society. Half of them say their work depresses them and 43 per cent have problems sleeping because of their work.[73]

In Japan a 1999 survey by the Citizen Watch Company found that Japanese workers are more likely to go without breakfast, spend long hours commuting, hardly talk to their spouses, and get less than five hours sleep at night than workers twenty-five years ago.[74] A 1993 Gallup poll found that Americans feel more rushed than Japanese (see Table 13.1).[75]

TABLE 13.1 THE US RUSH FACTOR

US surveys	1965	1975	1985	1992
People 18–64 years old 'always feeling rushed'	24	28	35	38

Source: R. Gittins, 'Work: the Long and the Short of It', *Sydney Morning Herald*, 8 September 1999, p. 19.

Only 30 per cent of American workers said they were satisfied with the number of hours they worked compared with 45 per cent in 1976.[76] The proportion of all workers surveyed wanting to work shorter hours went up from 47 per cent in 1992 to 63 per cent in 1997.[77] Three-quarters of Americans surveyed in 1996 said they got less than eight hours sleep a night and 40 per cent said they got less than six hours. Half of those surveyed thought they should be sleeping longer.[78]

Almost half of Americans surveyed felt they didn't have enough time to spend with their spouses and 39 per cent felt they didn't have enough time to spend with their children.[79] One economist, Victor Fuchs, found that US parents were spending 10–12 hours per week less with their children in 1986 compared with 1960. Another found that many children have to look after themselves.[80]

Long working hours mean that people have to sacrifice some of the things they would rather be doing:

> Predictably, they are spending less time on the basics, like sleeping and eating. Parents are devoting less attention to their children. Stress is on the rise, partly owing to the 'balancing act' of reconciling the demands of work and family life.[81]

People with dependent children notice the lack of leisure most acutely,[82] although top salary earners are able to buy services for domestic activities which they lack the time to do themselves. Purchased domestic services include housekeeping, meals, 'valet birthday parties' for their children, and novel services from agencies such as Grandma Please that provide a listening and homework help service for children of busy parents. According to Suzanne Franks in *Having None of It*, 'this sector represents the work-rich buying other people's time for themselves'.[83] Such services are not an option for the poorly paid, particularly working women, who must somehow juggle family responsibilities with work commitments. Franks describes how the 'nineties hyper-woman is more likely to lie awake at night compiling endless mental lists of all the things that need to be done the next day' and emerge totally exhausted at the end of each day.[84]

Overwork can lead to tiredness and lack of sleep, which can in turn cause a loss in 'creativity and decision-making abilities'. A person may become irritable and depressed or even paranoid. In fact, most people in modern economies don't get enough sleep or at least they get much less sleep than people in previous centuries. Fatigue is also an increasing factor when workers are expected to work long and irregular hours.[85] In Australia, hundreds of truck drivers fall asleep whilst driving long trips without sufficient rest.[86]

The Southern European practice of afternoon siestas has been stigmatised as indicative of a lack of work ethic, but sleep researchers have found that an afternoon nap is not only natural for the body but helps people to be more productive and creative afterwards. The whole idea of having too much sleep is very much a consequence of the work ethic, which views sleep as unproductive and something that should be kept to a minimum.[87]

An insurance analysis by WorkCover found that overwork and stress at work caused claims amounting to $60 million annually against Australian employers for conditions such as depression, anxiety and sleep disturbances. The number of claims was increasing by 40 per cent each year.[88] The ACTU survey found that 49 per cent of those surveyed said they had 'suffered health problems because of their work conditions'.[89]

Overwork and tiredness can also lead to accidents that can kill and maim those who work with dangerous equipment and chemicals. In Australia alone,

3,000 people die each year from the work they do: 'For every two people dying on the roads, there are three who die after being crushed, burned, drowned, or injured by chemicals at work.'[90] Tiredness can also put other people at risk, as pointed out by the *Medical Journal of Australia* which argues that doctors are putting themselves and their patients at risk by working long shifts at hospitals.[91] The ACTU survey found that 25 per cent of workers surveyed had experienced accidents or near misses at work because of working arrangements.[92]

In Japan they have a word to describe death from overwork. *Karoshi*, or 'Salaryman Sudden Death Syndrome', is a well-documented phenomenon involving men, mainly white-collar workers on a salary, who suffer early deaths. It is defined as a

> condition in which psychologically unsound work processes are allowed to continue in a way that disrupts the worker's normal life rhythms, leading to a buildup of fatigue in the body and accompanied by a worsening of preexistent high blood pressure and a hardening of the arteries, finally resulting in a fatal breakdown.[93]

It is estimated that 10,000 Japanese people, generally aged between 34 and 61, die each year from overwork, as many as die in car accidents.[94] In Japan, loyalty to one's employer is extremely important and this loyalty 'is often measured by the time spent at one's desk'. Japanese workers are reluctant to leave the office before their boss does, so subordinates suffer down the line if those at the top work long hours. '*Karoshi* victims labour for weeks without adequate rest, then collapse and die without warning.'[95]

In the US the effects of work are less dramatic but manifest themselves in stress, heart disease, hypertension, depression, gastric problems and many other health problems related to stress, exhaustion and lack of sleep. A third of American adults say they are stressed almost every day and a similar proportion feel rushed much of the time.[96]

Tired and overworked employees are not necessarily the most productive or creative employees either:

> Employees with no time to think, making careless mistakes, can cause the organization to be less innovative and less productive in the long run. Contrary to popular belief, always being in a hurry to get something done is not productive. A frantic routine leaves no time for just thinking. Creativity doesn't flow if not enough time is made available for it. A productive and successful worker needs the time to sit back, ponder the big picture, and take the long-term view.[97]

Some of the costs of overwork, and subsequent exhaustion, were described by Charles Handy in *Director* magazine:

The symptoms of tired behaviour are well established; it isn't the bleary eyes or the dropping jaw, it is the imperative to make things simpler in order to operate. We do this by polarising issues into black and white, right or wrong, no greys or in-betweens; we do it by stereotyping people and situations to fit them into familiar boxes which we know how to deal with; we shorten the time horizons and postpone all the difficult decisions until another day. When tired, we also talk rather than listen – it helps to keep us awake; we also let emotion rather than reason come to the fore, and to keep us going we look to drink and other stimulants.[98]

Despite all this, Handy says, 'We do need that adrenalin. We need our deadlines, targets and the pressure to deliver. Without them I, personally, find that I sink into lethargy and self-doubt.'[99]

CONCLUSION

People are being squeezed for time and they don't like it. Most workers around the world seldom have a free choice about how many hours they work: it is dictated by employers or by financial circumstances. The good jobs are full-time, long-hour jobs and the part-time jobs are low paid, insecure, with no benefits and poor working conditions (see Chapter 8).

In an editorial in *United States Banker*, John Milligan states that 'American business has fostered a work ethic so consuming as to be damaging to family values', acknowledging that he feels 'almost un-American to complain about long hours and sacrifice'.[100]

A few people, usually professionals or executives, have been able to change their work patterns voluntarily even though it meant taking income reductions, so that they could work reduced hours. These people are referred to as 'downshifters'. But such people are few and far between although between 40 and 66 per cent of workers tell surveyers they would like to work fewer hours even if it means a bit less pay.[101] For most people 'downshifting' is not an option, either because they do not feel they can afford an income reduction, or because meaningful, reasonably paid, alternative employment is not available. It is not in employers' interests to have workers working shorter hours.

As Juliet Schor points out, 'Capitalism has brought a dramatically increased standard of living, but at the cost of a much more demanding worklife.'[102] And much of what we spend our money on is made necessary by, or is compensation for, all that work.

256

NOTES

1 Quoted in Ernie J. Zelinski, *The Joy of Not Working: a Book for the Retired, Unemployed, and Overworked* (Berkeley, California: Ten Speed Press, 1997), p. 25.

2 Diane Fasel, *Working Ourselves to Death: the High Cost of Workaholism, the Rewards of Recovery* (San Francisco: HarperCollins, 1990), pp. 2, 9.

3 Quoted in Zelinski, note 1, p. 24.

4 Paul Wallich, 'The Analytical Economy', *Scientific American* (August 1994); Robert Gilman, 'A New Relationship with Time', *In Context* (1994).

5 'Undue Diligence: Workaholism in the US', *The Economist*, Vol. 340 (24 August 1996).

6 Barrie Stevens and Wolfgang Michalski, 'Long-term Prospects for Work and Social Cohesion in OECD Countries: an Overview of the Issues', in Stevens and Michalski, *OECD Societies in Transition: the Future of Work and Leisure* (Paris: OECD, 1994), p. 17.

7 Juliet B. Schor, *The Overworked American: the Unexpected Decline in Leisure* (New York: Basic Books, 1991), pp. 1–5, 29.

8 Kenneth Roberts, *Contemporary Society and the Growth of Leisure* (London: Longman, 1978), p. 33.

9 Larry Reynolds, 'America's Work Ethic: Lost in Turbulent Times?', *Management Review*, Vol. 81, No. 10 (1992); Schor, note 7, pp. 29–31; Charles Handy, 'Living Fast, Dying Rich', *Director*, Vol. 48, No. 1 (1994), p. 65.

10 Schor, note 7, pp. 21–9.

11 Zelinski, note 1, p. 4; Handy, note 9, p. 65.

12 'No Free Lunch Is Fast Becoming No Lunch', *Facilities Design and Management*, Vol. 15 (1996), p. 12.

13 Analytical Studies Branch, 'Why Has Inequality in Weekly Earnings Increased in Canada' (Statistics Canada, 1999). http://www.statcan.ca/english/Vlib/Research/ana80/htm.

14 Suzanne Franks, *Having None of It: Women, Men and the Future of Work* (London: Granta Books, 1999), p. 69; Stewart Lansley, *After the Gold Rush: the Trouble with Affluence: 'Consumer Capitalism' and the Way Forward* (London: Century Business Books, 1994), p. 177; Caroline Daniel, 'Working to Live or Living to Work?', *New Statesman*, Vol. 127 (10 April 1996), pp. 24–5.

15 Handy, note 9, p. 65; Frederick A. Palumbo and Paul A. Herbig, 'Salaryman Sudden Death Syndrome', *Employee Relations*, Vol. 16, No. 1 (1994).

16 Lansley, note 14.

17 '40-Hour Week Officially Dead', *Sydney Morning Herald* (7 March 1998), p. 9.

18 Adele Horin, 'All Work, Low Pay', *Sydney Morning Herald*, 27 December 1997, p. 6s.

19 Dierdre Macken, 'Revolt of the Wage Slave', *Sydney Morning Herald*, 30 May 1998, p. 6s.

20 ACTU, 'Working People Want a Balanced and Secure Working Life: ACTU Survey Reveals Many Don't Have One' (ACTU, 1999). http://www.actu.asn.au/national/media/media99/990902survey.htm.

21 Barry Bluestone and Stephen Rose, 'Overworked and Underemployed: Unravelling an Economic Enigma', *The American Prospect* (March–April 1997).

22 *Ibid.*

23 'The 1997 National Study of the Changing Workforce', *Shorter Work-time News* (20 August 1998).

24 Franks, note 14, pp. 90, 92.

25 'Undue Diligence, note 5.
26 *Ibid.*
27 Reynolds, note 9.
28 Franks, note 14, p. 176.
29 Schor, note 7, pp. 26–7.
30 Nadya Labi, 'Burning Out at Nine?', *Time* (23 November 1998), p. 86.
31 Schor, note 7, p. 44.
32 Marshall Sahlins, 'The Original Affluent Society', in Neva R. Goodwin, Frank Ackerman and David Kiron (eds), *The Consumer Society* (Washington, DC: Island Press, 1997), pp. 18–20.
33 *Ibid.*, pp. 19–20.
34 Schor, note 7, p. 6.
35 Robin Theobald, *Understanding Industrial Society: a Sociological Guide* (New York: St Martin's Press, 1994), p. 88.
36 *Ibid.*, pp. 87–8; Schor, note 7, pp. 47–8.
37 Schor, note 7, p. 47.
38 *Ibid.*, p. 51; P. Bernstein, *American Work Values: Their Origin and Development* (Albany, NY: State University of New York Press), p. 44; Anders Hayden, 'The Price of Time', *New Internationalist* (November 1998), p. 16.
39 Schor, note 7, pp. 52–7.
40 David J. Cherrington, *The Work Ethic: Working Values and Values That Work* (New York: AMACON, 1980), p. 3.
41 Schor, note 7, pp. 59, 72.
42 *Ibid.*, pp. 59–60.
43 *Ibid.*, p. 67.
44 Bluestone and Rose, note 21.
45 Diane Dujon, 'The Ethics of Work', *Dollars and Sense* (January–February 1998), p. 26.
46 Schor, note 7, p. 68.
47 Helen Trinca, 'It's Just not Working', *Sydney Morning Herald*, 7 November 1998, p. 7.
48 Franks, note 14, p. 72.
49 ACTU, note 20.
50 Richard Zelade, 'The Habits of European Executives', *International Business*, Vol. 11, No. 4 (1998), p. 6.
51 Schor, note 7, pp. 69–71.
52 Quoted in 'A Culture That's Got to Change', *Accountancy*, Vol. 112 (1993), p. 56.
53 'Unpaid Overtime: the American Workplace's Dirty Little Secret', *Shorter Work–time News* (20 August 1998).
54 Roberts, note 8, p. 4.
55 Edward Gross, 'A Functional Approach to Leisure Analysis', in Erwin Smigel (ed.), *Work and Leisure: a Contemporary Social Problem* (Connecticut: College and University Press, 1963).
56 Zelinski, note 1, p. 52.
57 Joffre Dumazedier, *Toward a Society of Leisure*, translated by Stewart McClure (New York: The Free Press, 1967), pp. 15, 72–4.
58 Gross, note 55.
59 Clive Jenkins and Barry Sherman, *The Leisure Shock* (London: Eyre Methuen, 1981), p. 242.
60 Sebastian de Grazia, *Of Time, Work and Leisure* (New York: Anchor Books, 1964), pp. 192–8.

61 Jenkins and Sherman, note 59, pp. 14–15; Robert Gilman, note 4.

62 Roberts, note 8, p. 31.

63 Schor, note 7, p. 1.

64 Harold Wilensky, 'The Uneven Distribution of Leisure: the Impact of Economic Growth on Free Time', in Smigel (ed.), note 55.

65 Roberts, note 8, p. 90.

66 Zelinski, note 1, pp. 52–3.

67 Leland Ryken, 'Teach Us to Play, Lord: We Have Long Affirmed the Protestant Work Ethic. We Need a Leisure Ethic to Match', *Christianity Today*, Vol. 35, No. 6 (1991), p. 20.

68 Zelinski, note 1, pp. 4–6.

69 David Dale, 'Stressed Out – We Work and Rest More but Do Less', *Sydney Morning Herald*, 17 December 1998.

70 ACTU, note 20.

71 Michael Posner, 'Whatever Happened to Spare Time: 'the Protestant Ethos in Turmoil', or Why We Cannot Stop Working', *World Press Review*, Vol. 38 (September 1991), p. 26.

72 Daniel, note 14, pp. 24–5.

73 Brian Dean, 'The Puritan Work Ethic' (Anxiety Culture, 1999). www.anxcult.dircon. co.uk/puritan.htm.

74 Michael Millett, 'Sorry Darling, No Headache, Just Too Busy', *Sydney Morning Herald*, 12 June 1999.

75 Desiree Cooper, 'Whistle While You Work' (Metrobeat, 1997). http://www.cln.com/charlotte/newsstand/c090697/metro.htm.

76 Murray Weidenbaum, 'A New Social Contract for the American Workplace', *Challenge!*, Vol. 38, No. 1 (1995).

77 'The 1997 National Study of the Changing Workforce', note 23.

78 Robert Wuthnow, *Poor Richard's Principle: Recovering the American Dream Through the Moral Dimension of Work, Business and Money* (Princeton, NJ: Princeton University Press, 1996), p. 22.

79 *Ibid.*, p. 22.

80 Schor, note 7, pp. 12–13.

81 *Ibid.*, p. 5.

82 Wuthnow, note 78, p. 23.

83 Franks, note 14, p. 74.

84 *Ibid.*, p. 177.

85 Ron Callus, 'Employers Flex Their Muscle on Hours', *Sydney Morning Herald*, 3 August 1999.

86 Andrew Hopkins quoted in Chris Richards, 'Dying to Work', *Background Briefing, ABC Radio*, 8 June 1997.

87 Aric Sigman, 'Caught Napping in the Office', *Personnel Management*, Vol. 3, No. 11 (1992), p. 15.

88 David Humphries and Julie Delvecchio, 'Stressed Workers Cost Companies $60 Million', *Sydney Morning Herald*, 26 January 1998, p. 1.

89 ACTU, note 20.

90 Chris Richards, 'Dying to Work', *Background Briefing, ABC Radio*, 8 June 1997.

91 Marion Downey, 'Long Hours "Are Putting Doctors, Patients at Risk"', *Sydney Morning Herald*, 15 June 1998.

92 ACTU, note 20.

93 Palumbo and Herbig, note 15.

94 Posner, note 71, p. 26; Kim Bush, 'Work Time, Free Time', *In Context* (Winter 1994).

95 Palumbo and Herbig, note 15.

96 Schor, note 7, p. 11.

97 Zelinski, note 1, p. 43.

98 Handy, note 9, p. 65.

99 *Ibid.*, p. 65.

100 John W. Milligan, 'Family Values', *United States Banker*, Vol. 105, No. 8 (1995), p. 4.

101 Stephanie Gallagher, 'You Can Afford to Quit', *Kiplinger's Personal Finance Magazine*, Vol. 52, No. 5 (1998); 'Undue Diligence'. note 5.

102 Schor, note 7, p. 10.

◇14◇

Conclusion

When the accumulation of wealth is no longer of high social importance, there will be great changes in the code of morals. We shall be able to rid ourselves of many of the pseudo-moral principles which have hag-ridden us for two hundred years, by which we have exalted some of the most distasteful of human qualities into the position of the highest virtues. We shall be able to afford to dare to assess the money motive at its true value.
John Maynard Keynes[1]

There is something ridiculous about producing unnecessary trinkets and various other products just to keep people busy working.
Ernie J. Zelinski[2]

Has the time not come to employ some mechanism other than work as the basis for distributing the wealth of a nation and for cementing the social bond?
Dominique Méda[3]

The gains in living standards in affluent countries are now being eroded by the degradation of the quality of life that is accompanying the capitalist imperatives of work and production. The environment is being degraded and rates of depression, suicides, and drug taking are all increasing in the most affluent countries.[4] Graham Burrows, a professor of psychiatry, suggests that much depression is work-related and also associated with a feeling of powerlessness. The World Health Organisation predicts that by 2020 stress will account for half of the top ten medical problems in the world.[5]

Despite a booming economy during the Clinton years, ordinary American citizens did not feel any better off. The *New York Times* headline, 'Paradox of '94: Gloomy Voters in Good Times' summed it up.[6] Over 45 million American adults (and not an insignificant number of children) are taking medications to treat depression, anxiety, stress and other psychological 'disorders'.[7] In Australia, suicides amongst young people are increasing[8] and family doctors are treating more depression.[9] A study of thousands of British civil servants found that the further down the hierarchy workers were, and the less control they had over the job, the sicker they were likely to be.[10]

Work is clearly not healthy for individuals and the products it produces are no longer healthy for the planet. Yet governments everywhere pursue policies aimed at encouraging more jobs, preferably jobs in the private sector aimed at producing things that people will pay for individually. Despite the dysfunctionality of the work ethic it continues to be promoted and praised, accepted and acquiesced to. It is one of the least challenged aspects of industrial culture, one that has also been incorporated into other cultures and political ideologies such as socialism.

Gramsci used the term 'hegemony' to describe the phenomenon by which the majority of people accept the values and political axioms that ensure their own subordination to the ruling elite. This hegemony is not stable and requires constant reinforcement. Reinforcement occurs through social conditioning, aided by leading social institutions, as well as the rejection and marginalisation of those who propose radical change. It requires the promotion of the virtues of the existing system and the denigration of alternatives as unworkable, disastrous, undesirable. Ralph Miliband observes that:

> The smooth functioning of capitalist democracy requires that the working class should accept the general validity and legitimacy of the social order; that it should believe that any grievance or demand that it may have is remediable within the confines and by traditional procedures of the political system; and that it should be convinced that any radical change in existing arrangements must be highly detrimental to its best interests.[11]

Many institutions have taken part in this process of ensuring a capitalist hegemony. Miliband notes that 'One important reason why the claims [of a capitalist democracy] can be advanced with a certain measure of plausibility and confidence is that the enterprise of indoctrination proceeds neither from a single source nor from a single doctrine or body of thought.'[12]

In this book we have seen that the work ethic, in its various forms, has been promoted by the churches, the schools, the media, political parties and government bureaucracies. Various professional and academic groups have taken part, particularly social scientists, economists, writers, and later the advertisers and public relations experts. While many of these institutions and individuals believed themselves to be independent of business leaders, at the higher levels of the social hierarchy, particularly, political 'soundness' has usually been a necessary requirement for advancement.

The work ethic has evolved over time to suit changing social conditions. From its religious origins, as a calling and moral duty to God, it evolved into a secular success ethic and the basis for justifying inequalities in wealth in society. For the upwardly mobile, work still has meaning as a road to success. But the work ethic that is advocated to those who have little chance of success is an ethic of work as responsibility to the family and the nation. This latest manifestation of the work ethic is most pronounced in the rhetoric of welfare reforms, in the language of obligation, responsibility and dependence.

Throughout the evolution of the work ethic, hard work has been associated with good character and virtue. Work has become the central feature of most people's lives, the source of their self-identity, income, status, and the respect others give them. It gives them their purpose and provides them with social relations and a structure to their day.

And just as important as being a motivator for work, the work ethic with its associated beliefs of individual responsibility, and the promise of fair rewards for hard work, has legitimised the social structure of inequalities. It has been the lens through which social inequalities have been viewed. It says that those who are poor deserve to be so because they lack a work ethic; those who are rich also deserve to be so because they have worked harder and taken better advantage of opportunities which are available to everyone. (The promotion of the work ethic and its impact on ideas and beliefs is shown in the diagram on page 264.)

The acceptance of capitalist values by workers has been more effective than force or coercion in ensuring a passive, compliant workforce. This has been done by ensuring that the virtue of work and wealth, and the resulting social order, have come to be seen as natural, desirable, morally right and inevitable. It is because of this that people consent to spending most of their waking days working for someone else.

> We have become a nation of employees. We are dependent upon others for our means of livelihood, and most people have become completely dependent upon wages. If they lose their jobs they lose every resource, except for the relief supplied by the various forms of social security. Such dependence of the mass of the people upon others for all of their income is something new in the world. For our generation, the substance of life is in another man's hands.[13]

Alan Wolfe notes in *The Seamy Side of Democracy* that 'various ideologies have associated with them certain values; if people uphold these values, belief in

263

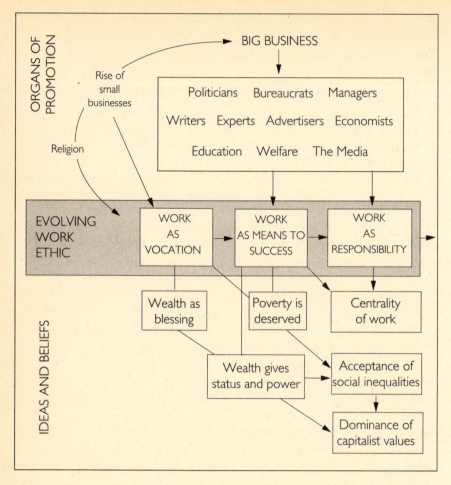

the ideology will almost automatically follow.' Although he does not list it as one, the work ethic is key value from which capitalist ideology follows. Wolfe lists individuality and competitiveness as key values in a capitalist society, because they work 'to prevent collective action for social change' and reinforce the status quo.[14] Yet both individualism and competitiveness in a capitalist society have their origins in the work ethic, as this book has demonstrated.

The values associated with the work ethic have permeated every institution of modern industrial societies; schools, government, the media, churches, family, unions, clubs. The dominance of these values has been driven by business interests with the help of large donations, infiltration of these institutions by businesspeople, and the use of public relations and advertising.

But it has also been made possible by the cooption of key intellectuals, including economists, scientists, psychologists, sociologists and others, who have all provided an intellectual rationale and demeanour for ideological beliefs.

Earl Shorris, in his book *The Oppressed Middle*, discusses how

> The most insidious of the many kinds of power is the power to define happiness. It is the dream of merchants, despots, managers, and philosophers, because whoever defines happiness can control the organization and the actions of other men: he not only assigns aspirations and desires, he constructs the system of morals by which the means of achieving happiness is judged.[15]

In a work-dominated society, happiness must be earned through hard work. The suffering and boredom associated with work is the price one has to pay in order to attain happiness.[16] Shorris goes on to say that the 'enforcing aspect of happiness is its impossibility'. It is only whilst people are seeking happiness that they can be manipulated and expected to behave predictably. A person who is happy is more likely to be independent and free of other influences. A business-minded person in an affluent society defines happiness in ways that encourage acquisitiveness, wastefulness 'and social competition through displays of material wealth'.[17]

In such a society, many people participate in this definition of happiness so that they can sell their own services and goods. Managers 'prove the system' by enjoying 'more of the signs of happiness' than those beneath them, and by the status and power they have over their subordinates. Each step up the social hierarchy offers the aspirant a small reward in terms of status, power and income, a proof of the eventual happiness in store for those who keep climbing: 'The aspirant is pushed and pulled toward his dream of managerial happiness, constantly having to renew his faith in the definition given to him by his managers to overcome the disappointments that dominate his life.'[18]

The deceptively enticing promise of consumer goods, never fulfilled, is also a reason why many workers are willing to put up with dismal working conditions. The lack of alternatives for unskilled workers and the scrambling to keep up by more affluent workers go some way to explain people's passive acceptance of their jobs, no matter how unpleasant. But they don't explain the continued work ethic people often display nor their embracing of a political and social system in which they are the losers.

Employers have specific and mutually recognised powers over their own employees through their ability to reward and punish workers. They are able to control what people do for a large part of their waking hours, when they are at work. But employers, as a social class, also have more subtle and unspecified powers over employees. They have what John Kenneth Galbraith calls conditioned power, the sort of power that people are often unaware of:

> The acceptance of authority, the submission to the will of others, becomes the higher preference of those submitting. This preference can be deliberately culti-vated – by persuasion or education. This is explicit conditioning. Or it can be dictated by the culture itself; the submission is considered to be normal, proper, or traditionally correct. This is implicit conditioning.[19]

Such conditioning means that people internalise submission as part of their own sense of what is good and moral behaviour. Rewards and punishments may reinforce this behaviour but it appears to be self-motivated.[20] Religious organisations have long practised this sort of authority through the condi-tioned power of belief.

The conditioned power of wealthy businesspeople is hidden behind a governmental decision-making structure. The existence of a parliamentary democracy that overtly makes decisions and governs provides the legitima-tion, as Habermas refers to it, for advanced capitalism, since on the face of it parliamentary democracy enables the participation of the masses in the social system.[21] The power of businesspeople to shape our culture, our aspirations and our purpose in life, and to ensure that we work for their benefit, remains largely hidden.

The political consensus in capitalist societies does not require an absence of alternative ideologies or radical thought; in fact, the existence of opposi-tion helps legitimate the prevailing ideas as the outcome of a pluralistic and democratic process. All that is required is that the competition for ideas is 'so unequal as to give a crushing advantage to one side against the other' as is the case in capitalist societies.[22]

At the start of the twenty-first century there are very few challenges to the centrality of work. John White notes in his book on the philosophy of work that 'a striking feature of most of the philosophical writings on work ... is their lack of interest in challenging' the centrality of work. He finds this particularly surprising in those who take a liberal vantage point since the cen-trality of work constrains people's lives so much: 'It seems so patently at odds with the ideal of autonomous well-being that one cannot imagine how radical thinkers could support it.'[23]

A major problem with envisaging alternatives to a work-centred life is that many people have become so reduced by their work focus that they have dif-ficulty envisaging what they would do if they had a lot of extra time. Most people spend almost all of their time working, resting from work, or spending the money they earned working. A life that is not fully taken up with work and consuming seems to offer not only boredom but also purposelessness.

Langdon Winner in his book *Autonomous Technology* took this to an extreme when he said:

> Automation is now much more than a speculative fantasy. Its capacity for the liberation from toil must be balanced against the prospect that man will find himself functionless in his own world.... In the world of mechanical or electrochemical 'dystopia' people would be left with absolutely nothing to do or be....[24]

It would be a sad world indeed if people's only function in it was to produce goods for consumption, if this was the highest they could reach for. Yet this seems to be the case today. The centrality of work in the lives of many people reduces their ability to find meaning in anything else. If work was not so predominant we could develop multiple potentials in children at school, encouraging play, creativity and experimentation. Non-vocational subjects such as philosophy and history and politics would become more popular at university. People would have time to develop their relationships with family and friends.

Part of the problem is the amount of time that work takes up, a problem recognised by the ancient Greek philosophers who observed that 'productive' work reduced people's ability to pursue politics, art and philosophy. Staffan Linder has argued that increasing wealth and productivity has led to a scarcity of time, as goods take time to use and enjoy and time to maintain. As time pressures increase, time spent waiting, thinking, visiting sick people and in personal maintenance is resented and cut down. It is for this reason that affluence has not led to the satisfaction of material needs and cultural development. Instead the shortage of time has led to hectic lifestyles, while idle time and time spent on cultivating the mind and spirit have been sacrificed.[25]

Fred Hirsch, in *Social Limits to Growth,* also talked about the scarcity of time that arises from increased consumption levels and earning the money to pay for them. Social relations such as friendship lose out under the pressure of time, since making and keeping friends is very time-consuming.[26] As the Shorter Worktime Network of Canada points out: 'Family, friendship, community, democracy – all these take time.' They suggest that the cost of lack of time in our society 'is a deficit in the healthy, socially positive development of children' and that these costs will manifest as 'government services to children – increased child protection and apprehension case loads, increased rates of youth delinquency and need for correctional facilities, etc.'[27]

Time shortages also exacerbate environmental problems as people don't have time to walk, cycle or catch public transport so they use their cars. Cars are the most energy-intensive and polluting forms of transport.[28] In the US public transport use has declined since 1945, and today 80 per cent of all passenger travel is made in private cars. And the highways they run on require four times as much land and energy to construct as railway lines.[29] People don't have time to cook so they buy processed and packaged food. They don't have time to enjoy nature so they buy packaged leisure.[30]

But time shortages are not the only consequence of the predominance of work in our lives. Work can also sap our energy and our desire to develop our potential as people. There is some evidence that routine boring jobs with no individual discretion or autonomy undermine the ability of those workers to exercise out of work hours the qualities they are unable to exercise at work. Some workers are unable to counteract the dulling affects of work during their leisure time and so avoid intellectual stimulation.[31]

Whether or not dull work breeds dull leisure, after eight hours at the office followed by a frantic rush home in peak-hour traffic few people have much energy left for anything more than dinner and television. The average Australian, according to the Bureau of Statistics, spends four in every five minutes of passive leisure with audiovisual media, particularly the television, radio and CDs.[32]

An Australian worker described how even an average workday can leave little room for other activities:

> At the end of each day you are buggered, physically buggered. You're just sort of shattered. And it takes a couple of hours when you get home of sitting down to get over it. There is no hope of being able to play with the children. I go to bed at about nine or ten so that I can get up in time to be back at work by seven in the morning. We are just work machines. They tell you that you are working for BHP for only eight hours a day, but basically you are working for the Company twenty-four hours a day.[33]

Those on high incomes also tend to be preoccupied with work. Diane Fasel, in *Working Ourselves to Death*, notes the dearth of literature on work addiction, what John O. Neikirk has called 'the pain others applaud'.[34] Whilst other addicts are stigmatised, workaholics are often admired and praised as a 'sort of paragon of virtue'[35] who is bound to succeed. Fasel also dismisses some of the myths surrounding work addiction: that only high-powered executives and yuppies become workaholics, for example, or that workaholics are happy and superproductive.[36]

Yet work addiction seems to be what employers look for in an employee. John Wareham explains to employers, in an article on 'Spotting the Hard Worker', how to choose the person who is driven by a work ethic: 'Conscientious workers usually see overtime and weekend work as opportunities to go the extra mile and get ahead in the world. They talk about feeling guilty when not engaged in some productive activity.'[37]

People who work too much and are constantly busy have little time to contemplate or to question. Anxieties are suppressed and critical thought inhibited. One is simply caught up in day-to-day affairs. To some extent keeping busy enables people to get on with lives that they don't want to think about. Work, like other addictions, enables people to cope with their fears and problems by ignoring them, not facing up to them.[38] One businessman, Thomas Asacker, noted:

> It seems that most of the people I run into simply want enough money and free time for things like annual vacations, watching television, surfing the Net, or kibitzing about this or that. Questioning the way things are and trying to improve them appears to be nothing but a waste of their 'downtime'. Business people seem particularly prone to this status quo way of living. We're running so fast that we often forget to stop, take a breath, look at the map, and question the route.[39]

Modern workers rush about so much that they don't have time to stop and consider what the point of it all is. A preoccupation with work means that they are less likely to be fully aware of life's pain, emptiness and contradictions. Fasel takes this further: 'When you are fully alive, you let yourself feel the pain of living in an environment where we pollute our water and air, where we risk nuclear annihilation, where relationships are fragmented, and so on.'[40]

Lack of time for contemplation ensures that most people will not challenge the social system. A job keeps a person busy and 'channels energies that might otherwise be disruptive' into work that is specified and supervised by others.[41] Workers are not left with long hours of inactivity during which they might begin to feel purposeless and start questioning the order of things. The 'constant low-level attention' required for television and movie watching, radio listening and newspaper reading doesn't allow people to be alone with themselves.[42] They are always busy and doing something, too busy to concern themselves with larger social issues, even if they are directly affected. The quest for money unites people as unquestioning instruments of the industrial production system.

A Canadian Buddhist observes:

> consumer society is moved by people who are in flight. Having no authentic personality they hide their emptiness from themselves and others with the accoutrements now so familiar, from mechanical gadgets to designer clothing to computer games. Totally ignorant of the exercises of meditation and renunciation that would enable them to find themselves, they lead active, busy lives that get them through their years, in plentiful social contact with others vainly seeking to fill the gap caused by the missing contact with themselves.[43]

Work need not be so all-embracing and time-consuming. But the endless production of consumer products necessitated by a work ethic, our acceptance of the quest for ever-increasing profits as the highest motivation, and our granting of status and power to those who provide us with jobs that enable us to fulfil these goals, prevents us pursuing alternative, superior goals and a better quality of life.

It is a combination of social conditioning and daily busyness which prevents a deeper questioning of the direction in which modern societies are going. There are various choices for the future. If work is merely a means to an end it is time to re-evaluate what those ends are. And if production and consumption are no longer of paramount importance, indeed destructive to our social and environmental wellbeing, then we need to re-evaluate the influence that we allow corporations to have over social institutions and government policies.

We also need to find new ways of judging and valuing each other which are not dependent on work and income. The search for social status is an important determinant of people's behaviour and most excess consumption and work is driven by it. The question is, can enough people see through the conditioning that we are subject to and recognise that it is detrimental to our future?

England's dream of industry
Is on the wane at last.
And ancient dreams of wisdom's sheen
Are waxing from the past.
As old dreams die upon the earth
Another comes to birth.[44]

NOTES

1 John Maynard Keynes, 'Economic Possibilities for Our Grandchildren', in J. M. Keynes, *Essays in Persuasion* (Macmillan, 1931).

2 Ernie J. Zelinski, *The Joy of Not Working: a Book for the Retired, Unemployed, and Overworked* (Berkeley, California: Ten Speed Press, 1997), p. 36.

3 Dominique Méda, 'New Perspectives on Work as Value', *International Labour Review*, Vol. 135, No. 6 (1996).

4 Antony Kidman, 'Education is the Key to Helping the Depressed Cope', *Sydney Morning Herald*, 3 August 1999.

5 Cited in Geoff Strong, 'The Darkness Within', *Sydney Morning Herald*, 17 July 1999, p. 39.

6 Clifford Cobb, Ted Halstead and Jonathan Rowe, 'If GDP Is Up, Why is America

Down?', *The Atlantic Monthly* (October 1995).

7 Andrew Kimbrell, 'Breaking the Job Lock' (Utne Reader Online, 1999). http://www.utne.com/

8 Marion Downey, 'Suicide Rises as Spending Falls', *Sydney Morning Herald*, 11 February 1999.

9 Stephen Cauchi, 'GPs Treating More for Depression: Study', *The Age*, 30 October 1999.

10 Cited on Norman Swan and Len Syme, 'Mastering the Control Factor, Part One', *The Health Report, ABC Radio*, 9 November 1998.

11 Ralph Miliband, *Capitalist Democracy in Britain* (Oxford: Oxford University Press, 1982), p. 54.

12 *Ibid.*, p. 78.

13 Frank Tannenbaum, quoted in A. R. Gini and T. J. Sullivan, 'A Critical Overview', in Gini and Sullivan (eds), *It Comes with the Territory: an Inquiry Concerning Work and the Person* (New York: Random House, 1989), p. 4.

14 Alan Wolfe, *The Seamy Side of Democracy: Repression in America*, 2nd edn (New York: Longman, 1978), pp. 115–17.

15 Earl Shorris, *The Oppressed Middle: Politics of Middle Management* (Garden City, NY: Anchor Press, 1981), pp. 17–18.

16 Brian Dean, 'The Puritan Work Ethic' (Anxiety Culture, 1999), www.anxcult.dircon.co.uk/puritan.htm.

17 Shorris, note 14, pp. 22, 25.

18 *Ibid.*, pp. 26–7.

19 John Kenneth Galbraith, *The Anatomy of Power* (London: Hamish Hamilton, 1984), p. 24.

20 *Ibid.*, p. 35.

21 Nicholas Abercombie, Stephen Hill and Bryan S. Turner, *The Dominant Ideology Thesis* (London: George Allen and Unwin, 1980), pp. 16–17.

22 Ralph Miliband, *The State in Capitalist Society* (London: Quartet Books, 1969), p. 164.

23 John White, *Education and the End of Work: a New Philosophy of Work and Learning* (London: Cassell, 1997), p. 40.

24 Langdon Winner, *Autonomous Technology: Technics-Out-Of-Control as a Theme in Political Thought* (MIT Press, 1983), p. 33.

25 Staffan Burenstam Linder, *The Harried Leisure Class* (New York: Columbia University Press, 1970).

26 Fred Hirsch, *Social Limits to Growth* (London: Routledge and Kegan Paul, 1977).

27 Shorter Worktime Network of Canada, 'Lost Time: Time, Work and Family' (Shorter Worktime Network of Canada, 1999). http://www.vcn.bc.ca/timework/losttime.htm.

28 Jonathan Harris, 'Consumption and the Environment: Overview Essay', in Neva R. Goodwin, Frank Ackerman and David Kiron (eds), *The Consumer Society* (Washington, DC: Island Press, 1997), p. 272.

29 Clive Ponting, 'Creating the Affluent Society', in Neva R. Goodwin, Frank Ackerman and David Kiron (eds), *The Consumer Society* (Washington, DC: Island Press, 1997), pp. 289–90.

30 Harris, note 27, p. 272.

31 Gini and Sullivan, note 12, pp. 27–8.

32 Australian Bureau of Statistics, 'How Australians Use Their Time, 1997' (Australian Bureau of Statistics, 1997), http://www.abs.gov.au.

33 R. J. Kriegler, 'Workers and Bosses', in Craig R. Littler (ed.), *The Experience of Work*

(UK: Gower Publishing, 1985) , p. 153.

34 Diane Fasel, *Working Ourselves to Death: the High Cost of Workaholism, the Rewards of Recovery* (San Francisco: Harper Collins, 1990), p. 2.

35 W. Oates, quoted in Adrian Furnham, *The Protestant Work Ethic: the Psychology of Work-Related Beliefs and Behaviours* (London: Routledge, 1990), p. 158.

36 Fasel, note 34, Chapter 1.

37 John Wareham, 'Spotting the Hard Worker', *Across the Board*, Vol. 33 (January 1996), p. 49.

38 J. R. Waddell, 'The Grindstone', *Supervision*, Vol. 54, No. 12 (1993)

39 Quoted in Thomas A. Stewart, 'Gray Flannel Suit? Moi?', *Fortune* (16 March 1998), p. 76.

40 Fasel, note 34, p. 111.

41 Paul L. Wachtel, *The Poverty of Affluence: a Psychological Portrait of the American Way of Life* (Philadelphia, PA: New Society Publishers, 1989), p. 245.

42 Sebastian de Grazia, *Of Time, Work and Leisure* (New York: Anchor Books, 1964), p. 324.

43 Cited in Nathan Keyfitz, 'Consumerism and the New Poor', *Social Science and Public Policy*, Vol. 29, No. 2 (1992).

44 Richard Gosden, unpublished poem, 2000.

Bibliography

HISTORY OF THE WORK ETHIC

Alger, H. (1900). *Bound to Rise or Up the Ladder.* Chicago: Saalfield Publishing.

Anthony, P. D. (1977). *The Ideology of Work.* London: Tavistock Publications.

Applebaum, H. (1992). *The Concept of Work: Ancient, Medieval, and Modern.* Albany, NY: State University of New York Press.

Bernstein, P. (1997). *American Work Values: their Origin and Development.* Albany, NY: State University of New York Press.

Chandler, A. D., and Tedlow, R. S. (1985). *The Coming of Managerial Capitalism: a Casebook History of American Economic Institutions.* Homewood, Illinois: Richard D. Irwin.

Cherrington, D. J. (1980). *The Work Ethic: Working Values and Values that Work.* New York: AMACON.

DeVitis, J. L., and Rich, J. M. (1996). *The Success Ethic, Education, and the American Dream.* Albany, NY: State University of New York Press.

Fullerton, K. (1973). 'Calvinism and Capitalism: an Explanation of the Weber Thesis'. In R. W. Green (ed.), *Protestantism, Capitalism and Social Science: the Weber Thesis Controversy* (2nd edn, pp. 8–31). Lexington, Mass.: D. C. Heath and Co.

Halévy, E. (1960). *England in 1815* (E. I. Watkin and D. A. Barber, trans.). (1st paperback edn). (Vol. I). London: Ernest Benn.

Hammond, J. L. and Hammond, B. (1937). *The Town Labourer 1760–1832* (Left Book Club edn). London: Victor Gollancz.

Hengel, M. (1974). *Property and Riches in the Early Church: Aspects of a Social History of Early Christianity* (John Bowden, trans.). (British edn). London: SNM Press.

Marshall, G. (1982). *In Search of the Spirit of Capitalism: an Essay on Max Weber's Protestant Ethic Thesis.* London: Hutchinson.

Tawney, R. H. (1938). *Religion and the Rise of Capitalism: a Historical Study.* Harmondsworth: Penguin Books.

Thomis, M. I. (1974). *The Town Labourer and the Industrial Revolution.* London: B. T. Batsford.

Thompson, E. P. (1980). *The Making of the English Working Class.* London: Penguin.

Tilgher, A. (1931). *Work: What It Has Meant to Men Through the Ages* (Dorothy Canfield Fisher, trans.). London: George G. Harrap.

Ward, J. T. (1975). *The Age of Change 1770–1870*. London: A. and C. Black.

Weber, M. (1967). *The Protestant Ethic and the Spirit of Capitalism* (Talcott Parsons, trans.). (2nd edn). London: George Allen and Unwin.

WORK ETHIC IN THE TWENTIETH CENTURY

Ali, A. J. (1995). 'Work Ethic and Loyalty in Canada'. *Journal of Social Psychology*, 135 (1), 31–7.

Bleakley, D. (1983). *Work: the Shadow and the Substance*. London: SCM Press.

Cherrington, D. J. (1980). *The Work Ethic: Working Values and Values that Work*. New York: AMACON.

Chinoy, E. (1992). *Automobile Workers and the American Dream* (2nd edn). Urbana and Chicago: University of Illinois Press.

Colson, C. and Eckerd, J. (1991). *Why America Doesn't Work*. Dallas: Word Publishing.

DeVitis, J. L. and Rich, J. M. (1996). *The Success Ethic, Education, and the American Dream*. Albany, NY: State University of New York Press.

Eisenberger, R. (1989). *Blue Monday: the Loss of the Work Ethic in America*. New York: Paragon House.

Fasel, D. (1990). *Working Ourselves to Death: the High Cost of Workaholism, the Rewards of Recovery*. San Francisco: Harper Collins.

Franks, S. (1999). *Having None of It: Women, Men and the Future of Work*. London: Granta Books.

Furnham, A. (1990). *The Protestant Work Ethic: the Psychology of Work-Related Beliefs and Behaviours*. London: Routledge.

Gini, A. R. and Sullivan, T. J. (1989). 'A Critical Overview'. In A. R. Gini and T. J. Sullivan (eds), *It Comes with the Territory: an Inquiry Concerning Work and the Person* (pp. 1–35). New York: Random House.

Lipset, S. M. (1992). 'The Work Ethic, Then and Now'. *Journal of Labor Research*, 13 (1), 45–54.

Maccoby, M. and Terzi, K. A. (1989). 'What Happened to the Work Ethic?' In A. R. Gini and T. J. Sullivan (eds), *It Comes with the Territory: an Inquiry Concerning Work and the Person*, (1989 edn, pp. 65–77). New York: Random House.

MéDa, D. (1996). 'New Perspectives on Work as Value'. *International Labour Review*, 135 (6), 633–43.

Pascarella, P. (1984). *The New Achievers: Creating a Modern Work Ethic*. New York: The Free Press.

Posner, M. (1991, September). 'Whatever Happened to Spare Time: "The Protestant Ethos in Turmoil", or Why We Cannot Stop Working'. *World Press Review*, 38, 26–7.

Reynolds, L. (1992). 'America's Work Ethic: Lost in Turbulent Times?' *Management Review*, 81 (10), 20–5.

'Undue Diligence: Workaholism in the U.S.' (1996). *The Economist*, 340 (7980), 47–9.

Watson, T. (1987). *Sociology, Work and Industry*. (2nd edn). London: Routledge and Kegan Paul.

Wuthnow, R. (1996). *Poor Richard's Principle: Recovering the American Dream Through the Moral Dimension of Work, Business and Money*. Princeton, NJ: Princeton University Press.

Yankelovich, D. and Immerwahr, J. (1984). 'Putting the Work Ethic to Work'. *Society*, 21 (2), 58–76.

Zelinski, E. J. (1997). *The Joy of Not Working: a Book for the Retired, Unemployed, and Overworked*. Berkeley, California: Ten Speed Press.

MANAGING AND MOTIVATING WORKERS

Andrew, E. (1981). *Closing the Iron Cage: the Scientific Management of Work and Leisure*. Montréal: Black Rose Books.

Baritz, L. (1974). *The Servants of Power: a History of the Use of Social Science in American Industry*. (Reprint edn). Westport, Connecticut: Greenwood Press.

Blackburn, K. (1996). 'Preaching "the Gospel of Efficiency": The Promotion of Ideas about Profit-Sharing and Payment by Results in Australia, 1915–1929'. *Australian Historical Studies* (107), 257–80.

Carey, A. (1995). *Taking the Risk Out of Democracy*. Sydney: UNSW Press.

Davis, C. (1996, Autumn). '"You Are the Company": the Demands of Employment in the Emerging Corporate Culture, Los Angeles, 1900–1930.' *Business History Review, 70*, 328–62.

Fones-Wolf, E. A. (1990). 'Beneath Consensus: Business, Labor, and the Post-War Order'. Unpublished PhD thesis, University of Massachusetts.

Gee, J. P., Hull, G. and Lankshear, C. (1996). *The New Work Order: Behind the Language of the New Capitalism*. Sydney: Allen and Unwin.

Littler, C. R. and Salaman, G. (1985). 'The Design of Jobs'. In C. R. Littler (ed.), *The Experience of Work* (pp. 85–104). UK: Gower Publishing.

Mills, C. W. (1948, December). *The Contribution of Sociology to Studies of Industrial Relations*. Paper presented at the Proceedings of the First Annual Meeting of Industrial Relations Research Association.

Sampson, A. (1996). *Company Man: the Rise and Fall of Corporate Life*. (Paperback edn). London: Harper Collins Business.

Taylor, F. W. (1911). 'The Principles of Scientific Management', *Scientific Management*. Westport, Connecticut: Greenwood Press.

Theobald, R. (1994). *Understanding Industrial Society: a Sociological Guide*. New York: St Martin's Press.

Thompson, P. (1983). *The Nature of Work: an Introduction to Debates on the Labour Process*. Hampshire, UK: Macmillan Education.

Viteles, M. S. (1953). *Motivation and Morale in Industry*. New York: W. W. Norton and Co.

Watson, T. (1987). *Sociology, Work and Industry*. (2nd edn). London: Routledge and Kegan Paul.

Whalley, P. (1986). *The Social Production of Technical Work: the Case of British Engineers*. Hampshire: Macmillan.

Whyte, W. H. (1960). *The Organization Man*. (2nd edn). Harmondsworth: Penguin.

Zussman, R. (1985). *Mechanics of the Middle Class: Work and Politics Among American Engineers*. Berkeley: University of California Press.

UNEMPLOYMENT, WELFARE AND THE WORK ETHIC

Blair, T. (1997). 'Welfare Reform: Giving People the Will to Win'. *Vital Speeches of the Day, 63* (18), 549–52.

Bright, R. A. (1978). 'Dole Bludgers or Tax Dodgers: Who Is the Deviant?' In P. R. Wilson and J. Braithwaite (eds), *Two Faces of Deviance: Crimes of the Powerless and the Powerful,* (pp. 161–76). Brisbane: University of Queensland Press.

Brotherhood of St Laurence (1974). *Why so Harsh on the Unemployed? a Second Discussion Paper.* Fitzroy, Victoria: Brotherhood of St Laurence.

Casse, D. (1997). 'Why Welfare Reform is Working'. *Commentary,* 104 (3), 36–41.

Colton, M., Casas, F., Drakeford, M., Roberts, S., Scholte, E. and Williams, M. (1997). *Stigma and Social Welfare: an International Comparative Study.* Aldershot, UK: Avebury.

Cooper, M. (1997, 2 June). 'When Push Comes to Shove'. *The Nation,* 264, 11–5.

Corn, D. (1997, 5 May). 'Welfare, Inc.' *The Nation,* 264, 4–5.

Deacon, A. (1977, 17 November). 'Scrounger Bashing'. *New Society,* 355–6.

'Dethroning the Welfare Queen: the Rhetoric of Reform' (1994). *Harvard Law Review,* 107 (8), 2013–30.

'Ending Welfare: Were We Wrong?' (1997). *The Progressive,* 61 (10), 8–9.

Feagin, J. R. (1975). *Subordinating the Poor.* Englewood Cliffs, NJ: Prentice-Hall.

'Finding a Place for the Jobless in Discrimination Theory'. (1997). *Harvard Law Review,* 110 (7), 1609–26.

Gosden, R. (1997, June–July). 'Shrinking the Dole Queue'. *Arena Magazine,* 29, 39–41.

Jackson, D. (1997, March). 'Why Do Stereotypes and Lies Persist?' *Nieman Reports,* 51, 44–5.

Janigan, M. (1995, 4 December). 'Wading into the Welfare Mess'. *Maclean's,* 108, 32ff.

Kaus, M. (1986, 7 July). 'The Work Ethic State: the Only Way to Break the Culture of Poverty'. *The New Republic,* 22–33.

McCrate, E. (1997, September/October). 'Hitting Bottom: Welfare "Reform" and Labor Markets'. *Dollars and Sense,* 34–5.

Miller, G. (1991). *Enforcing the Work Ethic: Rhetoric and Everyday Life in a Work Incentive Program.* Albany, NY: State University of New York Press.

Morris, L. (1994). *Dangerous Classes: the Underclass and Social Citizenship.* London: Routledge.

Ogborn, K. (1986). *Workfare in America: an Initial Guide to the Debate* (Discussion Paper No. 6). Woden, ACT: Department of Social Security.

Peterson, J. (1997). 'Ending Welfare as We Know It: the Symbolic Importance of Welfare Policy in America'. *Journal of Economic Issues,* 31 (2), 425–51.

'The Muddled Maths of Welfare to Work'. (1997). *The Economist,* 342 (8007), 25–6.

Walters, W. (1997). 'The "Active Society": New Designs for Social Policy'. *Policy and Politics,* 25 (3), 221–34.

'Welfare as They Know It'. (1997). *Harper's,* 295, 24ff.

Williams, L. A. (1997). 'Rethinking Low-Wage Markets and Dependency'. *Politics and Society,* 25 (4), 541–50.

Windschuttle, K. (1975–76, December–January). 'Dole Bludgers: How the Media Created a Phoney Scandal'. *New Journalist,* 18–24.

'Working for Whose Welfare?' (1996). *Canada and the World Backgrounder,* 62, 20–1.

ATTITUDES TO SOCIAL INEQUALITY

Asma, S. T. (1993). 'The New Social Darwinism: Deserving your Destitution'. *The Humanist,* 53 (5), 10–2.

Connell, R. W. (1977). *Ruling Class Ruling Culture: Studies of Conflict, Power and Hegemony in*

Australian Life. Cambridge: Cambridge University Press.

Davies, A. F. and Encel, S. (1970). *Australian Society: a Sociological Introduction*. (2nd edn). Melbourne: Cheshire.

Galambos, L. (1975). *The Public Image of Big Business in America, 1880–1940*. Baltimore: The John Hopkins University Press.

Galbraith, J. K. (1956). *American Capitalism: the Concept of Countervailing Power*. (Sentry edn). Boston: Houghton Mifflin.

Galbraith, J. K. (1984). *The Anatomy of Power*. London: Hamish Hamilton.

Galbraith, J. K. (1992). *The Culture of Contentment*. London: Penguin.

Jones, G. (1980). *Social Darwinism and English Thought: the Interaction Between Biological and Social Theory*. Sussex: The Harvester Press.

Josephson, M. (1962). *The Robber Barons: the Great American Capitalists 1861–1901*. London: Eyre and Spottiswoode.

Kitch, M. J. (1967). *Capitalism and the Reformation*. London: Longman.

Lane, R. E. (1962). *Political Ideology: Why the American Common Man Believes What He Does*. New York: The Free Press.

Marchand, R. (1998). *Creating the Corporate Soul: the Rise of Public Relations and Corporate Imagery in American Big Business*. Berkeley: University of California Press.

Miliband, R. (1982). *Capitalist Democracy in Britain*. Oxford: Oxford University Press.

Miliband, R. (1969). *The State in Capitalist Society*. London: Quartet Books.

Mills, C. W. (1956). *The Power Elite*. Oxford: Oxford University Press.

Schwarz, J. E. (1997). *Illusions of Opportunity: the American Dream in Question*. New York: W. W. Norton.

Sloan, J. W. (1997). 'The Reagan Presidency, Growing Inequality, and the American Dream'. *Policy Studies Journal*, 25 (Fall), 371–86.

Tedlow, R. S. (1979). *Keeping the Corporate Image: Public Relations and Business, 1900–1950*. Greenwich, Connecticut: Jai Press.

Wachtel, P. L. (1989). *The Poverty of Affluence: a Psychological Portrait of the American Way of Life*. Philadelphia, PA: New Society Publishers.

Whalen, C. J. (1996, September). 'The Age of Anxiety: Erosion of the American Dream'. *USA Today*, 125, 14–16.

Wolfe, A. (1978). *The Seamy Side of Democracy: Repression in America*. (2nd edn). New York: Longman.

EDUCATION AND THE WORK ETHIC

Aronowitz, S. (1998, March–April). 'The New Corporate University: Higher Education Becomes Higher Training'. *Dollars and Sense*, 32–5.

Blakers, C. (1992). 'School to Work: Transition and Policy'. In M. Poole (ed.), *Education and Work* (pp. 54–71). Hawthorn, Victoria: Australian Council for Educational Research.

Boutwell, C. E. (1997). *Shell Game: Corporate America's Agenda for Schools*. Bloomington, Indiana: Phi Delta Kappa Educational Foundation.

Bowles, S. (1973). 'The Integration of Higher Education into the Wage-Labor System'. In M. B. Katz (ed.), *Education in American History: Readings on the Social Issues*, (pp. 139–60). New York: Praeger.

Bowles, S. and Gintis, H. (1976). *Schooling in Capitalist America: Educational Reform and the Contradictions of Economic Life*. New York: Basic Books.

Chomsky, N. (1988). 'Toward a Humanistic Conception of Education and Work'. In D. Corson (ed.), *Education for Work: Background to Policy and Curriculum*, (pp. 19–32). New Zealand: Dunmore Press.

Clark, D. M. (1997). 'The Trouble with Business–Education Partnerships'. *Techniques,* 71 (9), 70.

Cohen, D. K. and Lazerson, M. (1973). 'Education and the Corporate Order'. In M. B. Katz (ed.), *Education in American History: Readings on the Social Issues*, (pp. 318–33). New York: Praeger.

Corson, D. (ed.). (1988). *Education for Work: Background to Policy and Curriculum*. New Zealand: Dunmore Press.

Deutschman, A. (1992, 10 August). 'Why Kids Should Learn About Work'. *Fortune,* 126, 86–9.

Dolainski, S. (1997, May). 'Partnering with the (School) Board'. *Workforce, 76,* 28–30+.

Fones-Wolf, E. A. (1994). *Selling Free Enterprise: the Business Assault on Labor and Liberalism, 1945–60*. Urbana and Chicago: University of Illinois Press.

Giglio, L. and Bauer, L. (1998). 'School-to-Work Programmes and Partnerships'. *Educational Horizons,* 76 (2), 65–8.

Hall, J. R. (1993, May). 'Education is Everyone's Business'. *Chief Executive,* 24–7.

House of Representatives Standing Committee on Employment, Education and Training. (1997). *Youth Employment: a Working Solution*. Canberra: Parliament of the Commonwealth of Australia.

Kaplan, G. R. (1996). 'Profits R Us: Notes on the Commercialization of America's Schools'. *Phi Delta Kappan,* 78 (3), K1–K12.

Kennedy, R. D. (1994). 'Let Candles Be Brought: the Case for Business Involvement in Education'. *Vital Speeches,* 60 (8), 248–50.

Meister, J. C. (1998). *Corporate Universities: Lessons in Building a World-Class Work Force*. (Revised edn). New York: McGraw-Hill.

Molnar, A. (1996). *Giving Kids the Bu$iness: The Commercialisation of America's Schools*. Boulder, CO: Westview.

Noah, H. J. and Eckstein, M. A. (1988). 'Business and Industry Involvement with Education in Britain, France and Germany'. In J. Lauglo and K. Lillis (eds), *Vocationalizing Education: An International Perspective*, (pp. 45–68). Oxford: Pergamon Press.

Poole, M. (ed.) (1992). *Education and Work* (pp. 111–32). Hawthorn, Victoria: Australian Council for Educational Research.

Sinclair, U. (1924). *The Goslings: a Study of the American Schools*. (1st edn). Pasadena, California: Upton Sinclair.

Spring, J. H. (1972). *Education and the Rise of the Corporate State*. Boston: Beacon Press.

Wagner, C. G. (1998). 'Making it in America: Education Trumps Background in Determining Status'. *The Futurist,* 32 (1), 16–7.

White, J. (1997). *Education and the End of Work: a New Philosophy of Work and Learning*. London: Cassell.

CHANGING NATURE OF WORK

ACTU. (1999). *Working People Want a Balanced and Secure Working Life: ACTU Survey Reveals Many Don't Have One*: http://www.actu.asn.au/national/media/media99/990902survey. htm.

Bagnall, D. (1999, 2 February). 'All Work No Jobs'. *The Bulletin*, 11–5.

Bluestone, B. and Rose, S. (1997, March–April). 'Overworked and Underemployed: Unravelling an Economic Enigma'. *The American Prospect*, 58–69.

Bullock, C. (1998, 25 October). 'A Flexible Future'. *Background Briefing, ABC Radio*, 2RN.

Church, G. J. (1987, 7 September). 'The Work Ethic Lives! Americans Labor Harder and at More Jobs than Ever'. *Time*, 130, 40–2.

Gee, J. P., Hull, G. and Lankshear, C. (1996). *The New Work Order: Behind the Language of the New Capitalism*. Sydney: Allen and Unwin.

Lum, J. (1997, Sept–Oct). 'Sweatshops are Us'. *Dollars and Sense*, 7.

Palumbo, F. A. and Herbig, P. A. (1994). 'Salaryman Sudden Death Syndrome'. *Employee Relations*, 16 (1), 54–61.

Ransome, P. (1996). *The Work Paradigm: a Theoretical Investigation of Concepts of Work*. Aldershot: Avebury.

Reilly, P. and Tamkin, P. (1996). *Outsourcing: a Flexible Option for the Future?* Brighton: Institute for Employment Studies.

Richards, C. (1997, 8 June). 'Dying to Work'. *Background Briefing, ABC Radio*, pp. 2RN.

Roberts, K. (1978). *Contemporary Society and the Growth of Leisure*. London: Longman.

Samuelson, R. J. (1992, 16 March). 'Overworked Americans?' *Newsweek*, 119, 50.

Schor, J. B. (1991). *The Overworked American: the Unexpected Decline in Leisure*. New York: Basic Books.

Sennett, R. (1998). *The Corrosion of Character: the Personal Consequences of Work in the New Capitalism*. New York: W. W. Norton.

'The 1997 National Study of the Changing Workforce'. (1998). *Shorter Work-Time News* (11), http://www.silcom.com/~rdb/swt/swt-11.htm.

Weidenbaum, M. (1995). 'A New Social Contract for the American Workplace'. *Challenge!*, 38 (1), 51–5.

Whalen, C. J. (1996, September). 'The Age of Anxiety: Erosion of the American Dream'. *USA Today*, 125, 14–6.

CONSUMERISM AND THE WORK ETHIC

Bell, D. (1976). *The Cultural Contradictions of Capitalism*. London: Heinemann.

Clapp, R. (1996). 'Why the Devil Takes Visa'. *Christianity Today*, 40 (11), 18–33.

Cross, G. (1993). *Time and Money*. London: Routledge.

de Grazia, S. (1964). *Of Time, Work and Leisure*. New York: Anchor Books.

Durning, A. T. (1992). *How Much Is Enough: the Consumer Society and the Future of the Earth*. London: Earthscan.

Ewen, S. (1976). *Captains of Consciousness: Advertising and the Social Roots of the Consumer Culture*. New York: McGraw-Hill.

Galbraith, J. K. (1970). *The Affluent Society*. (Revised 2nd edition). Harmondsworth: Penguin.

Goodwin, N. R., Ackerman, F. and Kiron, D. (eds) (1997). *The Consumer Society*, (pp. 229–36). Washington, DC: Island Press.

Hunnicutt, B. K. (1988). *Work Without End: Abandoning Shorter Hours for the Right to Work*. Philadelphia: Temple University Press.

Marchand, R. (1985). *Advertising the American Dream: Making Way for Modernity, 1920–1940*. Berkeley: University of California Press.

Packard, V. (1960). *The Waste Makers*. Harmondsworth: Penguin.

Packard, V. (1961). *The Status Seekers: an Exploration of Class Behaviour in America.* Harmonds-worth: Penguin.

Russell, B. (1983). 'In Praise of Idleness' (1932). In V. Richards (ed.), *Why Work? Arguments for the Leisure Society* (pp. 25–34). London: Freedom Press.

Schor, J. B. (1991). *The Overworked American: the Unexpected Decline in Leisure.* New York: Basic Books.

Shorris, E. (1994). *A Nation of Salesmen: the Tyranny of the Market and the Subversion of Culture.* New York: W. W. Norton.

Whitwell, G. (1989). *Making the Market: the Rise of Consumer Society.* Melbourne: McPhee Gribble Publishers.

Zweig, F. (1976). *The New Acquisitive Society.* Chichester: Barry Rose.

Index